GROTON, CONN. —SOUTHEASTERN BRANCH LIBRARY —UNIVERSITY OF CONNECTICUT—
FEB 6 1969

George R. Marek, for many years Vice President and chief executive officer of the RCA Victor Record Division, is a native of Vienna. Most of his sources were, naturally, in German, and he visited and interviewed surviving members of the Strauss family as well as dozens of men and women who had worked with the composer. Mr. Marek's previous books have included: *Puccini—A Biography; Opera as Theater*, a critical study; *The World Treasury of Grand Opera*, and others.

ALSO BY GEORGE R. MAREK

A Front Seat at the Opera
Puccini—A Biography
Opera as Theater
The World Treasury of Grand Opera

Also by George R. Marek

A Front Seat at the Opera
Puccini—A Biography
Opera as Theater
The World Treasury of Grand Opera

George R. Marek, for many years Vice President and chief executive officer of the RCA Victor Record Division, is a native of Vienna. Most of his sources were, naturally, in German, and he visited and interviewed surviving members of the Strauss family as well as dozens of men and women who had worked with the composer. Mr. Marek's previous books have included: *Puccini—A Biography*; *Opera as Theater*, a critical study; *The World Treasury of Grand Opera*, and others.

RICHARD STRAUSS

The Life of a Non-Hero

BY

GEORGE R. MAREK

SIMON AND SCHUSTER
NEW YORK

PUBLISHED BY SIMON AND SCHUSTER
ROCKEFELLER CENTER, 630 FIFTH AVENUE
NEW YORK, NEW YORK 10020

FIRST PRINTING

LIBRARY OF CONGRESS CATALOG CARD NUMBER: 67-10524
DESIGNED BY EDITH FOWLER
MANUFACTURED IN THE UNITED STATES OF AMERICA
BY H. WOLFF, NEW YORK

The author wishes to express his appreciation to the following for permission to reprint previously published material:

Richard Aldrich, review of Strauss's concert February 28, 1904, copyright 1904 by The New York Times Company. Reprinted by permission.

Sir Thomas Beecham, A Mingled Chime, *G. P. Putnam's Sons, copyright 1943 by Sir Thomas Beecham.*

Norman Del Mar, Richard Strauss, *Barrie & Rockliff.*

Geraldine Farrar, Such Sweet Compulsion, *The Greystone Corporation.*

Lawrence Gilman, review of "The Egyptian Helena" in the New York Herald Tribune November 7, 1928.

Hugo von Hofmannsthal, Selected Plays and Libretti, *edited and introduced by Michael Hamburger. Bollingen Series XXXIII-3. Pantheon Books. Page lxvi.*

Harry Graf Kessler, Tagebücher 1918-1937, *Insel-Verlag.*

Ernst Krause, Richard Strauss Yearbook 1959-60, *Boosey and Hawkes Publishers. (Excerpt translated by GRM.)*

Erich Leinsdorf, "The Genius of Richard Strauss," copyright © 1965 by The Atlantic Monthly Company. Reprinted with permission.

Edward Lockspeiser, Debussy, *The Macmillan Company, copyright © 1962 by Edward Lockspeiser.*

Thomas Mann Briefe 1889-1936, *S. Fischer-Verlag and Alfred A. Knopf, Inc. (Excerpt translated by GRM.) The Thomas Mann letters will be published in English by Alfred A. Knopf, Inc.*

Ernest Newman, Testament of Music, *Alfred A. Knopf, Inc.*

J. B. Priestley, Literature and Western Man, *Harper & Brothers.*

Mrs. John Barry Ryan, for permission to quote a letter from Otto H. Kahn to Richard Strauss dated May 29, 1908.

L. C. B. Seaman, From Vienna to Versailles, *Coward-McCann, Inc., copyright © 1956 by L. C. B. Seaman.*

George Bernard Shaw excerpts quoted by permission of the Harvard College Library and The Public Trustee and The Society of Authors, London.

Richard Strauss, Betrachtungen und Erinnerungen, *edited by Willi Schuh, copyright 1949 by Atlantis-Verlag.*

Richard Strauss, Briefe an die Eltern 1882-1906, *edited by Willi Schuh, copyright 1954 by Atlantis-Verlag.*

Richard Strauss, "Daphne," copyright 1938 by Richard Strauss; renewed 1965. Used by permission of Dr. Franz Strauss, copyright owner, and Boosey and Hawkes, Inc., Sole Agents. (Excerpt translated by GRM.)

Richard Strauss and Hugo von Hofmannsthal, A Working Friendship, *copyright © 1961 by William Collins Sons & Co., Ltd. Reprinted by permission of Random House, Inc.*

Igor Stravinsky and Robert Craft, Themes and Episodes, *Alfred A. Knopf, Inc., copyright © 1966 by Robert Craft and Igor Stravinsky. Copyright © 1962, 1963, 1964, 1965 by Igor Stravinsky. Copyright © 1964, 1965 by Robert Craft.*

Deems Taylor, Of Men and Music, *Simon and Schuster, copyright 1937 by Deems Taylor.*

Edmond Taylor, The Fall of the Dynasties, *copyright © 1963 by Edmond Taylor. Reprinted by permission of Doubleday & Company, Inc.*

Hannah Vogt, The Burden of Guilt, *Oxford University Press.*

Stefan Zweig, Die Welt von Gestern, *Atrium-Verlag. (Excerpt translated by GRM.)*

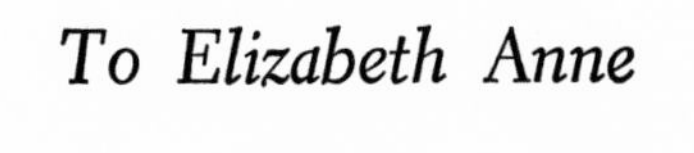
To Elizabeth Anne

CONTENTS

ADMISSIONS AND ACKNOWLEDGMENTS

The book is a biography and an inquiry. I have attempted to present a paradoxical man in the round. And I have attempted to inquire and to explain why it was that this great talent declined, why Strauss failed in his later years. In pursuing the answer to this question, it was necessary to consider the composer linked to his times and his world. It was necessary to portray him against the background of events, the debasement of German culture, the tottering of the European foundation. In Strauss's biography, background often becomes foreground. Segments of that history in and through which Strauss lived help to elucidate the man.

Though the book is often critical of Strauss, it is, I hope, objective. Oscar Wilde wrote: "Every great man nowadays has his disciples, and it is always Judas who writes the biography." I have been neither a disciple nor, I trust, a Judas.

The book does not pretend to be a full examination of the *music* of Richard Strauss. Such an examination has been performed several times by several critics, such as Norman Del Mar, Richard Specht, William Mann, and others. Though the major works are discussed—how can one write about a man without paying attention to his work?—several of Strauss's minor compositions are not even mentioned. In short, I was looking at the man more than at the music.

Many people have helped me and many thanks are due to Karl Böhm, Gustl Breuer, Robert Breuer, Hugo Burghauser, Norman Del Mar, Charles Gerhardt, Donald J. Grout, Lotte Klemperer, Irving Kolodin, Heinrich Kralik, Ernst Krause, Dan H. Lawrence, Walter Legge, Erich Leinsdorf, Gregor Piatigorsky, Victor Reinshagen, Joseph Rosenstock, Artur Rubinstein, Willi Schuh, Leopold Stokowski, Alice Strauss, Franz Strauss, George Szell, Walter Toscanini. My thanks are due also to the publishers Boosey and Hawkes for the loan of the later scores. Particular thanks are due to Henry Simon, editor of Simon and Schuster, who took the liveliest interest in my manuscript, rough and finished, and made many valuable suggestions.

Most of the documents I have freshly translated from the German. When for one reason or another I did not do so, I indicated the source of the quoted passage.

A list of the principal sources consulted will be found at the back of the book.

George R. Marek

New York, April, 1966

FOREWORD

The Enigma of Richard Strauss

In the Uffizi Gallery in Florence there hangs a self-portrait by the seventeenth-century painter Carlo Dolci. It is a curious work. He pictures himself as a gentleman, a man obviously of means, yet thoughtful and introspective, his eyes looking upon the beholder with a wistfulness which does not exclude a certain amount of fashionable haughtiness. His hair is carefully coiffed, his cloak of the latest cut, and the ruff he wears over it is of impeccable white. At first glance one would say, "This is a banker or a diplomat." But that is not all there is to the portrait. This man of ease holds in his hand another portrait, once again a self-portrait. In that second, smaller picture he sees himself as a very different creature; he shows himself as the craftsman, the professional, the artist at work. He is unshaved, unkempt. A pair of spectacles sits on his nose at an awkward angle, and the nose itself is no longer aristocratic but merely long. His mouth is half open with strain, no trace of melancholy smile remaining. On top of his head with the disarranged hair rests a simple, serviceable cap. His eye, now intense and critical and no longer in the least faraway, gazes at an unseen canvas.

Dolci cannot be counted among the greatest artists. But for once —that is, in this painting—he touches greatness; he shows us vividly the division between man and artist, separating visually the man of the world from the man of the workshop. Now calm in elegant resignation, he becomes the next moment the laborer possessed of his labor who forgets to comb his hair or shave his face.

The biographer of Richard Strauss may take note of this division. It is peculiarly applicable. Strauss was a gentleman, a man of the world and to a certain extent at least a man of fashion. He was as well an artist of high devotion and great intensity. The division is as sharp in Strauss as it is in Dolci.

But to paint a likeness of Strauss we need a triple portrait, not a double one. There is the man; there is the composer. There is in addition the executant musician. Fully half of his working days were spent as a conductor, and a considerable period was spent in the artistic management of an opera house. Other composers were performers as well, though mostly in their formative years: Brahms and Schumann were pianists, Wagner, Mendelssohn, Berlioz conductors, Franck an organist, Elgar a violinist. But, with the possible exceptions of Mahler and Liszt, no composer was more active than Strauss in serving other men's music. We cannot do him justice unless we pay some attention to this other role.

Even if we paint three portraits and put them all together we may not succeed. Strauss is a difficult subject for biography. He lived in the age of paper, and the documents about and by him are copious. But he was a reserved man, and the documents are circumspect, not to say obfuscating. Strauss, once he became famous, was careful of what he said and wrote. He hid more than he revealed. One has to dig underneath the documents.

In accepting this task we can console ourselves with the knowledge that, though we can shed considerable light on a personality that in the existing biographies has been dealt with respectfully but by and large superficially, in the last analysis the nature of the artist must remain unanalyzable. One may pile the Pelion of deductions on the Ossa of biographical minutiae and yet not arrive at complete understanding. One can examine a public figure from diverse points of view—the historical, the social, the psychological, the merely anecdotal, or the point of view that each brush stroke or each pen stroke or each note set down is autobiographical and that therefore we must look solely to the work if we are to interpret the man. Each of these points of view can teach us something. All together they will not teach us everything.

We are all familiar with the fact that the nature of the artist is split by contradictions. That could be said of most human beings, gifted or not, except that the clashes and paradoxes seem more extreme in those who have been endowed with a gift. At least we know more about these contradictions, for we take the trouble to find out. We know that Dostoevski, who looked so deeply into the human soul and who was so eloquent a champion of the downtrodden, the misfit, and the persecuted, hated the Jews. We know that the painter David, who contributed so much to the patriotism of the France of the eighteenth century, was a turncoat and a sycophant. We know that Wagner was a man whom you would not have trusted with either your money or your wife. We know that Tolstoi, whose *War and Peace* is a paean of profound kindness, could be cruel to those nearest to him. We know that Titian employed dubious measures to assure himself of a monopoly of the most lucrative commissions to be found in or out of Venice. Michelangelo has been called—by Rudolf and Margot Wittkower in *Born Under Saturn*—"avaricious and generous; superhuman and puerile; modest and vain; violent, suspicious, jealous, misanthropic, extravagant, tormented, bizarre, and terrible; and this list is far from being complete."*

It is hardly a major revelation, therefore, to say that Richard Strauss was an artist of contradictory character, even though the German biographies I have read make him out to be a man of exceptional evenness. The contradictions in him are manifold, peculiar, and well covered up. As in Dolci's portrait, the gentlemanly figure looms large. That is exactly how Strauss wanted the world to see him: the gentleman genius, with the stress on the former.

Strauss showed no obvious eccentricities. He did not shout in rapture, he did not indulge in outbursts of temper; he did not have to savor the odor of rotting apples in order to compose; he did not have to wear a velvet jacket. He did not betray his friends (though he had few); he did not borrow money without any intention of giving it back; he did not in despair throw any of his manuscripts into the fire (perhaps it would have been better had he done so with a few of them); he did not have a violent love affair with a Shakespearean actress; nor are there any juicy marital scandals to relate about him. He did not believe that he was sent into the world

* In this inquiry into "the character and conduct of artists" the authors also discuss Dolci's self-portrait.

to lead it to redemption. He did not create while tossing feverishly in a transport of disease, nor did he lie fallow for long periods of discouragement. He was most of the time the craftsman with his spectacles on his nose, proceeding at a determined but orderly pace.

Strauss was married only once. It was a love match. Pauline de Ahna was a singer whom he met while she was a student and who became one of the superb interpreters of his songs. In later life she tried to become a "great lady." She gave herself airs. After that virtually all who knew Pauline cordially disliked her. She ruled the roost firmly. He let her rule the roost, accepting bondage docilely. Deems Taylor, the American critic and composer, interviewed Strauss in Garmisch while Taylor was music critic of the New York *World*. They had tea in the garden, and afterward Strauss took him and another man who had accompanied Taylor into the house to show him his home. As Strauss "approached the threshold of his own home, he paused and wiped his feet carefully upon a small square of dampened doormat that lay before the door. Advancing a step, he wiped his feet once more, this time upon a small dry doormat. Stepping across the doorsill he stopped and wiped his feet for a third and final time upon a small rubber doormat that lay just inside the door. A weight fell from my shoulders that will never again rest upon them. Strauss may be a good conductor and a great composer, and I shall always respect him, but I could never again be afraid of him. For in that moment I saw, for a flash, the truth. Here was no Titan or demigod; before me stood only a married man."*

How does this fit in with the man who wrote the music of *Don Juan?* How reconcile the punctilious businessman—and Strauss was a good businessman—with the composer of *Don Quixote?* How are we to explain the difference between the dry dignitary, correct in dress and demeanor, and Strauss, the composer of the final scene of *Salome?* The man who saw the sun rise on Zarathustra's mountaintop—how could he be content with three-room domesticity? He seems to have been little in sympathy with the aims and program of the new psychoanalysis, was in fact so little interested in it that he made no special effort to become acquainted with Sigmund Freud, though both men lived in Vienna. Yet he responded

* Deems Taylor, *Of Men and Music.*

at once to Hofmannsthal's translation of Sophocles' *Elektra* into the twentieth-century idiom of the twisted psyche. The man who was able to organize the tour of an orchestra and was aware of the last penny of expense that such a tour entailed, and the composer of mystic, dream-drenched songs, exquisite in their musical poetry —how could they have been one and the same? One of the most attractive features of his personality was his self-deprecating humor. Humor he has in his music, but how, then, are we to rationalize the fustian of those sections of *Ein Heldenleben* which deal with the hero's critics and the hero's battles?

These contrasts do not fully account for the puzzle that is Richard Strauss. The chief enigma with which he confronts us is the decline of quality in his musical output. He started high, after several derivative early works, and kept up the standard for many years. Then suddenly he lost the touch, he compromised, he was satisfied with less than the best. He lost his self-critical faculty, and partly believed, partly forced himself to believe, that his *Egyptian Helena* and *Arabella*, and, worse still, the *Danae* and *Friedenstag*, stood on the same plane as *Till Eulenspiegel* and *Der Rosenkavalier* and "Morgen." All great composers produce some work that is less than the best. Great composers who lack sharp self-criticism produce work of very uneven quality, Berlioz being a notable example. Some artists are restless experimenters and are driven to try for the new, even if that new is not so nourishing as the old. That can be said of Stravinsky or Picasso. But Strauss after a certain point did not try for the new. He was often content to repeat formulas and to substitute orchestral tricks for musical substance. I am not of the opinion that all of his works after *Ariadne* are worthless. In the sand there are stuck some shining ideas, here and there. But what a lot of sand one has to wade through! Curiously, his last works, the four last songs and the late orchestral work, *Metamorphosen*, are suffused with a warm, soft glow of sunset; the light shines once more, even if only in reflection. Still, his decline was precipitous and prolonged, so precipitous indeed that his case is almost unique in the history of music. What was the reason for this decline? Did he just burn himself out or, as I believe, were special causes responsible?

These problems will have to be solved if a biography is to aid us in understanding Strauss better. He is worth understanding. He is among the last composers who are truly alive in the music lover's affection, among the last who are heard again and again in concerts and on records. Of the men who worked in the last decade of the nineteenth and the first decades of our century, we hear Mahler, we hear Debussy, Puccini, Bartók (whose best works came later), Stravinsky; we hear less now of Elgar, of Delius, of Vaughan Williams, of Scriabin, of the early Schönberg, of Sibelius. Of Rachmaninoff only the piano works remain, not the symphonies. Mahler's star is in the ascendancy. So is Bartók's, I believe. But of all these composers Strauss remains the most beloved, the one who says most to the public at large (Puccini means a lot only to the operatic public and he was primarily a nineteenth-century composer)—and he gives signs of continuing this popularity.* Militant modernists now consider him old-fashioned. He is not that to those of us who possess a peaceful view of music.

That we still treasure him—and within limitations will continue to treasure him for who knows how long—is undoubtedly due to the characteristic that Strauss is the last of the romantics. Surely that is what he was, the last figure of a festal processional frieze, and not a forerunner. In spite of his musical language, which seemed at one time so cacophonous, in spite of the subjects of his tone poems and operas, which seemed at one time so daring, in spite of the innovations he did introduce into the language of the orchestra, he was a figure of the romantic dusk, not a figure of dawn. He was one who gathered onto himself the rich tradition of the nineteenth century and brought this tradition to an end in a riot of humor, melody, and color.

* In a survey made by the American Symphony League of the 1963/4 season Strauss ranks seventh among "Most Performed Composers (standard)": Beethoven, Mozart, Brahms, Tchaikovsky, Wagner, Bach, Strauss. This ranking takes into account only orchestral concerts. If performances of operas and songs were to be considered, Strauss might well rank even higher.

1

The State of Music in Germany

Richard Strauss was born in Munich in 1864. It was the year after Manet had exhibited his *Le Déjeuner sur l'Herbe* and had thereby not only created a resounding scandal but had drawn "the sharpest dividing line in the history of painting since the French Revolution," according to John Canaday in *Mainstreams of Modern Art*. It was the year that Tolstoi began to sketch out the work that was to occupy him for eight years to come, *War and Peace*. It was the year Zola enjoyed his first literary success, *Contes à Ninon*, and Charles Dickens published *Our Mutual Friend*.

Berlioz had recently managed to get a part of his shapeless opera, *Les Troyens*, produced. Brahms, already successful, played his new "Paganini Variations." Liszt was shortly to turn his collar around and become the "Abbé Liszt," Verdi was revising his early *Macbeth*, Smetana was putting the finishing touches to his opera, *The Bartered Bride*, Stephen Foster died a pauper's death in New York, and Offenbach was on his way to becoming a millionaire (in French francs at least) with the production of *La Belle Hélène*.

It was the high autumn of the romantic period of music. In the two decades during which Strauss became a young man and a young composer, this autumn was to cool, but now it was still balmy and rich. The spring that had preceded it occurred at the beginning of the century, when Beethoven and Schubert composed the great music of the romantic age, and Bellini, Rossini, and Weber its mellifluous melodies. The summer followed around the middle of the century, a time when romanticism was at its bright zenith and musical genius was as prodigally strewn about as was pictorial genius in the Renaissance. Between 1840 and 1850 one could have heard new music in profusion, new music by Donizetti and Meyerbeer, Berlioz and Mendelssohn, Chopin and Schumann, Wagner and Verdi, Gounod and Glinka, Liszt and the young Johann Strauss, Jr.

It looked then as if musical wealth was never going to diminish, the light never to darken, the fruits never to dry, the sounds never to cease.

It was a long autumn, an Indian summer following a long summer. While Strauss was a schoolboy, *Aida, Boris Godunov,* and *Carmen* appeared in the opera house, Tchaikovsky's Fourth Symphony and Brahms's First Symphony in the concert hall, Grieg's *Peer Gynt* music in the theater. The man whose music and philosophy were to bear the strongest influence on Strauss forged to fame; his ambition was fulfilled and his exalted plan became reality. A little over a month before Strauss was born, Richard Wagner had slipped to the bottom rung of his career. His *Tristan and Isolde* unproduced, with no prospect of ever realizing his dream of a theater in which the Ring drama could be adequately presented, with the patience of friends and publisher exhausted, he had hidden himself in a hotel in Stuttgart. Almost everywhere—in Vienna, Mainz, Dresden, Zurich—creditors were waiting to seize him. Having abused the hospitality of his well-wishers, he did not know where to find asylum. No additional appeals, however eloquent or insistent, seemed productive. A few days after his arrival in Stuttgart, when he was beginning to worry how he was going to pay his hotel bill, he was informed that a visitor from Munich was downstairs and desired to see him. Who could it be? Surely another creditor. While he was deliberating how to give the caller the slip, the visitor sent up word that he had come as a delegate of His Majesty Ludwig II, King of Bavaria. Wagner suspected a ruse but reluctantly made an appointment for the next morning. He slept little that night, steeling himself for the trouble that he was sure was to come on the morrow. The next day the visitor called. It was the day of rescue. That afternoon Wagner left for Munich. He paid his hotel bill with a snuffbox that had been given to him in Russia. His railroad ticket had to be bought by a friend.

A king had summoned him with the expression of idolatrous admiration and the promise of full artistic and financial support. Wagner the failure became Wagner the force.

On June 10 of the following year, *Tristan and Isolde* was given in Munich. Bülow, whom Wagner had appointed as court conductor, led the première, as he was to lead a new staging of *Lohengrin* two years later and the première of *Die Meistersinger* three years later, all in Munich.

The King's motives may have been sick. The King's longing was to escape from government to legend, from the reality of Munich to the imagined mountain of Montsalvat. The King's love was centered less in music than in the man. Indubitably his response to music was inseparable from his wish to dream himself back into an age of knighthood. Balancing an Arthurian lance suited him better than balancing a Bavarian budget. Whatever were the propulsive forces, Wagner now had what he needed and Wagner's music was now launched in exemplary performance. A concentration of rays shone on Bavaria's capital: the sun of the new music appeared brightest there. Some found this sun harsh and ugly, some hot and heady. None could ignore it.

In the performance of other music as well, music less controversial, the beautiful city on the banks of the Isar played an active part. Its standards were high. The orchestra had been brought to a level of quality by Franz Lachner, friend of Schubert, who had worked with it since 1836. (He retired in 1865 and Bülow took over.) The opera house was guided by Karl von Perfall, who became intendant in 1867. At the beginning of Wagner's sway in Munich the composer liked Perfall; later Perfall was to become "a thorn in Wagner's flesh" and still later prove himself an obstacle to Strauss's career.

Was Munich's musical culture unique? What was going on in other German cities? In what musical atmosphere did Strauss grow up? What was the condition of music in the Germany of the sixties?

We had better not speak of "Germany." The unification of the country was to follow later. It is more accurate to speak of the German-speaking audiences living in various states, the states and principalities being politically divided and indeed often inimical to one another. To these audiences music was, if not a necessity, at least a comfortable and expected adjunct of life, as secure a ritual as the Sunday walk in the woods. They looked on music as their birthright. If Faust's plaint that "two souls, alas, dwell in my breast" is applicable to every man, it is peculiarly applicable to a German. One soul strives for the precisely ordered ideal, the beautiful, the emotional—all qualities of music—while the other soul is earthbound, dull, bigoted, chauvinistic, arrogant, and often cruel.

The German mixes nectar with beer. He combines a particularly irritating Philistinism with an open-minded sensitivity to the new in art. (Compare the reception that was accorded to new composers in Germany to the hostility shown to almost any French composer who dared to say something new.) If this be a paradox, it is true all the same, and it is particularly true of music. The German is at home with music. In a sense—and we must not generalize too widely—music, and especially instrumental music, has been the artistic expression most congenial to the German, as painting to the Italian and drama to the British.

Wagner would have denied—and did deny—this. Many of his diatribes against the state of music in Germany contained truths. The middle-class burgher ensconced behind his mug of beer understood nothing of "true art" (by which Wagner meant his art) and wanted only the most superficial entertainment, which to Wagner meant "foreign" music such as Meyerbeer's or Rossini's. Yes, of course provincialism was prevalent. When and where is it not? But when Wagner claimed that the German middle and upper classes were not receptive, that the theaters were debauched, that all musical activity needed regeneration from the ground up, he was indulging in special pleading. It was not so bad as all that.

The fact is, as Wagner was shortly to discover for himself, that there existed a large public for music, that this public was an enthusiastic one, though within a relatively narrow compass of taste, and that standards of performance throughout the land were not altogether abysmal. The fact is that Munich was not unique in being a musical city.

The city to which most German musicians aspired was the Prussian mecca, Berlin. The Royal Orchestra of this, the largest German city, had as early as 1811 earned Weber's admiration for its "power and precision." Some seventy years later when Richard Strauss first went to Berlin—he was then twenty—he wrote to his father: "The orchestra is very good, splendid wind players and enormous fire and dash."* Four years later, as a young conductor, Strauss wrote: "The Philharmonic Orchestra is the most intelligent, accomplished, and alive orchestra I know."†

Berlin had two opera houses which commanded, if not always the best artistry, the most generous subvention. Dresden specialized in opera. Wagner had worked there at the Hoftheater. *Rienzi, Der Fliegende Holländer*, and *Tannhäuser* saw their world premières at this theater. Leipzig's famous Gewandhaus orchestra could trace its origin back to the middle of the eighteenth century and had been led by Mendelssohn, the first of the stellar conductors. A curious custom, worth mentioning in passing, prevailed at the Gewandhaus: The violin and viola players always stood while performing, and it was not until ten years after Arthur Nikisch became its head that they were allowed to sit down.‡

Music was being played not only in the larger cities. It is a characteristic of German life that music was decentralized. Each principality had its own little orchestra. Each grand duke, each local court, budgeted a yearly sum to support a "band" (*Kapelle*) and a theater, the theater in most cities being a combination opera house and place where spoken plays, particularly the German classics, were performed. These subventions were granted because many of these potentates were men of some culture. Occasionally they were granted because it was the politically expedient thing to do. Occasionally they were granted because musical and theatrical activities shed representational luster and the theater was a place in which one could show off new uniforms. Occasionally a duke loved an actress. Whatever the reason, one could find orchestras and theaters in Riga, Karlsruhe, Braunschweig, Stuttgart, Frankfurt, Darmstadt, Hanover, Kassel, and other cities. The young Strauss's early journeys took him, in addition to Berlin, to Dresden, Meiningen, Hamburg, Frankfurt, Wiesbaden; and everywhere there was music.

By twentieth-century standards the quality of these smaller local

---

* Letter of February 29, 1884.

† Letter to his father, January 24, 1888.

‡ Bülow, too, would often make part of the orchestra play in a standing position.

orchestras was not very high. Still, orchestral playing had progressed since the early years of the century, when one orchestra, that of Leipzig, had elicited general admiration for its ability to shade simple dynamics, executing a crescendo and a diminuendo. The orchestras had grown fuller since the days when Liszt gave the première of *Lohengrin* (1850) with a total of thirty-eight men—and this was at Weimar, an exceptionally enlightened town—or earlier when the Opera in Dresden allowed Weber thirty-five orchestral players. However, in the sixties it was still a sparse ensemble that grappled with a Beethoven symphony or the new music of Wagner. The point is that they did grapple with it: it is indicative both of Wagner's mounting fame and of the courage of German orchestras that two years after the première of *Die Meistersinger* in Munich the work could be heard in Dresden, Dessau, Karlsruhe, Mannheim, Weimar, Hanover, Leipzig, and Berlin as well as in Vienna.

The style of orchestra playing—insofar as one can tell from contemporary descriptions—tended toward the heavy. Dramatic passages were executed with heft—*wuchtig* is the German word for it. The drums pounded and the basses dug in. Slow tempos were *very* slow; that was the way to carve out the sentiment. In fast passages the strings indulged in a bit of "noodling"; the individual notes were not so important as the general impression. But the sound of the violins was warm, the brass, trained in martial strains, played assertively, the woodwinds produced a sweet tone, the cellists played luxuriantly with their heads ducked; and if it was all rather foursquare and heavy as German furniture, there were as yet few who wanted the style changed. The orchestras played "the classics," emphasizing as was to be expected the German romantic classics. They played a great deal of new music as well, much of it dreary. One thinks of the sixties and seventies as the time of Wagner and Brahms. One forgets that there was a host of composers around who took themselves very seriously and were taken seriously. Who now remembers Wendelin Weissheimer or Alexander Dreyschock or even Peter Cornelius or Joseph Joachim Raff or Josef Rheinberger? The last named was a passionate anti-Wagnerian. Wagner said of him that he was obviously a much better composer than he himself, for Rheinberger composed punctually every weekday from five to six, while he, Wagner, could compose only when an idea occurred to him.

In the concert halls Raff and Ludwig Spohr were particular favorites. Mozart was less frequently played than he is today and Bach much less frequently, in spite of the resurrective work that Mendelssohn had begun.

Orchestral players were court employees and as such they benefited by an assurance of permanence in their position and by a pension plan. They were dependent on the annual grant, and it could and did happen that some duke or other would arbitrarily decide to reduce expenses.* Generally, however, the orchestras were kept intact and musicians kept working as long as they could hold a bow or blow a reed. Conductors jibbed at the number of graybeards in the ranks of the orchestra and demanded more skillful replacements. But a player could not easily be dismissed. The musicians worked very hard, shuttling often between concerts and the theater, where they were required not only to take part in operatic performances but to play incidental music for the drama. Their salaries were just enough to keep them in food and lodging. Even the various *Kapellmeister* were threadbare men, and, with due allowance for the fact that living in Germany was inexpensive, they nevertheless had to exercise a timid frugality to make ends meet. The twenty-two-year-old Strauss, already noted both as a conductor and as a composer, was offered a three-year contract in Meiningen at a yearly salary of 2,000 marks ($500).†

Because of the frequency of musical performances of one kind or another, rehearsal time was limited. We read with amazement that Bülow conducted the "Eroica" in Meiningen "magnificently," but without a rehearsal. Strauss himself conducted in Weimar a performance of *Die Meistersinger*—suddenly substituted for a canceled *Tristan*—"without a rehearsal of any kind."

Resident orchestras and opera companies did not account for all the available music. The prominent orchestras toured. There were traveling opera companies, organized for profit. A good deal of chamber music was played. In the sixties and seventies pianists such

* It happened to Strauss in Meiningen in 1886.

† In present purchasing power this would be approximately equivalent to a salary of $5,000.

as Brahms and Clara Schumann made new converts to the romantic piano literature, while Bülow, in addition to his conductorial activities, continued to play the piano sonatas of Beethoven "as no one had played him before."* Liszt had retired from active concert life, but his pupils carried on the tradition, among others Carl Tausig, perhaps Liszt's greatest pupil (who, however, died before he was thirty in 1871), and Sophie Menter, born in Munich, whose "singing hand" Liszt had praised. Among violinists Joseph Joachim is best remembered; he, the friend of Brahms and the founder of the Joachim Quartet, played with "extraordinary technique" and without any of the tricks to which violin virtuosos were prone since Paganini.

While Strauss was being trained as a conductor, the state of music in Germany underwent a change. At first gradual, it was to have a significant influence on Strauss's concept of orchestral writing; it was to influence him as a composer, and conversely he was to influence orchestral ability. The change was to be found in new standards of virtuosity, new demands made on the expressiveness of the orchestral body, demands for nimbleness and lightness and much solo work, demands that were to be fulfilled with the help of a new generation of men at the helm, leaders of the orchestra miles removed from the humdrum *Taktschläger* (time beaters) and the routine *Kapellmeister* who functioned in the early part of the century.

The conductor as the interpreter came to the fore. The orchestras were pulled up by the force of his baton. It was he who became the "virtuoso," the man whom audiences loved or at least respected. It was his personality that became important; it was the pros and cons of his interpretations that were being discussed. While in the long run this was not an unmixed blessing, it did serve to show to the public the masterpieces of orchestral music in a new and fresh light. It gave the composer new opportunity to write works the complexity of which would have been unconquerable a few short years before.

Wagner must be given credit for much of this development. Propelled not only by the exigencies of his own music but by his ideas

---

* Attributed to Liszt.

touching the business of conducting, as well as by the example he himself set, there now coursed around his planet new stars: In addition to Bülow, there were Hans Richter, Anton Seidl, and Hermann Levi. More new conducting talent was soon to follow: Gustav Mahler, Karl Muck, Felix Mottl, Arthur Nikisch, Franz Schalk, and Felix Weingartner were all contemporaries of Strauss.*

The musical developments of the latter half of the century were aided by economic and political developments. For Germany it was both an era of prosperity and an era of growth of national consciousness. The industrialization of the country, while not so marked as the progress of Great Britain under Queen Victoria, did continue apace. The burgher became stouter, and the laborer, while still underpaid, ate better and had a few flowers in his window box. It was an era of comparative peace, interrupted by two minor wars and one major but brief war in which the Germans emerged victorious.

Bismarck was both the builder and the pilot of the ship of the national German state. The ship had been built at some cost. Wilhelm I, King of Prussia, believed that Prussia was destined to lead Germany and that he himself was destined to lead Prussia. Bismarck quite agreed. The only possible road toward this goal had to resound with the tread of marching feet: power was the means to leadership and a strong army was the means to power. The Prussian army was developed to shining and lethal efficiency. First it humbled Austria, which had dared to want to play a leading part in Europe. Soon after, Prussia easily rubbed out the opposition of other German states, particularly the southern states. But though conquered, the south of Germany and particularly Bavaria still resisted unification. In Munich a Prussian was considered a "foreigner." (The press called Bülow that.) The Iron Chancellor then conceived the plan of how the states could best be unified:

> Bismarck was convinced—and later made no bones about saying so—that the rift between the northern and southern Ger-

* Mahler was four years older than Strauss, Muck five, Mottl eight and Nikisch nine, Weingartner and Schalk a year older. Arturo Toscanini was three years younger, but this culminating representative of the conductor's art did not conduct in Germany until the twentieth century.

> man states could best be healed by "a national war against the neighbor people, our age-old aggressor (France)." With the help of a doctored press report—the famous "Dispatch from Ems," an early classic in the manipulation of mass media—he maneuvered the French Emperor, Napoleon III, into declaring war on Prussia. All the German states rallied to Prussia's defense in a national crusade, and three months later the victorious German armies were besieging Paris, where the republic had been proclaimed. German might, German unity, and Prussian hegemony all received a memorable consecration at Versailles on January 18, 1871; the German Empire, including all the German states and the freshly annexed French provinces of Alsace and Lorraine, was solemnly proclaimed in Louis XIV's Hall of Mirrors, and the King of Prussia became Kaiser Wilhelm I.*

The French having been overrun, the cannons were put in storage and Bismarck was declared the first Chancellor of the Reich. On October 16, 1871, the German Reich's Parliament was opened by the Kaiser, who said—and he may even have believed it for the moment—"The new German empire will be a reliable shield of peace."†

The new German Reich consisted of four kingdoms, five grand duchies, thirteen principalities, and three free cities. These were to have a voice in government. Actually in the Federal Council Prussia held seventeen of the forty-three seats, "so that in effect this body was gradually reduced to a distinguished debating society."‡

This Prussian-dominated nation was convinced that the German represented virtue, cleanliness, and goodness; if anybody disagreed he had better be persuaded by a bullet. National pride pervaded everything and mirrored itself in the steel of the bayonets and the polish of the boots.

It mirrored itself as well in cultural consciousness and in musical life. The Germans believe not only that music is "their" art but

---

* Edmond Taylor, *The Fall of the Dynasties.*

† One remembers Verdi's outraged letters during the Franco-Prussian War, such as the one to Clarina Maffei on September 30, 1870: ". . . And that King who is always talking about God and Divine Providence, with whose help he is destroying the best part of Europe! He thinks he is predestined to reform the morals and punish the vices of the modern world! ! ! What a fine messenger of God he is!"

‡ Taylor, *op. cit.*

that music is a moral force. To them this, the freest of the arts, the one least bound to the real world, is both a representational achievement and a text for a sermon. They judge a work of music not solely as to whether it is or is not good music but also whether its objective is a worthy one. The Ninth Symphony must be better than the Seventh. *Die Zauberflöte* is a better opera than *Così fan tutte,* not because its music is better but because it deals with a lofty theme, while the libretto of *Così* is frivolous.

In the Teutonic view music, at its best, contains not only moral but patriotic value. That was an additional reason why the cultivated German should tend it and care for it. When Bayreuth opened in 1876, it was recognized as an event of high national importance, even by those who were not in sympathy with Wagner's aims, though none could have foreseen that on a far-off day the devil would cite Wagner's music for his purpose.

Ten years after that inauguration, Liszt was to die at Bayreuth, Brahms was to present the fourth of his four symphonies—and Strauss was to compose his first tone poem. In that decade we can note once again an increase in the size and quality of orchestras, and a marked increase in the size of audiences.

When Bayreuth opened, Strauss was a schoolboy twelve years of age. He was born about five weeks after Wagner had come to Munich. The date of his birth is June 11, 1864. He was born in a house located in the central part of Munich, Altheimereck No. 2. The Strauss apartment occupied the second floor, the rest of the house being the Pschorr brewery. (See page 31.) The house was destroyed in World War II. Today Altheimereck No. 2 is a small, jerry-built building containing a cheap nightclub, and nothing there marks the birthplace of Munich's famous son.

Strauss not only was born into a musical family, his father encouraging him from the moment that he showed musical aptitude, but he grew up in a period that was fortunate for a German musician. Germany's national ambition helped to elevate him early to a figure of fame, though his works at first scandalized the conservatives and shocked the bourgeois. More important, there was available to him a multiplicity of forums in which he could not only expose his wares but present himself as an executant musician.

Yes, Strauss was fortunate, in more ways than one.

2

Youth

One of the men who held up a warning hand against Strauss's first free-striding compositions was his own father. Professional musician though the father was, and through performance versed in contemporary music, we find him on a number of occasions pleading with his son to mend his musical ways, to return to the pre-Wagnerian old style, to abjure convoluted polyphony, to avoid supercharged orchestral effects, and to be less "clever." Even at the beginning of the composer's career, when Richard was twenty years old, Franz, the father, wrote to the son: "Please, my dear Richard, when you create something new, take care that it be melodic, not too difficult, and pianistic. I am more and more convinced that only melodic music makes a permanent impression both on musicians and laymen. Melody is the life-enhancing element of music."* Two years later he responded to a letter in which Richard reported the effect on him of a performance in Meiningen of the "Eroica" under Bülow. Richard wrote that that performance "was the most magnificent thing you can imagine; even though our orchestra does not possess the sheen of the one in Munich, though the house is bad acoustically, though in the Finale the violins made a small blunder, it was a performance the like of which I shall never hear again. In the Funeral March each note contained a spirit and a soul such as I never thought possible for an orchestra to produce. And

* Letter of February 11, 1884.

the Finale: I can only say that for the first time in the Finale the whole light of Beethoven's sun emerged. If Beethoven had heard it, he would have said, 'Now I understand the greatness of my music.' I was so moved that after the last movement I sat in the Green Room and cried like a baby. I was alone with Bülow. He embraced me and kissed me. I shall never forget it."*

To this outpouring of youthful enthusiasm the older man replied: ". . . I was astonished, for I am not used to such enthusiasm from you . . . I am glad to hear about your adoration of the 'Eroica.' I beg you to take this eternally young work of genius as your example and ideal. The greatness of a work lies solely in its lofty simplicity. Think of the ancient Greeks! That is not to say that one needs to imitate, but one needs to train one's thoughts toward noble clear simplicity . . ."†

Simplicity and clarity are what he was unable to hear in his son's works. When the tone poem *Macbeth* appeared on the scene, Father Strauss wrote: "I counsel you, though with a heavy heart because I know the advice is not going to be heeded, to revise *Macbeth* once more, and carefully. Throw out all that superfluous weight of instrumental fat. Give your listeners a better opportunity to hear what you really want to say."‡

Don Juan pleased him better. He found in it "independence . . . a good design . . . no insecure groping . . . fire and spirit, brilliantly orchestrated." However! However, Franz believed that this highly emotional tone poem "suffers from too much cogitation. . . . In all your compositions I find too much reflection. . . . With your great talent you could afford to cede a little braininess to emotion. And I do not mean sentimentality. The work is terribly difficult and only very good orchestras will be able to play it. I think without harming the work it could be much less difficult. There are too many incidentals which interfere with the main theme, so that occasionally one does not see the forest for the trees. Keep in mind that you are not writing for professionals. I confess to you that my own head became heavy when I heard the music for the first time. I could only make sense out of it at the

---

* Letter to his father, January 31, 1886.
† Letter of February 2, 1886.
‡ Letter of October 17, 1890.

second hearing, in spite of the fact that I had previously read the score several times. . . ."*

So it went even after Strauss had become a famous composer. "Please be a bit more miserly with the brass"; "In your new works, avoid excess of polyphony"; "Take pity on the poor members of the orchestra!"

The exhortations we find in the letters must have been repeated in many a face-to-face discussion. They were rather more pronounced than the normal disapproval by the older generation of what the younger generation is doing, more severe than a father's headshaking question of what in the world his son is up to. They sprang from the conservatism of Franz Strauss, a conservatism so ingrained that, as the son wrote reminiscingly, the later Beethoven, beginning with the Finale of the Seventh Symphony, was to his father suspect, no longer "pure music," redolent of that Mephisto, Richard Wagner. Yet if we can look at Franz's remarks in the light of yesterday, when Richard's first important works were new, and forget the greater "wisdom" which knowing the outcome confers on us, we can see that Franz's fears were not altogether stupid, his views not altogether senseless. Neither the charge of overly luxuriant polyphony nor the charge of "too many incidentals" is groundless. The father's taste was too limited to evaluate all that was new and remarkable in his son's music; but he saw what was questionable. It goes without saying that in his composing Richard did not pay the slightest attention to Franz.

Franz seems to have been a real personality, though one would hardly have called him a likable man. He is usually dismissed as a cantankerous curmudgeon. Ludwig Nohl, a writer who reported on the first performance of *Die Meistersinger* in Munich, speaks of him as a "musician of the old school destitute of anything approaching refinement." Strauss himself said that his father "would have deemed it dishonorable to revise an artistic judgment which he once made up his mind to be the correct one." He also noted that his father was "short-tempered, choleric, tyrannical." This is scant filial tribute. Yet the evidence suggests that far from the composer's resenting his father, the relationship between father and son

* Letter of March 4, 1891.

was one of love, albeit a distant love. Franz's convictions were so strong one had to grant them a certain respect. A photograph taken in his old age shows him to look like an old cavalry officer, his eyes still truculent, his handlebar mustache still bristling.

Franz Strauss was the first horn player in the Munich Court Orchestra. According to even grudging contemporary testimony, he was a virtuoso of the instrument, an extraordinarily fine musican. He taught at the Royal School of Music. He had lost his first wife and two children during a cholera epidemic and had then married a second time. Richard's mother was his second wife. Josephine Pschorr was the daughter of a family of wealthy brewers and had brought to the marriage a comfortable fortune. Pschorr beer was then and is today one of the most popular beers in a city that specializes in beer. Franz's marriage relieved him of the necessity of having to live within the limits of a musician's salary, and no doubt his financial independence contributed to the independence of his opinions and actions. He seems to have been the spokesman whenever the orchestra had something to complain about. He fought with conductors. He was tetchy in his criticism of new music. In short, he was the Peck's Bad Boy of the orchestra.

Richard was born in a comfortable home. As a child and as a young man he never knew the pinch of want nor the meanness of genteel poverty. There was money sufficient not only for the necessities but also for certain luxuries, such as summer vacations. Neither father nor son was extravagant. As a young man Richard tried to live on his earnings, but the Pschorr family was quite ready with financial assistance when the genius in the family needed it.

Though Franz Strauss belonged, at least partly, to the world of the theater, his standards of behavior were as bourgeois and as ultraconservative as his musical taste. He brought up his two children —three years after Richard, a girl was born, Johanna, called Hanna by the family—using the customary code of the German paterfamilias. That is to say that he was the ruler of the home, the domestic court of last appeal, a Kaiser within four walls. He was full of wise saws and modern instances, which he did not hesitate to pass on to his son. When Franz's letters discuss how Richard should behave in society and toward "the ladies" they are at their tritest.

All could not have been easy and light in the relationship between the parents; the mother began to suffer from nervous depressions, which became so severe that she had to be sent to a sanatorium, where she spent at least a short time. Richard Strauss in later life remembered her as a gentle, soft-spoken woman "poetically inclined," so sensitive that any artistic experience proved turbulent, and she could read but sparingly. After evenings spent at the theater or concert she suffered with insomnia. She was happiest when she sat in the garden of her brother—"Uncle Georg"—and did needlework. Though she came from a cultivated and music-loving family, she does not seem to have been the intellectual equal of her husband. Her portrait taken in later life shows the countenance of a resigned, sad woman, her lips compressed, a German *Hausfrau,* ungainly, unmodish and stout, a woman seemingly bereft of feminine vanity.

Franz absolutely loathed Wagner and behaved toward the composer with offensive rudeness, not only because he had no use for his music but also because he had no use for Wagner the man. *Tannhäuser* was still bearable, *Lohengrin* sickly sweet; as for the later works, then under production, they were not to be endured. As to Wagner the man, one cannot altogether blame Franz for being repelled, for Wagner at the time showed, with his new-found power, his least attractive side to the citizens of Munich. He was not only deeply embroiled in the Cosima scandal, but as the favorite of the King he insisted on meddling in Bavarian politics, as well as lording it over the Opera and the orchestra, turning these institutions into a Wagner theater. The reforms and stricter discipline demanded by him and Bülow were just, or would have been had they been less egocentrically oriented. But demands for reform are hardly ever popular, and the Bavarians thought that their artistic institutions were good enough. The players would rather eat sausages than consume so much difficult new music. Two currents swirled around Wagner during this Munich period, one of fanatical enthusiasm and one of deep suspicion. Franz's suspicion was very deep. It was of course within Wagner's power to have Franz dismissed. He did no such thing, though the two men quarreled on more than one occasion. For, whatever Franz's opinion, he played Wagner's music beautifully. Bülow and others remembered the melting tone he summoned in the *Tristan* and *Meistersinger* horn passages. Once during a rehearsal Wagner was passing through the orchestra and remarked jokingly, "Always dour, these horn players." Franz replied, "We have every reason to be."

Franz's relationship with Bülow was not much better. Bülow said of him, "The fellow is intolerable. But when he blows his horn, one cannot be angry with him." At the end of one long rehearsal Strauss declared that he was tired and could play no more. Bülow, who himself was irritable and short-tempered, shouted at Franz, "Then go and apply for your pension." Strauss picked up his horn, went to the intendant, and asked for his pension, "because Herr von Bülow has so ordered." Perfall had to use all his tact to smooth over the incident. Bülow complained that "the intrigues of a Strauss" and others of his ilk made his life so difficult "that I can no longer maintain my subjective, personal indifference to them."* Later Strauss and Bülow became reconciled; this was after Bülow had taken an interest in Richard's music.

Franz Strauss's hatred of Wagner endured to the end of his days. The day after Wagner's death in 1883, before beginning a rehearsal under Hermann Levi, the orchestra stood for a moment in silent tribute to the dead composer. Franz Strauss alone kept his seat.

It was in the atmosphere of "orthodox" music that the boy Strauss grew up. His father's gods were Mozart above all, then Haydn and Beethoven, Schubert, Weber, Mendelssohn, and Spohr. Until Richard was sixteen years old, these were the composers who nourished his imagination. As to his general education, it was the normal one given to a good German boy going to a good German school. It was humanistically slanted, following a Teutonic orientation. A German education included, in addition to the belief that the best music was German music, a thorough knowledge of the classics of German literature—Lessing, Schiller, Goethe and the lyric poets—and a fair acquaintance with the plays of Shakespeare in their translation by Schlegel and Tieck, a translation so adroit that the Germans very nearly consider Shakespeare to have been a German poet. In the visual arts the taste was more international, excluding the French. How could the Germans help themselves, Germany's quota of Dürer, Cranach, Grünewald, and a few

---

* Letter to Wagner, April 8, 1869.

artists of the highest rank being insufficient? Richard Strauss early became familiar with Italian Renaissance art and the great painters of the Netherlands. He had opportunity to see masterpieces in Munich's marvelous museum, the Alte Pinakothek. He never lost his interest in painting. Strauss was an educated man, rounded in the arts. We shall have opportunity later to acknowledge the breadth of his culture.

He was quite a good student, and by the time he was graduated from the Gymnasium at eighteen he had learned a lot of Latin, a little Greek, and very little French.

But along with these pleasant heritages, Strauss absorbed in his father's house some of the Teutonic prejudices. Musically Italy was not worth bothering about. Verdi was a vulgar composer, turning out barrel-organ tunes. One had to be suspicious of the French: aside from Molière and Napoleon, France had produced hardly any great men, the people being entirely frivolous. These clichés, narrow though they were, were innocent enough. More serious and more consequential was the prevalent anti-Semitism, to which the father fully subscribed. (We can imagine how he must have suffered playing for the conductor Hermann Levi.) When making music with Richard, Franz insisted on strict observance of the tempo. If Richard did not satisfy him, his favorite censure was "You hurry like a Jew." Franz may have disagreed with everything Wagner and Bülow stood for, but on one subject they were in accord. It is sad and disgusting to see manifestations of virulent prejudice in a man like Bülow. Over and over again he curses the Jews. To give but one example of several, he writes to Wagner:

> I am seeing the dark side: I no longer believe in the possibility of our being saved from general degradation—i.e., Judaization—the disease has spread too far. And since the positive forces in State and society—nobility, Army, clergy—are no longer very powerful, regeneration can only come through the masses. But they would need a bellwether, and, there again, none but a Jew would be able to qualify for the mission. So we should have to wait for the coming of the opposite of a Messiah—namely, one who would fasten his people to the cross.*

* *Ibid.*

This is an obvious rehash of Wagner's unappetizing hash, and Bülow was being more papal than the Pope. All this and more was inculcated into the young Richard.

As a very young child Richard showed a responsiveness to music. When he was six he composed a little Christmas song. There was no question that Richard was destined to follow a musical career. No other was even considered. But it stands to the credit of the father that he suppressed any ambition to make a child prodigy of Richard. Rather, Franz saw to it that his son's musical education proceeded slowly and was well rounded.

His musical proclivity was acknowledged by his teachers in the Gymnasium, which Strauss entered when he was ten years old. He seems to have had at least one sympathetic teacher, who wrote of the eleven-year-old boy: "There aren't many students who show as much sense of duty, talent, and liveliness as this boy. . . . He learns quite easily. Whatever he does learn gives him pleasure and inspires him to greater industry. His attention in class is good; nothing escapes him. Yet he can hardly sit still a minute, and the school bench is for him an odious object. Good humor and merriment sparkle from his blue eyes day after day. . . . Every teacher must love such a boy; it is difficult not to betray one's predilection. Strauss is a potential musical talent."*

His attention in class could not have been *that* good. There is extant a notebook in which on the back of a mathematical exercise he sketched a violin concerto. Richard loathed mathematics, though later when he became financially successful he could add very well!

Much of his early youth was spent with the numerous members of the Pschorr family. Josephine had four sisters, all of them married and all of them living in Munich. One aunt, Johanna, was his favorite. For her, who was a good singer, he wrote a number of songs. He was then fifteen years old.

Only the introspective writer bent on minute autobiography may be expected to set on paper his remembrance of things past, and do so in a way that offers us a trustworthy record. Strauss did not do so. What were the transitory troubles of his development? Did he as a boy and young man suffer and struggle and thus acquire under-

---

* Quoted in Franz Trenner (Ed.), *Richard Strauss: Dokumente seines Lebens und Schaffens.*

standing and compassion? Was his a happy childhood? The evidence is scanty, but whatever evidence there is points that way, to a childhood replete with a serenity wrapped in enough money, the security of belonging to a family of importance in town, and the protection of the solidarity that prevailed among the members of the Pschorr family. His inner life seems to have been as serene as his outer life. With all the work that a young gifted boy was expected to do, and with all the education that was crammed into his head, there was time for leisure, time for summer and winter vacations spent in the surroundings of Munich, a countryside blessed with exceptional beauty, with blue-green fields, with cold still lakes and high but not unfriendly mountains. Richard Strauss retained in later life a love for high places. He preferred the mountains to the sea. As a boy he enjoyed winter sports. He was proficient on skates. This pleasure in a winter warmed by the round-bellied tile oven of the Biedermeier style echoed itself long after in scenes of *Arabella* and *Intermezzo*.

However, lest this reconstruction of youth seem too idyllic, it is well to remember that the German school system of the period would appear to us today a cold gray system and that, whatever were its advantages in making the boys and girls toe the mark and learn a lot of miscellaneous facts, it did not dispense understanding or a view of the world that led to tolerance. Nor did it encourage any sort of give-and-take between pupil and teacher. The teacher quoted above may well have been an exception—there are good teachers to be found in any system—for the average teacher of the Munich Royal Gymnasium was a dreary official whose small salary was compensated for by his own large sense of importance. Teachers were trained to be martinets, and schools were run like military barracks. When the teacher entered the classroom the pupils stood stiff at attention. This gesture symbolized the general stiffness, as did the little book, "the Class-Book," in which the teacher marked down any pupil's infraction of the rules, as did the division of learning into precisely timed periods during which a precise amount of the curriculum had to be traversed. Discipline above all! Stefan Zweig, in his autobiography, *Die Welt von Gestern*, speaks of "the unconscious bitterness" which this system created in young minds. "We had to learn the prescribed portion and submitted to exams to determine if we had learned it; not once during the eight years did a teacher ask what we might wish to learn; guiding inspiration, for which every young man secretly yearns, was completely absent." There is no evidence that Strauss's schooling created in him "unconscious bitterness." On the other hand, there is no evidence that Strauss took anything but dry data away from school. His "guiding inspiration," good and bad, came from his home, a home in which music reigned.

When Strauss was eleven, his father set him to learning the fundamentals of music in earnest. He studied musical theory with F. W. Meyer, who was a friend of Franz's, an important member of the orchestra, occasionally serving as its conductor. He had begun instructions on the piano much earlier, first tentative lessons being given to him when he was four and a half years old. His teacher was August Tombo, who was a harpist in the orchestra. It was Tombo who went to Wagner to tell him that the harp part in the Fire Music of the *Walküre* was unplayable. Wagner paid him the compliment of asking him to correct the score as Tombo thought best. Benno Walter, another colleague from the orchestra, gave him instruction on the violin. Strauss never really mastered either instrument, though he became reasonably proficient as a pianist. These men, all colleagues of his father, passed on to the young boy the principles of German music, trained him in the classic sonata form, and sternly administered the do's and don't's of traditional harmony.

What he took in he gave out. Quite early the composer began to compose, quite early did he begin to cover a quantity of notepaper, trying his 'prentice hand at many and several forms of music, for Strauss was nothing if not prolific. These student compositions are derivative, of such a nature that they must have pleased his father and given no inkling that the composer was later to bite the hand that had musically fed him. Norman Del Mar has given us an affectionate analysis of several of these beginnings, such as a set of piano miniatures redolent of Schumann, Beethoven and Mendelssohn, a piano sonata "for all intents and purposes one of Mendelssohn's *Lieder ohne Worte*";* a set of variations for horn and piano com-

* Norman Del Mar, *Richard Strauss: A Critical Commentary on His Life and Works*, Vol. I.

posed for his father by the fourteen-year-old boy; quantities of songs; and during the last year of school, when excerpts from Sophocles' *Electra* were being acted by the class, a chorus from *Electra* which was duly performed at the graduation exercises. Did Strauss remember this when, almost thirty years after, he turned to Hofmannsthal's *Elektra?* Later (1882) came a violin concerto, a horn concerto, and a cello sonata for which Joachim congratulated him. The list of early compositions is long.

Within the family these compositions did not lack for admiration. With all his other activities, Franz also served as the guiding spirit and leader of an amateur orchestra. They gave concerts regularly, followed by discussion, beer, and sausages. Franz introduced his son's compositions into the repertoire; in due course these twenty-seven or thirty gentlemen rehearsed Richard's First Symphony (in D minor). A composer must hear his music performed if he is to make progress; Strauss was given such opportunity early. Surprisingly the young man's symphony was deemed good enough to merit a professional performance: Hermann Levi scheduled it for one of the regular subscription concerts of the Munich Musical Academy. Johanna Strauss recalled that her father, who was playing in the orchestra, was all on edge, while the young author (seventeen years of age) appeared to be completely self-possessed. The symphony was politely applauded. Strauss later disowned it and begged his father not to send the score to anyone.

On graduation from the Gymnasium, Strauss enrolled at the University of Munich to take a few humanistic courses in aesthetics, philosophy, history of civilization, and Shakespeare. This was in the winter of 1882. In the summer of that year, Franz Strauss was bidden to go to Bayreuth to play in the first performance of *Parsifal.* He took his son along. (The story goes that Franz went only because Levi asked him to go; it was a *quid pro quo.* In return for Levi's performing Richard's symphony, Franz had to consent. But this story is not authenticated.) What impression the work made on Richard we do not know, nor how many of the sixteen performances he heard, nor whether he was there at the last performance (August 29), when Wagner noticed that Hermann Levi was in pain during the third act and, slipping unobserved into the orchestra, took the baton from the ailing conductor and led the work to its end. This was the last time that Wagner appeared as a conductor.*

Whatever were Strauss's reactions, it is certain that in his early years the father's taste was reflected in the son: Richard started out in life as a convinced anti-Wagnerian. One of Richard's school friends was another music student, Ludwig Thuille. Later Thuille moved to Innsbruck, and Richard used to write to him and give him his impressions of the music he heard in Munich. This is what he reported about a performance of *Siegfried,* heard when he was fourteen: "I was bored out of my mind. It was gruesome boredom, so horrible that I cannot describe it. Really awful! The beginning is a long drum roll . . . which growls in the deepest regions. It sounded so stupid that I laughed out loud. There isn't a trace of consequential melody. I tell you, there is such disorder as you cannot imagine. At this point [Act I, when Mime asks Siegfried if he knows what fear is] a cat could have croaked and the rocks could have turned into scrambled eggs out of pain over the disgusting dissonances. . . . The only thing which was halfway right was the song of the Forest Bird. . . ."† And so on, at great length and with youthful vehemence.

Similarly, he found *Lohengrin* unworthy. He wrote to Thuille: "The introduction consists of a humming of violins in a high range, in A major. You can hear it but it sounds terribly sweet and sickly, as does the whole opera. Only the story is good."‡ The harmonies of *Tristan,* at first piquant to the ear, became as "tiring as a steady diet of lobster mayonnaise."§ And, with the assurance of inexperience, he uttered the prophecy "You may be certain that ten years from now not a soul will know who Richard Wagner is."

All the same, he was soon to know who Wagner was; rather, what his music meant. He began to study the score of *Tristan;* in company with another student, he played through it. Franz in his dressing gown entered the room and the "hated sounds" ceased.

* Since in Bayreuth the orchestra is unseen by the audience, no one in the audience had an inkling of what had happened.

† Quoted in Max Steinitzer, *Richard Strauss.*

‡ Letter of February 22, 1879.

§ Letter to his father, February 1, 1884.

But not for long. How indeed could he have escaped the fascination of this "music beyond music," which by this time permeated the atmosphere of all musical Germany and indeed of the world?

The paradox that underlies Strauss's creation is this: that only after he broke away from the classic scheme, only after he broke away from his father's teaching, only after he turned from being an anti-Wagnerian to being the admirer of the sage of Bayreuth, which he was to remain all his life, only after he had bathed himself in the dangerous stream of the tetralogy, did he learn to swim strongly. Wagner lifted him beyond Wagner.

The year after his first visit to Bayreuth, Richard, now nineteen years old, was sent away from home so that he might see more of the world—or at least more of Germany—receive fresh impressions, compare the musical life of other towns with that of the city which, though its music was excellent, was yet not the major capital. Most important, the journey was to aid him in making contacts with those who might prove useful to his career. From this period we have the first of the series of letters to his father—as well as the letters of admonition which the older man wrote to the younger—which contain Richard Strauss's observations on paintings seen, theaters attended, opera and music heard. In December of the year of 1883 (a year that was marked by Wagner's death in Venice on February 13) he went to Berlin, stopping on his way in Leipzig and Dresden. In Dresden he was thrilled by the famous Gallery and particularly by Raphael's *Sistine Madonna*, which he likened "to the pianissimo G-major point in the beginning of *The Consecration of the House* Overture."* Berlin, he found out soon, was a city very different from his Munich. It was a city where wine was drunk, rather than beer, a city in which the well-to-do ate lobster rather than sausages. The Prussian social gesture was a clicking of the heels, a rapid, stiff bow from the waist. Its language was precise and clipped, a dialect very different from the comfortable, careless, and mouth-filling Bavarian which Strauss had heard as a child.

As the Berliners looked down upon all other Germans, considering themselves as a kind of private bodyguard of His Serene Majesty the Kaiser, so did they look up to any man who wore a uniform.

---

* Letter to his father, December 12, 1883.

The Prussian officer was the lord of the manor. The splendor of official uniforms was matched by the splendor of the women's gowns, all this to underscore the belief that here was the center of a world to come, the crossroads of all Europe.

Being Germans, they needed to enrich the show with substance. The intellectual life of Berlin could exist and grow alongside the political. Men of mind were almost as much in demand as men of muscle; the spectacles of the studious were as proudly worn as the monocle of the military.

The pomp and gaiety that pervaded Berlin were conspicuously displayed. All was well in the Prussian edifice, at least on the street floor. From the basement there arose, now and then, some grumblings, as yet hardly disturbing. Bismarck was still the chief executive of the Reich, and the Kaiser, now quite old, its undisputed warlord. Yet against Bismarck, against the truculent policy of Wilhelm I, indeed against Prussian hegemony in general, voices were beginning to be raised. In 1878, because of an attempted assassination of the Kaiser by a Socialist, a severe bill to repress socialism had been brought into Parliament. It had then been rejected, but it was followed by new disturbances and by consequent reprisals, such as the suppression of liberal clubs and newspapers and new proposals of gagging bills. There were violent debates, which availed nothing. Restriction of liberty led to an increase of emigration. Between 1875 and 1884 emigration from Germany (especially from Prussia) increased fivefold. But all this was not too important, a dissonance not strong enough to be heard against the patriotic chorus.

The first winter Strauss spent in Berlin was to him a winter of content. He was young, personable, even handsome, with his large blue eyes which looked coolly upon the world, a forehead that was soft and pale, set off by a crop of dark wavy hair. He was tall and thin and gangling, but he carried himself erect. The young man was quickly invited here and there, his father having unlocked the doors of artistic Berlin society for him. He was installed in a "beautiful room . . . in the liveliest and most beautiful part of a beautiful city (where at least six lines of horsecars meet),"* though the

* Letter to his father, December 26, 1883.

room was located in a girls' school, and he was occasionally disturbed in his work by the giggling of the school misses. Not only homes but social functions were open to him, and for a time he made the rounds of balls, *redoutes,* masquerades, and charade parties. He was, as was to be expected, very much taken by the young women he met, who possessed a worldliness new to him and who could not only dance but also discuss Spinoza as well as voice an opinion on the question of whether or not God existed. (At least some of them could discuss this.) Richard was all the more socially acceptable because he had learned to play cards. Already at that age he was a good Tarok player. Later he changed to what was to remain his favorite game, Skat.*

His father was well satisfied: "I note with pleasure that you are moving in good social circles; this is of great use to you in your worldly development. . . . Try not to give offense. You express yourself too impetuously: don't be too forward."†

Professionally Richard was what Gilbert would have described as a "pushing young particle," running from musical pillar to musical post, calling on this cellist and on that pianist, this critic and that journalist, playing his cello sonata at a social evening—that is, he played the piano part and reported with no modesty whatever that it was "colossally applauded"—seeking a recommendation from one well-wisher to be passed on to the next. He made the acquaintance of such men as Joseph Joachim; Karl Klindworth, pianist and pupil of Liszt, who fashioned the piano reduction of the Ring; Hermann Wolff, the famous impresario and concert agent, "a valuable acquaintance"; Philipp Spitta, the biographer of Bach; and the conductor Ernst von Schuch, who was later to lead the premières of several of Strauss's operas. He heard the great Eugen D'Albert play the piano. He went to concerts and the opera on free tickets and to

* All his life he was a passionate cardplayer, constantly looking for Skat partners and opponents worthy of his mettle. When he was on concert tours, he played a great deal of poker, though rarely for very high stakes. He never mastered bridge, which in his later years had displaced Skat as the favorite German card game. Strauss liked to win! Piatigorsky recalls that Strauss, with whom he played Skat, engaged him often and suspects that the reason lay not only in his good cello playing but his poor ability as a cardplayer.

† Letter of January 10, 1884.

the theater whenever the parental allowance, which he was determined not to overspend, permitted.

In short, he was twenty, and he knew precisely what he wanted. Each step he took, each move he made, each prominent person he cultivated, served his purpose, that of becoming a successful composer. As yet he had no thought of becoming a conductor.

Three youthful compositions are yet to be mentioned, for each of them plays a certain importance in Strauss's early career. His first complete orchestral work is a "Festival March"; it represents a remarkable feat of sheer nerve, if nothing else, considering that it was composed in 1876 by a twelve-year-old boy. It is his first published composition and now bears the number Opus 1. The "March" was published only because Uncle Georg Pschorr offered to pay the cost of bringing the work into print. Young Richard approached Breitkopf and Härtel, one of Germany's two leading music publishing houses—nothing less would do—and they did publish it, having nothing to lose.* Shortly after, when Strauss offered them another work without subvention, they refused it. Franz Spitzweg, a relative of the painter and an intimate friend of Bülow's, decided that this young man had talent and accepted him. The reward of such perspicacity proved historic: all of Strauss's early tone poems went to Spitzweg's firm, J. Aibl, a small publishing house. (The firm was merged in 1904 with the Austrian publishing house, Universal-Edition.)

The second work is a series of eight Lieder (Opus 10) composed when he was eighteen. The last of these eight is "Allerseelen" (All Souls' Day), a little miracle of bittersweet evocation, daring harmonically and melodically, and presaging Strauss's most beautiful later songs.

The third work is the Serenade for Wind Instruments in E flat (Opus 7). Its importance lies in the fact that it attracted the attention of the man who was to play a decisive part in Strauss's life, Hans von Bülow.

Because the career of Strauss is ineluctably linked to Bülow's

* Several biographers state that Breitkopf and Härtel refused the "March." Evidently this is an error. The "March" was published by them and is still in the Breitkopf catalogue.

sponsorship, because Strauss owed much to the older man, and because Bülow himself is one of the most challenging of characters in musical history, it might be well at this point to digress from the mainstream of the biography and sketch a portrait of the man whom Strauss called "the mirror of all the shining virtues of the executant artist."

Bülow

Most illustrious of the pianists who followed Liszt; most provocative of the conductors who brought new insight to the interpretation of the major works of musical literature; an artist praised to the sky and condemned with contumely; a musical personality high in demand but so uncomfortable that his going was as welcome as his coming; exigent with his public yet courting the public's favor; a worker of ferocious energy who yet could sink into periods of flabby lassitude; a friend capable of unselfish generosity yet one who could wound with savage sarcasm; a man who hid behind the manner of an admiral the self-accusation of failure, feasting at the banquet of fame yet always remaining hungry; receptive to new social ideas and at the same time bigoted and intolerant; humorous and lachrymose, cowardly and courageous; the most important proselytizer for music to appear in the latter half of the nineteenth century—that was Hans Guido Freiherr von Bülow.

By the time Richard Strauss met him, he had experienced enough triumph and suffering to fill to the brim the destiny of most men. He was fifty-four and world-renowned; Strauss was twenty and unknown.

Bülow looked more like a French statesman than like a German musician; one could imagine him getting to his feet in the Chambre des Députés and freezing his opponent with frigid aphorisms. He was elegant of bearing. A high-domed head with a long neck sat on top of a thin small body. He held himself exaggeratedly erect. He walked with a quick and nervous step, his pointed goatee, now graying, stabbing the air before him. Young Strauss, who was anything but timid, told his father that he was looking forward to the meeting with fear.

Bülow was born in Dresden. He began to study the piano at the age of nine, his teacher being Friedrich Wieck, the father-in-law of Robert Schumann. Prompted by his parents, he made a halfhearted attempt to break away from music by studying jurisprudence. The law bored him. He plunged himself ever deeper into the world of sound, probing diverse styles and forms of music. German though he was, his musical sensitivity was internationally oriented, his taste comprehensive. Early he became a musical progressive, enthusiastically championing the cause of the new music of Liszt and Wagner. When he heard Liszt conduct a performance of *Lohengrin* in Weimar, he made up his mind that music, not the law, was to be his life, and he sought out Liszt for his teacher. Soon he became a successful pianist, a virtuoso of the first rank, traveling up and down the Continent.

Though he was born in Dresden, he considered himself a Prussian, belonging to the Junker class. He could be very Prussian when it suited him, only to act contrary to Junker tenets the next moment. He admired Bismarck inordinately, seeing in the Chancellor the savior of the German nation, at the same time that he was left in his political leanings. In 1848 he was all for the revolution, and later in the sixties he sympathized with the Socialists. He despised the mob and yet sided with "the people," whatever he may have meant by "the people."

He married Liszt's daughter Cosima when he was twenty-seven. The facile judgment has it that the marriage was a relationship in which Bülow was as much attracted to the father as to the daughter, that he married the daughter to marry the father. There is truth in that but it is not the whole truth. In the early years Cosima and Hans were drawn to each other by bonds of deep affection, if not of love, and by an affinity of intellectual interests, for Cosima—as well as Bülow—had a mind that was eager for every form of artistic aggrandizement. It was only later that they began to drift apart. Cosima was disappointed: she had expected Bülow to become a great composer, and the more intimately she became acquainted with Wagner's work—particularly when Wagner played for them portions of the *Meistersinger* score—the more she realized that her ambition could never be fulfilled. As she was more and more drawn to Wagner the artist, so did her love for Wagner the man ripen, finally to become the be-all and end-all of her life. It is true as well that Bülow stood in awe of Cosima and that this awe was not conducive to parity. In later years he wrote, "She was too important a woman for her first husband."

To Richard Wagner Bülow was devoted with a dedication that was almost parasitical, an adoration that filled his whole being, which neither the loss of his wife to Wagner nor the slime the world slung at him could diminish. Not once during the time that Cosima lived with Wagner—Bülow knew about it; he was far from the conventional cuckolded husband*—nor during the time when divorce proceedings were instituted nor at any time thereafter did Bülow speak out against his friend. Wagner forced him, for a time at any rate, to become an exile; but it was only the fact itself that he bemoaned, not the man who had caused it. To his dying day Bülow remained faithful to his idol.

Throughout most of his life, his activities were fourfold. He combined his pianistic career with that of conducting. As we have seen, Wagner called him to Munich as the principal conductor of the Royal Opera. Third, he was a teacher. He was, fourth, a composer, producing a quantity of feeble music. The two works that were most frequently performed in the day of Strauss's youth were his *Nirvana*, a symphonic tone poem in the style of Liszt, and his incidental music to Shakespeare's *Julius Caesar*. They have been forgotten.

Perhaps his interests were too manifold for his own peace of mind. Except when he was sunk in despair, and perhaps even then, he was constantly studying, reading, writing, discussing, philosophizing, planning. Liszt put it to him strongly: "What Rossini told

---

* See Ernest Newman's analysis of this point in *The Life of Richard Wagner*, Vol. III, Ch. 21. Newman's conclusion: "The theory, then, that Bülow was 'deceived' must, on the totality of the evidence in our possession, be ruled out. He had seen for a long time that it was the hand of fate that had drawn Wagner and Cosima together; and it was from the noblest motives that he lent himself to the ignoble deceit it became necessary for all three to practice if Wagner, and with him the prospects of his art in Munich, were not to be brought down in ruin."

me in Milan, that in his nature too many elements were mixed, that is true of you. You have the stuff in you for a dozen careers: musician, pianist, music director, composer, writer, editor, diplomat, etc. But you must take your time. And you need a sense of humor."*

A sense of humor he may not have had, but he surely possessed prodigious wit. That wit shows itself in his letters (he was in correspondence with many of the famous men of his time), which are unconventional missives written in a free-roaming impressionistic style and are filled with German, French, English, Italian, Latin, Greek, and occasionally Polish and Russian quotations. He employed his wit often to a sour purpose. But he could also storm the barricades for a quixotic cause. Like Cyrano:

> *He attacks the false nobles, the false saints,*
> *The false heroes, the false artists—in short,*
> *Everyone!*

His pronouncement that there are only two kinds of conductors, those with the score in their heads and those with their heads in the score, has become a standard epigram. As to interpretation, his advice was as simple as it was useless to any conductor of smaller stature than his: "Once you really know the score," he said, "interpretation comes by itself." He once addressed a lady in the first row who was fanning herself: "Madame, if you must fan yourself, do so in rhythm." His judgment on a mediocre pianist was: "His technique enables him to conquer every easiness with the greatest difficulty." ("*Dieser Mann hat eine Technik welche jede Leichtigkeit mit der grössten Schwierigkeit überwindet.*") He hung in his dressing room a picture of the *prima ballerina.* He was not in the least interested in ballet, he explained, but he worshiped the lady because she was the only female in the opera house who did not sing flat. In Vienna he was approached by a casual acquaintance who said coyly, "I bet you do not remember me, Herr von Bülow." Bülow looked at him and replied, "You have won your bet." He devastated a pupil who had played ineptly by telling her that she ought to be swept out of the classroom not with a broom but with a broomstick. Even

---

* Quoted in Richard Du Moulin-Eckart, *Hans von Bülow*.

his praise, Brahms said of him, had the effect of salt in the eyes; it smarted.*

He flailed about him without regard for his own safety. Indeed, he had a positive genius for making himself disliked, time after time finding the one action or the one word calculated to give the strongest offense. Early in his activity in Munich, a discussion took place as to whether the pit for the orchestra could be enlarged. It was pointed out to him that to do this a couple of rows of the stalls would have to be removed. His reply was "Then there will be a few fewer bastards in the audience."† The remark was promptly reported to the newspapers.

He particularly disliked the intendant of the Berlin Opera, Georg Hülsen. In a popular concert in Berlin he programmed the March from Meyerbeer's *Le Prophète* and announced that he was going to demonstrate how this march should be played and how it was *not* played at the "Hülsen Circus." A sharp insult, which caused another uproar.

What was he like in front of his audiences? When he was in the vein he electrified them, creating a communion of rarest enjoyment. He commanded them as well as his orchestra. Every member of the audience felt: "Up there stands a man of iron, of inexorable will, and what he is offering us is the highest art affords." He had the faculty, essential to all great musicians, of making music exciting, of kissing it into life. Audiences shouted and wept at his concerts. Woe to the late arrival! Bülow would turn and annihilate the offender with a look. He demanded and got absolute silence and would not begin if a rustle could still be heard. Once when a few female members of the audience continued to chatter he turned and, glowering menacingly, said, "Ladies, remember, you are not saving Rome." He made great demands on the audience's attention span. He would conduct for the first part of his concert the Ninth

* The aphorism of the three B's—Bach, Beethoven, Brahms—is attributed to him as well. Another excellent epigram of his is untranslatable but will amuse German-speaking readers. He said of a prize-winning composition, "*Je preiser gekrönt, desto durcher fällt es.*" Still another: " '*Kunst*' *kommt von* '*können.*' *Wenn es von* '*wollen*' *käme hiesse es* '*Wulst.*' "

† This is a free translation. He actually used the word *Schweinehunde,* which to a Bavarian is the strongest epithet one can use. He then tried to extricate himself from the affair by saying he had used the word in the North German sense: in Prussia the word had less force. Nobody believed this Pickwickian evasion.

Symphony of Beethoven; then intermission, and for the second part of the concert he would play the Ninth Symphony of Beethoven! He would program three Beethoven symphonies at one concert; he would as a pianist play on one evening all five of the last Beethoven sonatas. Yet in another mood he was quite willing to give "popular programs," filling the evening with showpieces.

He was prone to make speeches to the audiences, often gracious and charming. He liked to teach. Sometimes he would talk nonsense; once, speaking of Beethoven, he dedicated the music to Bismarck, linking him to Beethoven! But he could also harangue the audience and behave boorishly. Then, according to Amy Fay, a pupil of Liszt, "his face seems to say to his audience, 'You are all cats and dogs, and I don't care what you think of my playing.' "* The American critic James Huneker heard him perform in Philadelphia the Tchaikovsky B-flat Minor Concerto, of which Bülow had given the world première in Boston the previous year, in 1875. The presence of the conductor, wrote Huneker, seemed superfluous, "as Bülow gave all the cues from the keyboard and distinctly cursed the conductor, the band, the composition, and his own existence."† Perhaps this was but a manifestation of his doubt in himself: "If dissatisfaction with oneself is a salient characteristic of genius, then I could lay a large claim to genius," he wrote.

After the catastrophe in Munich, when Wagner's relations with Cosima became public knowledge, where was he to turn, how was he to continue his career in a country where the newspapers held him up to ridicule not only as a duped husband but, as the general phrase had it, "the favorite of a king's favorite"? He sank into a despair out of the depth of which he wrote to his friend Bechstein,‡ "Oh God! How alone and friendless am I now! If only all were over —it would be best if some pitying soul were to make me a gift of a sufficient quantity of prussic acid! Is there no accommodating apothecary in Berlin? I would will him my whole library and whatever else I possess."§ One sees that he was not free of dramatizing self-pity. Was he alluding to Romeo's "true apothecary"?

* Quoted in Harold C. Schonberg, *The Great Pianists.*

† Quoted in Schonberg, *op. cit.*

‡ The owner of the Bechstein piano firm and one of Bülow's oldest friends.

§ Letter of August 5, 1869.

But he did not succumb. Life in him was too strong, the will to work too powerful, the love for music too demanding. After a sojourn in Basel, he went to live in Florence for a time. He found there sympathetic and intelligent friends, great success as a pianist, and eventually the companionship of a young Italian girl. All the same, this arch-German could not stay away forever from the fatherland. He did go to America, touring extensively as a pianist and conductor (1875-76), where he played no fewer than 139 concerts. Two years later he resumed residence in Germany. After engagements in various cities—Baden-Baden, a brief return to Munich, Amsterdam, London, St. Petersburg—he accepted at the beginning of 1880 the position of court musical director (*Hof Musik-Intendant*) in Meiningen.

Meiningen was able to retain him for five years, an unusually long period for so restless a soul. There he wrought miracles with the orchestra. In that little town, aided by the support of the music-loving Duke of Meiningen, Georg II, he brought the orchestra to a perfection such as had hardly been known and was not soon to be known again. He made of Meiningen not only a "Beethovenopolis" (his own expression) but the place where several of Brahms's new compositions were first performed. He made the orchestra memorize the music, a feat hardly duplicated since. In Meiningen he found whatever personal happiness this tortured man was capable of. He married for the second time (1882), an actress, a charming and pretty woman. Her name was Marie Schanzer.

Though the amount of work he did in Meiningen was formidable, it did not satisfy all his need for work. He at first planned the continuation of a piano tour, the object of which was to raise money for Bayreuth. His Bayreuth benefit recitals had already produced a considerable sum of money, 28,000 marks, and he had drawn on his own savings to bring that sum up to 40,000 marks, which he had set as his goal.* But then he reconsidered the project, not only because he could hardly stay away long enough from Meiningen but also because he had signed a petition drawn up by a rabid anti-Semite, one Dr. Bernhard Förster (who later became the husband of Elisabeth Nietzsche), a petition to the Reichstag which

* The sum was eventually refused by Wagner.

demanded that German Jews be made second-class citizens.* Bülow now realized that as a concert pianist he must expect a falling off of "about half of his audience," for the concert public was "made up of more Jews than Germans."†

It was at the height of his fame as a conductor in Meiningen that Strauss met him, though the meeting took place in Berlin, where Bülow had taken the orchestra on tour. In the programs he was planning he had included young Strauss's "Serenade." Here he demonstrated that he could overcome personal prejudice as well as change a musical judgment. He could hardly have wished to do a favor to the son of a man whom he could have remembered only with dislike. Nor had his first opinion of Richard Strauss's music been favorable. Spitzweg had asked for Bülow's judgment about some piano pieces by Strauss. Bülow had replied: "The piano pieces by R. Str. I disliked profoundly—unripe and precocious. Lachner [conductor in Munich but a very mediocre composer] is a Chopin in fantasy compared to this. I miss the spirit of youthful invention. In my view we have to deal here not with a genius but, at most, a talent such as comes a dime a dozen [*60 aufs Schock*]."‡ Yet, confronted with a new sample of the young man's work, Bülow changed his mind. On February 7, 1884, Strauss was able to write home: "Bülow will perform my Serenade!!!!" The four exclamation marks indicate that it was no ordinary news that he was conveying.

While Strauss was waiting for this performance to materialize, he opened the newspaper one morning and read with a shock that another and quite unimportant conductor, one Benjamin Bilse, had announced the première of the selfsame "Serenade." Strauss was beside himself. He had known nothing about it. He ran immediately to Wolff, the impresario, who assured him that he too knew nothing about it and that he had not given Bilse the manuscript. In a fury, Strauss went to the concert. He could not prevent the performance, which was "very bad, much too slow, and the orchestra not together."§ Yet the work had a success of sorts, though Strauss took

---

* Wagner had had the good sense not to sign the petition, possibly because he was then involved with Hermann Levi, Angelo Neumann, and Joseph Rubinstein.

† Letter to Hans von Wolzogen, September 10, 1880.

‡ Note of October 22, 1881.

§ Letter to his father, February 19, 1884.

no pleasure in this, his only concern being that Bülow should hear about it and cancel his performance "in blind anger."

As it turned out, Bülow did not take the work off the program, but the performance was postponed one day and was then conducted not by Bülow but by the assistant conductor of the Meiningen orchestra, Franz Mannstädt. Bülow, however, was in the audience and showed his approval by applauding vigorously. After the concert Strauss thanked him and asked whether he might now play a new overture and symphony for him. Bülow declined; he had no time. He had to practice the piano, as he was thinking of going on a concert tour. Strauss's reaction to this was "If I were Brahms, he would sit down at three o'clock at night, drink a cup of black coffee, and study the score."* Perhaps later Bülow would do the same for him, Strauss hoped. Yet he must have been pleased with what he had obtained, because in addition to hearing his work played by the excellent orchestra, he now heard Bülow talk kindly of Strauss's father. To Richard's astonishment, Bülow remembered Franz as "a fine musician with a most beautiful tone. Marvelous phrasing and declamation. 'I learned a lot from him. Write him and tell him so.' "†

A further result of the meeting was that Bülow commissioned Strauss to write a work specially for the Meiningen orchestra. Strauss at once set to work, and in the summer he had ready the Suite for Wind Instruments in B-flat Major (Opus 4). Bülow made a few suggestions for changing the sequence of the four movements, but in the end he declared himself satisfied. He then proposed that after the work had been rehearsed in Meiningen it should be performed on the occasion of a visit of the orchestra to Munich; and more, that at a morning performance before an invited audience the young composer himself be asked to conduct it. Strauss had never held a baton in his hand, but he was quite willing. He asked when he could rehearse the piece, and received the astonishing reply that the orchestra on tour had no time to rehearse. To refuse Bülow's invitation was unthinkable, so there was nothing to do but try to conduct, or at least make a pretense of

---

* Letter to his father, February 29, 1884.
† *Ibid.*

doing so. The incident must have slightly tarnished Strauss's self-esteem, at least temporarily. But worse was to follow.

When before the concert Strauss called for Bülow at his hotel, it was at once evident that Bülow was in the foulest of humors. As they mounted the stairs of the Odeon Concert Hall, he stormed against Munich, protesting that he still felt the wounds that Munich had inflicted on him and Wagner; he railed against Perfall; and he called the Odeon a cross between a church and a stock exchange. In short, Strauss recollected, "he was as exquisitely unpleasant as only he could be when he was angry."

Strauss conducted in a state of semiconsciousness. He could remember afterward only that he had committed no out-and-out blunders. Bülow refused to listen to his young protégé's conductorial debut. Smoking one cigarette after another, he paced furiously up and down the Green Room. When Strauss came back, his father, profoundly moved, entered from the opposite door in order to thank Bülow. At the sight of Franz, Bülow broke out. "Like a furious lion he pounced upon my father. 'You have nothing to thank me for,' he shouted. 'I have not forgotten what you have done to me in this damned city of Munich. What I did today I did because your son has talent and not for you.' Without saying a word my father left the music room from which all others had long fled when they saw Bülow explode. This scene had, of course, thoroughly spoiled my debut for me. Only Bülow was suddenly in the best of spirits."*

Though Bülow was Strauss's most illustrious advocate, there were others who recognized the budding talent. The Serenade for Wind Instruments that led to the Strauss-Bülow meeting had been performed over a year earlier than the Berlin concert by the conductor Franz Wüllner, who was by no means a nonentity. Here and there in Germany's decentralized musical life musicians looked attentively at Strauss's work. One could hardly remain unaware of his existence, for he poured out one piece after another—an overture in C Minor, a piano sonata in B Minor, a cello sonata in F, a violin concerto in D Minor, a horn concerto in E flat—all rather academic,

* Richard Strauss, *Erinnerungen an Hans von Bülow.*

all professionally put together, but none of them really original or convincing. His early classical training, though it endowed him with competence, had to be surmounted before he could say something original. It is astonishing how much notepaper he used up in early tries. Spitzweg was publishing these things one after the other. The publisher demurred a little and told Bülow that he was losing money. "Stick with him," counseled Bülow. "In five years you will make money with him." An accurate prophecy: in five years the première of *Don Juan* took place.

But where was the symphony? (Strauss's early attempt hardly counted.) A German composer had to have a symphony to his credit to call himself a composer. Strauss now tackled the form in earnest and produced in about three months the Symphony in F minor, which he himself thought vastly superior to his first, now disowned, brainchild. It is, however, not very much of a symphony. It has an attractive enough Scherzo but a very weak Finale, and the whole thing is Mendelssohn and Schumann mixed and diluted, with a few drops of modern harmonic bitters added.

This was the first work that carried Strauss's name overseas; it was given on December 13, 1884, by the New York Philharmonic under the direction of Theodore Thomas. Thomas was a man avid for new music, an open-minded experimenter and in more ways than one a pioneer in presenting good music to American audiences. He organized an orchestra of his own, traveling up and down the land on what he called the "Thomas Highway." He gave summer outdoor concerts of a serious character. ("At last," he said, "we are rid of the cornet.") He served as the leading spirit of the Cincinnati May Festival, and he had had charge of the concerts given in connection with the Philadelphia Centennial of 1876. (For the Centennial he commissioned Richard Wagner to compose a special work. Wagner consented, but named a high price, which he was paid. He then sent in "The Centennial March." Thomas rightly considered it a potboiler and never forgave Wagner.) In the course of a visit to Europe, Thomas had called on his old friend Franz Strauss. He was shown the manuscript of the symphony and he immediately agreed to perform it.

The first German performance followed a month after the American première, on January 13, 1885, under Franz Wüllner. Strauss went to Köln for the rehearsal and wrote his parents: "Papa will open his eyes when he hears how modern the symphony sounds. Perhaps it contains a bit too much counterpoint. But it all ebbs and flows so well that it is a pleasure."*

And now an extraordinary bit of luck came to Strauss's aid. Bülow's assistant conductor, Mannstädt, was called to Berlin as the head of the Philharmonic Orchestra—"to give outdoor concerts indoors," Bülow said deprecatingly—and Bülow now had the post. He was besieged by candidates, among them Weingartner and Mahler. But Bülow had an idea of his own. He asked Spitzweg whether "Richard the Third" would be interested in the post. (That was his name for Strauss, because Richard the First was Wagner and after Wagner he couldn't very well call anybody Richard the Second. The best he could do was Richard the Third.)

It is remarkable that Bülow would take such a chance. Strauss was not a conductor, not as yet anyway, and Bülow knew nothing about Strauss's ability as an executant musician, let alone as a trainer of an orchestra. Did Bülow play a hunch? Or did he feel that he could teach the composer? Or did he just like Strauss's personality and want the young man near him? Perhaps all three motives played a part. At any rate, he proposed the opportunity, and Strauss replied that it was "the most joyous surprise imaginable." It would be "a most valuable and ideal position." He hoped modestly that he could "perhaps occasionally conduct preliminary rehearsals." What attracted him most was the chance "to be able, by attending all your rehearsals, to study closely your interpretation of our symphonic masterpieces."†

Bülow then proposed his candidate to the Duke of Meiningen, calling Strauss "an uncommonly gifted young man (as well as the grandchild of the famous beer Pschorrs), whose only fault is his youth." Knowing that the Duke's daughter, Princess Marie, could influence her father in the musical affairs of the city, Bülow advised Strauss to call on the Princess and "captivate her musically." Marie was an accomplished pianist and an enthusiastic member of the

---

* Letter written from Köln, January 12, 1885.

† Letter to Bülow, May 26, 1885. A facsimile of this letter appeared in the review *Die Musik* of January 1905.

Choral Society. Strauss did call on Marie. And the Duke gave his approval.

At the age of twenty-one (though Bülow had told the Duke that Strauss was twenty-two), Strauss obtained his first regular employment. In September 1885 he moved to Meiningen.

4

Toward Brahms and Wagner

His experience in Meiningen was to prove both richer and shorter than he had expected. He was now under Bülow's tutelage and in daily contact with the conductor. The Bülows took Strauss into their home, fed him roast rabbit, venison, and pot roast, and whatever other heavy dishes pass for good cooking in Germany; instructed him how to behave toward the Duke; taught him how to make friends with the orchestra. Frau Bülow advised him how to ingratiate himself with the female members of the chorus. Bülow was in his positive phase. He inspired and exhorted the acolyte, he bubbled with epigrams, he roamed through scores with the enthusiasm of a hunter, and he who could suddenly turn hermit now turned host, inviting one and all to his house. At teatime and after concerts Strauss heard Bülow discourse on music and philosophy, the talk flowing on till past midnight. He met a variety of musicians and actors—as well as a few "gay actresses"—for, small though Meiningen was, it was a music and theater center. And soon after his arrival he met Brahms.

He observed Bülow at work and was himself almost immediately put to the practical business of leading an orchestra and preparing works for performance. Bülow rehearsed every day from ten to one, conducting everything from memory, and Strauss sat there, the score before him, attentive to every nuance. So indelible was the impression of those concerts that in later years Strauss remembered:

> The way in which he set before us the poetic meaning of Wagner and Beethoven was utterly revealing. Nowhere was there a trace of capriciousness: all flowed through inner logic from the form and content of the work itself. His temperament, which carried all before him, was linked to strictest artistic discipline, fidelity both toward the spirit and the letter of the work (the two being identical to a greater degree than is generally supposed). After punctilious rehearsals he presented the works so cleanly that I still consider those performances the summit of orchestral playing.*

(Does this smack of youthful idolatry? Strauss's estimate of singers and musicians was on the whole cool and considerate. He never expressed himself with like fervor about any of the dozens of conductors with whose work he became familiar—until many years later he heard Toscanini conduct *Salome.*)

Meiningen repertoire was not of course limited to Beethoven and Wagner. Brahms was one of Bülow's current enthusiasms. He held open house for Brahms: whenever Brahms wished it, Bülow was ready to play his music or to test a new composition by him. Several of Brahms's major works—the Third and Fourth symphonies, both of the Overtures, and the Second Piano Concerto—were tried out in Meiningen before Brahms committed them to publication. Within the first few weeks of Strauss's stay, Strauss heard Brahms's First and Third symphonies, the *Academic Festival* and *Tragic* overtures, and both of the piano concertos. A little later, Strauss himself conducted Brahms's Violin Concerto.

Strauss was, in fact if not in title, soon promoted to full-fledged conductor. Toward the middle of October Bülow dashed off on one of his journeys and asked Strauss to take over the study of Brahms's new A Major Serenade. His formal debut as a conductor occurred on October 18, though it was but a partial debut. The concert was a strange one, with a longer program than those to which we are now used. Bülow conducted the *Coriolanus* Overture and Beethoven's Seventh; Strauss played the piano part of Mozart's C Minor Concerto with a cadenza fashioned by himself. Bülow had asked him to learn this, though Strauss was far from an accomplished pianist. Learn it he did—no musical undertaking seems to have frightened

---

* Richard Strauss, *Erinnerungen an Hans von Bülow.*

the young man—and play it he did in such a manner that after the first movement Bülow, who conducted, whispered to him, "If you can't manage to succeed at anything else, you can always become a piano player." For the second part of the concert, Strauss conducted his own F-Minor Symphony. Evidently the audience got its money's worth, though it is difficult to understand how they could have absorbed a new symphony after so long a musical banquet. Brahms was present. His laconic comment on Strauss's symphony was "Quite pretty, young man." He then told Strauss that his polyphony was overly complicated, warned him against "thematic pranks," and recommended that he study Schubert's dances for their simple directness.

From Munich Franz was watching his son's progress with one prideful and one anxious eye. Every move that Strauss made was reported to the father, and Franz was not backward with advice: "Dear Richard, you have to get over this habit of conducting with snakelike arm movements. It looks ugly, particularly when one is as tall as you are. It is not even pleasing when Bülow does it, and he is small and graceful. . . . Such mannerisms may provoke laughter in the audience and detract materially from the good impression of your work. When conducting, the left hand should do nothing except turn the pages of the score, and if there is no score, it should remain at rest. The guiding of the orchestra lies in the use of the baton, and a glance. . . . I ask you therefore, dear Richard, to follow my counsel and not to 'carry on.' You have no need of it." As to his composing: "I was very happy over the counsel which Brahms gave you about the use of counterpoint in your music. My dear son, I beg you to take this true and honest advice to heart. It grieves me deeply to see that in all of your new compositions you were more interested in contrapuntal artifice than in natural healthy invention and development."* (And so on at great, great length.)

This proved too much even for the obedient son. He replied in a letter to his mother: "How does Papa know that I 'carry on' when conducting? I am no clown."† Just the same, he was not a graceful conductor at the beginning. A Danish periodical of the period described him humorously as "a pale, long-haired young man who

---

* Letter of October 26, 1885.

† Letter of October 28, 1885.

looks as if he had dined for the last two weeks on newborn lamb and drunk nothing but Karlsbad water." While conducting he "made movements as if he were seasick."

While Strauss was rehearsing the Brahms Serenade, Marie von Meiningen came to watch Strauss at work, being accompanied by several of her regal relatives and their retinue. This was a custom permissible to reigning princes and their families. They liked to break in on rehearsals, partly perhaps because it whiled away a morning, partly—as in Marie's case—because they were genuinely interested, and partly because, like most of us, they were stage-struck and enjoyed a peek behind the scenes. The conductor then had to stop what he was doing and ask whether their Royal Highnesses would care to hear anything special. Even Bülow submitted to this short-order service, at least when he was in good humor. When he was not, he could be quite rude to the visitors. Strauss inquired whether Marie wished to hear a particular composition. "Yes," she replied, "I should like to hear *The Flying Dutchman* Overture." Strauss had only the vaguest acquaintance with this overture and had never seen the full score. In great embarrassment he stammered, "I have never conducted the overture." With a malicious smile which seemed to imply "What kind of conductor is this?" Marie replied, "Well, then, the *Freischütz* Overture. At least you know that one." At this, Strauss took his courage in his two hands and said, "No, I'll try *The Flying Dutchman*." A score was speedily found. Since the orchestra knew the piece, Strauss had to do nothing more than beat time, which he did "with the courage of despair." The overture went "snappily," and the unexpected audience declared itself satisfied. "I scored my first success as a conductor," Strauss wrote his father, "and that with a work by Wagner."*

These were for Strauss days of intense enjoyment, because they were days of intense activity. Bülow was an exacting taskmaster as well as a natural teacher. He shaped the raw fledging into a conductor within the space of a month, an astonishingly short apprenticeship. In addition to his orchestral duties, Strauss rehearsed the ladies' chorus (and drew from Franz the admonition "Be equally charming to all the ladies, don't show favoritism . . . don't listen

* Letter of October 14, 1885.

to gossip"); gave Marie von Meiningen piano lessons; played and heard others play chamber music; read a great deal, the books being supplied to him by Marie Bülow; studied French, and practiced the piano.

In short, he experienced and stilled that omnivorous hunger for learning which is a telltale mark of growing talent. He shared Bülow's enthusiasm for Brahms. Meiningen was agog in those October days, for Brahms's latest symphony, the Fourth, was to have its world première. Brahms was feted and dined and honored. He was invited to Princess Marie's house, where the Prince of Hessen, with three members of the orchestra, played the whole of his B-flat Quartet twice, to Brahms's "unconcealed horror." This man of a prickly gruff exterior—Bülow called him "the bear"—never liked concerts entirely devoted to his music, "and wished that at the end they would add 'a proper piece by a proper musician.' "* At least so he said. One can never be sure what were Brahms's true feelings and thoughts. He hid what he felt. Under that self-deprecating manner lay a nervous vulnerability that could swamp his genuine kindness with mischief. Strauss described him as "cool and catty" (*maliziös*), curiously indifferent to the precise nuances in the playing of his symphony— "You can play it this way or that," he said to Bülow—yet deeply concerned with the success of his work, though he pretended to belittle both the work and its success.

The première of the Fourth took place on October 25, 1885, Brahms conducting. It turned into a triumph for Brahms. The following day he conducted his *Haydn Variations* and the *Academic Festival Overture*. During the overture Bülow played the cymbals and Strauss the timpani, more or less as a lark, though Bülow took it very seriously and became highly nervous. Strauss described the Fourth as "a giant work, great in concept and invention, masterful in its form and in the structure of its periods . . . new and original and yet from A to Z genuine Brahms: in a word, an enrichment of our art."†

Demanding and complex though Strauss's musical experiences were, they could not prevent him from throwing himself into another enthusiasm, the love for the stage. Though years were to pass

* Walter Niemann, *Brahms*.

† Letter to his father, October 24, 1885. He wrote this before the première.

before that enthusiasm was to come to fruition in Strauss's operas, the sense for the theater and the dramatic instinct were implanted in Strauss in the Meiningen days. He could hardly have had a better indoctrination. The repertoire theater in that little town, a private company formed and directed by the Duke, was as famous throughout Germany as was Bülow's orchestra. Duke Georg was what the Germans call a *Theaternarr* (a fool for the theater), having been led to this world by the actress Ellen Franz, his morganatic wife. What the two accomplished made history. With a relatively small troupe of players (but a relatively large sum of money) they developed the "Meiningen style," which was one of completely integrated ensemble playing in which every small role, every episodic detail, was masterfully handled, the supernumerary as carefully directed as the leading player, as much thought being given to Osric as to Hamlet, to Burleigh as to Maria Stuart. It was in Meiningen, almost for the first time, that the three-dimensional stage was effectively used, different levels rising from the stage floor, the actors' movements flowing over these levels. Costumes were of rich materials and designed with minute attention to historical correctness. Props were as far as possible authentic, every drinking cup, lance, and sword of the period. The style of acting was one of extreme passion and orotund declamation. That style was to have an important influence on the Moscow Art Theater.*

Later the Meiningen style deteriorated into fussiness, but in Strauss's day it was at the height of its vigor. Whenever Strauss could spare an evening, there he was, drinking it all in. When he finally departed from Meiningen, and went to court to take his official leave, he was told that the Duke was particularly sorry to see him go—here Strauss was ready to bow politely—because he was the best *claqueur* who had ever operated in the Meiningen theater.

An unexpected development propelled Strauss into a prominence for which he probably was not ready. Bülow, who really was not happy unless he made a deadly enemy once a month, quarreled with Brahms. His anger may have been justified but he retaliated in a strange way. The Fourth Symphony had been an enormous suc-

* One of the last graduates of the Meiningen school was the great German actor Albert Bassermann. His father August had been manager of the theater and one of its leading players.

cess, so much so that Bülow used it as a showpiece for the orchestra on its tours. Bülow was particularly anxious to conduct it at a forthcoming concert in Frankfurt. He suddenly learned that Brahms had announced that he himself would conduct the symphony in that city with the Frankfurt orchestra. It is not clear what Brahms's reason was for committing so boorish a discourtesy toward a man to whom he owed nothing but gratitude. One of Brahms's biographers conjectures that "it appears quite possible that, displeased with the plodding excessively detailed interpretive technique of Bülow, which tended to upset the continuity of the music, Brahms wanted to bring forth his own concept, more simple and robust; or perhaps he wished to offer his work firsthand to his friends in Frankfurt, who were not overly fond of Bülow."* Neither explanation can exonerate Brahms.

Bülow behaved as foolishly as the composer. He not only fumed and stormed at Brahms, but, feeling that his prestige with the orchestra had been undermined, he handed in his resignation.† Brahms tried to apologize, calling himself "thoughtless and inconsiderate." "Stupidity and everything else—thy name is Brahms," he wrote to Bülow.‡ The Duke tried to change Bülow's mind, without success. Bülow departed on December 1, 1885, the real reason for his departure lying in his unceasing restlessness. And Strauss became his successor.§

Though Strauss, according to Bülow, conducted "with unbelievable security," he could hardly have been ready to step into Bülow's shoes. He threw himself into the task with vigor, and programmed such major works as Mozart's Requiem, Beethoven's Second, Schubert's "Unfinished," Berlioz' *Harold in Italy*, as well as a new symphony by his friend Ludwig Thuille. But it soon became obvious that the Duke had lost some of his enthusiasm for the orchestra. A keen rivalry had always existed between the theater and the orches-

---

* Hans Gal, *Johannes Brahms: His Work and Personality*.

† There was a mixup as well about the period of a vacation for Marie Bülow, who was active at the Meiningen Theater. She resigned. But this difficulty could have been resolved.

‡ Letter of November 19, 1885.

§ More than a year after the incident, Bülow was in Vienna. Brahms called on him at his hotel. Bülow being out, Brahms left his card, with a musical quotation on it from *The Magic Flute*: "Shall I never see you again, beloved?" Bülow accepted this advance, and their friendship was restored.

tra. There was talk now of reducing the size of the orchestra. Strauss was not—as yet—a box office draw; he may have felt that to move on was the better part of valor.

Before Strauss left Meiningen, he had formed a close friendship with a man whose influence was to prove almost equal to that of Bülow, and in certain respects more decisive. This equivocal personality was Alexander Ritter, a man who—in the planetary system the center of which was the sun of Wagner—moved in an inner circle but remained a cold star, shining in reflected light. It was Alexander Ritter who led Strauss to Wagnerism. It was he who changed Strauss's outlook as a composer.

Ritter was one of the five children of Julie Ritter, a woman to whom posterity owes a debt of gratitude. Early she recognized Wagner's genius, and in a noble and unselfish way she made him a modest allowance, which enabled Wagner to continue his work on the Ring poem. This she did though she had five children to support. She increased this allowance when, considerately, a rich uncle of hers died and left her well off. She did not live to see the Ring completed, dying in 1865, though she did live to see Wagner become a powerful figure under the protection of Ludwig. Her son Alexander had been trained as a violinist and later became a conductor.

Ritter had been a member of Liszt's circle in Weimar, had known Wagner well, and had married Wagner's niece Franziska. For a time he had fallen on unsuccessful days and tried to make a living by running a music store. Bülow, who had befriended him long before, had rescued him from the life of a merchant by giving him a place among the violins in the Meiningen orchestra. Considerations of friendship counted for little with Bülow if music was involved. This was an exception, for Ritter was a second-rate violinist. He was as well a second-rate composer. He composed a number of tone poems and two short operas, one of which, *Der faule Hans* (Lazy Hans), was premiered in Munich at the time Strauss moved to Meiningen. His music is a feeble echo of Liszt and Wagner.

There was nothing feeble about his personality. Now at fifty-two —he was exactly as old as Brahms—with his long beard and mane of abundant hair, with large eyes that frequently darkened in what he thought righteous anger, he seemed like a Teutonic Zeus.

He did not merely speak, he made pronouncements; he did not merely give an opinion, he set it forth as law. Ritter was one of those arch-Germans in whom a wide and never-ceasing education, much reading and ruminating, coagulated into a hard core of beliefs and prejudices which nothing could soften, nothing reshape. It was to be expected that he would be an ardent Wagnerite. His passion for Wagner did not confine itself to Wagner's music or Wagner's dramatic theories but embraced all of Wagner's ideas from vivisection to pan-Germanism. There was no foolishness Wagner had uttered which this disciple did not consider gospel. On the other hand he held Brahms in small esteem. "One has to study Brahms carefully," Ritter said, "until one notices that there's nothing in it."*

Ritter had drunk deep as well at the springs that had nourished Wagner's philosophy. He worshiped Schopenhauer, he believed in the regeneration of German art through the participation of "the folk," and he daydreamed of German legends, ascribing to them mystical significance, cosmically valid. German plays and German operas needed to be rooted in German legend and distill ethical teachings. Nothing less would do. He was, one will not be surprised to learn, a venomous anti-Semite, outdistancing the Master in Germanic arrogance. And there was only one Master. Ritter never swerved from the conviction, expressed to him by Bülow in a letter written almost twenty years earlier, that "All that is still ideal and worth preserving in the German spirit lives in this one head."†

Ritter continued what Bülow had begun, Strauss's conversion to Wagner. Once the friendship was formed, that conversion was inevitable. Strauss became a member of the club, abiding by all the rules. It is clear that Strauss, though he was "uncommonly gifted" (Bülow's estimate) as a young man, was at the same time uncommonly impressionable, and that his artistic development needed the traversal of several phases before it could become independent. Phase one was the classicism fostered by his father; phase two Bülow's view of music, which led to the influence of Brahms; and now, the latest, the sorcery administered by a Merlin trained in all the tricks of Bayreuth.‡

---

* Quoted in Max Steinitzer, *Richard Strauss.*

† Letter of July 31, 1866.

‡ Most of the correspondence between Ritter and Strauss had been lost. One day a

Ritter believed, as did Wagner, that music could, and at its best should, express an underlying poetic idea, that if it did not tell a story it ought at least to heighten and intensify a poetic concept. Ritter spoke of "music as expression" (*Musik als Ausdruck*). There was nothing very startling in all this. Composers from time immemorial had known that music could express a non-musical idea, just as they had known that music need *not* express a non-musical idea. What need to spin theories? Ah—but we are forgetting that it is a German specialty to give a fine-sounding phrase to a simple idea. Ritter was not the first nor the last to codify the convenient. The slogan "Music as expression" served Strauss well as he turned to the tone poem. These tone poems, having Liszt and Wagner as spiritual ancestors, now could encompass a wider range of non-musical concepts than had hitherto been thought possible.

Before the tone poems Strauss had, so to speak, to get Brahms out of his system. Strauss did not compose much during the months he spent in Meiningen, and it is difficult to see how he could have had the time to do so. But the two works which do belong to the Meiningen period, *Wanderers Sturmlied* (The Wanderer's Storm Song)* and *Burleske* (Burlesque), are clearly works for which Johannes stood godfather.

The Wanderer's Storm Song is composed for orchestra and a six-part chorus, the words being an adaptation of a poem by Goethe. The poem is a youthful one, an aftermath of Goethe's love for a young girl, Frederika Brion, the daughter of a pastor. Goethe gave her up and told her so; then in despair he roamed through the woods and fields, penning this strange rhapsody, the burden of which is that the artistic creator must walk through life alone, essentially an outcast. It is a theme dear to German romanticism; one meets it again in Thomas Mann's *Tonio Kröger*. Goethe himself disowned the poem in later life; it is hardly one of his major works. Strauss's setting, though showing undoubted skill in the handling of the voices and a certain dramatic force in orchestral writing, is on

---

packet arrived at Garmisch. Frau Strauss, who regularly examined the mail, thought it was just another manuscript, unsolicited, for an opera libretto. It was her custom to return such offerings without opening them and she did so now. It proved to be the letters of the two men. The packet was lost on the return trip.

* He had begun this composition in the summer of 1884, just before Meiningen.

the overblown side. Romain Rolland called it "a work in the style of Brahms, consciously constructed of conventional thoughts."

The *Burleske* is quite another matter. It is the *Till Eulenspiegel* of the piano concerto. Here for the first time, and in spite of the fact that a certain string passage within the work sounds like something from Brahms's Fourth Symphony, Strauss set original and titillating ideas before us. As the title implies, the *Burleske* is a spoof of a serious concerto, its mood alternating between dulcet passages and impish cavortings. It is lively, witty, and good-natured. Its very opening, a motive given to four unaccompanied timpani, makes one sit up and take notice, and this motive is put to humorous use later on. Here, too, we find a waltz, the first of those provocative and dissonantly tilted waltzes that abound in Strauss's work. The only trouble with the *Burleske* is that it is too long; even in his later work Strauss sometimes does not know when to finish a joke. All the same, the *Burleske* is delightful and deserves greater popularity than it enjoys.

Strauss composed the piano part of the *Burleske* for Bülow. Bülow repudiated it, saying that he had no intention of sitting down and learning so complicated a piece of nonsense. Strauss became discouraged with the work, particularly because a run-through with the orchestra in Meiningen, in which he himself attempted to play the piano part, ended in a shambles. He laid it aside. More than four years later, when Strauss made the acquaintance of the pianist and composer Eugen D'Albert, he resurrected the piece. D'Albert played its first performance on June 21, 1890. But Strauss was still not sure of its worth, and only in later life did he become fond of it: he included it in his last London concert, in October, 1947.

New attempts were being made to recapture Bülow for Meiningen, and he did conduct one or two guest performances. But it became apparent that he would not return and equally apparent that, not having a star conductor available, the Duke planned to reduce the orchestra from forty-nine to thirty-nine men. The Duke, however, offered Strauss a prolongation of his contract. An orchestra of thirty-nine seemed a bit too meager for the young conductor. Just at that time Strauss heard from Munich: Perfall offered him a post, the post of third conductor at the Opera. It was hardly a windfall, and Strauss realized at once that he was likely to be a small fish in a big pond. How was he to decide? He turned to Bülow, who was in St. Petersburg, and put the matter before him. It was unlikely, he wrote, that something better would come along. He was tempted to accept the post, since the prospects for the Meiningen orchestra seemed meager. But he would not take a step without Bülow's approval. Would Bülow therefore be kind enough to give him his counsel? Bülow replied:

> The problems of counterpoint in the Ninth [Symphony] would be easier to solve than to impart by letter decisive advice in matters of such prime importance as you lay before me. My impulse would be to advise you to stay on for the time being, in the interest of the Duke as well as of the Ex-*mine*-ingen orchestra. But it really depends on what part the Duke is disposed to play in the full cultivation of music on the banks of the Werra.* Therefore put the question straight in the highest quarters. . . . If you want to go to Munich out of patriotism or homesickness—well, that is your business. But I in your place should refuse for the time being. You are one of those exceptional musicians who need not serve from a private on upward; you have the stuff in you to be promoted at once to a commanding officer. *Pas de zèle*—delay! Do not run the risk—perhaps it is not much of a risk for your lively spirit—of becoming a Philistine, a lout, a snob on the banks of the Isar. . . . In any case, you will be appreciated all the more if you do not immediately say yes. . . .†

But nothing better came along, and without Bülow Meiningen no longer seemed attractive. Reluctantly and with some misgivings, Strauss said yes, signing a three-year contract with Munich, which was to begin with the first of August, 1886.

The farewell from the Meiningen orchestra (April 3, 1886) was a sentimental one. Strauss delivered a little speech paying tribute to the man who had built the orchestra. Then, without an audience present, he conducted Bülow's *Nirvana*. A telegram was sent off to Bülow.

Before assuming his new post, Strauss felt that he had well earned a vacation. He longed to go to Italy, "the land where the lemons are in bloom," which ever since Goethe had been the goal

---

* The river that flows through Meiningen.
† Letter of December 23, 1885.

of German artists in search of an antidote for too much Germanism. Strauss's father and Uncle Georg helped to finance the trip. Stopping only to spend a week with his family, he set out on his first Italian voyage.

In Bologna he stood before the picture of St. Cecilia by Raphael. He wrote to his father that in contemplating this picture, with its entranced saint gazing toward a heaven in which angels gaily make music, the tears came to his eyes. In Bologna, too, he heard *Aida* and called it "Redskin Music" (*Indianermusik*). He liked Rome best, as Mendelssohn had before him, and spent hours in the Vatican and the Campidoglio and the Forum. He was so enraptured by the Forum that he forgot mealtime and, sitting on one of the marble fragments, wolfed down two oranges. He met the painter Lenbach, who turned out to be a brilliant conversationalist. He tried Italian opera once more, attending a performance of *The Barber of Seville*, and thought, "I will never be converted to Italian music."* (He was soon to change his mind.) He identified all he saw with himself, as the creative mind does. Of Michelangelo's *Last Judgment* in the Sistine Chapel, he observed, "Granting the magnificence of Michelangelo, Papa would certainly take it amiss were I to employ in my music his foreshortenings and contortions."†

Like Goethe, he made his pilgrimage to the Campagna and like Goethe he mused on the glories of the Roman past. He had a rather frightening adventure, a stormy voyage by sailboat from Amalfi to Capri. Arrived at Capri, he climbed the high rocks, and, with the angry ocean below him lighted by a purple sinking sun, he felt transfigured. In Naples he heard a "tolerable" performance of the Verdi Requiem and overcame his prejudices enough to admit that the music was "pretty and original." In Florence, like the typical hurried tourist, he ran in one morning to the Medici Chapel, the Baptistry, the Uffizi, *and* the Pitti Palace!

Not all of his experiences were pleasant. Not only did he feel he was being overcharged right and left, but whatever possessions he did not guard were stolen: he lost his leather suitcase in Naples, his laundry in Rome, and even his little Baedeker in a theater. As he wrote to Bülow, "Such a bumbling German as I, not knowing a

---

* Letter to his father, April 27, 1886.
† Letter to his father, May 7, 1886.

word of Italian and very little French, alone and for the first time in Italy, quite overwhelmed by the magnificent landscape and art—such a fellow is an easy prey for the Italians, who could quite compete with any Jew."*

All of these Italian impressions, the inspiring and the sour, he gathered together to give them voice in his first tone poem, *Aus Italien.* The composition is in four movements: first, The Campagna; second, Among the Ruins of Rome (this he sketched while sitting in the Baths of Caracalla); third, On the Beach of Sorrento; and fourth, Neapolitan Life. As a tone poem, *Aus Italien* stands between the old and the new, being still anchored in classic tradition but showing the new, wider spectrum of the Straussian orchestra. It elicited praise from the master of orchestral coloration, Debussy himself. But *Aus Italien* is by no means a good work and strikes us today as naïve. Strauss mistook the popular song "Funiculi Funicula" for a genuine Neapolitan folk song and used it as the basis of the last movement, giving the whole movement a vulgar taint. *Aus Italien* stands far below in quality to those other impressions brought home by a German composer of about the same age, Mendelssohn's "Italian" Symphony.

Nonetheless, *Aus Italien* was sufficiently novel to create opposition and cause headshaking when the following year Strauss conducted its première in Munich (March 2, 1887). "Some applauded furiously," he wrote to a friend. "Others hissed energetically . . . I felt enormous pride: the first work which aroused the opposition of the multitude; it cannot be insignificant."†

Strauss asked permission to dedicate the work to Bülow. Bülow answered that though it was his custom to decline such dedications, in this case he accepted it with enthusiasm, the work having been honored by the fact that it did arouse opposition.

After Italy, Strauss visited Bayreuth. Through Ritter he was able to meet Cosima, who began to take an interest in him. He heard *Parsifal* and *Tristan.*

Toward the end of the summer, then, he returned to Munich to assume his new post. He remained in Munich for three years. During that period he suffered much discouragement. He was made to

* Letter of June 23, 1886.
† Letter to Lotti Speyer, quoted in Ernst Krause, *Richard Strauss: Gestalt und Werk.*

do considerable hackwork and prepare and conduct operas of secondary quality. He wanted to refresh tired performances and tried to prod lazy and arrogant singers, without, however, having sufficient authority to make them toe the mark. How disheartening it was to be a reformer without power! In short, he met the usual fate of the third conductor of the opera house, running into the usual operatic intrigue and indifference. He was not helped by the first conductor, Hermann Levi, who was often sick, wanted peace, and anyway had not much use for the whole Strauss family; nor by the second conductor, a mediocrity, Franz Fischer by name, who was in solid with Perfall.

The first operas handed to Strauss were Boieldieu's *Jean de Paris,* Cherubini's *Der Wasserträger* (*Les Deux journées*) and Marschner's *Der Templer und die Jüdin.* He felt something less than enthusiasm for these pieces of entertainment, though Bülow told him that years ago these operas had given him pleasure, being "absolutely clean scores" and representing opportunities to learn "elegance and grace (without affectation)."* He was also given *Così fan tutte.* This merely shows in what small esteem this opera was then held. It was judged a trivial work, one of Mozart's failures. It was Strauss himself, in later years, who resurrected *Così;* conducting it until late in life, he led the public to a re-evaluation of the bewitching comedy.

Another work they fobbed off on the third *Kapellmeister* was Verdi's *Un Ballo in Maschera* (given in German, of course, as *Der Maskenball*). Studying the score, he began to change his mind about Italian music. "It gives me much pleasure," he wrote to Bülow; "and insofar as it was possible with only one orchestral rehearsal, I conducted the work approaching the spirit you once showed in your famous performance of *Il Trovatore.*"† But what were considered the real plums of the repertoire, the major Wagnerian works, Mozart's *Figaro* and *Don Giovanni, Fidelio,* and so on, were pre-empted by either Levi or Fischer.

Though Perfall had summoned him, Strauss could no more come to a good working relationship with the famous intendant than had

* Letter of June 27, 1886.
† Letter of December 13, 1886.

Wagner or Bülow before him. Ernest Newman called Freiherr Karl von Perfall "a person of the most comprehensive dilettantism."* He was the author of a play "which had a dazzling run of three performances." He was as well a composer of operas, all equally unsuccessful. Though undoubtedly an able diplomat and skilled at the complicated task of running an opera house, and, at least in his younger days, genuinely concerned with the cultivation of German art, he was so stuffy a man and so conservative that the newer tendencies were foreign to him and he resisted every breach of custom. He had just about made his peace with Wagner's music when along came Strauss. The more daring Strauss became, the more Perfall disliked him. Once, in an irritated mood, Strauss called Perfall "Baron Durchfall." (The word means both "failure" and "diarrhea.")

Strauss, it is clear, was not a comfortable man to have around an opera house, where unfortunately a conductor is needed who knows the routine and will not be too exacting. Perfall had no appreciation of the caliber of his employe, though Strauss was a glutton for work and learned the scores of a dozen operas. Furthermore, Perfall did not take kindly to Strauss's frequent absences. Strauss's growing reputation made it possible for him to be invited hither and yon, often to conduct his symphony, soon to conduct *Aus Italien.* Already in the early part of 1887 we find him in Frankfurt, in Hamburg to visit Bülow,† in Köln. The next winter he was in Milan, where he gave two concerts. There he met Arrigo Boïto, who, always in the vanguard of new tendencies, greeted him with enthusiasm. He met also the distinguished Antonio Bazzini, the director of the Milan Conservatory and one of the teachers of Puccini. It may be interesting to give the program Strauss conducted in Milan, if only to show a typical example of the kind of program-making then prevalent (three overtures in one evening!):

---

* Ernest Newman, *The Life of Richard Wagner*, Vol. III.

† He had of course to ask permission for such time away from duty. Bülow, urging him to get such permission, wrote him on December 15, 1886: "Tell the immortal author of *Junker Heinz* [an opera by Perfall] that I promise, should he give his permission . . . not to intrigue against the performance of the above-mentioned questionable box-office piece."

Weber	Overture to Euryanthe
Richard Strauss	Second Symphony*
	Intermission
Beethoven	Overture to Leonore No. 1
Glinka	Kamarinskaya
Wagner	Prelude to Die Meistersinger

To his parents he wrote: "I am the lion of the hour . . . Everybody enchanted by my compositions and my conducting."† To Bülow he wrote more modestly: "The newspapers praise me far beyond my deserts."‡

In Leipzig he made the acquaintance of Gustav Mahler, of whom he said that he was one of the "few modern conductors who understand modifications of tempo; he has the right ideas, particularly about tempi in Wagner (as opposed to the currently accredited Wagner conductors)."§ By this he meant chiefly Levi, with whom his relationship was forever vacillating between respect and antipathy. Levi, though he was sacrosanct, having received the Master's approval, and though he was unquestionably a fine conductor, was a nervous and unstable personality. There exists a letter by Strauss to Bülow written in white heat in which Strauss storms against Levi's performance of the Ninth Symphony, calling it "the most villainous and atrocious transgression against a work of art which I have ever experienced."|| The letter reads as if it were prompted not only by honest indignation but also by his general state of being out of tune with his surroundings. He felt himself, he wrote in the same letter, "surrounded by intrigue, hatred, and envy." Fischer grabbed the conducting of everything worthwhile within sight, with the exception of *Carmen*, which was awarded to Strauss and which he conducted, he confessed, imitating Bülow to the letter.

In the summer of 1887 he spent a few days' vacation in Feldafing, a resort about an hour away from Munich, where the

* The Scherzo was encored.
† Letter from Milan, December 9, 1887.
‡ Letter from Munich, December 26, 1887.
§ Letter to Bülow, October 29, 1887.
|| Letter of December 26, 1887.

Pschorrs had a villa. Across the street lived the family of General de Ahna. The General was a cultivated and well-to-do scion of an old and noble family. He was a music lover, had a good baritone voice, liked Wagner's music, and loved to sing, though strictly as an amateur, Wolfram's "Evening Star." He had two daughters, the elder of whom, Pauline, had inherited her father's musicality, had a fine soprano voice, and was a graduate of the Munich Conservatory. She was a pretty girl with a good figure, a complexion the color of pure pale honey, and the most abundant chestnut hair imaginable. She wore her hair up, giving additional height to her tall figure. Her long face was a trifle equine, though when lit by her smile it seemed actually beautiful. She knew she was attractive, she was self-assured, and she was proud of her family background. Musical by instinct, she was not overly intellectual, not highly educated. She was two years older than Strauss—when they met he was twenty-three and she twenty-five—and radiant with youth. Strauss fell in love with her. It was his first serious love* and was to prove his last.

It was natural that he, the Herr *Kapellmeister* and composer, should become her teacher. He urged her to pursue a professional career, assured her that she was sufficiently gifted to become a major singer, played his music for her, studied Elsa and Elisabeth with her, and discussed his own theories and ambitions. They were soon inseparable, though seven years were to elapse before they got married.

To this period belong the first of the many songs in which Strauss expressed his love for her and which she was later to interpret. In this group of songs is to be found Strauss's most popular song, "Ständchen" (Serenade), (though "Traum durch die Dämmerung" is a close second in popularity). It is a masterpiece, a moment of fragrant lyric inspiration, words and melody being in perfect conjunction, a song which may keep company with the most beautiful Lieder of Schubert and Brahms.

The following year, after the Munich season had come to a close, Strauss went once again to Italy, and in Bologna heard a performance of *Tristan and Isolde*. He realized that "the whole *Tristan* is a

* There is some indication that Strauss had previously been in love with Dora Wihan, wife of a cellist in the Munich orchestra. But the evidence is not certain. See page 79.

most beautiful *bel canto* opera." To this belief he was to adhere in his conducting of *Tristan*.

Apart from a violin sonata in E flat,* which is influenced by both Brahms and *Tristan* (it even contains a quotation from *Tristan*), Strauss now concentrated on two major orchestral works, the tone poems *Macbeth* and *Don Juan*. These works, truly revolutionary in their time, did not immediately find a conductor willing to brave their difficulties, and this braking of the run of his success, along with the situation in Munich, prompted him to write in a melancholy vein to Bülow: "For the time being, *Macbeth* lies resignedly in the drawer of my desk. The dissonances set down in the score try to devour one another. *Don Juan* probably will keep it company soon."† He then stated his artistic creed at length, echoing the ideas he had exchanged with Ritter. He was convinced that the path of programmatic music was the path he had to pursue, even though it might turn out to be a dead-end street. "If one wishes to create a work of art consistent in mood and structure, if such a work is to give the listener a plastic impression, then what the author wanted to say must have been formulated plastically in his own mind. This is only possible through the fructification by a poetic idea, whether or not a program is furnished along with the composition."

The real purpose of the letter was to induce Bülow to think more kindly of *Macbeth*. Bülow had at first disliked it. But Bülow, impatient with aesthetic prattle, took a red pencil and wrote across the letter: "Theory gray or green—in practice, what's important is to write beautiful melodious music."

Things in Munich came to a crisis. It was caused by an action on Perfall's part, which at the least showed a complete lack of kindness but may actually have been a perfidious move, done with malice aforethought. Levi being still in ill health and absent, Strauss was entrusted by Perfall with the revival of Wagner's first opera, *Die Feen* (The Fairies). With great conscientiousness, he studied and rehearsed the work. Just before the première, Perfall sent for him and announced that the first performance—the first work, Strauss said, that he was truly permitted to produce from the ground up

* Heifetz made a beautiful recording of this sonata.
† Letter of August 24, 1888.

and would have enabled him to show all of which he was capable—was to be taken away from him and given to Fischer. Stunned by this blow, Strauss first sent a telegram and then a long letter to Bülow. He reported the gist of the interview with Perfall: the intendant felt that it was not a question of talent but of seniority. Further, he did not at all like the way Strauss conducted; he imitated Bülow. He had a few unkind words to say about Strauss's youthful presumption, expecting more than was his due. Strauss wanted to resign at once. It is probable that Strauss's resignation was exactly what Perfall wanted.

Bülow urged him not to resign but to stay and to bide his time. All this was but the darkness before the dawn. By the time his contract was up, he, Bülow, would find the right post for Strauss. Patience!

Bülow was as good as his word. He recommended Strauss to the conductor in Weimar, Eduard Lassen, and to Hans von Bronsart, the intendant of the Weimar Opera. True, Weimar was a much smaller town; true, his salary was no more than he had earned in Munich, a mere 3,000 marks. Nor was the orchestra as full as he needed—only six first violins. All the same, Strauss recognized that both men were the finest type of idealistic musicians, and in several conversations they made him feel wanted. Weimar, the town of Goethe and Liszt, was renowned among German cities for its favorable artistic climate. It was as well a pretty little town, with its green and rosy gardens. But indeed Strauss would have accepted almost any position away from what he then called "the cesspool of the Munich theater."

A further indignity was in store for him before he left Munich. The news reached him in Wiesbaden that his father had been pensioned. Franz was due for retirement, but he was given no warning, the notice being merely posted on the bulletin board. Somebody read it and brought the news to Franz while he was sitting in a coffeehouse. There were no official farewells, no acknowledgment of his services, no decoration bestowed by the government, no ceremonies else—merely a cold period set to the career of a man who had made himself disliked. Perhaps it was Perfall who played the part of the "churlish priest," though Strauss blamed the "rhythm Jews" (*Taktjuden*), meaning Levi, of course.

Before he assumed the post at Weimar, he went to Bayreuth, where through Bülow's recommendation he had been engaged as musical assistant. Shrewd Cosima had seen to it that this young talent, this ardent Wagnerian, should be harnessed to her cause. She soon honored him with her friendship and frequently invited him to Wahnfried. He felt free and happy in the atmosphere of Bayreuth, avoiding the company of Levi as much as possible. He heard Felix Mottl and Hans Richter conduct. Pauline joined him. Under her lover's enthusiastic tutelage she had made great strides as an artist. Cosima found her attractive. After the festival was finished, Cosima instructed both of them in the interpretation of *Lohengrin* and *Tannhäuser.* Strauss, eager, content, and ambitious, absorbed it all.

He was now ready for Weimar and the post he was to hold for over four years, exciting, significant, and fruitful years. In Weimar he found sympathy and understanding and the opportunity to stage and conduct works for which he felt a real affinity, yet reserving sufficient time for occasional guest conducting and for a strengthening of his creative talent. Bronsart and Lassen were as one with him in the search for ideal performances, and though the ideal was not often reached, though indeed the means were limited and provincial, the seriousness of purpose was always there.

The breadth of the operatic repertoire Strauss now attempted was astonishing. He began with *The Flying Dutchman* and *The Magic Flute,* he went on to *Lohengrin,* using the knowledge he had gained in Bayreuth, and to *Tannhäuser.* Gluck's *Iphigénie in Aulis,* Nicolai's *Merry Wives of Windsor,* Lortzing's *Waffenschmied,* Marschner's *Hans Heiling,* Weber's *Freischütz* and *Euryanthe,* and Bellini's *Norma*—all these works came under his baton and were illumined by his musical intelligence and dramatic instinct. Soon Pauline joined him, and she sang Pamina and Elsa as well as Elisabeth. Her presence spurred him on to an increasingly profound comprehension of Wagner. Even without her, the conducting of Wagner remained for him a ritual of high purpose. Then and for some years after, he conducted Wagner standing; he sat for other operas (including his own).

In addition to his work at the opera house, Strauss gave orchestral concerts in Weimar. Since he himself was now thinking in the idiom of the tone poem, his concerts were so heavily weighted in favor of programmatic music that, as he reported to his father, Bronsart shook his head. No wonder, replied his father: "Your programs are more than an ostrich can digest. There are other composers besides Liszt, Wagner, and Berlioz whose works have a right to be heard. Do Mozart, Haydn, Spohr, etc., no longer exist for you?"*

Now that Strauss was encouraged by success, working with an orchestra that liked him, favored by the proximity of the woman he loved, steeped in music to which he felt himself akin, buoyed by the perception that the time was propitious for a new voice, that new conditions existing as the century drew to a close demanded new expression, his talent began to take free strides. Before we follow his strides, it might be well to present a summarizing portrait of Strauss at this time of his youth. What was he like in the days when the world was before him, what was he like when he left Munich in his middle twenties, what was he like when he joined the band of progressives and set out to conquer? The clearest self-revealing sketch at hand is in the form of a letter he wrote not to his father or to his mentor but to somebody else with whom he had been closely connected and who was young, as he was. This rather mysterious person was Dora Wihan, whose name has previously been mentioned. In later years Strauss never spoke of her, yet it is certain that as a young man he loved her and it is probable that they were lovers. We know little enough of Dora. She was the wife of the solo cellist of the Munich orchestra, Hanuš Wihan, a man nine years older than Strauss, who was a friend of the Strauss family. As a very young man—he was about nineteen—Strauss wrote a cello sonata for Wihan (Opus 6) which Wihan performed. To Dora he dedicated a little piano composition. Dora was a very beautiful girl, four years older than Strauss, and musically gifted. After four years her marriage to Hanuš ended in divorce. But whether Strauss had anything to do with the breakup is questionable. Wihan went to Prague as professor at the Conservatory and there formed the Bohemian String Quartet, which gained some renown. What happened to Dora is uncertain. She went to America, lived for a time in

* Letter of October 20, 1889.

Dresden and Greece, worked as a piano teacher, and died in 1938. It is probable that Strauss destroyed most of her letters to him, save one very short one. Before her death she expressly ordered that Strauss's letters to her, as well, should be burned. But this one letter she gave as a gift to a female friend in Dresden. It is now owned by Ernst Krause of Berlin (author of a biography of Strauss).*

MY DEAR GOOD DORA:

How shall I begin my letter? With sorrow over your letter, with thanks for your congratulations on my name day, with a recital of experiences? Really, I don't know: the fact is that your letter, my sweet Dora, has moved me deeply and saddened me, since it has postponed to an unforeseen future the prospect of my seeing you again. Oh God! What wooden expressions for that which I feel! I ought to comfort you. But how? I can't write to you that "it isn't as terrible as all that, Meister." [Eva's words to Hans Sachs, slightly paraphrased by Strauss.] Nor that time will heal all wounds. It is really time which deals the wounds. Heavens! Now I try to make epigrams—isn't it awful!!!!

Enough of that! You think that in later years you will come to visit me; I recommend a song to you, as yet unperformed, by one Richard Strauss, entitled "Patience," Opus 10, A-flat Major. Apropos, have you received the piano score of the *Italian Fantasy?* If that gives you even a little comfort, I should be happy. To write you at this time that things go well with me will perhaps irritate you. Yet it is true; the artist Richard Strauss is in excellent shape, particularly since he ceases to be the Munich Hofmusikdirector. After breathing the miasma of a swamp for three years, the fresh air benefits me. True, it is difficult for me to leave Munich, away from my family and from two friends such as Ritter and Thuille, to whom I have become so attached as you would find it difficult to imagine. But I must away! My whole future depends on my not falling prey to the swamp fever of Munich. With the help of Ritter, I have now acquired a stronger viewpoint of art and life. After groping for so long, I now feel firm ground under my feet. I can now dare to begin the fight against the Jews and the Philistines. Just think! I have joined the ranks of the Lisztians! In short, it

* The letter was only partly published in Krause's book. The complete text has been reprinted in the *Richard Strauss Jahrbuch 1959/60.*

is hard to imagine a more progressive viewpoint than the one which I now hold. I feel wonderful; a new clarity has overcome me. But how can one write all this? You must come and see me. Would you recognize me again?

Now I want to answer your questions: I am employed in Bayreuth as "assistant," piano rehearsals, etc. Recently I made the acquaintance of Frau Wagner, who is quite interested in me. I even enjoyed the privilege of going to a *Freischütz* with her. How that came about is a very funny story. The good Levi very comically fell into a ditch which he had dug for me! How was it in Berlin? So wonderful as you cannot imagine. Ritter, Thuille, and I, with the motto

Dear God, are we fine folks!

[An approximate translation of a bit of Bavarian dialect which Strauss set to music]

The Ninth was indescribably beautiful, the *Tannhäuser* overture absolutely fabulous. I still tremble when I recall the sound! Bülow conducted like a god, though sometimes he behaved like a clown; at other times he was enormously touching. (The leathery St. Johannes* was there as well.) "Two souls dwell in his breast." The poor man! God, how much I have to tell you! And yet you do not come!!! By the time you do, I will have forgotten everything.

If all this seems madness to you, yet there is method in it! Oh my God! Now I am suffering from "quotitis." (That is the newest expression invented by Thuille, quite in the Berlin spirit.)

Bülow is safely in America to earn some money. Where am I going? If you promise me to write to nobody and to say nothing, for it must still remain a deep secret—to Weimar, with Lassen and under Bronsart as intendant. What a splendid change from Munich! To the city of the future, Weimar, to the post where Liszt worked so long! I have great hopes. Bronsart is an excellent fellow, a man of honor from head to foot (quite like Perfall†) and very progressive (quite like Perfall†). And besides, Lassen is old and tired and looks forward to relief of his labors (quite like Fischer†). My pupil Zeller is engaged as Heldentenor, starting next September; one of the first operas which I will conduct there will be Ritter's *Der faule Hans*, with Zeller in the title role. Then his newest one-act opera,

* Brahms.

† This is of course meant ironically.

Wem die Krone? In short, I believe it will be wonderful. Bronsart is also head of the Tonkünstlerverein. He invited me a few days ago, in case Nikisch is detained in Leipzig, which seems probable, to conduct, in addition to my *Italian Fantasy,* the first two concerts of this season in Wiesbaden, 27th and 28th of June; including *L'Enfance du Christ* by Berlioz. Not so bad, is it? Yes, the artist Strauss is doing very well. But can happiness never be complete?

On my return from Berlin, I stopped in Meiningen and had my *Macbeth* played for me four times. Steinbach had already studied it. It sounds grim, but I think it will make an impression on profound souls! At the moment, I am arranging it for four hands and hope to bring it out next spring. As to the text of my opera, I have the first act and part of the second act, to the end of the great love scene, tentatively ready. (That means until I revise it again.) Ritter likes it very much.

In addition, I have sketched out a new tone poem, to be entitled probably *Death and Transfiguration.* I plan to begin to write the score right after Easter.

Apropos! If you have finished reading the writings of Wagner which I sent you, please be kind enough to send them back to me. I would like to have them all bound! The Dostoevski books as well, please!

One thing more. If you knew how eagerly I read your letters, you would not say anything about *"distractions par une comtesse."* She is, by the way, a charming creature, a fool for the Music of the Future, and one of the few great admirers of your Richard. In that connection, I recall a charming saying by Wagner. In a letter to Uhlig, he praises Ritter's sister Emilie as a model woman and he adds: Women are our consolation. Every woman is born as a personality. Every man is born as a Philistine, and it takes a long time if ever before he works himself up to being a personality. Well, why shouldn't I then [be interested in *"la comtesse"*]? I gain for "our" art a true partisan. Our art, it must be admitted, is miles removed from what these days is called music.

And now heartfelt thanks for your dear wishes, you good and faithful creature. I add, speaking from the heart, that I hope no wish shall ever be granted to me which runs contrary to yours. You really must not leave me alone for so long. God! I have been hoping for two years. I have been hoping only to be forced now to close the book of hope with the words "It cannot be." But I don't want to wax maudlin.

If my new composition contains more dissonances than your little ears can tolerate, you are not to sulk!

Farewell! Continue to love me. And this time don't let me wait so long for an answer.

Your old faithful R.

Munich 4/9/1889

5

Free Strides

Every artist is a member of his society. Every artist is part of the world. Though he may revolt against it, as Wagner did; though he may cloister himself, as César Franck did; though he may be as irresponsible as that son of a sunny people, Rossini; he yet belongs to communal life and he cannot escape the prevailing winds, those winds which carry the seeds of current ideas. Strauss, perhaps more than any other major composer, lived in the world. His home environment and upbringing had shaped him into a middle-class burgher, though a burgher who was intellectual and receptive, and much more sensitive than the smug citizen whom Goethe in *Faust* has saying:

> Nichts Bessers weiss ich mir an Sonn- und Feiertagen,
> Als ein Gespräch von Krieg und Kriegsgeschrei,
> Wenn hinten weit in der Türkei,
> Die Völker aufeinander schlagen.
>
> (*There's nothing pleasanter on a Sunday or holiday*
> *Than a little talk about war and its alarums,*
> *As far away some place in Turkey*
> *Nations battle one another.*)

All the same, Strauss was a good German citizen as well as a German artist, knew what was going on both in the arts and in politics, and was influenced by the mundane as well as by the eternal. He read both Nietzsche and the daily newspaper.

What was going on? In the two decades into which fall the creation of Strauss's major works—1890 to 1910—hope flourished, middle-class prosperity boomed, and Germany became a world power, developing more significantly than other European nations. This period of two decades is set within a longer era of peace. Though occasionally rocked by small wars—far enough away ("some place in Turkey") not to disturb the citizen—Europe enjoyed a forty-year peace, which lasted from the end of the Franco-Prussian War to the beginning of the First World War.

Around the turn of the century Europe drew a cleaner breath than it had for years. In Germany, particularly, the people had been given new confidence first by Bismarck, then by Wilhelm II. To be sure, the poor people in the basement from time to time raised an audible clamor; at a certain moment the clamor became loud enough so that the legislators could no longer ignore it. There had been a revolt by the Socialist party and the discontent led to the repeal—in 1890, the same year that the pilot of the empire, Bismarck, was dropped by Wilhelm—of the stringent anti-Socialist muzzling law which Bismarck had sponsored. To be sure, Karl Marx had published part of his creed (in 1894), but few people read it, and in the years of national consciousness the laborer soon lay down again with the capitalist. Dissension was outshouted by hip-hip-hurrah patriotism.

The Germans were united in their faith in Germany and in their Kaiser, who dreamed gaudy dreams of imperialism. The mills of a nation's gods grind exceedingly slow, and it was many years before the Wilhelmian policies met retribution. A whole generation passed, Wilhelm was permitted to cheat and trick and spend more and more money on building the machinery of war, while professing his love of peace.

That bad actor with the bad arm, that vain majordomo who changed his uniform more often than a *cocotte* changes her dress, that hysterical speechmaker who enjoyed blasting forth with grandiose words but was a coward—nobody stopped his plots and counterplots, which had as their central purpose setting England against France, France against Russia, and every European nation against every other so as to leave Germany in the center. The other European nations produced their own conniving, and the Kaiser was allowed to prate about "a place in the sun," he was allowed to build a formidable navy in competition with England, and he was allowed to complain about being "ringed in" when in point of fact his spiked helmet poked beyond the frontier, east and west.

As Virginia Cowles puts it in *The Kaiser:* "The personality of Germany as a nation was almost perfectly represented by the personality of the Kaiser as a man. Germany was threatening and blustering one moment, pained and reproachful the next. Germany was able, tempestuous, and unwise, a country with a chip on its shoulder, longing for prestige and acclamation, prone to dark moods of dejection that turned overnight into menacing arrogance."

Whatever disturbances occurred—such as the Boer War, in which Germany played a casual role—took place on foreign soil. The fatherland remained inviolate. There was peace in that able, tempestuous, and unwise country, peace in a uniform, but nevertheless peace so assertive that young people grew up vigorously and savored the joy of life, demanded and received new art and artists, became freer in their feeling and thinking. Yes, even in a Germany under an imperial censorship, a new freedom of expression flourished.

The new writers were occupying themselves with two tendencies that, though seemingly opposite, often merged, occasionally in the same head. One tendency led toward a greater awareness of social conditions, a recognition of the problems of economic existence, of seeing life without romantic spectacles, of protest against poverty and the misery that lives in a factory. As the nation's prosperity increased and the middle-class, middle-aged citizen put marks in the savings bank, the newer artists raised the voice of conscience, pleading the cause of the injured and indigent, and lashing out at society's hypocrisy. The social drama and the social novel came to the fore. But alongside of this daylight art there developed another tendency. This other tendency was a journey into a dreamworld, putting on not only rose-colored glasses but glasses tinted blue and purple. Fantasy flourished, as did the poetry of mood. The importance of the fleeting impression, the hidden sudden stimulus, and the lack-logic impulse was explored in verse and novel. Writers dreamed through half-closed lids. These dreams in words employed a luscious imagery and played with love, love transient and insubstantial. The erotic was frankly set on paper, straitlaced prudery unlaced, the charm of the physical described, sometimes with a good deal of self-conscious provocation. It is astonishing how often the word "dream" occurs in the literature of the period, even before 1900, when Freud published *The Interpretation of Dreams.*

Ibsen exercised a powerful influence on the German naturalistic writers. *A Doll's House, Pillars of Society,* and *An Enemy of the People* were all new and were social manifestoes as well as plays; so was the daring *Ghosts.* So was *Hedda Gabler* (1890). All these were read and pondered over by the German dramatist Gerhart Hauptmann, soon to emerge as Germany's leading dramatist, who combined both tendencies in his sphere: within the space of two years he published the socialist play, *The Weavers* (1892) and the dream fantasy, *Hannele's Assumption* (1893).* Strauss all his life admired Hauptmann (who lived to the ripe old age of eighty-four), though several attempts at collaborating on an opera came to naught.

The poets who were splashing color onto verse took their inspiration from the French. These "symbolists" and "decadents" and "impressionists," or whatever they were called, made vice a virtue. It was often only a paper vice under a paper moon. But it was taken seriously by the youth of the nineties, it horrified the elders, and would have horrified Kaiser Wilhelm had he ever read a line of contemporary poetry. The eldest of these French poets and the one endowed with the most brilliant talent was Pierre Charles Baudelaire, whose only volume of verse, *Les Fleurs du mal* (Flowers of Evil), appeared first in 1857 and was later enlarged. Stéphane Mallarmé followed (*L'Après-midi d'un faune*), and declared that poetry must learn from music, Wagner's music particularly. Arthur Rimbaud wrote of a phantasmagorial world. These French poets were associated with Stefan George, the fine German poet who formulated the doctrine of "art for art's sake." A much lesser talent, but then considered important, was the poet and novelist Otto Julius Bierbaum,† whose erotic novel *Prinz Kuckuck* enjoyed the success

---

* The opportunity to be heard was offered Hauptmann by Otto Brahm, guiding spirit of the new "Free Stage" (*Freie Bühne*). Brahm was the one who brought Ibsen's *Ghosts* before the German public (1889).

† He is the author of the poem "Traum durch die Dämmerung."

of scandal. In Freud's home town, as well as in Germany itself, new talents were rising. Less than four years after Strauss's *Don Juan* appeared, Arthur Schnitzler put *Anatol* on the stage, a series of scenes with a Viennese Don Juan as its central protagonist. To Schnitzler the riddle that lay at the core of the world was man's relationship to woman. It was a riddle always to be asked, never to be solved. The "land without limit" was the enamored heart, be its pulse fleeting or enduring.

Music, too, was in a state of change. Classic romanticism was still strong: Tchaikovsky's *Pique Dame* (1890), Dvorak's *Symphony from the New World* (1893), and, with all its newness, Verdi's *Falstaff* (1893) belong to the tradition. But Mahler's First Symphony (1888), Debussy's setting of Baudelaire songs (1890), and his *Prélude à L'Après-midi d'un faune* (1892) speak a new, post-Wagnerian language, one influenced by the world of *Tristan*.

All of this newness, this desire for experimentation, this curiosity to reach a hitherto closed bourn, this delving into subconscious strata of the mind, this love of color, this inducing of a dream state, this exploration of the use of sex in art, acted on and were absorbed by the young Richard Strauss, who composed three of the tone poems on which his fame rests before he was thirty years old. He had begun the composition of *Don Juan* while he was still in Munich; now he played the score on the piano for his new well-wishers, Bronsart and Lassen. They urged him to present it at a concert that very season, Lassen particularly being "quite beside himself with admiration."* During the rehearsals, the orchestra "huffed and puffed, but did its job famously."† One of the horn players, dripping with perspiration, asked Strauss in what way they, the musicians, had sinned that God now visited such a scourge upon them. Yet they all dived into the whirlpool score with great enthusiasm, and the "hornists particularly blew with utter death-defiance!"‡

The first performance took place on November 11, 1889. It proved to be a historic occasion. We may imagine the excitement of the audience sitting up straight in their chairs as they heard the first

* Letter from Strauss to his father, November 10, 1889.
† *Ibid.*
‡ *Ibid.*

bars, when the strings throw out that bold upward leap, as if the hero were to bound in one jump to the center of the stage. We may imagine the delight of the listeners as they heard for the first time the seductive theme of love sung by the oboe, from which they were then roused by the proud assertion of the theme of Don Juan himself. As the last sounds died away, the audience began to shout its approval. Five times Strauss had to acknowledge the applause. There was an insistent clamor for a *da capo,* which the composer shrewdly did not grant.

The news spread immediately. Bülow was in Weimar and reported that *Don Juan* had a "quite extraordinary success."* Frankfurt, Dresden, and, later, Berlin asked for the composition. From being more or less a local celebrity, Strauss became a figure of some national importance; himself young, he became one of the spokesmen of the young generation. He had touched a beating vein, he had expressed in music what the writers were expressing in words, had found a new language with which to speak openly of erotic desire, of voluptuousness, of rebellion. Both virility and femininity are to be found in the score and with it, at the close, weariness and satiety, death in a useless duel. How well did this accord with the spirit of the times! But even today *Don Juan* remains capable of delighting us with its prideful beauty. When we compare this music to that which Strauss had composed before, we understand that it "seems incredibly remote from that of the Good Boy of the Conservatoire displayed in the opus numbers before this opus 20."†

As the reader knows, *Don Juan* was the second, not the first, of the tone poems the Good Boy composed. It was preceded by *Macbeth.* This is an inferior work, with which Strauss himself was not fully satisfied, especially when Bülow criticized it: Bülow objected specifically to the end, which in the first version was a triumphal march of Macduff. Strauss revised the work, laboring on it off and on for four years, and the revised version was not heard until a year after *Don Juan.* Later Bülow presented it in a concert in Berlin. *Macbeth* was then wildly acclaimed. By that time the ground for Strauss's success had been prepared.

It is significant that Strauss took the inspiration for his *Don Juan*

* Letter to Marie von Bülow, November 13, 1889.

† Donald Francis Tovey, *Essays in Musical Analysis,* Vol. IV.

from a verse treatment of the legend by a poet who, though he lived in the eighteenth century, was akin to the contemporary school, a predecessor of the Stefan Georges and the Rimbauds. This strange poet was Nikolaus Lenau, a turgid talent, moody and metaphysical, who wrote: "I build no temples out of ruin. Passion is always and only the new passion . . . and when it knows itself it knows nothing of repentance." Lenau died insane, and his *Don Juan* is an unfinished drama. But enough of it remained to furnish Strauss with a text. Strauss's *Don Juan* has no definite program, though Strauss used portions of the poem as a foreword to the score. The poem serves merely as a general guide to the character who denies that surfeit of pleasure is possible, who is driven by the storms of desire, finally to end bleakly, "the fuel consumed, the hearth cold and dark." No plot is told in the music, no stone guest appears, no specific victims are described, though the section known as the Carnival Scene parallels a passage in Lenau, and the death of the Don in a duel, when he wearily lets fall his rapier at the point of conquering his adversary, can be sensed toward the end.

It was inevitable that music so new should call forth some protests. The redoubtable Hanslick, for example, not in the least made cautious by his many mistakes and Tory to the end, felt that *Don Juan* was nothing but a "tumult of blinding color splotches, a stuttering tonal delirium," and wished that more such tone poems would be composed because they would all the quicker cause "a return to healthy, musical music."* Such opposition only served to firm Strauss's fame.

Even before the première of *Don Juan*, Strauss had finished the second of his major tone poems, *Tod und Verklärung* (Death and Transfiguration). Before discussing this tone poem, we must take up the story of Strauss's life and observe the less attractive side of his behavior.

It is natural that he should have found new confidence in himself. That confidence was buttressed by his success at the opera in Weimar. In the season of 1889-90 he restudied and restaged what he wanted to present as a model performance of *Lohengrin*. He

---

* Written in 1891. Quoted by Nicolas Slonimsky in *Lexicon of Musical Invective.*

worked with indefatigable zeal to bring to his audience a cleansed version of the familiar opera—Pauline sang Elsa and this served as an additional incentive—and he succeeded so well that Cosima overwhelmed him with compliments. But life was not free of stresses and strains. Bülow appeared in Weimar and proved to be in his cantankerous phase. He didn't want to have anything to do with Franz Strauss, who was in Weimar on a visit. Bülow played brilliantly—"none of the younger ones can compare himself with him," Strauss acknowledged*—and conducted a Brahms concert. During the rehearsal he gave vent to a "drivel speech," during which he invited the orchestra to "give a cheer for Brahms."† Strauss was now quite under Ritter's and Cosima's influence and refused to join in. This occurred a few days after Bülow and Strauss were together in Berlin, where Bülow presented *Don Juan* to the important Philharmonic audience. In spite of the fact that the work once again scored an enormous success and that the metropolitan critics wrote long articles praising the music, Strauss felt that Bülow had thoroughly mishandled it, that he had failed to penetrate the sense of the tone poem, and that he wouldn't listen to the slightest of the composer's suggestions for its performance. Perhaps Strauss secretly resented a few derogatory remarks Bülow had made, perhaps he was goaded to anger by the meddling Ritter, perhaps he had caught Bülow's nervousness, or perhaps he was merely suffering from an attack of swelled head—whatever the reason, he now burst out in denouncing the friend to whom he owed everything.

Who was to blame for Bülow's bad performance? According to Strauss—of all people, the Jews! Bülow had become friendly with an "ugly Jewish circle." They had made him vain, spoiled his artistic probity and tempted him toward affectation and exaggeration. Though Strauss admitted that Bülow had worked like a Trojan to rehearse *Don Juan*, he brought "before the public merely an interesting piece of music, but not my *Don Juan*. Bülow no longer understands poetic music, he has lost the touch. That Bülow conducted at all was merely a business trick of Wolff [the impresario, who was a Jew], who wanted to show that Bülow could champion

* Letter to his parents, February 16, 1890.
† *Ibid.*

brand-new symphonic works and thus deal a blow to the Wagner Club."* Proof was to be furnished that the "firm of Wolff deals not only in standard articles but in the very newest."† Strauss goes on to justify his anger by telling his father that he has no desire "to become a famous composer through misunderstanding," that he "wishes to serve his art honestly and is not afraid of failure," provided that his message is carried to the public forum correctly and rightly.‡

Even granting that Bülow's musical understanding did not encompass Strauss's new works and that he could make little of *Don Juan* (which is doubtful), Strauss's denunciation was, to say the least, a sign of petulance. With all his humor Strauss could be humorless; with all his modesty he could be arrogant. These contradictions showed themselves early and were to persist. An open break between the two men was avoided, but the band of friendship now contained a knot that was never to be quite untied. Almost two years later Strauss apologized. He wrote to Bülow, who had announced that he would perform *Macbeth*, that he was overjoyed to hear the news of so generous a project; he had feared that "because of his own changed artistic views" Bülow was "no longer as close to him as of yore."§ He assures Bülow that in spite of the intrigues around them "nothing, nothing in this world, could extinguish or even diminish my boundless love, admiration and deep gratitude to you."||

Fine words, and no doubt fully meant. Still, to his father Strauss called Bülow "a complete reactionary" who at one time had been a progressive, not from inner conviction but because "the powerful personalities of a Wagner and a Liszt, and the opportunity to do battle" had pushed him in that direction.¶

The ways of the two men separated. Strauss still wrote Bülow from time to time in terms of old respect and affection, he still made a special trip to hear Bülow conduct the Ninth, and just before Bülow's death he visited him in Hamburg (January, 1894).

---

* Wagner now stood for conservatism!

† Letter to his father, February 2, 1890.

‡ *Ibid.*

§ Letter to Bülow, January 30, 1892.

|| *Ibid.*

¶ Letter to his father, February 23, 1891.

The only new work of Strauss's with which Bülow could yet become acquainted was *Death and Transfiguration.* Less than a year before his death, Bülow wrote to Spitzweg: "Would to God that it could again become possible for me to take an active interest in [Strauss's] development. After *him* [Brahms], by far the most individual and richest personality! . . . God protect his physical well-being, then his psyche will be safe."*

When Bülow wrote this letter, he knew he was a sick man, though he did not know how sick he was. Urged on by Marie, Strauss, and other friends, Bülow sought health in the sun and embarked on a journey to Egypt. Strauss saw him for the last time, and for a brief moment only, in the railroad station in Berlin. Bülow reached Cairo more dead than alive. There, far away from home, the brilliant self-made pariah died on February 12, 1894.

But much of what Bülow had taught him remained in Strauss. That included the passion for making music.

Strauss's conducting schedule in Weimar would have laid an ordinary mortal low, even a young mortal. It seems to be a peculiarity of conductors that they thrive on hard work; only inactivity disintegrates them. The record of longevity among successful conductors is noteworthy. (Perhaps the exercise keeps them in trim.) Strauss had inherited Bülow's passion for detailed rehearsal, his inexorability in demanding the best of which musicians and singers were capable, his selfless as well as selfish devotion to a musical task. His career in Weimar was a triumph of enthusiasm over matter. Marie Gutheil-Schoder, then a young singer in Weimar (later she was to become one of the finest interpreters of Strauss roles and a famous Octavian), remembered that he formed the town into "the center of the musical life of Germany."† This he accomplished with limited means, singers of limited talents, and a small, though valiant, orchestra. Some time later (in 1892), after he had hit his stride, he reported the schedule of a "few busy days" to his parents: Tuesday night *Tristan;* 11:30 at night to Leipzig. Wednesday 10 to 2:30 first rehearsal for a Liszt concert. In the evening back to Weimar. Thursday conducted *Lohengrin* in Eisenach. Return to Leipzig one

* Letter to Spitzweg, Hamburg, April 2, 1893, quoted in Max Steinitzer, *Richard Strauss.*

† Marie Gutheil-Schoder, *Erlebtes und Erstrebtes.*

o'clock at night. Friday, rehearsal 10 to 1 and 3 to 6. Saturday, general rehearsal; concert in the evening. Program: Liszt *The Ideals*, Schubert-Liszt *Wanderer Fantasie* (with Siloti as pianist), *Mazeppa*, afterward *Death and Transfiguration*. He wrote: "I am a little bushed, but well, gay, and in good spirits. I enjoy such battles. . . ."*

Nonetheless, whether from overwork or not, he fell seriously ill in May, 1890, a cold developing into pneumonia. At one point he was on the danger list. He said to a friend that he could reconcile himself to the thought of death, but before he died he would like to have conducted *Tristan*. During his sickness he used to repeat long passages to himself, and as soon as he was convalescent he took up the score of *Tristan* and grappled with the problem of producing the work in a house without a sunken orchestra pit. During the summer he went to Bayreuth, where Pauline sang Elisabeth, and where Cosima mothered him and would not allow him to exert himself. He complained that she wouldn't let him conduct, the doctors having told her that he needed to husband his strength, and that she treated him as if he were a little child.

As soon as he returned for the new season in Weimar—he protested that he was quite well again, though he was not—he began rehearsals for the production of *Tristan*. It was a heavy task he loaded on the orchestra, and though orchestral rehearsals began in October, it was not until January 17 of the following year, 1892, that the performance took place. Father Strauss was once again ready with advice: "*Tristan* will cause you much work and worry. I'll be glad when it is all over. Do not hold overlong rehearsals. It's no use tiring everybody, for then a lethargy sets in which works to the disadvantage of the project. A rehearsal of five hours is too long. *Tristan* contains no moments where one can coast and pull oneself together . . . I know it from my own experience. . . . Consider that your orchestra is small and everyone has to contribute to the utmost of his power. And quite a few of the orchestra members are elderly and cannot stand such extraordinary exertions. Be sensible, dear Richard!"†

Whatever might have been the shortcomings of the perform-

* Letter from Leipzig, March 12, 1892.
† Letter of January 7, 1892.

ance, which was uncut, it is certain that it pleased Strauss. He told Cosima that it was the most beautiful day of his life. The inner kinship he felt with the work, his boundless admiration for it, he retained to his dying day. The performance in Weimar was merely the first of innumerable performances he conducted. Many years later, in 1933, when the conductor Fritz Busch wrote to him, "Just think! *Tristan* now begins to weaken at the box office," Strauss answered, "If there is only one person left who pays for a ticket for *Tristan, Tristan* has to be performed. That one person is the last living German."* Two years later, when Strauss was corresponding with Joseph Gregor, who had sent him his book *History of the World Theater,* Strauss wrote that Gregor had failed to recognize the importance of *Tristan,* that to him the work represented the last conclusion of Schiller and Goethe and the highest fulfillment of the two-thousand-year-long development of the theater. As an old man he lived for a time in Switzerland, fleeing from war-torn Germany. He carried the score of *Tristan* always with him, as a sort of talisman.†

In June of the *Tristan* year he once again fell ill, this time with pleurisy and a very severe bronchitis. Had he not been completely cured of the previous illness? Had the new exertions taken their toll? There he was, pale, frightfully thin, coughing, and once again the doctors feared for his life. There was but one cure then for respiratory diseases: getting away to the sun. Once again Uncle Georg came to the rescue with a generous gift of 5,000 marks. Strauss set off for Greece and for Egypt. He was to be away for some eight months, and the diary he kept during this journey has been preserved. Greece proved to him the same important experience that it proves to all men who have eyes to see and minds to think historically: it vivified his sense of beauty. He became, so to speak, personally acquainted with Zeus and Aphrodite. Henry Miller (in his *Greece*) wrote that falling in love with Greece is the easiest thing in the world: "It is like falling in love with one's own image." The world of antique Greece was later to appear in his work, though sicklied o'er with the pale cast of the world of Freud. For the time

* Quoted in Ernst Krause, *Richard Strauss.*

† I owe this fact to Victor Reinshagen, the Zurich conductor, who knew Strauss well during his Swiss sojourn.

being, he marveled, enjoyed, admired, journeyed from blue mountains to blue seas, spent time on the Acropolis and in the museums as well as with the people. In short, he followed the well-worn path of the traveler. But unlike the ordinary traveler, and like the artist, he saw everything in relation to his art. "The talent sucks the man," said Emerson, and, equally, the man ingests everything to feed his talent. In Olympia, gazing at the Hermes of Praxiteles, Strauss thought of Bayreuth! He compared Greece, with its pervasive sense of beauty—a sense developed through "so unimportant a stimulus as races and wrestling matches"—to the beauty that one man, Wagner, "placing himself far above his people," created. "Here a great people, there a great genius."

From Greece he journeyed to Egypt, then to Sicily, and back to Italy. There he visited Bülow's daughter Blandine and her husband, spent more leisurely days in Florence than he had previously, and finally returned, fresh in mind and spirit, completely cured. In his trunk was the almost completed manuscript of his first opera.

He spent the rest of the summer with Pauline before attacking the new season in Weimar. There, on December 23, 1893, he led the première of an opera the merits of which he had instantly recognized, Humperdinck's *Hänsel und Gretel.* Pauline played Gretel with "abandoned fun." It was a charming Christmas present for the audience at Weimar.

By that winter the second of Strauss's famous tone poems, *Death and Transfiguration,* had become a concert attraction widely programmed, at least in Germany. Even outside of Germany it had achieved fame: the Philharmonic Society of New York, for example, had given it on January 9, 1892, under Anton Seidl. Strauss himself conducted its première at a festival of new music in Eisenach, on June 21, 1890. Once again he scored a pronounced success.

Indeed, *Death and Transfiguration* became, for many years at least, the most popular of Strauss's tone poems. Unlike *Don Juan,* it tells a defined story, one invented by the composer and put into words by him. Strauss considered the explanation in words necessary to the understanding of the composition. He therefore asked Ritter to turn his prose sketch into poetry. This Ritter did twice. Being dissatisfied with the first version of the poem, Ritter elaborated it, and it was the second version that was set at the head of the score when the tone poem was published. Both versions are pedestrian poetry, for Ritter was no better a poet than he was a composer.

Death and Transfiguration, though at the end it treats of a mystery that cannot be described, except in men's imaginations, though it deals with the journey to the undiscover'd country, is extraordinarily graphic in its mortal aspect, in that part above all which describes the sufferings of the sick man. Is it not remarkable that a man physically healthy and positive in his outlook on life, a man in his twenties (he was twenty-five when he began to compose the poem, as we have seen from the letter to Dora), should be occupied with the thought of death and disease and dissolution? More remarkable, that he should be able to sound these thoughts in so convincing a manner? It is the last thing one might have expected from the well-balanced Strauss. A sentimental biography has traced the origin of *Death and Transfiguration* to the serious illness that befell the composer. This is a fine story, except that it could not possibly be true, Strauss having fallen ill over a year and a half after he had completed the composition and having been in excellent fettle while he was composing it. No, the artist can turn toward dark broodings in the midst of felicitous circumstances, and vice versa. Not outward circumstances were responsible but, at least partly, the spirit of the times, that dream-drenched epoch that explored darkness and death.

For *Death and Transfiguration,* in spite of all its pictorial quality, is wrapped in a dreamlike aura. We sense this at once in the soft introduction—a beautiful and original passage, though it owes a debt to *Tristan*—where the mood is established by the uneasy and irregular pulse of the soft strings while the flute heaves a pathetic little sigh.* One "sees" the sick man twisting uncomfortably in his bed. Extraordinary is the transition from this feeble and febrile mood to the next one of smiling recollection, the patient enjoying a moment of happiness before the pains begin in earnest. The smiling melody is shortened; it begins frantically to fall over itself, suddenly to be swamped by the onrush of suffering. That suffering is

* Toscanini used to labor to get this rhythm just right. He once walked out on a recording session, completely spent, because the orchestra could not play it to his satisfaction.

depicted with almost clinical accuracy. Has there ever been in music a description as bold as this writhing pain, these hammer blows against the brain, these contortions of nerves? The "Death" itself is handled with consummate musical mastery, Strauss leaving us no doubt as to the exact moment when the fell sergeant makes his arrest. To me the "Transfiguration" seems less noble, less successful, than the preceding material. It has been said that Strauss was unable to handle the sublime, that he "succeeded throughout his creative career in inverse proportion to the degree of sublimity to which he aspired."* It seems to me, however, that the "Transfiguration" sags not because of lack of reach but because Strauss was not deeply concerned with religion or the religious. He lacked involvement with God. He felt none of the passion of faith. Whenever he touches the religious, as for example in certain phrases uttered by Jokanaan in *Salome*, he becomes unconvincing. It was in psychological probing that his interest lay; it was in the expression of characters, the more curious the better, that his talent showed itself. In the earthbound portions of *Death and Transfiguration* his genius soars, while in the ascent to the sky he falls like Daedalus.

In its time *Death and Transfiguration* was a disturbing work of the new art, and Romain Rolland was quite right when he called it "one of the most disturbing." In technical daring it represents an advance over *Don Juan*. In one respect only is it simpler than the earlier tone poem: Strauss here used less percussion. This pleased his father, who used to call the percussion section "the kitchenware."

As in the case of *Don Juan*, there were voices raised against this music, as well as for it. One of these was Debussy's, who had liked Strauss's earlier music. He felt that though Strauss was "one of the most assertive geniuses of our times," the composition was built out of undistinguished material. He wrote: "In the cookery book, under 'Jugged Hare,' will be seen this wise recommendation: 'Take a hare.' Richard Strauss proceeds otherwise. To write a symphonic poem he takes anything."†

---

* Norman Del Mar, *Richard Strauss: A Critical Commentary on His Life and Works*, Vol. I.

† Quoted in Edward Lockspeiser, *Debussy: His Life and Mind*.

The composer retained a special love for *Death and Transfiguration;* he not only quoted a theme from it in *Ein Heldenleben* but at the end of his life, in one of the last songs—"Abendrot" (Sunset)—he alluded to it.

For a long time Strauss had been ambitious to create an opera. Where better could he use "music as expression," how better enlarge the symphonic poem to include words and characters? Because he was under Ritter's influence, the subject he chose had to be mystic, didactic, elevating, derived from the legendary, its hero self-sacrificing, its locale placed in medieval Germany, the "folk" taking an important role; in a word, Wagnerian. And nothing would do but that he, like Wagner, write his own text. Strauss worked on this text for several years, constantly seeking Ritter's advice. He lacked literary talent and it turned out to be a sore task, but he kept on doggedly writing and revising. *Guntram* is stuffed with underdone ideas, its central one being a man's redemption. The very title is Wagnerian, combining Gunther and Wolfram, while other characters in the opera are called Freihild and Friedhold.

The plot, too, is a farrago of Wagnerian ideas. It may be useful to recount it briefly, if only to show how far Strauss's successful operas departed from such quasi-religious balderdash:

The locale is the Germany of the middle of the thirteenth century. Guntram has distinguished himself by aiding a group of poor peasants who are refugees from war-torn homes and are being persecuted by the young Duke Robert. Guntram meets a mysterious figure, Friedhold, who is an emissary of a league dedicated to noble works, a league that calls itself "Champions of Love" (obviously modeled on the Knights of the Grail). Spurred on by idealism, Guntram decides to carry the message of love to the tyrant Duke Robert, to attempt to soften his angry heart. As he turns to go, Freihild rushes in. She is Robert's wife, but not partisan to Robert's spirit. She abhors oppression and has now broken away from a life that has become intolerable to her. She sees no way out but suicide. Guntram prevents her from throwing herself into the lake. He tries to calm her, while she speaks bitterly of her loveless marriage. Freihild sees in Guntram a mere strolling minstrel and scornfully bids him go to the Duke for his reward for saving her life. Guntram is deeply offended but clings to Freihild until, beside herself, she strikes him in the face.

The second act plays at the Duke's court. Guntram and Freihild have fallen in love. Freihild's father, the Old Duke, calls on Guntram to give the assembly a taste of his art by singing a song. (The situation is similar to the second act of *Tannhäuser*.) The song in praise of peace which follows is so eloquent that it stirs all his listeners with the exception of Robert, who pours ridicule on Guntram. Freihild cannot bear this and comes to Guntram's defense. In a fury, Robert condemns Guntram to be whipped and imprisoned. Just then a messenger arrives with the news that the rebellion has regained strength and is on the point of threatening the castle. There is a violent altercation, Guntram and the young Duke draw their swords, and Guntram kills him. Freihild is now free, but Guntram realizes that by his act of violence he has become unfaithful to the doctrine of peace, unfaithful to his profoundest conviction.

The Old Duke bitterly invites Guntram to complete his destruction and slay him as well. Guntram, overcome with horror, lets his sword drop. Freihild declares her love for Guntram while he is arrested and removed to a dungeon.

In the last act, Guntram is in prison, tormented by his thoughts. Freihild appears to him; a long love scene ensues. But Guntram knows that he must renounce Freihild, and this renunciation scene represents the climax of the opera. At this moment, the mysterious Friedhold appears. The two men face each other. The latter, as the representative of the league, demands that Guntram present himself to be judged. But Guntram has now arrived at a differing creed: only he himself can expiate his guilt, only he himself can determine the course that his soul must pursue. God is within him, not outside. He takes leave of Freihild and goes out into the wilderness, no longer a knight, no longer a member of a league, but only a sinful human being searching for his salvation. The idea of man seeking God within himself and being in open conflict with organized religion derives from Nietzsche, whom Strauss was reading while he was writing the revised version and whose polemic against Christianity Strauss found much to his liking.

In the first draft Guntram does reappear before the league. Only later did Strauss arrive at the solution that asserts individual responsibility. In rejecting the league Guntram becomes, so to speak, his own priest. When Ritter, who was a Catholic, read the revised version of the text, he was incensed.* He felt that this new ending was "an immoral mockery of every ethical creed," that Strauss had robbed the opera of artistic unity, that he had become unfaithful to Wagner's philosophy as expressed in the Master's *Religion and Art*, and that in short the opera had become worthless. Strauss tried to persuade Ritter of the fitness of what he was doing, covering eleven closely written pages to explain. To no avail. Ritter never forgave Strauss and, disappointed, turned away from the composer, much to the benefit of Strauss's later development.

The music of *Guntram* is better than the text. Some of the qualities that are to be found in the later operas are here present in the rough, particularly passages of soaring melody for the soprano voice. But the whole score does not amount to an interesting or original opera, several passages being so close to *Tristan* as to be almost ludicrous.

Guntram was performed in Weimar on May 10, 1894, with Pauline in the part of Freihild. It had a mild *succès d'estime* but, though it was later given in Munich, it was soon dropped from the repertoire. It is probable that the theme itself contributed to its failure. People had had enough of redemption and renunciation and of men forming mystic societies to bring goodness into the world while orating like Gurnemanz. Strauss could never see it that way. He was quite sure that the failure of *Guntram* was due to intrigue among the critics. He even defended the text (as late as 1945) and said that though perhaps no masterpiece, it was no worse than the text of *Il Trovatore*. In 1940, after almost half a century, he pre-

* The essence of Strauss's creed, which so offended Ritter, is to be found in Guntram's words:

Mein Leben bestimmt
meines Geistes Gesetz;
mein Gott spricht
durch mich selbst zu mir

(My life is governed
by my spirit's law;
my God speaks to me
through myself!")

pared a new version, much abridged. This version was performed both in Weimar and in Berlin, again without leaving a mark. Strauss possessed enough wry self-criticism to construct in the garden of his house in Garmisch a "grave" for Guntram. "There he lies," said a homemade tablet, "cruelly slain by the symphonic orchestra of his own father. May he rest in peace."

Two days before the première of *Guntram*, Pauline and Strauss made their engagement official. The story of how this came about is a charming anecdote which has been told by Lotte Lehmann in her book *My Many Lives*.

The incident occurred during a rehearsal of *Tannhäuser*. (I have heard the story told as occurring during a rehearsal of *Guntram*. No matter.) Pauline made a mistake, and an argument arose between her and Strauss, who was conducting. At the height of the argument she lost her temper altogether, threw the piano score, which she was holding in her hand, right from the stage onto his head, shrieked, and, quitting the stage, rushed to her dressing room. This was a piece of insubordination that shocked everybody present into speechlessness. Strauss, terribly angry, laid down his baton, interrupted the rehearsal, and stalked into Pauline's room. Through the closed door wild shouts of rage could be heard. Then, suddenly, silence. Who had killed whom? A delegation of the orchestra approached the door, and one of them knocked timidly. Strauss opened the door and listened while one of the musicians stammered, "The orchestra is so horrified by the incredible behavior of Fräulein Pauline de Ahna that they feel they owe it to their honored conductor Strauss to refuse in the future to play in any opera in which she might have a part." Strauss regarded the musicians smilingly. Then he said, "That pains me very much, for I have just become engaged to Fräulein de Ahna."

Was the quarrel a lovers' quarrel as much as a musical one? It is not an unreasonable surmise. Pauline and Strauss had now known each other for seven years. Perhaps during the argument in the dressing room she pointed this out; perhaps she asked what her future with him was to be. Perhaps, like a pretty woman sure of herself, she used a display of temper to force a showdown. At any rate, Strauss and Pauline were married on September 9, 1894, in Weimar. As a marriage tribute Strauss brought her an imperishable gift: a group of songs, among which were "Cäcilie," "Heimliche Aufforderung" (Secret Invitation) and "Morgen" (Tomorrow). They stand among the highest examples of Strauss's work and among the finest of all German Lieder. How beautiful is "Morgen," with its delicate, sun-drenched expression of love's fulfillment! We can "see" as well as feel the two people walking hand in hand along the beach. Even if in future generations all of Strauss's major works should become obsolete—which is not likely—even if our taste in orchestral music should change radically, Strauss will remain immortal because he wrote such songs as "Morgen," "Traum durch die Dämmerung," and "Ständchen."

Before Pauline and Strauss were married, they went once again to Bayreuth. This time Strauss was allowed to conduct. He led *Tannhäuser* with Pauline as Elisabeth. Cosima, who had heard the final rehearsal of *Death and Transfiguration* and was unable to make much of it, was supposed to have said to him; "Well, well, so modern—and yet he knows how to conduct *Tannhäuser!*"*

One further incident is worth mentioning of the history of *Guntram.* Strauss sent the score of the opera to Verdi. He had by now changed his mind about at least some of Verdi's works. He particularly admired *Falstaff.* He wrote to Verdi that he could not find words to describe to him the great impression which the extraordinary beauty of *Falstaff* had made on him, and that as a slight token of his admiration he was sending him the score of *Guntram,* hoping that Verdi would accept it. Someday he hoped to speak to Verdi personally and "discuss music" with him.†

Verdi replied promptly: "Dear Sir: A few days ago I received a work which you so kindly sent me and which enjoyed such a success. I am now on my way to Milan, where I shall spend a few days, and therefore I do not have time to read your score. Yet, dipping into the score here and there, I perceive that your *Guntram* is a work fashioned by a knowing hand. It is too bad that I cannot understand the text, not because I wish to pass judgment (this I

---

* She had previously called *Don Juan* "an incredible thing, compared to which other symphonic compositions are milk toast."

† Letter to Verdi, January 18, 1895.

would not dare to do), but rather because I wish to admire and to share your pleasure. . . ."* In its courtesy and modesty as well as in its noncommittal distance the letter is typical of Verdi. Strauss never met Verdi personally but he preserved the letter all his life.

---

* Letter from Genoa, January 27, 1895.

6

Three Tone Poems

As he had been earlier in Meiningen, so Strauss was now restive in Weimar. The pattern of his behavior proved similar then and later: he would plunge himself into a task, accomplish wonders in the early stages, be all eagerness and enthusiasm; after a while, he would slacken his interest, see deficiencies magnified, become bored even, and begin to long for a change. When this mood was upon him, it was invariably others who were at fault, it was invariably his co-workers and his superiors who were the cause of his dissatisfaction, conditions too narrow, the public "incapable" (as the playwright John Webster called his audience). He did not recognize, nor did he want to recognize, that the cause lay within his own nature; a nature driven by ambition, which, drinking work as if it were water, could never know surfeit of activity nor set limits on projects and plans. Strauss, the executant musician, needed the excitement of the concert hall, the frantic activity of the opera stage, the approbation of audiences. As soon as he had achieved that approbation in one place, he was ready to move on. He wrote to his father: "As a conductor one needs the success of the moment, as a composer one has to *be* somebody. Nothing else matters."* He needed both "the success of the moment" and the consciousness of being somebody creative. The first need was as strong as the second. He said once that his real profession was conducting, composing

* Letter of February 6, 1894.

being his secondary task. We need not take him altogether seriously, and yet be certain that he loved to walk out on the stage. That is the reason, as much as financial gain, why in the course of his career he set out to impress almost every civilized city in Europe and America, why his concert tours were extensive, why he dashed off to one place and the other, why he braved long train rides and bad hotels.

Already in the summer of 1892, that is, before he embarked on his Mediterranean journey, he hinted to Bülow that he was no longer in perfect accord with Bronsart. The intendant, he said, had brusquely refused to advance his position. Such an advancement would have brought with it an increase in his remuneration, which indeed was quite small. Moreover, Bronsart did not agree "with the subjective way in which he conducted Beethoven" (whatever that may mean). "I am going to move on," he wrote to Bülow, "and now I am curious as to where."*

He could hardly have foreseen where this change was to lead him. When he was in Egypt, he received from his father a letter containing unexpected news. Franz reported that Levi had written him a note in which he asked Franz urgently for an immediate and confidential interview. The two men met in a café, and to Franz's astonishment Levi proposed that Strauss return to Munich, this time in a position equal to his own, that is, as chief conductor. Before broaching the matter to Strauss, he, Levi, wanted to know first, whether Strauss would adopt a friendly attitude toward Levi, and second, whether Strauss's state of health would be equal to the task. Levi said that he had discussed the idea with Fischer, the other conductor at the opera, and reluctantly (we can imagine how reluctantly) Fischer had agreed that if Strauss were to accept, it would be necessary to make him artistically and financially Fischer's superior. Levi himself seemed dispirited, wrote Franz, and uncertain of his own future. Levi had hoped to become co-director of the opera house with the present manager, Ernst von Possart. The powers in charge, however, opposed a double regime, a regime rendered even less clear-cut by the fact that the august and now aging Perfall still exercised much influence. Disappointed in his

---

* Letter from Munich, June 30, 1892.

hope for advancement, Levi now took stock and considered how best to make his own position secure. He felt he needed a co-worker both capable and loyal to him, who could help hold the artistic level high, share some of the work, contribute new ideas, and bring stability to an opera house riddled with politics and constantly in danger of sinking into mediocrity. Only then could Levi feel tranquil, only then could he hope for a peaceful atmosphere for the few remaining years of his activity. (That, more or less, is what Levi said to Franz. It seems probable, however, that the real reason why Levi, the brilliant and cultivated conductor, was not entrusted with the direction of the opera lay in his own unstable personality as well as in his frequent illnesses.) Two other conductors were being considered for the post. One was Weingartner, who, however, was contractually bound elsewhere. The other was Mottl, a personal friend of Levi's, who, however, had married a woman of equivocal reputation; this made his welcome in a Munich, which had recently experienced the Wagner-Cosima marital scandal, dubious.

The one hesitancy Levi felt about Strauss, and he said so frankly to Franz, was his fear that Strauss was completely under the influence of Ritter. Levi knew that Ritter hated him. What, asked Levi, had Ritter against him? He had never done anything to hurt Ritter. Franz's reply is a model of holier-than-thou attitude. He answered that Ritter was an anti-Semite; what could you expect?

During the interview Levi tried to woo Franz (and through him Strauss, of course) by dropping a derogatory remark about Perfall. Franz writes: "To kick a dead horse is hardly noble, even if that horse happens to be an ass. As to Ritter, I remarked that though you were very friendly with Ritter, you would preserve your independence."* Levi kept repeating that he demanded that Strauss adopt "a friendly attitude toward *him*." Franz replied, once more self-righteously, that his son knew of no wrong he had committed toward Levi, and that any such implication was calumny. Finally Franz assured him that Strauss would return from his stay abroad in perfect health.

Why in truth did Levi want Strauss at his side, in spite of the boorish anti-Semitic rudeness Strauss had shown to Levi, virtually

---

* Letter of March 16, 1893.

cutting him dead in Bayreuth? We may take Levi at his word when he said that he needed a younger and a capable co-worker, so that he might still "work along for a few more years." He was motivated as well by an idealism that set the goal above personal considerations; he was willing to enlist a man unsympathetic to him personally, if he could help nourish the musical life of his beloved Munich.

Why did Strauss go back to Munich with the shadow of the frock-coated Perfall still hovering over it? Why was he willing to return to what he had called the morass? It is not difficult to guess that first, the larger authority in the larger city attracted him; second, he knew that Levi was soon to retire (he did retire two years later) and he hoped he would then have the opportunity to be in sole command; third, his new salary was attractive, beginning at 7,000 marks (roughly twice what he received in Weimar) and increasing every year; fourth, by contract he would be handed the choicest plums of the operatic literature, including the Mozart and Wagner works; and finally, there was a prospect of having *Guntram* performed if he did go to Munich. Perhaps this last reason was as strong as any.

So back he went, assuming the post in 1894.

Strauss was exactly thirty when he returned to Munich. We need not follow his conductorial activities too precisely, for they were more of the same as in Weimar. He was active both in the opera house and in the concert hall, and he had at his disposal fuller means, a larger orchestra, and better singers. He added to his repertoire *Die Meistersinger*, and he inaugurated a festival of Mozart operas, Levi conducting *Figaro* while he took over *Don Giovanni* and *Così*. As to *Die Meistersinger*, he never established with that comedy the intimate and personal relationship he felt toward *Tristan*. All the same, he conducted it superbly and with a light touch. One of his contemporaries compared Strauss's interpretation of *Die Meistersinger* with Hans Richter's. He said that Richter approached the work from the viewpoint of Hans Sachs, Strauss from the viewpoint of Walther von Stolzing.

Almost alone he was responsible for the resurrection of *Così fan tutte*. He said that "Of all the dramatic works of Mozart, *Così* had been considered a stepchild, and that the average verdict deemed it to be one of the weaker works. Even Richard Wagner believed that the text was poor and that it bound Mozart's wings."* Even granting, added Strauss, that the plot was not particularly brilliant and rather strained credulity, da Ponte's text contained fine psychological touches that gave Mozart the opportunity to create in music two enchanting characters and to distinguish these characters one from the other, the sentimental and conscientious Fiordiligi from the gayer, more mercurial, yet more realistic Dorabella. He pointed to the fine irony of the style here created by Mozart, the mixture of the humorous and the pathetic, the parodistic and the sentimental. To be sure, it was a difficult work to give; but when it was justly done, then the work became "gorgeous," one replete with captivating stage effects.†

On another occasion, Strauss made a most felicitous remark about *Così*. He was discussing the duet for the two women after the lovers pretend to have departed (No. 18, Act I). There the ladies are, not knowing how to carry on or what to do with their spare time. Strauss said that it took real genius to compose boredom and not make it boring.

As a conductor, Strauss was being invited here and there, and for the first time outside of Germany's borders. In the first three years of his second engagement in Munich, we find him in Berlin, in Switzerland, in Hungary; we find him giving a concert in Moscow (where he played *Death and Transfiguration* and *Till Eulenspiegel*); in Brussels, in Antwerp, Amsterdam, London, and, in 1897, for the first time in Paris, a city he was to visit frequently thereafter. Wherever he went, he was welcome, but perhaps his most vociferous reception came in Barcelona, where, after playing the "Eroica," the Prelude to *Die Meistersinger*, and the Prelude to *Guntram*, he gave the Spanish audience his *Don Juan*. The result was pandemonium. "This kind of applause is new to me. The people here must be used to it from the bullfights," he wrote to his father‡—and he had to repeat the entire tone poem.

Pauline accompanied him on many of these journeys, and she

* From notes Strauss wrote for the *Neue Freie Presse* in Vienna in 1910 on the occasion of a revival of the opera.

† *Ibid.*

‡ Letter of November 12, 1897.

herself took part in several concerts. He was happy with her. The marriage had turned out well. Her bubbly disposition, her sense of fun, her irreverence toward the pompous gestures of the age, along with her complete reverence for him, her love of gossip and her eagerness for travel and adventure delighted him. She was still coquettish, pretty, assertive, hot-tempered. As yet that temper had not degenerated into vulgarity.

But there was a cloud on the horizon: Pauline did not find favor with Strauss's parents. Whether Franz disapproved of "the actress," or whether Pauline behaved disrespectfully to the old despot, or whether it was just a common case of in-law jealousy, whatever the reason, there were quarrels and grievances voiced on both sides, until one day (the date is uncertain, for Strauss was so wrought up that for once he did not date his letter, although he was usually punctilious about dating) he wrote his mother a letter that gave vent to his anger and took Pauline's part. This letter is very different in tone from that which Strauss used habitually to his parents, and he addressed it to his mother, perhaps hoping to find her more responsive than his father:

> Many thanks for the beautiful lilac plant. It gave me much pleasure. But, really, it would give me more pleasure if my continuous endeavors to effect an understanding between my wife and my family were not so totally unsuccessful. I assure you that my wife intends sincerely to correct her faults, faults which are minor and harmless and of which she herself is aware. You, on the other hand, I must note with sorrow, are not willing to understand the peculiarities of her nature nor to condone them. When I realize that gossip, miserable, lying, old woman's gossip, suffices for you to raise such awful accusations against Pauline as you did this morning and to nullify all of my endeavors, as well as Pauline's, to arrive at an understanding, then I must ask myself if it wouldn't be better to cease any relationship between Pauline and you. To be sure, Pauline's nature is impulsive, violent, and brusque. But at bottom she has a good, childlike, and naïve nature. Even with the best will in the world, she can't quickly and radically change the way she behaves. That behavior doesn't please you: very well, from now on she wants to avoid disturbing your peace and tranquillity—even though at the bottom of her jealous heart she feels true

> love and admiration for you. I haven't the slightest intention of continuing to explain, unfortunately unsuccessfully, the character of my wife while you don't take the least trouble to get to know her. . . . In short, I propose that you erase your rambunctious daughter-in-law from the family book and content yourself with your much more accommodating son-in-law [Hanna's husband]. Both Pauline and I want dearly to see you, my beloved parents, peaceful and happy. I conclude with much pain that that cannot be the case, so long as the woman whom after much deliberation I have chosen as my wife, and whom in spite of her faults I love and admire, irritates you and embitters your life.
>
> Pauline is ready to make this concession to your peace of mind. If, as I fear, you really want it, she will submit to voluntary banishment from your family circle and remain by the side of her husband. . . .*

The letter is ascribed by Dr. Willi Schuh, the Strauss scholar, to the year 1896. If it was written late in 1896, it was written while Pauline was pregnant, and perhaps that fact is at least partly responsible for its tone of injury. As with so many family quarrels, so was this quarrel patched up, and later Strauss continued to write to his parents (his father lived on another nine years) warm and chatty letters. But Franz never became fond of Pauline.

Strauss's only child was born on April 12, 1897.† The time of pregnancy had been exceedingly difficult for Pauline. The baby was born late, and the doctor had falsely diagnosed twins. Pauline suffered great pain. She had indeed been in danger of her life, but this fact was hidden from Strauss, who in the last few days before her giving birth was away on a concert tour. He received the news of the birth of his son in Stuttgart. The date happened to coincide with the first anniversary of Ritter's death, so Strauss gave his son two names, Franz, after his father, and Alexander, after his friend. Strauss was beside himself with joy. He adored the baby from the first moment on and he was proud of Pauline for having endured her suffering "heroically." Her first words when she awoke from the

---

* This letter is from Willi Schuh (Ed.), *Briefe an die Eltern, 1882-1906.*

† Cosima sent a congratulatory telegram saying "Please not Zarathustra as mentor. Offer my services as governess."

anesthesia were "Doctor, would you like a cognac?" "As a housewife," wrote Strauss, "her first thoughts were about the physician, not about herself."*

During the tour that made him miss Pauline's delivery, he played a new composition, *Enoch Arden*. It is a melodrama for speaker and piano; the poem by Tennyson is recited and underscored by music, the music characterizing each of the protagonists—Enoch himself, Enoch's rival, and Annie Lee, "the little wife to both." The work has only slight musical interest. In its time it was a great success, chiefly because the narrator of the poem was Ernst von Possart himself, a popular and distinguished actor, then intendant of the Munich opera and Strauss's chief.†

The important works that belong to the second Munich period are the three tone poems, *Till Eulenspiegel, Thus Spake Zarathustra,* and *Don Quixote*. These, along with a number of songs—including the famous "Traum durch die Dämmerung" (Dream at Dusk)—are the fruit of three years of compositional work. Considering how little time Strauss had at this period for composing and how complex the three tone poems are, they demonstrate again that Strauss, once he was seized with an idea, could develop and execute music with extraordinary rapidity. Each of the three is different from the other in mood and feeling; each is ineluctably linked to the poetic idea the composer wished to convey; each is "music as expression." Of the three, in my opinion, *Till Eulenspiegel* is the most successful and *Zarathustra* the least. *Don Quixote,* though it has never reached the popularity of *Till* or *Death and Transfiguration* or *Zarathustra,* is a challenging composition, in the long run perhaps the most rewarding of Strauss's orchestral works.

Two of the three tone poems are prevailingly humorous in character. As a humorist—if we understand by that term an artist who not only could create funny works but could voice grave thoughts lightly—Strauss excelled. He might occasionally merely crack a joke, even a crude one, using for it so ingenuous a musical device as a wind machine or a child's rattle. But he was capable of mastering the difficult art of touching our understanding through "still

---

* Letter to his parents, April 16, 1897.

† Possart appeared in New York in 1910 in a repertory of plays. He was a fine Iago, Shylock and Mephistopheles.

smiles," to quote Carlyle's phrase. He was not a social humorist. He did not present a "speaking picture of the follies and foibles of a nation," which Voltaire defined as true comedy. (Except perhaps in *Feuersnot* he never satirized the Germans or the Germany of his time.) He was rather a private humorist; as such he gave us his best musical portrayals, portrayals three-quarters gay, one-quarter sad, such as Till and Quixote and the Marschallin and Zerbinetta. Is it not all the more strange that this ironic German could quite turn off his sense of humor and, attempting to set philosophy to music or music to philosophy, bring forth a work that makes a noise about Nietzsche? A great distance in "reasonableness" (if I may so express myself) separates *Till* and *Zarathustra.*

Till Eulenspiegel is a figure who occurs in one guise or another in the literature of many nations. Whether he is called "Pelele" in Spanish or "Háry János" in Hungarian, whether he acts as a servant to two Italian masters or as a barber of Seville, his is the sly triumph. He was invented because there was need for him: he shows that the simple are superior to the educated, the poor cleverer than the rich, that the strolling beggar is able to best the seated dignitary, that the liar often speaks the truth, and that he is strongest armed who can summon impudence. This is so obviously untrue of real life that it had to be fabricated by fable for the benefit of the little people and the titillation of the mighty.

There is no general agreement as to the origin of Till. He, who might appear in a painting by Brueghel, is usually considered to hail from the Netherlands and is supposed to have lived in the fourteenth century. The stories of his adventures were circulated in the German-speaking countries in the sixteenth century, and they accorded with the growing resistance of the peasant and the laborer toward church and state. "*Eulenspiegel*" in German means an owl's mirror. Whether the owl here serves as a symbol of wisdom and the mirror as a reflection of man's foibles is uncertain. He appears under the name of Howleglass or Owlglass in English literature of the sixteenth century.

Till is called a *Schalk.* That means not quite a prankster, not quite a buffoon, not quite a rake, but a combination of all. He traveled throughout the land, appearing at fairs and village meetings. He worked his mischief on the rich, played his jokes on priests, cheated tradesmen, interfered with newly married couples, and spread confusion wherever he went. Occasionally he appeared to settle disputes, such as the time when the inhabitants of a village could not determine how many they were—whoever counted forgot himself with becoming modesty—until Till came along and solved the problem by including himself. He was something of a philosopher as well. When you went downhill, he said, you must be sad, thinking that you need soon plod uphill again; and when you climbed uphill you must smile, thinking of the next stretch that led downhill. Till could answer such questions as how many grains of sand there were on the beach and how many days had elapsed since the world began. He posed as a famous painter at the court of Hessen and obtained the commission to paint the Duke's portrait. In due time he showed him a blank canvas and told the Duke that the painting could be seen only by those who were legitimately born. (One perceives how ancient is the story of the Emperor's clothes.)

To German children Till is as well-known a character as Lewis Carroll's Alice is to English children. Strauss was familiar with Till from childhood on. He liked Till so much that at one time he was considering an opera on the subject, and he went so far as to have a libretto sketched out. He settled for the tone poem, one which after *Death and Transfiguration* gave him a change of pace: instead of treading the slow steps appropriate to a sickroom, Strauss now cavorts.

I believe *Till* to be an altogether brilliant composition enriching music by one of its comparatively few successful humorous works. For once there is not a blot of bathos, not a stretch of "philosophic" meandering, hardly a touch of the commonplace. It is melodiously easy and charming, even though Till creates an unholy racket when he storms through the marketplace and breaks the dishes. The design, which is in rondo form, returning at its end to its beginning, is as right as a ring. The poem is not too long and not too short. Its episodes are varied and consistently entertaining: Till disguised as a priest preaching a musical sermon as greasy as one of Tartuffe's speeches, Till "glowing with love," Till humming a folk ditty. And so on until Till's final capture, the process by which he is judged, his condemnation, his being strung up at the gallows, the mockery he can summon even at the point of death, his expiring squeak—all these are so set forth that we seem to see the events pass before our very eyes. In a word, *Till* is a heartwarming and happy masterpiece.

Beethoven said that music was a higher revelation than philosophy. Can music reveal philosophy? One hesitates to say that it cannot, for one ought not to set limits to the art. But the attempt to reveal a philosophical thought process, the attempt to portray in sound a specific philosophical system or detailed philosophical teaching, must end in failure. Music cannot translate; direct translation from the didactic to the emotional becomes impossible. At best such music must use words as explanatory subtitles. Insofar, then, as Strauss deals with the philosophical teaching of Nietzsche, with his intellectual convictions, Strauss tries to give us a creation that cannot stand on its own feet.

Nietzsche is not a lucid writer, and *Zarathustra* is probably the least lucid of his works. He has been widely misunderstood, by Hitler's intellectual stooges on purpose. His Superman is not a mindless and bigoted warrior armed to the teeth. He is a being who, through breeding, education, hard thinking and harder egotism, rises above mediocrity and conformity. His road lies beyond good and evil; all means that will propel man along it are recommendable. To reach the higher state, such "weak" institutions as advocate the sanctity of humanity in general must be destroyed. Christianity must be destroyed, democracy, "this mania for counting noses," abolished.

"Nietzsche has been refuted by every aspirant to respectability; and yet he stands as a milestone in modern thought, and a mountain-peak in German prose," wrote Will Durant in *The Story of Philosophy*. His most beautiful prose is to be found in the prose poem *Also sprach Zarathustra*. Here Nietzsche clothes ideas in robes of multicolored language. He sings as he teaches, he rhapsodizes as he expounds.

To the extent that Strauss attempts the impossible he fails. Not only does he fail but he becomes pretentious. To the extent that Strauss is inspired by the cadence of Nietzsche's language, by its poetic aura, he succeeds with his own. He did deny wanting "to write philosophical music or to portray Nietzsche's great work musically," and said that the poem was to be regarded as "my homage to the genius of Nietzsche." Contradicting himself almost in the same sentence, he added, "I meant rather to convey in music an idea of the evolution of the human race from its origin, through the various phases of development, religious as well as scientific, up to Nietzsche's idea of the Superman."* Strauss had a way of saying one thing and meaning another, and he sometimes and rather capriciously denied a programmatic content after he had previously spelled it out.

The tone poem's sections are clearly titled with "chapter headings." But if we did not know them, we could not identify them. The plan to present "an idea of the evolution of the human race" is beyond him and may be beyond music. It reads—but it does not sound. What, without an explanation, are we to make of such a curious heading as "*Von den Hinterweltlern*"? It is a difficult word to translate and has been frequently mistranslated: such as "Primitive Man" or "Backward Man" or "Inhabitants of the Unseen World." To Nietzsche it meant man undeveloped, ignorant, unfired by a will to power, man before he takes the first step on the road. What has it to do with music? Nothing. How can we consider seriously an attempt to express in music the world of science? Strauss suggests that world by presenting us with a fugue beginning in the lower reaches of the orchestra and employing all the notes of the chromatic scale. But that, erudite though it may be, is a trick; it has nothing to do with science, and we are left with a fugue, which we either like or dislike as a musical composition.

But, as I have suggested, whenever Strauss lets Nietzsche guide him toward feeling, *Also sprach Zarathustra* is successful. Such concepts as "Of the Great Longing," "Of Joys and Passion," "The Grave Song," and perhaps and loosely "The Convalescent" are adaptable to musical usage.

Within *Zarathustra*'s thirty-three minutes there are to be found moments of superb beauty and passages of gripping intensity, side by side with amorphous sections and intramural cleverness that impresses only German musicologists—and no longer even them. Even they have given up the game, so popular at one time, of read-

---

* Notes written for the first Berlin performance.

ing profound meaning into every note and germinal motive of the composition.

There is the stunning opening of the sunrise, obviously inspired by the beginning of Nietzsche's work: Zarathustra, leaving his solitude and standing in the dawn, addresses the sun: "You great star! What would your fate be if you had no one for whom you could shine?" This opening, using the simple C-Major triad, serves as one of the key motives, its three notes occurring again and again within the score. One cannot avoid the suspicion that Strauss wrote it with the brain, not the heart, to demonstrate to us how complex a "philosophical" structure could be built with the squarest brick. The first section is the one that deals with man in his primal condition. Since unenlightened man was deeply obsessed with religion, Strauss here quotes the traditional Credo. Even so sensible a commentator as Norman Del Mar believes that that quotation is "palpably cynical."* How "palpably"? We could hear nothing cynical in this did we not know that Nietzsche was opposed to religion, that he was opposed to the creed that blessed the meek, and that Strauss not only agreed with him but was attracted toward Nietzsche by that very opposition.

The section entitled "The Convalescent" is a marvelous scherzo, gay, light, and dazzling. But the "Dance Song" that follows is a rather ordinary Viennese waltz, complete with *Schmalz* and *Schwung.*

The "Song of the Night Wanderer" contains the conciliatory climax of the tone poem. Then, with its harmonies growing lighter, the music rises to a beautiful "Epilogue," which ends the composition in a close of peace. (This is quite contrary to Nietzsche's conclusion.)

There you have it, a work of curious anomalies, divided against itself. It overwhelms you with opulence and bores you with stuffiness. It lifts you with its inspiration and lectures at you in professorial tone. It is both fulsome and fabulous. It contains both romantic exuberance and doughy pedantry. It includes some of the best and some of the worst of the composer. With its virtues and its faults, both impressive, it could be called "Thus Spake Richard Strauss."

---

* *Richard Strauss: A Critical Commentary on His Life and Works,* Vol. I.

The two celebrated Spanish dons, Juan and Quixote, are citizens of the world. They roam over countries, nationalities, and time. *Don Quixote* is Spain's most valuable contribution to the sum of international literary wealth. Cervantes' novel, while dealing a death blow to the medieval way of thinking, while smiling Spain's chivalry away, as Byron said, kindled a spark in the most diverse imaginations. Cervantes' influence can be found in Fielding's *Tom Jones* and Laurence Sterne's *Tristram Shandy,* in Dostoevski's *Idiot* and Chekhov's *Uncle Vanya.* In the pictorial arts, *Don Quixote* has inspired Daumier, who kept returning to the theme again and again, Doré, Goya in the period in which his vision was obsessed by witches and demons, Dali, and Picasso. In music, *Don Quixote* has served Purcell in England, a host of operatic composers in Italy (including Donizetti), Mendelssohn in Germany, Massenet in France, Rubinstein in Russia, de Falla in Spain. *Don Quixote,* like Ulysses, can be forever interpreted afresh.* Strauss's tone poem is a wonderfully successful interpretation. It is imaginative but clear. Once we know the title of the tone poem, we can see Quixote and Sancho Panza in our imagination and we don't need commentary or a detailed guide through the episodes. The music has what is needed to make the Don come alive: irony and derision, affection and sympathy. This last is an important ingredient, for a good satire makes plausible that which it satirizes.

One feels that Strauss was enjoying himself. He is not straining for effects lying outside the domain of music and he is not dredging up artificial profundity. Complex, ingenious, and technically marvelous though *Don Quixote* is, it strikes one as natural and indeed as simple. Like *Till Eulenspiegel,* it is warmhearted. It is less gay than *Till,* the mixture of sadness and comedy being about three to one. Cervantes' novel would assay the same.

I do not know why this fine composition is not more popular than it is. In number of performances it lags behind the other four. It is a difficult work to perform, needing a cellist who knows how to play an unsprightly instrument in a sprightly fashion and a conductor who can do justice to both its wit and its warmth. (I have

* Ulysses, Don Juan and Don Quixote are all travelers. Are stay-at-homes less likely to capture our imagination?

heard *Don Quixote* often, but I have heard only one completely satisfactory performance, and that was Toscanini's.)

Don Quixote is a tone poem, though Strauss called it "Fantastic Variations on a Theme of Knightly Character," and though technically it could be called a concerto for cello and viola. Not all the variations are of equal quality. It cannot be said that the tone poem is unblemished. But the balance of genius to manipulation is much in favor of genius.

My own favorite is Variation Three, which begins with a funny conversation between the Knight and Sancho Panza. The second part of this Variation portrays the world of chivalry, a world of giants, dragons, and menaced maidens, as Don Quixote sees it in his mind's eye. The whole orchestra sings in delicate and tender tones. We find here the Strauss of the lovely songs. We understand the Knight and all misguided knights bent on whatever errand.

"Whether he was a fool or a wise man is not clear, but surely he entered heaven," concludes Cervantes of his hero. Strauss does him justice.

We may briefly set down the record of the reception of these three tone poems: They were all successful. *Till Eulenspiegel* was first performed November 5, 1895, in Köln, under Franz Wüllner, the conductor who had already shown a sympathetic interest in Strauss's work. It became almost at once a strong drawing card. *Zarathustra* was given the following year, November 27, 1896, in Frankfurt, under the direction of Strauss himself. It caused a little more headshaking by the critics, but once again Strauss pleased the public. Immediately there began to appear essays that related the music to Nietzsche's text; they awed rather than instructed people. But there was hardly a major orchestra that did not program the work.*

Hanslick of course hated the new tone poems, as he had hated *Don Juan* and *Tod und Verklärung*. Of *Till* he wrote that it was "a veritable world's fair of sound effects."† Of *Zarathustra* he wrote:

* Barbara W. Tuchman in *The Proud Tower* points out justly that Nietzsche lay at "the core of his time" and that Strauss's choice of subject was in tune with his time.
† Quoted by Ernst Krause in *Richard Strauss: Gestalt und Werk*.

"O Zarathustra, do not crack your whip so ominously! Don't you know that noise kills thought?"*

Don Quixote was likewise performed by Franz Wüllner in Köln, on March 8, 1898. One critic called it "the complete negation of everything that I understand music to be."† But it really did not matter. For every critic who scowled at Strauss's refractory impudence, there were two who proclaimed the significance of the tone poems. For every member of the audience who was puzzled, there were two who were enraptured and twenty who were curious. Applause resounded from Moscow to Paris and soon from London and New York. To name but one instance: two years after the première of *Zarathustra,* Strauss enjoyed, he said, "the greatest triumph of his career" in staid and stolid Amsterdam.‡ The Concertgebouw Orchestra, under Willem Mengelberg, honored him not only with a concert but by engraving his name in large golden letters in the hall itself, next to those of Wagner and Liszt. (To make room for this, poor old Gounod's name was obliterated.) After Mengelberg conducted *Death and Transfiguration,* the audience rose "as one man" in tribute to the composer. Then Strauss himself conducted *Zarathustra;* he was called "uncounted times" to acknowledge the applause. Read his report:

> It was the most beautiful performance of *Zarathustra* I have ever experienced; it had been rehearsed in sectional rehearsals for three weeks. It was fabulous! Add to that the hospitality of the Dutch—champagne and oysters three times a day. But in spite of all the affection which was tendered to me in the most touching way, I am quite glad to be home again—with roast veal and plain beer.§

Later Strauss dedicated the score of *Ein Heldenleben* to Mengelberg.

---

* Quoted by Franz Trenner, Roland Tenschert, *et al.*

† Franz Trenner (Ed.), *Richard Strauss: Dokumente seines Lebens und Schaffens.*

‡ Letter to his father from Berlin, November, 1898.

§ *Ibid.*

7

In the Metropolis

The nineteenth century expired with a shout, not with a whimper. It strode to its exit proudly and might well have raised a glass of champagne to the incoming century. The departing spirit had reason to be satisfied with itself. It had accomplished much: the lot of the working class had improved with industrialization, a few reforms had been introduced, the middle class had become more prosperous and a few of them very rich, a multitude of inventions had made life more comfortable. Though the factories pumped soot into the air and the new railroads set up a clatter, people did not mind; they gladly traded pure air for houses which, though stuffy, were well heated, gladly traded the petroleum lamp and the candle for the bright Welsbach burner. At the turn of the century strange and shiny new machines held out a promise of new money to be earned with new products. All that glittered seemed gold.

The century's achievements in art had been prodigious. Romanticism had refreshed art and reasserted its usefulness. Frank in tears and laughter, it had strengthened its hold on the plain citizen. Music, literature and painting had moved from the palace to the salon, and even to the single room. If in this move art had lost some refinement, it had gained in vitality and directness. Much of the most vital music we still enjoy is of nineteenth-century origin. As the century vanished, so did several of the musical geniuses who had been responsible for music's augmentation: Tchaikovsky,

Brahms, César Franck and Johann Strauss died in the last decade, Verdi in 1901.

Germany goose-stepped into the new century with especial optimism. It seemed to be in vigorous shape. It was bustling, working, pushing. The country that Bismarck had welded together held together. From year to year it had become more self-assertive, more proud. Bismarck had died in 1898. Before his death he had become reconciled with Wilhelm. He had called for "blood and iron," and this amalgam he had, through his own personality, mixed with arrogance. "Yet the arrogance was matched by the skill. That, his successors never understood. German policy after him had only the arrogance."* That arrogance increased in direct proportion to the buildup of Germany's military force. All but a handful of people believed that this accumulation of steel was to prevent war.

The adage that history repeats itself is now generally discredited. Yet we find a parallel between the history of European civilization in the early twentieth century and that of the decline of the Roman Empire. There, in the two centuries following the birth of Christ, the enormous empire enjoyed peace with but two brief interruptions. The Greco-Christian writer Aristides then called "the whole world a paradise, where men might travel safely from one end of the empire to the other, where, in place of war, cities competed with each other only in their splendor and pleasures." Shortly after, the Roman Empire began to crumble. Once it had begun to crumble it disintegrated quickly.

Germany did seem a "paradise," though hardly an innocent one. The young men of Germany considered themselves heroes and held themselves snappily erect, even if they had to wear corsets under their uniforms. They were humbly admired by their ladies, who accepted their role as *Hausfrauen*. Hadn't Kaiser Wilhelm laid down the dictum to his tepid queen and her female subjects: "*Kinder, Kirche, Küche*" (Children, Church, Kitchen)? Underneath all such slogan morality pullulated a lively traffic in prostitution. Homosexuality increased sharply.† But scandals were quickly extinguished, splendor was all around, rotund moral phrases filled

---

* L. C. B. Seaman, *From Vienna to Versailles.*

† The famous scandal involving, among others, Prince Philipp Eulenburg, the Kaiser's closest friend, was not made public till 1907.

the newspapers, and the opportunities to elevate one's "*Kultur*" were unceasing. One charming, though slightly prejudiced, observer, the young singer Geraldine Farrar, remembered:

> Imperial Germany of 1900 was a magnificent country, and Berlin quite measured up to one's earliest dreams of royalty and picturesque glitter. There was the military elegance of court life, the dynamic Kaiser, a dashing young Crown Prince, and divine music for only a few pennies to enchant one's enthusiastic spirit. Great names abounded in opera, concert and recitals. Dr. Karl Muck, the great Wagnerian authority; Dr. Richard Strauss, pre-eminent as conductor and composer; Leo Blech; Joachim's exquisite chamber quartet; Nikisch's glowing orchestral interpretations; Gustav Mahler, von Schuch and a host of others were guests in the Prussian Capital. Americans were popular. Teddy Roosevelt was a friend of the Kaiser, and it was said each tried to outdo the other in friendly overtures; in evidences of mutual esteem in the press headlines, at any rate. Our ambassadors were wealthy and charming, commercial relations were successful and all was *couleur de rose*.*

The general taste of this rose-colored era could hardly have been worse. Romanticism began to waddle, stuffed with sugary sentimentality. Paintings, music, architecture had to be big to be good. Franz von Stuck's sculpture *Amazon on Horseback* was considered important art. The buildings constructed in Berlin were neo-Greek palaces, decorated with fat symbolic friezes and surrounded by honor guards of bloated columns which supported nothing. In those buildings treaties were negotiated that were not meant to be honored, and agreements were concluded that were to carry Germany's commerce to the far corners of the world. Such as, in 1899, the new Trans-African telegraph and in the same year the Baghdad Railway. For high-sounding plans the Emperor had little trouble raising money: an issue of treasury bonds of 80,000,000 marks placed in the United States was quickly snapped up. Whatever business crises did occur, through overextended bank maneuvers and overproduction, were quickly settled, by decree rather than by economic adjustment. Once more the populace could admire the latest uniform of the Kaiser, once more recommenced the round of

* Geraldine Farrar, *Such Sweet Compulsion.*

ceremonial visits of the head of this state or that country, who thought it prudent to remain on the good side of Wilhelm; once more a splendid maneuver took place, a parade was passing.

The German writers of the turn of the century are now largely forgotten. Typical among them was the poet Detlev Freiherr von Lilienkron, who, himself a soldier, glorified war with eloquence. But it was in German literature, more than in the pictorial arts or in music, that protesting voices against gigantism and self-glorification were first raised. We have already noted this tendency in Hauptmann's social drama, to be followed by the social problem plays of his rival, Hermann Sudermann, by the daring though confused sexual writings of Frank Wedekind (*Spring's Awakening, Pandora's Box*, and others), and by splashing satires such as those of Ernst von Wolzogen, who was working with Strauss on a new opera, *Feuersnot*. Most of the lightness and charm that furnished an antidote to the pompous German writing of the period originated in Vienna. In 1900 Arthur Schnitzler published a short story which created a sensation: *Lieutenant Gustl.* It was one of the early stream-of-consciousness pieces of writing, detailing the thoughts of an army officer who, insulted by a common baker—from whom he cannot possibly demand satisfaction by challenging him to a duel—feels that the only way out of his dilemma, the only course open to him, is to commit suicide. In the morning he learns by chance that the baker has dropped dead during the night—and so there is no need for Lieutenant Gustl to feel his honor tarnished. It was a devastating satire. But it didn't diminish the general admiration for a fine uniform.

Another important document against the general smugness was brought forth by a young writer from Lübeck, himself a member of a bourgeois family: in 1901 there appeared a long novel called *Buddenbrooks*, by Thomas Mann. It delineated the decline of a great bourgeois family, paralleled by the rise of artistic sensitivity, artistic talent growing stronger as the family's commercial ability decayed. German readers read *Buddenbrooks* avidly—and then went back to trying to become as rich as the Buddenbrooks were.

This short (and oversimplified) sketch of conditions prevailing at about 1900 in the Wilhelmian era may be helpful in placing within a proper frame such productions as *Ein Heldenleben* and the *Sinfonia Domestica.* But before we arrive at these compositions, we must return to the chronicle of Strauss's life. He was now, in his middle thirties, to enter his most active period as an executant musician. He was now called to the capital.

In his memoirs, Strauss gives as his reason for departing from Munich the continued animosity which Perfall showed him. He recalled the Munich intendant always with bitterness and once went so far as to berate him as "a thoroughgoing villain." Strauss claimed that Munich had offered him a lifelong contract, that he was ready to accept such a contract, "but that at the last minute Perfall attempted to reduce the previously agreed-upon salary." Strauss at once departed for Berlin, where he was at once offered an engagement. The exactness of these recollections is questionable. Perfall was no longer acting in an official capacity, having retired as intendant five years previously. It is doubtful that he had the authority either to augment or reduce a salary or change a contract. The hidebound classicist liked Strauss's newest composition no better than his earlier ones. Still, Perfall was now seventy-four years old, and at such an age the fire of hatred, as the fire of love, does not burn quite so hot. It is certain that Perfall had previously approved Levi's choice of Strauss and that he had behind him years of experience with the "upstart." Would he now act precipitately?

It seems more reasonable to surmise that Strauss wanted to earn fresh laurels, that he wanted to conquer the capital, that he wanted to be at the hub of the Kaiser's sharp circle. Weingartner had relinquished his activities at the Berlin Opera, though he retained for some years the conductorship of the symphonic concerts of the Royal Orchestra. In November, 1898, Strauss became his successor, with the title of First Royal Prussian Court Conductor of the Royal Opera House of Berlin. Later (1901) he became music director of the Berlin Tonkünstler Orchestra in addition; this orchestra was devoted to the presentation of modern works by German and Austrian composers such as Bruckner, Mahler, Hans Pfitzner, Schillings, Hugo Wolf, Thuille, as well as a few foreigners, d'Indy, Charpentier, Paderewski, Smetana, Stanford, Elgar, and others. Eventually he had under his charge the musical direction of the Berlin Philharmonic as well. A wide sphere of activity indeed!

While he was considering the move from Munich, an offer came from New York. Anton Seidl, the conductor of the New York Philharmonic, had died in March of 1898, and the trustees of the orchestra proposed Strauss as his successor at the then fabulous salary of 40,000 marks. (In today's purchasing power, this would be equivalent to $50,000.) This was double what Berlin offered, but it was a short-term contract, and Strauss felt that the American position lacked security and that he preferred to stay in Germany to "strengthen his fame." He signed a ten-year contract with Berlin—the longest commitment he had yet made—with favorable terms: 18,000 marks for the first three years, 20,000 marks beginning the fourth year, two months' summer vacation, one month's winter vacation, a life pension of 4,200 marks after the expiration of the contract, and, in case of his death, a pension of 2,000 marks to his widow. These figures indicate Strauss's desirability as a musical attraction. In a letter to his mother he exulted: "What a pleasure, that at last I can thrown down the gauntlet to that gang in Munich who have treated me so miserably!"* We have by now become familiar with Strauss's way of justifying to himself what he wanted to do by denigrating others.

We find him, then, in the winter of 1898 ensconced with Pauline and their year-old baby Franz in Berlin, his apartment furnished by Pauline "with great care and excellent taste." Once again he threw himself into a conducting schedule that was unbelievably demanding, introducing himself to the Berlin public with a performance of *Tristan* on November 5, then conducting *Carmen* three days later, *Hänsel und Gretel* two days after that, *The Merry Wives of Windsor* the following day, *La Muette de Portici* the day after, and *Fidelio* two days after that.

As if all of this, plus composing, traveling, guest-conducting, were not enough, he now began, with the help of two friends,† the work of founding a society which had as its purpose the establishment of laws designed to insure better protection of the rights of the composer. It was at first called Genossenschaft Deutscher Tonsetzer (Fellowship of German Composers). It was to work for, first,

* Letter of April 14, 1898.

† One was Friedrich Rösch, whom Strauss had known since school days. He was an attorney who had become a composer. *Death and Transfiguration* is dedicated to him. The other was Hans Sommer, originally a physicist by profession, later a composer, chiefly of Lieder.

a sharpening and toughening of the German copyright act; second, an increase in authors' fees (royalties); third, an insistence on minimum fees for all concert and opera performances; and fourth, the establishment of a collecting and policing agency, which was to gather fees and royalties and to apportion them equitably to the members of the Fellowship. There was, said Strauss, need for such an organization, as composers were by and large poor businessmen and at any rate could neither negotiate all performance rights nor watch for unauthorized performances.

Strauss and his friends experienced no end of trouble putting this idea across. First he met with the opposition of his fellow composers, who were suspicious of one another and did not want to trust any association, even one of their own profession. (However, D'Albert, Humperdinck, Mahler, and Pfitzner were among those who supported the idea.) Second, there was the problem of where and how to raise the money necessary to run such an agency. (Strauss offered money to be considered as an advance against future royalties. Eventually the problem was solved by deducting a fixed percentage from royalties.) Third, and most important, certain politicians opposed the composers' demands and claimed that such unionization would militate against musical performances. One Eugen Richter, leader of the Liberal party, spoke against the plan in the Reichstag so eloquently that it was rejected. Strauss fumed: "He spoke against two hundred and fifty composers to get the votes of two hundred thousand restaurant keepers and members of singing societies. Everything is politics!"* Shortly after, he wrote: "You can't imagine what kind of Boeotians and duffers sit in our Parliament! Add to them those false and scurvy dogs, the vulgar arch-Jesuits of the Center, plus the chorus of hate of the Liberals and Freethinkers, the Sozi [Socialists]—"† But Strauss persevered.

It took almost seven years for the cause to be won. A practical way was found to keep track of and compensate for live performances, later of phonograph reproductions, and still later of radio transmissions. Out of the Fellowship grew the Anstalt für musikalisches Aufführungsrecht (AFMA), the Institute for Musical Per-

* Letter to his parents, May 6, 1901.
† Letter to his parents, May 21, 1901.

formance Rights, and out of that the powerful GEMA (Gesellschaft für musikalische Aufführungs und mechanische Vervielfältigungsrechte. Society for the Rights of Performance and Mechanical Reproduction.) It operates similarly to ASCAP (American Society of Composers, Authors and Publishers) in the United States. Though one may criticize certain monopolistic tendencies that have arisen in GEMA, one cannot doubt that its protective rules exert a beneficial effect, making it unlikely for another Schubert to starve to death.* Strauss's dedication to the cause may have been prompted by his wish to protect his ever-increasing income; nevertheless he was genuinely devoted to bettering the composer's condition and interested in the compositions of his contemporaries. His liberality in matters artistic was one of his attractive characteristics.

In the spring of 1899 he made an important new friend. Romain Rolland had called on him in Berlin, and the two men had sat and discussed music for an hour. They had instantly liked each other. Rolland was familiar with Strauss's work, partly through performances he had heard in his function as a roving correspondent for Parisian journals and partly through reading the published scores. Rolland, a year and a half younger than Strauss, was not yet a famous novelist; his chief work, the novel *Jean-Christophe,* was yet to be published (1904-1912). In *Jean-Christophe* he recreated at least the outward circumstances of this first meeting with Strauss: the young Jean calls on the composer Hassler for inspiration and guidance; Hassler's physical characteristics are identical with those of Strauss at that age.

Rolland, immersed in the world of music, literature, and the pictorial arts—he published several biographical and critical studies of composers and artists, including one on Michelangelo and one on Beethoven—was one of those free, pure, and rapturous spirits that we must and may admire more for their intentions than for their accomplishments. He was a dedicated man, dedicated to all beauty in whatever form and of whatever art, an idealist who believed that the freedom to admire beauty, the ability to respond to what great men had written or painted or composed, would lead

* Bartók's case was a tragic exception.

the world to brotherhood. He was very French, both in the sensitivity of his language, which was often so finely wrought and so rhapsodic that we sense his labor in forming his style, and in his occupation with the minute points of psychology. Though French to the core, he was drawn toward German thought, German "boldness," and particularly to German music. He felt that the salvation of Europe lay in a unity between and combination of all that was best in French and German culture. He worked toward that end almost to his dying day. Alas—he failed and he knew it! For a long period he hid away in a little room in Switzerland, his eyesight nearly lost, his dream of peace destroyed.*

Rolland was not a great writer, though *Jean-Christophe,* particularly the early volumes, inspired many of us when we were young. He lacked the follow-through, the staying power, the large view, which distinguish the great writer. He was almost too analytical to be creative. It was that ability to analyze, to appreciate, to wax enthusiastic, which drew more creative men toward him. Richard Strauss was well aware of these qualities. A friendship was formed between these two utterly dissimilar men which lasted for many years, which would cool occasionally but was never entirely broken. They met often when Strauss was in Paris, or Rolland in Germany, and their correspondence lasted intermittently from 1899 to 1926. There were years of silence, and years in which war interrupted their exchange. But then the two men took up the thread again, remaining on terms of mutual respect and liking, if not of close personal intimacy. Strauss did not desire, or was not capable of, intimacy with a friend.

Rolland, the more enthusiastic nature, overestimated Strauss's music, perhaps because he saw in it a means toward the *rapprochement* between French and German culture that he so ardently desired. His judgments, more those of a friend than of an objective critic, were often curious. He thought, at the beginning at least, the *Sinfonia Domestica* a masterpiece of Beethovenian proportions, he found *Schlagobers* delightful, but could not warm to *Ariadne* when he heard it in Vienna. He preferred *Ein Heldenleben* to *Don Quix-*

* He left Switzerland in 1938 and died in 1944 a month before his seventy-ninth birthday.

ote. The battle scene in the former was "the most admirable battle ever portrayed in music."* Though he was a strong advocate of Strauss's work, he was not blind to the weaknesses of Strauss's character and the limitations of his points of view. He wondered how Strauss, so intelligent, alive, and vital, could suddenly change into a man "possessed by the demon of indolence, of softness, of irony and indifference."† He saw clearly that Strauss was a German through and through, in spite of Strauss's claims (when convenient) to being an artist of no national adherence. Strauss, said Rolland, was held in thralldom by the melancholy of the north. In that he was like Nietzsche. He longed for the light of the south but perceived it merely through "the clouds and veils of German polyphony." He suffered from a touch of the German curse: imperialism—"like Nietzsche's Superman, the Wagnerian Siegfried, and Bismarck's politics."‡

Their most interesting correspondence occurred at the time that *Salome* was being planned for a production in Paris. Strauss asked Rolland's help in translating *Salome* into French. Rolland labored with selflessness to aid Strauss. To Rolland the proposed French translation was extremely faulty, provincial, non-French French, not worthy of the music. In vain did Rolland try to demonstrate to Strauss the difference between poetic, true French and the kitchen variety. Even Oscar Wilde, who was bilingual and had originally written *Salome* in French, was not, in Rolland's view, a true master of the language. It was too much to expect the foreigner, who after all was a musician and not a poet, to understand such subtleties. Rolland tried, nevertheless, and covered many pages with comments and hints for proper accents. He urged Strauss to study the score of *Pelléas* and Maeterlinck's language. Strauss could make very little either of Debussy's music, which he thought monotonous, or of the text. Finally, Strauss lost patience and asked why the French language sung differed from the spoken language; was that atavism or a dead tradition? Rolland roundly scolded him: "You are astonishing, you Germans. You understand nothing of our poetry, absolutely nothing, yet you judge it with imperturbable certi-

* Article in *La Revue de Paris,* June 15, 1899.
† Romain Rolland, *Correspondance; Fragments de Journal.*
‡ *Ibid.*

tude. Are you going to tell me we do the same in France? No. We do not judge your poets, because we don't know them. It is better not to know anything at all than to think one knows when one does not. . . . One has enough to do all one's life to make oneself master of one's mother tongue. If one really knew that profoundly, one would be a great man. The infinite nuances of a language such as French, which is the product of ten centuries of art and life, are the same nuances found in the soul of a great people. . . . You are too arrogant at this moment in Germany. You think you understand everything, so that you do not try to understand anything. So much the worse for you if you do not understand us! . . ."*

Strauss took it all. He replied in a conciliatory vein: "If you believe that I am too arrogant, you are not fair to me. Even if I am proud of our Richard Wagner (I know that this may appear ridiculous to the young French people), I do appreciate French culture sufficiently to want to understand it to the best of my ability and more than the average German. . . ."† And he continued to ask for linguistic advice.

Ein Heldenleben is the proudest of Strauss's compositions for the orchestra. His zest for life, his virile vitality, his being unafraid to sing a song of long breath, his erotic force, which is never turned aside by embarrassment, and finally, the ability to handle the huge orchestra, squeezing from it all the richness of its tonal resources, an ability so sure that he seems like a modern-day Cagliostro—all these are found in this, the last of the great tone poems. At the same time there are the faults already observed in *Zarathustra*. They become here enlarged partly because the subject is large and partly because he was infected by the spirit of the times, when the heroic was often synonymous with the pompous.

Ein Heldenleben seems to me to be truly a product of the Wilhelmian era, and it is so not only in title and program, which would not matter, but in musical content, which does matter. Aristophanes, in *The Frogs*, coined a word that has been translated as "bombastiloquent." It describes *Ein Heldenleben*.

Strauss worked on the composition during 1898, the year he

* Letter of July 16, 1905.
† Letter of July 16(?), 1905.

made extended concert tours, when he was acclaimed everywhere and when he accepted the Berlin offer. He spent the summer at the house of his father-in-law composing, and he finished the tone poem in Berlin. In reviewing the plan of the work, we find again the duality characteristic of Strauss. At first he speaks of *Ein Heldenleben* with self-deprecating humor. He writes to a friend that since Beethoven's "Eroica" was so little beloved of our conductors, he was composing a largish tone poem which was "to fulfill a pressing need . . . admittedly without a funeral march, but yet in E flat, with lots of horns, which are always a yardstick of heroism."* From being lightheartedly arch, he turned serious: it was to be a work depicting his struggles and reviewing his achievements. Why not autobiographical? He said to Romain Rolland that he did not see any reason why he should not write a work about himself; he found himself quite as interesting as Napoleon or Alexander the Great. Then he denied that the work was strictly autobiographical: it represented "not a single poetical or historical figure, but rather a more general and free ideal of great and manly heroism."† Why, then, the direct quotations from Strauss's own compositions in the score in the section "The Hero's Works of Peace"? Who but Strauss himself can this hero be?

I have called the work a product of the Wilhelmenian era. With its eight horns, five trumpets, and quadruple woodwinds, it seems to bear some relationship to those Berlin buildings, to those statues formerly to be found in the Siegesallee, supercolossal with the muscles showing.

The faults of the work lie in the sections "The Hero's Battlefield" and "The Hero's Adversaries." In the first, all that brass behind and on stage, all that battery of percussion, make up in noise what the music lacks in thought. It is cheap music, a Teutonic turmoil. Puzzling, too, is the theme for "The Hero's Adversaries." It is ugly, vulgar as well, and humorless; it is supposed to characterize the critics. Strauss, like every new composer, received his share of acid comments; there were some critics who disliked his music. But there were more who supported him; there were many who under-

---

* Letter written in 1898. Quoted in Norman Del Mar, *Richard Strauss: A Critical Commentary on His Life and Works*, Vol. I.

† Strauss's program notes.

stood him, and some who were enthusiastic. He had to suffer no such disdain as Wagner did in the early days. The reception of his compositions was kindness itself compared to the hostility shown to a Berlioz. He seems to have been so sensitive to censure that rancor bit into his soul; here he spewed out an ugly and venomous riposte, containing nothing of the humor that Wagner put into Beckmesser. In vain did old father Strauss write: "Those adversaries, in my opinion they transgress everything musical. Adversaries who behave so execrably—it is beneath one's dignity to notice them."*

The work's good parts are the beginning ("The Hero"), bold and stimulating as the beginning of *Don Juan,* the third section, "The Hero's Helpmate," and the final two sections. In "The Hero's Helpmate" we meet once again Strauss's favorite device of the solo violin playing a dialogue with the orchestra. Portraying the Hero's wife—as Strauss was to do subsequently in the *Sinfonia Domestica* and in *Intermezzo*—the solo violin displays many characteristics of mercurial femininity. The catalogue of feminine wiles goes on too long and the violin becomes discursive; but then the section melts into fine love music.

But it is the last two sections that in my opinion give the work its real quality. Here, in "The Hero's Works of Peace" and "The Hero's Release from the World," Strauss writes with unaffected inspiration. Peace and release are expressed in music that can assuage our own disquietude.

The first performance of *Ein Heldenleben* took place in Frankfurt on March 3, 1899, with the composer conducting from manuscript. It scored a good success. Some enraged listeners left the hall; most stayed to shout approval.

This was the last of the great tone poems. His next orchestral composition was entitled a symphony, though it is a sort of tone poem. Five years separate the *Sinfonia Domestica* from *Ein Heldenleben,* but it may be convenient to consider it here, partly because it too is autobiographical and partly because we can then turn our attention to Strauss as a composer of operas, which he was to

* Letter to Richard, June 1, 1900.

become for many years almost exclusively. We can dismiss the *Sinfonia* quickly enough; it has already been dismissed—or nearly so—from concert life.

No other orchestral work by Strauss has produced a sharper difference of opinion. Richard Specht, the German critic, thought it to be a "high point and that not only in the output of Strauss alone." "It is a work," he said, "with which he touches us as he does in no other of his tone poems. It is possible that in his other symphonic creations he was more brilliant, more seductive, more exciting, perhaps even more interesting; for this one we must love him. Here he expresses the best of his nature."* When he first heard the *Domestic Symphony*, Romain Rolland wrote to Strauss: "To tell the truth . . . I was a little shocked by your program, and it hindered me from judging the work itself. Then in the evening, at the concert, I really listened to it, forgetting the whole program; now I can tell you that it appears to me the most perfect work you have written since *Death and Transfiguration*, containing even greater richness of life and art." He then counsels him to have the work performed in Paris without a published program: "Leave music its mystery, leave the Sphinx his smile."‡ Strauss complied with Rolland's suggestions.

The derogatory judgments are equally strong. Somebody—I cannot now remember who but I think it was H. L. Mencken—called it "a cataclysm of domestic plumbing." Somebody else called it "one of the most embarrassing works in the history of music."‡ After a performance given by the Philadelphia Orchestra during the Strauss Centennial, one young critic wrote that it was a work of "abject emptiness," a work which "I cannot bring myself to discuss temperately."§

We must separate the music from the program. Once again we have Strauss laying down a definite program, then denying that it was definite, that it was supposed to describe his own domestic life, himself, his wife, his baby, and asserting that the symphony was meant to give a general musical picture of married life. The pro-

* Introduction to the published score, Edition Eulenburg.

† Letter of May 29, 1905.

‡ Wallace Brockway and Herbert Weinstock, *Men of Music: Their Lives, Times, and Achievements*.

§ Alan Rich in New York *Herald Tribune*, October 8, 1964.

gram is indeed embrarrassing, like a glimpse into a stranger's home on a Sunday morning before the breakfast dishes have been cleared away. The spirit of the tone poem is "*Kinder, Kirche, Küche,*" though—Strauss being Strauss—the *Kirche* is replaced by the bedroom.

If we can ignore the program, or manage not to be offended by its humdrum heartiness, we find that the music is not altogether worthless. "Not altogether" is the sad part of it. For the *Domestica* is a thing of shreds and patches, in which not even the themes hold together, but in which we find certain passages of the indomitable *élan* that Strauss could command and we find passages in which he summons the seductive sweetness that makes him the romantic composer he is. Needless to say, we find the old orchestral magic. The home is a noisy one, for Strauss thought it necessary to use five clarinets and bassoons and to add four saxophones to the already swollen orchestra. The most beautiful section of the work is the "Lullaby," followed by the "Adagio," an idyll of domestic bliss. But this must needs be cheapened by the outcry the baby raises, of which Hans Richter is supposed to have said that the gods in burning Valhalla did not make one quarter of the noise that one Bavarian baby made in his bath.

One wishes that the beauties of the work could be preserved. But one wishes more that Strauss had not written the work at all. A composer must be forgiven a weak production. But the *Domestic Symphony* is not an isolated weak production. It is a point on the graph that descends from the high mark of *Till Eulenpiegel* to the low mark of the *Alpensinfonie,* when years later he was once again to turn to a major symphonic attempt. This graph may be ascribed to two causes. The first lies in Strauss's characteristic of becoming disenchanted, not to say bored, with a form or a task he had mastered. His restlessness, which in his life expressed itself by his desire to go somewhere else, did not translate into the experimentation for which other restless artists strive. He was too easily tempted to substitute repetitive craftsmanship, even if it was high craftsmanship. (Perhaps another circumstance contributed to the patchiness of the *Sinfonia:* he was trying to finish it in time for his first American tour.) The second reason I have indicated in connection with *Ein Heldenleben.* Strauss was so much a child of his time, he was so worldly a composer, that not only the bombast of Germany seeped into him but also its comfortable smugness. During the battle section of *Ein Heldenleben,* the Hero wears a uniform. During the domestic caterwauling of the *Sinfonia,* Strauss wears a dressing gown, such as was worn by the German paterfamilias. He looks too well groomed, too self-satisfied.

Drawing the balance sheet so far, we find that Strauss had, by the time he was forty, given us nine tone poems. He had taken the inherited form and developed it with daring and liberality. The tone poems owe much to Wagner—their amorous expressiveness to *Tristan* particularly—but they are far from imitative works. They are fresh virtuoso pieces; to call them that is not to derogate them, for, as Paul Henry Lang wrote of them, "virtuosity carried to such a degree is art."*

Of the nine tone poems, four remain in the active repertoire of the orchestras of the world. They have become "classics." Will they remain so? I would guess that they will, for many years.

---

* *Music in Western Civilization.*

Feuersnot and First Trip to America

Though the failure of *Guntram* had made Strauss cautious, he did not for a moment lose his longing to compose operas. It could hardly have been otherwise, for he lived his life in the pit of the opera house, surrounded by *Figaros* and *Fidelios*, and experiencing over and over again the challenge and the hot satisfaction of an opera performance. In a sense his tone poems were operas without words, conceived dramatically, furnished with plot and story and engaged in character portrayal. After *Guntram* he considered several operatic projects, ranging from frivolous to serious. None of them seemed right. Of one fact he was sure, now that he no longer possessed the confidence of first youth: his literary gifts were not strong enough; he needed a collaborator.

He found him among the young men who had set out to mock the stuffiness of the Wilhelmian era. Along with Wilhelmian "worthy" poetry and plays, there appeared on the scene the products of a few "unworthy" men determined to make fun of *Kaiser, Kinder, Kirche, und Küche*. Hauptmann had shown them the way: in his comedy *The Beaver Coat* he had savagely satirized an arrogant and bullying little police official who never does find the thief of the fur coat. But Hauptmann was predominantly a serious dramatist and a poet; the others were predominantly casual comedians and at most poetasters, who threw darts at the *Gemütlichkeit*, the beery smugness, and—an easy target—the innumerable little laws which, to the satisfaction of most Germans, regulated almost every phase of life: laws that prohibited walking on the Berlin sidewalks more than three abreast or permitted the watering of window boxes only between the hours of four and five A.M.* These new talents were drawn especially to the Berlin theater. Berlin had become the center of Germany's theatrical life. Most of its twenty-five theaters offered classical fare. But one or two of them took a lesson from the French cabarets and presented variations of impudence on current themes. In the vanguard of the minor but merry talents stood Ernst von Wolzogen. He founded what he called *Das Bunte Theater*—The Motley Theater—and later a more important satiric theater, which he called *Das Überbrettl,* the Superplank.†

This turn toward frivolity was not of course confined to Germany, noticeable though it was in that stiff-legged country. What happened on the German literary scene happened as well in England, there as a protest against Victorianism, with the difference that while Germany produced but transient talents, in England two iconoclasts of genius came upon the scene: Oscar Wilde and Bernard Shaw.

Strauss met Wolzogen in Berlin. Did he have anything in the way of an opera to suggest, he asked. The author, anxious to connect himself with the composer, called Strauss's attention to an old Flemish tale.‡ It was the story of a capricious young girl who had drawn up her lover in a basket to her room, but had changed her mind when the basket was halfway up and had left him dangling there, a prey to the derision of the village. In revenge, the young man sought the help of a wise old magician, who extinguished all the fires in the village and announced that they could be lighted only by a flame that would spring from the posterior of a young girl. This folk tale was a bit too crass for staged representation, but it gave Wolzogen an idea. Let the story be set in Munich in an ancient time and let it serve as the opportunity to satirize the Philistines of Munich, who were of course Strauss's favorite *bêtes noires.* The lover was now to become a representative of the new art, the townspeople were to stand for the uncomprehending public, the

---

* *Life,* November 22, 1963.

† Bertolt Brecht was influenced by the *Überbrettl.*

‡ There is some doubt as to who suggested the subject to whom, several biographers stating that Strauss gave the idea to Wolzogen. The contrary is more probable.

girl the feminine element that inspires the artist, and the whole a hymn to art's power to give light and warmth.

Nothing would do but that the little story had to be stuffed with symbolic signficance. To add similarity to symbolism, Wolzogen now so shaped it that the resemblance to *Die Meistersinger* became obvious. Was that tribute or was it conceit? A little of both, no doubt.

The libretto Wolzogen finally submitted, which captivated Strauss, was called *Feuersnot*—Fire Famine. A strange young man has come to Munich. His name is Kunrad. He keeps very much to himself, and it is rumored that he is a magician. Some of the burghers think he is evil, but others are rather taken with him, for he is handsome and well-spoken. It is St. John's Eve, and the children and the townspeople are about to celebrate the traditional Munich summer festival. That consists of the lighting of bonfires, as high and merry as possible. (James Frazer gathered much information about these fire festivals in *The Golden Bough.*) The children are trotting from house to house, begging for all the available wood. The fire has a special meaning: any young couple who are in love and wish to become betrothed are to leap hand in hand through the fire and thus declare their troth. Kunrad, emerging from his house, observes the bustle of the town, listens to the impudent ditties sung by the children, and suddenly sees, among the young girls, the daughter of the mayor, blond Diemut. One glance suffices: he falls in love with her, forgets his reticence, asks her to leap through the fire with him, and without waiting for her answer approaches her and kisses her passionately. Diemut feels humiliated, or pretends to, in front of all the townspeople. She swears revenge. As night falls, Kunrad goes to Diemut's house, in spite of Diemut's warning that he will have to undergo punishment. Diemut lowers the basket from her balcony and bids him climb into it. Halfway up, Kunrad is left dangling. She refuses to pull the rope further. There he squats, while the whole town assembles to mock him. But now Kunrad addresses his tormentors. He tells them that always and forever those who ventured the new and the extraordinary were scorned, those who were brave enough to break the rules were harassed by the comfortable crowd, content to hide in the well-worn rut of life. (This whole chunk of "philosophy" is cribbed from *Die Meistersinger.*)

Appealing to his old Master, the Great Magician (obviously Richard Wagner), he calls for retribution. All fire, all light, is to vanish from the town. They are to be plunged into the darkness they deserve. His plea is heard. Suddenly the fire ceases, the lights go out, black silence envelops the town.

During this darkness, Kunrad manages to swing himself from the basket to the edge of the balcony. He climbs up and enters Diemut's room. She, needless to say, now welcomes the daring lover. The townspeople bemoan the evil that has befallen them, not knowing that Kunrad is with Diemut. At the right moment, and just as suddenly as the fires have been extinguished, the lights go on again, the fires burn as merrily as before, and Kunrad and Diemut appear on the balcony, united in love. Kunrad confesses that "All warmth springs from woman, all light is love."

Wolzogen's plot won't wash. He tries to weld a love story to a dissertation on art. The two elements of the poem do not go together, and Kunrad's sermon, which occupies the central part of the text, seems grafted on and fatuous. The text is couched in language that purports to be old German, as spoken by the "folk," but it is as forced as the artificially naïve usually is. A modern hand tries to write a medieval manuscript. Nor is the text particularly witty. It struts with elaborate puns. Kunrad refers to his redoubtable *Meister* whose "daring seemed to all of you too great and therefore you banished him, the Darer." (In German, "to dare" is "*wagen,*" and "the Darer" is *Wagner.** At least, it is so used by Wolzogen.) "But," Kunrad adds, "you will not rid yourself of the enemy—he returns ready for the fray." ("Fray" is *Strauss* in German). The poet then goes on to pun on his own name. Similarly, Strauss introduced Wagnerian quotations into the score, using among others the Valhalla motive to denote the old magician.

What, then, appealed to Strauss about the libretto? First, its eroticism; second, the revenge on Munich; and third (as I indicated), its second-cousin kinship to Wagner's comedy. Kunrad is an imitation of Hans Sachs, or rather a combination of Hans Sachs and Walther von Stolzing. The prominent burghers of Munich are the Meistersinger; the rest of the chorus, including the children, are

* Wagner himself punned on his own name. He called himself "the Waggoner."

the Munich equivalent of Nüremberg's population, and Diemut is Eva, a lot less moral but quite as blond.

The strange part about the whole affair is this: out of the self-conscious libretto Strauss fashioned a little opera which, though not a masterpiece, is full of warmth and sweetness and contains some very beautiful music. His second attempt at an opera is miles ahead of his first. It seems a youthful work, possessing the virtue of youth, though it is not immature. Strauss was thirty-seven when he finished *Feuersnot.* He finished it on Wagner's birthday, and the last page of the score is inscribed: "Completed on the birthday of and to the greater glory of the 'Almighty'! [meaning Wagner] Charlottenburg, May 22, 1901."

The best portions of the opera are those that deal with Kunrad's love: when Kunrad first sees Diemut, one feels Strauss warming to the task and becoming involved. The love scene itself bears the stamp of inspired Strauss. (That is why the love scene still appears occasionally on concert programs.) But there are other parts of the short work that are attractive. The children's choruses are light-hearted, as are the comments of the townspeople—for which Strauss occasionally uses old Bavarian folk melodies—and charming is the evocation of Midsummer Eve.

There are weak parts, such as Kunrad's speech and the ensemble that ensues after darkness sets in. Yet all together *Feuersnot* serves as a kind of study for *Der Rosenkavalier* many years before Strauss thought of a *Rosenkavalier.* He returned to its lightness after he had got the two tragic one-acters, *Salome* and *Elektra,* out of his system.*

When he had finished *Feuersnot,* the question arose as to where Strauss wanted first to present it. Early he decided against the première in Berlin. Not only did he not want to risk failure on what was now his home ground, but he knew that the bawdy subject and some of Wolzogen's daring verses might well offend official court prudery. Strauss was now a famous man and he could choose the opera house to which he wished to accord the privilege of the première. Two opera houses particularly vied for this privilege: Vienna under Mahler and Dresden under Ernst von Schuch.

* Thomas Beecham, who gave the opera in London in an English translation, was fond of the work. He called it "gay and audacious."

Strauss may have felt a certain history-minded attraction toward Dresden, because it was in Dresden that the Old Magician's early operas, *Rienzi* and *Der Fliegende Holländer*, were first performed. More important, Strauss knew Schuch personally, and valued him as a superb musician and as a man of progressive taste. Schuch was an Austrian, seventeen years older than Strauss, who had been working at the Dresden Court Opera since 1872 and had brought it to a fine level. Strauss valued Mahler as well. But both Strauss and Mahler feared the Austrian censorship, and Strauss indignantly objected to any bowdlerizing of Wolzogen's text. Altogether, the conditions seemed more propitious in Dresden than in Vienna.

But though Strauss made up his mind that it was to be Dresden, this did not prevent him from driving a sharp bargain. When Schuch offered a fee lower than the 1,500 marks Strauss wanted, Strauss threatened that he was going to give the opera to Vienna and berated Schuch with half-humorous, half-serious reproaches. He said he was going to change his name to Riccardo Straussino and have his works published by Sonzogno (the Italian publishing house of *Pagliacci* and *Cavalleria*) and then he could have anything he wanted from the German stages.

In the end, the whole matter was arranged satisfactorily: Schuch got the first performance and Strauss his fee. The première took place on November 21, 1901. It was a joyous success. The two authors were given an ovation, and Wolzogen appeared before the curtain sporting an aster the size of a tea saucer in his buttonhole. Immediately other German cities vied for the work, and in short order *Feuersnot* was given in Frankfurt (where it had an even more enthusiastic reception), in Vienna, in Berlin, and in Bremen. It took a little longer for the opera to arrive at Munich, the city it satirized. There it was heard in 1905, three years after the Berlin performance. In Berlin, however, it appeared that the Kaiserin disliked the work. After seven performances, and even though Strauss was now willing to soften the text somewhat, the work was forbidden by official edict. Wolzogen wrote to Strauss that Her Majesty did not wish to learn anything about the facts of life, after having given birth to a litter of seven children. The intendant of the Berlin Opera, Count Hans Heinrich Hochberg, himself a composer of operas, proved himself to be a man of courage and integrity. He immediately handed in his resignation, and he told Strauss that he would fight like a lion for the right of free presentation of the work. His protest was effective and the prohibition was countermanded. Strauss rather enjoyed the whole fracas, though by that time he had turned his attention to *Salome.*

The preparation and excitement attending the opening of *Feuersnot,* as well as the continuous string of concerts he was leading—a string that extended from the south of France to a full-fledged Strauss Festival in London (the first of several, June, 1903)—once again unbalanced Strauss's health. A man of lesser will might have become exhausted by the mere physical strain of traveling, long rehearsals, standing and waving his arms about, but Strauss needed but a slight pause in the gallop. So that he might recuperate, he spent two peaceful months on the Isle of Wight—he was at that time drawn toward England and the British—and by luck he found the weather splendid on an island where a cloudless sky is considered a curiosity. While he was on the Isle, he learned that he was to receive a doctor's degree from the University of Heidelberg, an honor which pleased him so greatly that he dedicated a new work to that famous institution of learning and dueling. This new work was *Taillefer,* a cantata to the words of the German poet Uhland. It is a gross composition, employing not only an army of a male chorus but a mass meeting of an orchestra. It has passed into deserved oblivion.

Knowing that he was going to make his first American tour shortly, he put the finishing touches on the *Sinfonia Domestica,* the work he wished to bring forward on that occasion. But he couldn't possibly just be content with the anticipation of this major journey and conducting a few operas in Berlin in the meantime. No, in December we find him running to London again and from there all the way to Poland, stopping off home to conduct, "in all haste, *Samson, Die Meistersinger,* and *Fidelio.*"

He was satisfying for his own particular needs the general desire for locomotion that gripped the people of the first decade of the twentieth century. People were travel-mad. Men and women were journeying hither and yon with new zest; new means of motion made news. In 1903 a Packard automobile completed in fifty-two days a journey from San Francisco to New York; it was the first time an automobile had crossed the continent under its own power. Later that year the Wright brothers made their first successful airplane flight at Kitty Hawk, North Carolina, though the flight lasted only twelve seconds. New ships were plying the Atlantic, and soon so many giant "express steamers" were available that the steamship companies found themselves caught in a competitive price war, which reduced the price of steerage passage to ten dollars.

America was still the land where money was handed to the famous on a silver platter. It had become more selective in the choice of celebrities and consequently the accolade of an American success had become more desirable. The idea of bringing Strauss over was Hermann Hans Wetzler's, a German musician who had been living in New York for some time, first officiating as an organist in Trinity Church and later establishing an orchestra of his own to present the "Wetzler Concerts." This venture was not very successful and lasted only a couple of seasons. Wetzler felt that the fame of Strauss, now generally regarded as the foremost living composer, would help his orchestra.

Quite unconcerned with the terrors of an Atlantic crossing in midwinter, Strauss and Pauline boarded the luxury steamer *Moltke* in Hamburg in February, 1904. He proved to be a hardier sailor than Pauline. And he was lucky enough to get a sharp skat game going, which whiled away the long hours. They arrived in New York after a very slow journey, the wind being against them all the way. There the usual reception—flowers, shipboard reporters, messages from city officials, a delegation from the orchestra—awaited him.* Three days after his arrival he made his debut as conductor in Carnegie Hall (February 27, 1904). Wetzler conducted *Zarathustra,* the excellent baritone David Bisham sang three of his songs, and he himself conducted *Ein Heldenleben.* At the second concert (March 4, 1904) he presented *Don Quixote,* the cello part being played by a young cellist named Pablo Casals.

What was he like as a conductor now, when he was forty years

* He gave an interview, which was published in the New York *Daily Tribune* on February 24, 1904. In part it said: "He had no compliments ready for either America or the Americans, and one of his first remarks, through his press agent, was that the religious side of *Parsifal* had been profaned by its production in this city. . . ."

old? Richard Aldrich, reviewing the concert in *The New York Times*, wrote:

> He is a young man of unpretentious appearance, slim, loose-jointed as he threads his way among the orchestra to the front of the platform, singularly lacking, indeed, in distinction of presence. His face, smooth except for an almost imperceptible mustache and surmounted by a remarkably high forehead, is grave and impassive; and notwithstanding the bald spot in evidence as he turns toward the orchestra, he looks his youth. His methods as a conductor are extremely reserved. His beat is quiet, but firm; he has few significant gestures, except at some of the most important climaxes when he summons the power of the brass instruments through an insistent beckoning with his left hand, of which otherwise he makes but small use. He seemed little concerned last evening over the vast complications of his score or over controlling the entrances and the nuances of the players, but directed with an almost matter-of-fact tranquillity and confidence. He evidently carries the substance of his music and all its manifold details easily in his head, for he made only casual references to the printed pages before him. In fact, a conductor who exhibits so little of the spectacular and so much of concentration in his work has not lately been seen here.*

This was the beginning of an extended tour, during which he not only conducted but also gave a series of recitals with Pauline. They went as far west as Minneapolis.

It cannot be said that Strauss's recorded impressions of America show any particular freshness of observation. He found America "magnificent yet a bit savage," its industry "grandiose," its "practical conveniences splendid," some of the "twenty-story-high giant houses even aesthetically pleasing," and New York "miserably paved."†

"The Americans certainly know how to honor one and are incredibly hospitable and charming," he wrote home. In Morgantown in Pennsylvania, where there was a German colony, he was handed the key of the city. In Cleveland he was given a silver cup.

---

* *The New York Times,* February 28, 1904.

† Letter to his parents from New York, March 2, 1904.

The Lotos Club and the Liederkranz Club in New York each tendered him a dinner. Receptions and parties followed one another, and, far from being fatigued, he seems to have swallowed the whole proceedings with pleasure. What the public, particularly outside of New York, seemed to like best were the song recitals with Strauss at the piano and Pauline singing and exuding charm. She was still very pretty and made the most of her beauty by artful costumes. She reported home that "A New York paper wrote that Mr. Strauss ought to write a symphony about the fabulous outfits of his wife."* The reviews of her concerts were generally good, except for those written by two critics in New York who—said Pauline with all the objectivity of an injured prima donna—"had been bribed by Melba and Sembrich."

In the last of the New York Carnegie Hall concerts (barring a special farewell concert on April 27, which was added later), the world première of the *Sinfonia Domestica* took place (March 21). Strauss had prepared the symphony most carefully in fifteen rehearsals. It was received politely and respectfully. It was not, as Strauss claimed, "a colossally enthusiastic success."† The reviews of the symphony make dull reading: nobody damned it, nobody really liked it.

Strauss conducted the New York Philharmonic in guest appearances, as well as the Chicago and the Philadelphia orchestras. His greatest artistic pleasure he derived from conducting the Boston Symphony. He had originally asked to be allowed to give a concert with the Boston but had been refused—one suspects because Wilhelm Gericke, the music director of the orchestra, was a bit jealous of Strauss the conductor. Henry Lee Higginson, the founder and patron of the orchestra, then invited Strauss after he had scored a pronounced success with the Philadelphia. At the last moment the project nearly foundered, because Higginson did not wish to pay the fee Strauss asked. Then the orchestra itself invited him to conduct the Pension Fund concert, and accordingly, on April 19, he conducted Beethoven's Eighth Symphony, the Prelude to *Tristan*, his *Don Juan*, *Don Quixote*, and the Suite from *Feuersnot*—a most ample program! He called the Boston "the most marvelous orches-

* Letter to Strauss's parents, March 13, 1904.
† Letter to his parents from Providence, R. I., March 22, 1904.

tra of the world. . . . Wonderful, both in sound and technique, of a perfection such as I have almost never experienced. The orchestra was filled with enthusiasm, because year in, year out, they have to play under a horrible shoemaker and yesterday they breathed freely."*

Wanamaker's, then one of New York's leading department stores, offered him the extraordinarily high fee of a thousand dollars to play two afternoon concerts in the auditorium of the store. Strauss consented and was promptly roasted by the German press for prostituting music by "appearing in a commercial establishment." Strauss replied: "True art ennobles any hall, and to earn money for wife and child is no disgrace to an artist."†

The Strausses' penultimate appearance was in Washington (April 26), where President Theodore Roosevelt and his wife received them. Roosevelt was an admirer of the Kaiser and sympathetic to all that was German. One may guess that the President was being polite to Strauss without particularly caring for his music.

After the farewell concert in New York, Strauss was once again besieged by journalists. He had complained right along that they had ascribed to him opinions he had never uttered and statements he had never made. It is true that the interview of a celebrity was at that time even less hampered by regard for truth than it is today. There was no dearth of cheap jokes about the cacophony of Strauss's music, one journalist calling the tone poem "Hell of a Leben." *The Musical Courier* published the following, probably apocryphal, interview:

SCENE—*Artist room at Carnegie Hall*

PERSONAGES:	RICHARD STRAUSS AND THE REPORTER
REPORTER:	Is that Trilby story true which came from Philadelphia last week?
STRAUSS:	No.
REPORTER:	Then Madame Strauss was not hypnotized by you into resuming her singing after she had fainted?
STRAUSS:	No.
R.:	But she did feel faint?
S.:	Yes.

* Letter to his father from Boston, April 20, 1904.

† Article in the newspaper A.M.Z., Berlin, April 20, 1904.

R.: What from?

S.: Hunger.

R.: You certainly spoke sharply to Madame Strauss on the stage.

S.: Yes.

R.: What did you say?

S.: "Wiener Schnitzel with spaghetti after the concert." That's her favorite dish.

9

Salome

Both the triumph and the degradation had passed for Oscar Wilde. The triumph had been spectacular. His comedies were performed to admiring and fashionable audiences; such aphorisms as "In married life three is company and two none" or "One should never trust a woman who tells one her real age"* were passed in clipped accents from lips to lips; his "creed of beauty" and jocund philosophy were discussed in shaded drawing rooms; and many a dandy in gray topper and gray gloves aspired to become another Dorian Gray. Wilde's popularity had been followed by the catastrophe in court, heaping on him such contumely, so thick a coating of filth and shame, as few public figures have had to bear. Now, only a few years after Wilde, abandoned and besotted, had died in Paris, the impudence of his work had lost immediacy and the justice of the judgment against him had come to be recognized as doubtful. The scandal no longer mattered. The man, preacher and pederast, was slipping into history. The work remained: Wilde was on the way toward becoming a classic.

It is extraordinary how quickly this came to pass. Only about ten years had elapsed since *Lady Windermere's Fan* had first been given in London; in those ten years that play, as well as *A Woman of No Importance, An Ideal Husband,* and *The Importance of Being Earnest* had become staples of repertory theater not only

* The first from *The Importance of Being Earnest,* the second from *A Woman of No Importance.*

in England but in many other countries and in Germany particularly. Even in the small German theaters audiences applauded *Ein Idealer Gatte* and *Lady Windermere's Fächer*. Wilde's plays have never lost their hold on German audiences and, except for *The Importance of Being Earnest,* which is a regular ingredient of London's repertoire, they are today more frequently given in Germany than in England.

What was in some ways his most daring work for the stage, *Salome,* had not been put before British audiences by the time Wilde died, and was not for many years thereafter. But it could be seen in Germany. There it was staged in 1902 in Breslau, of all places, and again in Berlin in 1903, by a young actor who had turned producer. Max Reinhardt had begun his long career as one of the most creative men of the theater by staging the work with a young and flaming actress, Gertrud Eysoldt, in the title role. She was to be associated with Reinhardt for many years to come and to excel in the plays of Ibsen, Maeterlinck, and Shaw.

How was it that Wilde swerved from his drawing-room comedies to pen an orgiastic rhapsody on a Biblical theme and that he did so not in his quicksilver English but in a perfumed French?* The impulse had come when he was staying in Paris, had read and been much impressed by Flaubert's treatment of the story in *Herodias,* and had seen a painting by Gustave Moreau. This surcharged picture, out-romanticizing the romanticism of Delacroix, whose disciple Moreau was, shows an almost nude woman, her jeweled cloak thrown back to expose her body, pointing ecstatically to the head of Jochanaan; the head appears to her as a vision surrounded by a nimbus dripping blood. Wilde was inspired to retell the story of the Judaean princess in a new way, the story which innumerable artists through the centuries had written or painted, because he saw himself as a poet of the forbidden, an Irish Baudelaire. He changed the story. In Flaubert Salome is merely the instrument of her mother's revenge, untouched by lust for Jochanaan. Wilde conceived her as driven by erotic desire, only half conscious of that desire yet paralyzed by it, a virgin consumed by "evil chastity." To Wilde nothing could be as sinful as innocence.

* Wilde was bilingual, though his written French was not that of a native.

Before writing the play, Wilde, as was his custom, told his ideas to a group of his Parisian friends, several young writers among them. As he talked and they listened, the play took shape in his mind. Afterward, back in his hotel room, he began to write. He wrote for hours and hours, heedless of the approaching dark, without stopping to touch food. It was midnight before he realized that he was feeling faint from hunger. He went across the street to a café, where there was a gypsy orchestra playing. He gave his order and then called over the leader of the orchestra. "I am writing a play," he told him, "about a woman dancing with bare feet in the blood of a man. . . . Play me something in harmony with my thoughts."* The gypsy band played. Wilde listened, returned to his hotel, and wrote on until he had finished the play the ensuing morning.

What he produced was no masterpiece and would today be an unused play were it not for Strauss's music. For all their lusciousness, his metaphors are too obviously calculated; for all the blazing colors of his language, what he has to say does not convince us as being high tragedy. The work is overladen and overripe, like a basket of tropical fruits that has been left standing. After the pomegranates and dates and mangoes one misses a plain apple. On the other hand, Wilde's imagination is as bold here as it was in *The Picture of Dorian Gray;* his nervous drive chases his characters to destruction under a sickly moon; Herod, Herodias, and Salome are fascinating because they are repulsive, and lives and deaths are played out so quickly that the repulsiveness does not turn into weariness. In short, the play has power, morbid and malodorous though it may be.

Though it was written in a transport, it is certain that Wilde, who was a practical man in matters theatrical, had a purpose in mind: that purpose was to write a drama for Sarah Bernhardt, one in which the Divine Sarah could show herself to British audiences. He read the play to Bernhardt, who at once accepted it with enthusiasm. Very soon after, it went into rehearsal. It was to open at the Palace Theater in London. The scenery was designed, the costumes executed, when suddenly the Lord Chamberlain refused a license

---

* Frances Winwar, *Oscar Wilde and the Yellow Nineties.*

for its production on the grounds (invoked before and since on the British stage) that Biblical characters could not be shown in a spoken play.

Wilde was beside himself. How dared the Lord Chamberlain oppose him, the "apostle of beauty" and favorite of British society? He threatened to renounce his British citizenship, to leave England forever and to settle in France. But he did no such thing. It was then decided that *Salome* was to be produced in Paris at Bernhardt's own theater, the Porte St. Martin. But now Bernhardt grew cautious, fearing that even in Paris public opinion might be against her appearing in so scandalous a role. She never did get around to acting Salome,* though the play was eventually produced in Paris (1896). The ban on its performance in England was not removed until 1931.

Strauss had first read the play in an adaptation by the Viennese writer, Anton Lindner. He was immediately interested, but the adaptation did not suit him, and he decided to go back to the original text by Wilde as translated into German by Hedwig Lachmann. It was this translation that Reinhardt used. Strauss went to see the play. The very first line— "How beautiful is the Princess Salome tonight!"—struck him at once as being apt for music. When a friend suggested that *Salome* might make a good operatic subject, he could truthfully answer that he was already at work on it.

He did not seriously plunge himself into the composition until after his return from America; he worked on it for the better part of two years. We must imagine him sitting at his desk and methodically setting such dithyrambic lines to music as "Thy mouth is like a band of scarlet on a tower of ivory." When he had an evening free from his conducting chores, he would stay with *Salome* until one in the morning, to arise the next day and, without hesitation, continue where he had left off. No outward transport, no wringing of hands, accompanied the composition of this frenzied work. He merely reported to his parents that he was "grinding away at it." What a phrase to use about such music! Seldom, I think, has so turbulent a creation been brought forth by so calm a creator. The manuscript is

* There is some confusion about this point, some sources stating that Bernhardt did appear in the play. To the best of my knowledge she did not.

set down in a neat handwriting, suitable for a Haydn minuet. He finished the score on June 20, 1905.

Strauss was from the first conscious of the controversial quality of the play. How could he not have been? Perhaps it was this very quality that attracted him to the subject, along with the fact that Reinhardt had turned *Salome* into a remarkable success; it ran for nearly two hundred performances. As an employe of the court, a functionary who operated right under the Kaiser's eye, Strauss worried about His Majesty's All Highest attitude.* He sounded out the Kaiser about the matter at a propitious moment: it was during an intermission of a performance of *Der Freischütz,* which Strauss was conducting. After the second act, the Kaiser summoned Strauss and complimented him on the excellence of the performance. Strauss replied that all he had done was to cleanse the score of its usual dust and false traditions. The Kaiser fancied himself a connoisseur of the arts, his criteria being the very heroic, the very sentimental, and anything favoring Germany. He had commissioned Leoncavallo to compose an opera on a German theme, and this, *Der Roland von Berlin,* had been given that very year, much to the satisfaction of the Kaiser and to the complete indifference of the public. Now, conversing with Strauss, the Kaiser suggested that a play by Hebbel, *Herodes und Mariamne,* might make a suitable text. Strauss replied that he was at work on a Biblical subject, that of Salome. The Kaiser could not very well raise any objection, having himself suggested a Biblical text. Strauss immediately communicated the result of the interview to Hülsen, the intendant of the opera house, who said, "There you are! Perhaps the Kaiser isn't so bad after all."†

Operatic history demonstrates that certain composers could write inspired music to uninspired librettos. One could instance such diverse examples as *Die Zauberflöte* and *Il Trovatore.* Strauss was not one of these, as his subsequent works prove. His sense of the stage searched for, and in his successful operas found, the dramatically

---

* "All Highest" was the form of address Wilhelm liked. A story circulated in Berlin said that the Kaiser's visit to church was reported as "The All Highest had an interview with The Highest this morning."

† Letter to his father, November 4, 1904.

right text. He recognized the possibility of *Salome*, though it is axiomatic that elaborate diction, language that occasionally out-Herods Herod, does not as a rule make for a good libretto. He perceived that the play ascended swiftly to four climaxes, each of which furnished material for music. The first is Salome's conceiving the sudden passion for the body of Jochanaan and her voicing of that passion. The second is Jochanaan's spurning of Salome. The third is Salome's plan for revenge, which includes the extracting of the solemn promise from Herod, and her dance. The fourth, the highest and most exacerbating, climax is the final scene, Salome's apostrophe and her death.

It is easy to see after the fact that the play "cried out for music," as Strauss himself observed. He did see it before the fact, and proceeded to prune the play of enough "literature" (Strauss's word) to make it a serviceable text. Eliminated were some of the theological disputes, the little lament that the Page utters over the body of Narraboth, and a few other passages. All that was essential to Salome herself was retained.

To put the matter in other words, Strauss found in *Salome* the elements necessary to him: a decadent eroticism, a strange ambience, a hectic conflict, and a main character—female—who, poisoned and poisonous, gave him the opportunity to deal with death and blasphemous transfiguration. It had to be a woman. It is a characteristic of Strauss's operas that the female characters spring to life, the men being comparatively pallid. One need only compare Salome to Jokanaan, Elektra to Orestes, Arabella to Mandryka, Zerbinetta to Harlequin, or Ariadne to Bacchus. He even fashioned female parts out of what might have been male roles: Octavian and the Composer.

Strauss played the nearly completed score to two men whose opinions he valued. He played it first for his father, whose reaction was the familiar caution. "Oh God," the old man said, "what nervous music! It sounds as if a swarm of ants were crawling in the seat of your trousers." Franz Strauss did not live to witness the triumph of the opera, for he died on May 31, 1905, at the age of eighty-three, to the last both admiring his son's genius and fearing for his future.

Gustav Mahler was the other. According to Alma Mahler, Gustav's wife, Strauss played and sang the entire opera with fine expression. (Romain Rolland, far from paying tribute to Strauss's ability as a player and singer of his own operas, said that he played and sang "very badly.") When he arrived at the place where Salome dances, Strauss said in a broad Bavarian accent, "That I haven't managed yet." Mahler wanted to know whether it was not dangerous to omit the dance in this fashion and to attempt to recapture the mood later on. Strauss answered with a smile, "Don't worry!" Mahler was overwhelmed by the work. That, at least, is how Alma told the story in her reminiscences.* She is not an altogether trustworthy witness, some of her stories being obvious exaggerations.

A month before he completed the score, he was ready to open negotiations with his friend Schuch. After *Feuersnot*, it was natural that Dresden should get the first opportunity. Schuch accepted with alacrity, though Strauss pointed out that *Salome* was about twice as difficult as *Feuersnot*. As Salome the two men chose a singer of prominence, and curiously enough one of ample girth, whom they had heard in Wagnerian roles. This was Marie Wittich, a Bayreuth Isolde. Strauss recalled the first rehearsal:

> At the first piano run-through the singers assembled in order to hand back their parts to the conductor—all except the Czech singer Burian, who, when asked last of all, answered, "I already know the role by heart." Bravo! At this the others felt rather ashamed and the work of the rehearsal actually started. During the acting rehearsals the dramatic soprano Frau Wittich went on strike. She had been entrusted with the part of the sixteen-year-old princess with the voice of an Isolde on account of the strenuousness of the part and the thickness of the orchestration—"one just doesn't write like that, Herr Strauss; either one thing or the other." In righteous wrath she protested, like any Saxon burgomaster's wife, "I won't do it, I'm a decent woman. . . ."†

The decent woman soon decided that the indecent role was too tempting to pass up. But two months before the date for the première, further troubles arose. Strauss learned that Frau Wittich had not as yet seriously studied the role. How could she master so difficult a part by the end of November? What is more, she had

* Alma Maria Mahler, *Gustav Mahler: Memories and Letters.*

† Willi Schuh (Ed.), *Richard Strauss: Betrachtungen und Erinnerungen.*

become fatter than ever during the summer. This worried Strauss less: "It doesn't matter," he wrote to Schuch. "Voice, Horatio, voice, and once again voice." But when the devil was she going to learn the role? By the end of October Strauss was still dissatisfied with the progress; he now threatened to withdraw the opera from Dresden. He told Schuch that Nikisch was already hard at work on the study of *Salome* in Leipzig and that Mahler had finally pushed the work past the censorship. (This turned out to be wishful thinking. Mahler had accomplished nothing.) Strauss gave Schuch a deadline: December 9—if not by then, he would give the work to whichever opera house could first get it ready.

We do not know how the suffering Schuch managed it, but he came through. The première of *Salome* took place precisely on the day of Strauss's deadline, December 9, 1905. Wittich, corpulent or not, sang the part of the sixteen-year-old princess forcefully, though she could not dance it, and as in many subsequent performances a dancer was substituted in the Dance of the Seven Veils; Karl Burian was a magnificent Herod, and Carl Perron was Jokanaan. (Later he created the role of Baron Ochs.)

Enormous was the excitement that pervaded all musical Germany and indeed all of Europe. Musical pundits, colleagues, people of the theater, and the socially prominent had come from far and wide to be present, and the audience, many of whom were of course familiar with Wilde's play, was in a high state of expectancy, an expectancy in which were mingled curiosity about hearing new music by the eminent composer and the fear—or the hope—that something shocking and scandalous was to be experienced. There was no scandal. The audience was swept away by the force of the music. They listened in absolute silence, broken only by a few whispers as the ballerina shed her veils and again as the severed head was handed from the cistern. For the final scene Schuch and his orchestra as well as Frau Wittich summoned every ounce of strength they possessed. The sound inundated the house and drew even the skeptical into its vortex. At the end of the performance the house went mad and vented its excitement in an ovation during which people stood on the seats, shouted, waved their hats, threw programs—and called the artists and composer before the curtain thirty-eight times.

Almost immediately the success leaped through Europe. Within two years *Salome* had been given in more than fifty opera houses, and not once or twice but frequently in each. By the end of 1907 Berlin could mark the fiftieth performance of the opera! The Kaiser disliked it. He sanctioned the production only after Hülsen, who obviously was nobody's fool, had thought up the idea of showing at the end of the opera the Star of Bethlehem shining on the backdrop. It signified the religious promise of the coming of the three Magi. *Salome* with a happy end? Wilhelm was supposed to have said that he liked Strauss but he was certain to do himself much damage with this opera. Strauss's comment: "From this 'damage' I was able to build my villa in Garmisch."

For the Berlin production Strauss attempted to obtain the services of the handsome young Geraldine Farrar. She declined regretfully, since she thought that her voice was not dramatic enough to encompass the role. She says in her reminiscences that Strauss offered to make changes suitable to her voice, and added, "You, Farrar, have such dramatic possibilities, can act and dance half naked, so no one will care if you sing or not."* If he did say that, then Strauss changed from his original intention: now he wanted not voice, as from "Auntie Wittich," but a figure. It is possible; Strauss knew how to cut his cloth.

In Italy the first performance was scheduled for Turin, and for this occasion the opera house had invited Strauss himself to conduct. Toscanini was rehearsing the new work for La Scala, and Gatti-Casazza, manager of La Scala, stole a march on Turin by making the dress rehearsal, scheduled for the day before the Turin performance, into a full-fledged performance. He was able to do so, since Toscanini had the opera ready. "With *Salome* he [Toscanini] achieved something rare even for him. He prepared the singers and the orchestra so painstakingly in their separate rehearsals and they responded so effectively to his instructions that when he brought all the elements together for their first joint rehearsal, he went through the entire opera without pause. Asked how it happened that he had not stopped, he said, 'There were no errors.' When Richard Strauss visited Milan to hear the production, Gatti-Casazza told him of

---

* *Such Sweet Compulsion.*

Toscanini's feat, and the composer, who knew how difficult this score was, would not believe it."*

The Paris première took place in May, 1907, again under Strauss's direction. The opera was given six times, and Strauss, who cared about such things, was pleased to receive the Légion d'Honneur. Artur Rubinstein, then beginning his career, met Strauss in Paris. He remembers him as being alternately "sleepy and lighthearted." When somebody called *Salome* unique, Strauss replied, "I can fabricate another one in no time at all."

London had to wait until 1910. After the great success of *Elektra,* Sir Thomas Beecham determined to give the earlier work. He was stymied, as Wilde had been, by the Lord Chamberlain. Beecham tells the story with great gusto in his autobiography.† To the arguments he advanced that Strauss was the most famous "and in common opinion the greatest of living composers," and that this work deserved to be heard, and that at any rate being given in German it would be comprehended by few, the Lord Chamberlain replied that he agreed, if Beecham would consent to certain modifications of the text. What were they?

> The first thing we did was to eliminate the name of John, who was to be called simply The Prophet; and having invested him with this desirable anonymity, we went on to deprive every passage between him and Salome of the slightest force or meaning. The mundane and commonplace passion of the precocious princess was refined into a desire on her part for spiritual guidance, and the celebrated line at the end of the drama, "If you had looked upon me you would have loved me," was transformed into "If you had looked upon me you would have blessed me." It is only fair to say that my collaborators in this joyous piece of nonsense were, in spite of their outward gravity, as exhilarated as myself; for we all of us alike felt that we were making a solemn sacrifice on the altar of an unknown but truly national god.

Furthermore, the severed head was to be eliminated and Salome was to be given a bloodstained sword. At this, the prima donna,

* Howard Taubman, *The Maestro: The Life of Arturo Toscanini.*
† *A Mingled Chime.*

Aïno Ackté,* a beautiful Finnish woman, protested, "objecting that the gruesome weapon would ruin her beautiful gown." They arrived at the compromise that Salome should have a large platter with a cover, "but that under no circumstances could any object, even the minutest, be placed beneath it, that might suggest by its bulging protuberance the presence of the precious head."

On the night of the performance the artists began by singing the deformed text. Than a curious change took place: ". . . gradually I sensed, by that telepathy which exists between the conductor of the orchestra and the artists on the stage, a growing restlessness and excitement of which the first manifestation was a slip on the part of Salome, who forgot two or three sentences of the bowdlerized version and lapsed into the viciousness of the lawful text. The infection spread among the other performers, and by the time the second half of the work was well under way, they were all living in and shamelessly restoring it to its integrity, as if no such things existed as British respectability and its legal custodians."

After the fall of the curtain, the party that had witnessed the performance from the Lord Chamberlain's box advanced on Beecham. His first impulse was to fly. To his astonishment, he heard effusive words of praise for the manner in which he and his colleagues had met and fulfilled their wishes. "To this day I do not know whether we owed this happy finishing touch to the imperfect diction of the singers, an ignorance of the language on the part of my co-editors of the text, or their diplomatic decision to put the best possible face on a dénouement that was beyond either their or my power to foresee and control."

Parenthetically, it may be mentioned that *Salome* was capable of creating another London furor much later, in the season of 1949-50, in a production created by Salvador Dali. His scenery and costumes were so scandalous that the affair led to the downfall of Peter Brook, who resigned under fire as the artistic director of Covent Garden.

---

* William Mann says in his book—*Richard Strauss: A Critical Study of the Operas*—that Strauss had an affair with her. I asked him where he got this information and he replied that a trustworthy acquaintance of Strauss told him and it was confirmed by one other person. Since I have been unable to find any documentary evidence I must consider the statement as gossip rather than fact.

New York saw *Salome* in 1907. Here too it caused a nine-day uproar, though whether through the shocking quality of the opera or because of the maladroitness of the impresario, Heinrich Conried, is questionable. Conried gave the public dress rehearsal, to which of course the directors of the Metropolitan, including the powerful J. P. Morgan, were invited, on a Sunday morning (January 20). Many members of the audience had come to the opera house directly from church. Morgan was revolted and said so. The next day there appeared a letter from a physician in *The New York Times:* "I am a man of middle life who has devoted upwards of twenty years to the practice of a profession that necessitates a daily intimacy with degenerates. I say after deliberation that *Salome* is a detailed and explicit exposition of the most horrible, disgusting, revolting and unmentionable features of degeneracy that I have ever heard, read of, or imagined." The audience at the première the day following was aware of all this.

The house was sold out at double prices. The performance began with an operatic concert, and the opera itself started around ten o'clock. Olive Fremstad sang. Once again the prima donna's figure made it advisable to have the dance executed by a ballerina. A few people left before the end, but whether because of the late hour or because of indignation cannot be determined. In the morning, *The New York Times* published a special report under the heading "How the Audience Took It": "Ten extra policemen were required last night to handle the crowds. . . . Many of the women in the Metropolitan Opera House last night turned away from the dance. Very few men in the audience seemed comfortable. . . . In the galleries men and women left their seats to stand so they might look down on the prima donna as she kissed the dead lips of the head of John the Baptist. Then they sank back in their chairs and shuddered." How the reporter could observe people shuddering in the darkened house he did not explain. H. E. Krehbiel, the critical dragon of the New York *Tribune,* was stung into emitting puffs of superheated prose, condemning the opera on moral grounds, though he acknowledged the force of some of the music. "Moral stench," "pestiferous work," "smarting eyeballs and wrecked nerves," "abhorrent, bestial, and loathsome," roared the dragon. All this influenced the directors. But—wrote Irving Kolodin in his *The Story of*

His mother,
Josephine
Pschorr
Strauss

His father,
Franz Strauss

BETTMANN ARCHIVE

Strauss at the age of ten

Strauss in his early thirties

Hans von Bülow, 1886

Strauss's wedding photograph

Strauss, Pauline, and their son Franz, 1910

Drawing by Max Liebermann

COLLECTION ANDRÉ MEYER, PARIS

Salome presents the head of Rosenkavalier-Strauss on a silver salver (Caricature by Georges Villa)

RIGHT: Strauss as conductor (Etching by Alois Kolb)

CULVER PICTURES, INC.

The old Strauss conducting

CULVER PICTURES, INC.

Gatti-Casazza, Alfred Hertz, and Strauss

THE LIBRETTISTS

LEFT:
Hugo von Hofmannsthal

OPPOSITE TOP:
Stefan Zweig

BELOW:
Clemens Krauss conferring with Strauss after the dress rehearsal of *Capriccio*, Munich, 1942

OPPOSITE BOTTOM:
Strauss and Joseph Gregor, 1938

ULLSTEIN BILDERDIENST

With Dr. Joseph Goebbels in Dresden

BETTMANN ARCHIVE

Strauss after World War II

CULVER PICTURES, INC.

Sir Thomas Beecham and Strauss in London, 1947

the Metropolitan Opera—"there is little doubt that the kiss bestowed by Salome upon the severed head was the *Casus belli* that led to the banishment of the work, especially since Fremstad performed the action with enormously voracious fervor, at the very front of the stage." Five days later it was announced that no further performances of *Salome* would be given, and neither the protestations of Conried nor the pleas of Alfred Hertz, the conductor, could change the directors' minds.

It is understandable that Strauss was less than pleased with the New York interdict. When later the Metropolitan was trying to obtain the rights to perform *Elektra,* they learned that Strauss had given the rights to the competition, to Oscar Hammerstein. Otto H. Kahn had by then taken over larger responsibility in the running of the Metropolitan. He wrote Strauss a conciliatory letter, attempting to change the composer's mind. This letter has only recently been published. Kahn pointed out that there was now a new regime at work, that Morgan had nothing more to do with artistic questions, that Gatti-Casazza, "who admires you very much," was the new general manager, and that the previous management had been responsible for the debacle:

> I can understand completely your "lust for revenge" against those responsible for the unfortunate *Salome* episode in New York. It is also quite understandable that you should regard "Orestes" Hammerstein as a ready tool for atonement, but permit me to point out that you are looking for Clytemnestra and her paramour in the wrong place.
>
> The responsibility for the *Salome* veto must be shared by the clumsiness of Conried and the honestly felt, but, in this case, totally inappropriate religiosity of Morgan. Conried tactlessly called the dress rehearsal for Sunday at eleven—the hour for church services—and invited "*tout* New York," thus attracting the attention and anger of churchmen, who stirred Morgan into action . . .*

It made no difference. Hammerstein got *Elektra.*†

The last of the famous opera houses to capitulate was the Vienna

---

* Letter of May 29, 1908, in the *Saturday Review,* May 30, 1964.

† He gave it in a French translation and the Elektra was Mariette Mazarin. She fainted after the first performance. All the same, she sang the part again six days later,

Court Opera House. Neither Mahler nor his successor could get the work past the Catholic-dominated censorship. Chiefly due to the endeavors of the Austrian Archbishop Piffl (an appropriate name!), the work was banned, though a visiting troupe played it in Vienna's second opera house. Not until 1918, after the First World War, did *Salome* enter the portals of the Vienna Court Opera. By then the Court Opera was no longer the Court Opera; it had become the Vienna State Opera.

While the popularity of the opera may have begun partly as a *succès de scandale,* audiences were neither so prudish nor so thick-skinned as not to recognize the work's originality and beauty. Several contemporary composers paid tribute to it. Dukas said that he had thought he knew something of the art of orchestration, but now he realized that there were many secrets which were to him undisclosed. Ravel spoke of its elementary force, of the burning hot wind of *Salome* which storms the soul. Busoni admired it. Cosima Wagner thought it was sheer madness.

The controversy helped. So did the caricatures that began to appear, as well as the jokes and anecdotes, most of them no doubt apocryphal. Strauss was supposed to have said to the orchestra, "Courage, gentlemen! The wronger it sounds, the righter it is." In a dispute with Schuch over a point of interpretation, Strauss asked, "Who after all wrote this opera?" Schuch answered, "*You,* thank God!" A cartoon appeared in *Le Témoin* in Paris in which a nude and sexy Salome exclaims, "Oh, if I had had the slightest notion, I would have asked for the head of Richard Strauss!"

What shall we say now of the opera, now that over a half century of familiarity has blunted its shock? Surely we no longer think of this as a mephitic score. Surely we are no longer incited to public protest. Necrophilism has not become a theme suitable for matinees; yet we have become accustomed to the theater's moving into the hospital, to its disclosure of disease in detail. If we are not afraid of Albee's *Virginia Woolf* how can we be afraid of Salome, even though she is set before us with music that intensifies the miasma of her corruption? Yet it is curious that two writers (both British!), William Mann and Norman Del Mar, recently used the

and five days after that she sang Elektra at a matinee performance and Salome in Massenet's *Hérodiade* that very same evening. Sopranos had stamina—in those days!

same word: they call the opera "nasty." Del Mar thinks that "after a performance of *Salome* one is left with a very nasty taste in one's mouth."* Is it possible? I have heard *Salome* dozens of times, and after a good performance I have experienced a sense of horror, of tragedy, of elation; occasionally I have been irritated by its faults. But never have I gone away with a "nasty taste." "Bitter," yes, but not "nasty," for *Salome* is a work of art and not a piece of pornography.

It is an important and valuable work of art. Think of the evocation of foreboding at the beginning of the opera; think of the poetic force of Salome's declaration of desire; think of the tone painting at such a moment as the springing up of an icy wind suddenly enveloping Herod; think of the orchestra's fury as Jokanaan descends into the cistern; think of the mounting fear of Herod set against the monosyllabic determination of Salome (a conflict expressed in operatic music of highest interest); think of the horrifying act of the execution, in which silence is set to music; at this point occur the notes for the double bass produced by pinching the string between the player's thumb and forefinger. Strauss said that these were to represent not the severing of the head but the moans of the mad Salome.† Let the forever-varying harmonies, the abundant, shimmering, shifting colors of the orchestra, the rumbling and the cries, the alternation between dissonance and consonant lushness, the long-breathed and ecstatic melodies strike your ear—and the power of *Salome* must be felt. Above all, there is the final apostrophe. Few passages in twentieth-century opera are as moving as this long monologue, the dark words of the girl who recognizes that the secret of love is deeper than the secret of death, a spiritually perverse but musically exalting "Liebestod," which culminates, after the words "I have kissed thy mouth, Jokanaan," in the shattering outcry by the orchestra.

That is not to say that the opera is not marred by faults, those lapses of taste and inspiration from which hardly any major work by

---

* Norman Del Mar, *Richard Strauss: A Critical Commentary on His Life and Works*, Vol. I.

† He got the effect from Berlioz, who speaks of it in his treatise on instrumentation. Strauss had revised this treatise, adding to it his own knowledge of modern orchestration. It was published in 1905, the same year as *Salome*, and is still considered a model of its kind.

Strauss is free. Gustav Mahler, who could not judge his own compositions, judged *Salome* acutely. He wrote to his wife: "It is emphatically a work of genius, very powerful and decidedly one of the most important works of our day. A Vulcan lives and labors under a heap of slag, a subterranean fire—not merely a firework! It is exactly the same with Strauss's whole personality. That is why it is so difficult in his case to sift the chaff from the grain."*

Yes, there is slag, there is chaff. Jokanaan is an unsuccessful figure, convincing neither as a gentle sufferer nor as an eloquent antagonist. Strauss once confessed to Stefan Zweig that he thought of Jokanaan as an unsympathetic character, that to him there was something ludicrous about a preacher in the wilderness. Did Strauss realize how flat and unprofitable the music associated with Jokanaan is? We have seen that religious ecstasy was not in Strauss's repertoire. Jokanaan sinks into banality when he preaches of the Sea of Galilee. Nor is the quintet of the Jews, which was supposed to be funny, truly humorous: the fugue is merely noisy.

Finally, there is the question of Salome's Dance. It has become fashionable now to deprecate it. I do not quite agree. It is obviously a set piece, perhaps composed with the intention of using it in the concert hall; it is certainly an afterthought, and Mahler's fear that Strauss would not be able to recapture the mood was not groundless. Strauss uses motives from the opera, but the theme specially composed for the Dance seems somewhat inapposite, a bit too "healthy." Altogether the dance seems a little vulgar; it exudes a tingle-tangle Orientalism. Or, to put it differently, its erotic appeal is *vieux jeu;* one may liken it to the Beardsley drawings illustrating Wilde's play. They were considered daring in the extreme, with their sexual symbols. Today they look like old-fashioned squiggles. Strauss is better than Beardsley, and the famous Dance does serve as an effective focal point, and does still manage to stimulate us with its orchestral excitement.

Strauss called *Salome* a scherzo with a tragic ending. He said too that one should conduct *Salome* as if it were composed by Mendelssohn. Both statements are nonsense. *Salome* is not a scherzo, and one could no more conduct it as if it were Mendelssohn than

---

* Letter written in January, 1907.

one could conduct the "Italian" Symphony as if it were Strauss. Undoubtedly he said it because he wished to counteract the excessive hysteria that pervades the conducting, singing, and acting of many performances of the opera.* He was right when he demanded that Salome should not move like an Egyptian belly dancer and that Herod should not slither all over the stage, bellowing in a nasal voice. All the frenzy that is needed lies in the music itself.

The frenzy of *Salome*, sexual, dramatic, and nerve-racking, leads into a peroration that fulfills the demand we can ask from art: that it nourish our desire for beauty. There is a reason why, after all the sensationalism has passed, *Salome* remains Strauss's second most popular opera.

---

* Birgit Nilsson's interpretation is restrained. She is, I think, the best Salome I ever heard—and I have heard many.

10

The Partner

The coffeehouses were the public libraries of Vienna. Each *Kaffeehaus* had its own clientele: the members of the opera claque gathered in one and the medical students in another, the *Fiaker* coachmen in one and the cavalry lieutenants in another, the struggling journalists in one and the arrived authors in another. But all coffeehouses had one thing in common: they had to make available a copious assortment of current newspapers, periodicals, and journals. These were mounted on wooden reading racks, and you could take possession of and hoard them for hours, just for the price of "*einen kleinen Schwarzen*," a demitasse of coffee. That was the cheapest thing you could order. (You also got free two glasses of the delicious ice-cold Vienna water.) The Austrian newspapers and periodicals, heavily censored, were short on news but long on literature; it was they, rather than the expensive books, that furnished the prevalent intellectual reading matter. In the late 1890's there began to appear in them a number of poems of sensitivity and beauty, which were signed Loris. The name was an obvious pseudonym. Who was Loris? The poets and writers in the vanguard, such men as Richard Beer-Hofmann, Felix Salten, Peter Altenberg, and Arthur Schnitzler, were curious. They guessed from the autumnal tone of the poetry that Loris must be an older man, a man of experience who had acquired mellow wisdom. Presently they discovered that the poetry had been written by a youth in his teens, that the reason for the pseudonym was that he was still attending school—

schoolboys were not permitted to publish under their own names—and that the real name of Loris was Hugo von Hofmannsthal.

At sixteen he began to write, at eighteen he was famous. Stefan Zweig described his appearance: "With his sparse and not quite developed mustache and his elastic figure he looked even younger than I had expected. His profile was sharp and his face, darkly Italian, seemed nervously tense. His deep, velvety, but very myopic eyes added to this impression. He threw himself into speech with one jump, as a swimmer does into familiar waters, and the longer he spoke, the surer he became of himself, the freer his gestures."*

His ancestors were Austrians, Italians, Swabians; one grandfather was a Jew. By the time Hugo was born, the family could be considered old and patrician; it had been ennobled and sported the "von" with pride. His father had trained for the law but had become a banker, and as such was highly successful. The elements were so mixed in Hugo that he was the very model of a pure Austrian, representative of the Austro-Hungarian Empire, which was constituted of heterogeneous nationalities and many languages. He was so fully aware of his Austrianism that he acknowledged not only the virtues of the inheritance but its defects as well. He knew better than to be taken in by the vaunted Austrian "*Gemütlichkeit*"; long before Hitler walked in and was welcomed he wrote of "Austrian brutality." He once drew up a table of comparison of the Prussian and the Austrian characters. If one peruses the right-hand column of this table, one obtains a view of Hofmannsthal's own nature:

The Prussian	The Austrian
Up to date in his views (cosmopolitan around 1800, liberal around 1848, now Bismarckian, almost without a memory for past phases)	Traditional in his views, stable almost for centuries
Lacks a sense of history	Possesses an instinct for history
Strength of abstractions	Little talent for abstractions
Incomparable in orderly execution	More quick on the uptake
Acts according to instructions	Acts according to fitness
Strength of dialectic	Rejection of dialectic

* *Die Welt von Gestern.*

More skill in expression	More balance
More consequential	More ability to adapt himself to conditions
Self-reliance	Self-irony
Seemingly masculine	Seemingly immature
Makes everything functional	Gives a social twist to everything
Asserts and justifies himself	Prefers to keep things vague
Self-righteous, arrogant, hectoring	Shamefaced, vain, witty
Forces crises	Avoids crises
Fights for his rights	Lets things go
Incapable of entering into other people's thoughts	Enters into other people's thoughts to the point of losing his character
Willed character	Playacting
Every individual bears a part of authority	Every individual bears a part of all humanity
Pushing	Pleasure-seeking
Preponderance of the occupational	Preponderance of the private
Extreme exaggeration	Irony to the point of self-destruction*

Since Hofmannsthal's parents were wealthy, he was never put to the necessity of earning a living. He was able always to live in reasonable luxury, at least until the German-Austrian inflation of 1920 swept away his fortune in a tornado of paper money. Then he asked his friend Carl Burckhardt to sell for him a van Gogh, a Picasso, and a sculpture by Rodin. This sale and the foreign royalties from his operas permitted him to live on halfway decently.

He lived in a little rococo castle of Austrian style in Rodaun, near Vienna. No modern touch spoiled its authenticity: he never permitted central heating apparatus to be installed in place of the white porcelain stove, and often he suffered from the cold of the Austrian winter. There was no modern bathroom in the entire castle. In his study he sat on an uncomfortable antique chair all white and gold, dressed in a severe black suit, and thought his thoughts and wrote his words. He kept a set of colored glass balls on his desk; he liked to look at them when he was writing.

His culture was prodigious. What did he not know? He was forever browsing among long-dead writers, particularly the dramatists,

* This analysis was published in the introduction to Hugo von Hofmannsthal, *Selected Plays and Libretti.*

from Middleton to Molière. He loved the antique, as Strauss did. He had a perceptive eye, and, though he professed himself unmusical, he responded to music and knew much music. He could recall all he knew. In moments of animation he could summon to his mind every book he had read, every picture he had seen.

He was familiar not only with the literature of his country and of Germany but also with the literature of France, England, Spain, and Italy, all of whose languages he spoke. Above all, he was a master of his own language, one of the supple stylists of German literature.

He was married to a woman who was "beautiful, exceptionally clever in a feminine way, courageous and humorous."* He had three children, two of whom are still alive. Fame and fortune, respect and love, surrounded him; yet he was given to terrible self-doubts, to brooding melancholy, to picayune touchiness. He was something of a snob, inordinately proud of his aristocracy and secretly ashamed of the Jew in his ancestry. This did not prevent him from marrying a Jewish girl.

Withdrawn and aloof, he hated crowds, including those that gathered for after-theater festivities. He refused to attend an official banquet after the première of *Ariadne auf Naxos*, if he would be forced to rub elbows with "smeary journalists and Stuttgart nonentities." Yes, he would come, but only if he were assigned to his own table with his own friends. "I am a liberal-minded person," he wrote to Strauss, "but when it comes to social intercourse I won't play along."† On the other hand, with all his contempt for the "smeary journalists," he was quite avid for publicity and quite willing to make propaganda for his work, penning many an essay and newspaper article to explain what he had in mind. And the weaker the work became, the stronger and longer became his explanations.

Vacillating between a knowledge of his worth and a sense of insecurity, he was quick to take umbrage, to imagine a slight when none was intended, to feel convinced that his work was not appreciated. Many a time Strauss had to soothe him, particularly when adverse criticism disturbed him, or worse, when Strauss himself was chary of praise. One time Hofmannsthal found out that Strauss had

---

* Willy Haas, *Hugo von Hofmannsthal.*

† Letter of October 9, 1912.

played some of the music of the *Joseph* ballet to a friend, but not to him, the co-author. He was hurt, sat down and wrote Strauss that during their conference in Berlin he, Hofmannsthal, had so much wanted to hear this music but could not bring himself to ask Strauss straight out to play it. Did Strauss not think it worthwhile to show his music to a man who understood little of music? Nevertheless, as the collaborator, wasn't he entitled to hear the music? Strauss answered: "You are a real Viennese. Instead of telling me simply, 'Dear Doctor, please play me something from *Joseph*,' you wait for a propitious turn in the conversation. When that didn't happen to arrive, you write me a letter later. Serves you right!"*

To an abnormal degree he was dependent upon the weather. A gray day was for him a lost day. When the south wind blew and carried heat, he suffered severe headaches. The barometer had to be steady before he could write. Yet he was never idle. A dozen projects were always gestating in his head. His ideas he sketched in helter-skelter fashion, covering every inch of paper across, around, diagonally, scribbling on margins. His handwriting is difficult to decipher. (Strauss's was always neat, even in the preliminary sketches.) In addition to his own output, which was considerable, he took an active part in such large enterprises as the establishment of the Salzburg Festival, he and Max Reinhardt being the guiding spirits.

To nourish his talent, he frequently became a vine clinging to strong trees, adapting other men's work: he drew on Sophocles, on Calderón (whom he especially admired), on Otway (*Venice Preserved*), on Molière, on the old morality play, *Everyman*. To that extent he was a collaborator, before Strauss. Perhaps, too, he was too erudite for his own creative good. Several of his works remained half-completed, most regrettably of all his *Andreas*, which is considered his masterpiece, and which indeed is a story of the most delicate implications set in a menacing Venetian atmosphere. He worked on this novella for more than ten years, then left it unfinished. Similarly he never managed to produce the final version of his major play, *The Tower* (*Der Turm*).

He was a mystic, though his mysticism did not exclude humor and insouciance, typically Austrian. He believed that reality was

* Letter of January 28, 1914.

nowhere, that illusion is all-pervading, that awake and asleep we dream, that we playact, that we are bound by ritual and legend and are least original when we think ourselves most independent. "Weariness of long forgotten races I cannot brush off my eyelids," he wrote. Like Schnitzler, he believed in the power of mood, and wrote of the havoc or ecstasy which an *Augenblick,* an instant, can cause in our hearts. Once he had come under the influence of Freud, he became deeply concerned with the interpretation of the psyche, though he examined his characters not by wielding a surgical lance but by placing a silver mirror close to their mouths. To an edition of Schnitzler's *Anatol,* Hofmannsthal (under the name of Loris) wrote some dedicatory verses, which characterized not only Schnitzler's but his own writing:

Thus we play theater,
Playact our own feelings,
Ripe before their time,
Tender and triste,
The comedy of our soul. . . .
A few listen but not all,
A few dream, a few smile,
And a few sip a sherbet. . . .

(Also spielen wir Theater,
Spielen uns're eignen Stücke,
Frühgereift und zart und traurig,
Die Komödie uns'rer Seele. . . .
Manche hören zu, nicht alle,
Manche träumen, manche lachen,
Manche essen Eis. . . .)

From poetry he turned to short stories and essays and to stage works. He was more than a little stagestruck, always wanting to be friends with actors and producers and scenic designers. Of his many plays, his comedy *The Difficult Man* (*Der Schwierige*) is most highly regarded. It deals with a man who is a representative of the old Austrian aristocracy. He is so afraid of being "vulgar" that he finds himself unable to express his own feelings or fulfill his own longings. Finally a girl of equal subtlety manages to win his love, though Hofmannsthal studiously avoids anything like a love scene in the entire play. The comedy seems to me totally local and limited, a piece of intelligent Viennese conversation without dramatic substance.

Was he a great writer? I think not. His lack of clarity, his lack of follow-through which permits the clock to run down, his inchoate mysticism, and a touch of theatricality in his verses prevented him from being more than a minor though a fine-grained talent.

Allardyce Nicoll, in his book *World Drama,* judges him "a blind prophet":

> In all his work Hofmannsthal reveals himself as a poet of high distinction, although a poet whom sheer love of beauty frequently leads astray and whose writings have but little message of hope. Despite his "philosophy," he is only a blind prophet whose ears are intoxicated with music.

J. B. Priestley, in *Literature and Western Man,* disagrees:

> He is ultra-sensitive, deeply serious; the mystical strain in him may not be strong, but it is not false, not a literary device like Maeterlinck's; and his feeling that catastrophe is on its way, that his world is doomed, has about it something genuinely prophetic. On the other hand, it could be argued that he retreated before this intuitive knowledge that the society and culture, of which he himself was the delicate final flower, were already dying, and that he turned in despair to Baroque masquerade and mystical yearning because he could not bring himself to recognize, in all its raw crudity and destructiveness, what had life in it instead of death. So he clings to the tradition he represents like a man tied to the mast of a ship that is breaking up. His search for "the way into life," perhaps his main theme once his prodigious youth had gone, suggests that he knows he has put himself outside it. But he cannot be dismissed as a figure, elegant and autumnal, of Viennese charm and final melancholy; there is in him more steely strength, more depth too, than that; unlike almost all his contemporaries, he is now gaining and not losing stature; and he is far from being merely the poet whose words we cannot hear, above the brass and percussion of the orchestra, in *Elektra* and *Der Rosenkavalier.*

It was this artist, of whom differing estimates are still possible, who formed a partnership that created the works for which he will be longer remembered than for his independent achievements. His words *can* be heard above the brass and percussion. Strauss wished it so: the words were important to him.

Why did Hofmannsthal accept the partnership? It goes without saying that he was far more than the ordinary librettist, and he was treated by Strauss as such. Strauss recognized his worth almost immediately. He wrote to him: "Your nature is so complementary to mine! We were born for each other and we will certainly accomplish something worthwhile if you remain faithful to me."* Hofmannsthal agreed: "It is more than a possibility, it is certain knowledge on my part, that we are destined together to create some, perhaps a number of works, which will be beautiful and remarkable."†

Their natures *were* complementary to each other. Hofmannsthal's Austrian refinement balanced Strauss's strong and occasionally tasteless German genius. On the other hand, Strauss brought to the collaboration something that drew out of Hofmannsthal what seemingly the poet lacked: practical recognition of the demands of the theater, the insistence on telling a story, the charge to sketch characters sharply, and, at least in the earlier works, the suppression of excessive mysticism. Hofmannsthal did not think too much of Strauss's dramatic taste, much as he acknowledged his musical taste. He waved aside suggestions for operatic subjects which Strauss put forth, sometimes gently and diplomatically, sometimes impatiently and brusquely; and, at least on one occasion, laid down the ultimatum that Strauss was either to stop talking about the particular plot he had in mind or he, Hofmannsthal, would give up the partnership. On the other hand, Strauss's intuition of what was possible to be done in opera, and what was not, prevented the poet from becoming too verbose or too vague, at least in the early period of the collaboration. The result is that Hofmannsthal's best plays, considered merely as plays, are the two librettos, *Der Rosenkavalier* and *Ariadne auf Naxos*.

When the collaboration began, Hofmannsthal was a highly reputed author. Yet the prospect of working with somebody on whom he could lean—even if that collaborator was a living man, rather than "literature"—must have helped to assuage his self-

* Letter of March 11, 1906.
† Letter of October 1, 1906.

doubts. Besides, he knew that there was a good chance here to spread his own reputation beyond national limits to the international realm of music. The poet is confined to his own language; the composer speaks the Esperanto of music. Moreover, there was the challenge posed by a new problem. To raise the worth of the operatic libretto was a congenial task to the stagestruck author. Strauss encouraged him: "You are the born librettist. In my mind that is a great compliment. For I consider it much more difficult to write a good opera than a good play."*

The partnership lasted for twenty-five years. It had its rocky periods, but in the main the two men worked together well. But as men their relationship was peculiar. With all the admiration of one for the other, and in spite of occasional bursts of genuine good will, they never really liked each other. The correspondence throws up cold waves of politeness and occasionally of something less than politeness, only rarely waves of affectionate friendship. In vain does one look for the communication of life's daily problems, those apart from work, or the banter usual among friends.

More than once, however, Strauss paid a tribute to his partner as artist, and almost always did the poet pay tribute to the musician. In 1924 Strauss wrote Hofmannsthal a charming letter on the occasion of Hofmannsthal's fiftieth birthday. Anything that he could tell him in words would be banal, "in comparison with what, as the composer of your wonderful poetry, I have already said to you in music. It was your words which drew from me the finest music that I had to give; this knowledge must fill you with deep gratification. Let therefore Chrysothemis, the Marschallin, Ariadne, Zerbinetta, the Empress, and, not least, H. [Helena]—'admired much and much reproved'—join me in calling on you and thanking you for all you have dedicated to me out of your life's work, and kindled in me, and roused to life."† A fine birthday gift!

Yet in many another, less festive, moment, Hofmannsthal sorely tried Strauss's patience—and vice versa. In 1917, after the failure of *Le Bourgeois Gentilhomme*, Strauss, testy and nervous, did lose his equanimity and angrily wrote Hofmannsthal's wife that "it really would not do to have Hugo merely brush aside my doubts with an

---

* Letter of July 6, 1908.
† Letter of January 29, 1924.

extravagant gesture." The least he had a right to ask was that Hofmannsthal read and ponder over Strauss's suggestions.* The quarrel was precipitated by Hofmannsthal's writing to Strauss that he found his suggestions for altering the work "beneath discussion . . . they demonstrate to me that your taste and mine are miles apart, at least as concerns matters of this kind. Pray let me have in due course your decision whether I am free to dispose otherwise of this Molière adaptation, of which I do not intend to alter one iota."† Strauss, after being angry, gave a soft answer. "Why do you immediately become bitterly angry when I make a proposal, even if you find it not worth discussing? One ought to be able to discuss anything at all, and particularly a work for the theater . . . I will readily admit that your taste is more cultivated than mine . . . But kill me if you like, I do not find anything more distasteful than plays which do not draw and are written for the proverbial five perceptive spectators."‡

Strauss held on to Hofmannsthal because he needed him. Yet the characters of the two men were too diverse for either to seek the other's companionship in leisure hours. That difference can perhaps be further instanced by the fact that Strauss was secretive and never wanted to talk about a project before it was ready. Hofmannsthal loved to talk about work in hand and regularly read the librettos to his friends, who regularly found the latest libretto excellent, "the best thing I have ever done."

They were formal with each other, using the polite form of address all through the years. Strauss addressed the poet as "Honored Herr von Hofmannsthal"; in a few letters he unbent sufficiently to call him "Dear Friend." But no more than that. They made a journey to Italy together; even this journey, which was undertaken for artistic reasons and not for pleasure, did not bring them close. As I have said, Hofmannsthal admired and respected the musician, but the man—well, he rather looked down on Strauss, who could be blunt and callous. Strauss could not understand Hofmannsthal's mercurial moods, the frequent headaches, the attacks of depression, the deep concern with which the poet observed Europe's political

---

* Letter of September 15, 1917.
† Letter of August 2, 1917.
‡ Letter of August 4, 1917.

morality declining. What did Strauss care about political morality? He was interested in getting on with the work; he was always demanding, "Where is the next act? Where is the next scene?"

As Hofmannsthal grew older, his melancholy deepened and he fled into lonelier isolation. Strauss kept driving on, his appetite for work being as insatiable as when he was young. There they were, one working moodily in Austria, the other methodically in his villa in Garmisch, and the circumstance that their personal meetings were relatively few has given us their copious correspondence, letters that allow us a fascinating glimpse into the workshop.

One other circumstance may have contributed to their seeing each other infrequently: the two wives did not like each other. Once Strauss had become famous and wealthy and had moved into his own villa, Pauline began to give herself airs. She frequently referred to the fact that she belonged to a titled family. The people she liked were not musicians or poets—even if the poet had a "von" before his name—but members of society, bankers and military celebrities. As a hostess she had now become pretentious, as a wife dictatorial. Her "Richardl" was to her the good-natured genius who could earn remarkable sums of money as well as flattering renown, but all the same as a man of elegance, as a man of charm, as a dinner-table conversationalist, well, really, he wasn't in it. He needed mothering; he needed to be taken care of, watched carefully, nursed along, spared all nuisances. But he needed also to be treated brusquely and bossed and sent about his business. "Go, Richardl, go compose," she would tell him and banish him to the workroom. The more he accepted her domination, the more waspish she became. He not only accepted it but he didn't mind in the least. The German language has an expressive word for a henpecked husband: *Pantoffelheld*, "hero of the slipper." The composer of *A Hero's Life* enjoyed the role. He continued to hold Pauline in unswerving affection even after she lost most of her looks and even though her behavior must have embarrassed him. Was he an uxorious philosopher or an indolent husband? A little of both. In his attitude loyalty combined with tolerance, love with laziness. As the years advanced, Pauline did not become easier to live with. She saw to it that the peach jam at breakfast was first-class, but the sweetness in her own personality dried up. She became parsimonious and kept everything in the house under lock and key, a bunch of keys dangling from her waist. As a *Hausfrau* she was capable even of interrupting her husband at his work. She sent him to the village to buy milk while he was composing *Elektra*, "the maid being busy washing the windows."* He went.

One of Hofmannsthal's intimate friends was the remarkable Harry Graf Kessler. In heritage and fortune, looks and behavior, an aristocrat of high order, he was one of those rounded, alive and responsive personalities whom nineteenth-century Europe bred once in a while. Though born a German, he was completely cosmopolitan in his outlook. Though born to a conservative tradition, he was strongly liberal and democratic in his political philosophy. He loved the arts, and was more than a dilettante. His home was in Weimar but he was always turning up in this city or the next, in London, Paris, or Rome. He knew many of the leading artists of the day; painters, authors (including Hofmannsthal) and musicians sought his company and counsel. The sculptor Aristide Maillol was a close friend. So was Edvard Munch, who painted his portrait. After the First World War, he took an active though ineffectual part in the government of the Weimar Republic, his name being linked with those of Rathenau and Stresemann. When National Socialism entered Germany, he immediately and voluntarily left the Third Reich. He went to Paris, never to return to Germany. From there he sent warnings against Hitler to the unheeding Germans; there he befriended the banished artists. He died in France in 1937, an almost forgotten exile.

We mention him here, though we shall have occasion to refer to him again, because he has left us in his diaries† a portrait of Pauline.

He attended a performance of *Elektra* in Berlin under Bruno Walter. After the performance, Pauline invited him and Max Reinhardt to supper at her home:

> At the dinner table Paulinchen showed her good and bad sides: In a motherly fashion she urged everybody to eat, particularly Max, who sat next to her and whose plate she kept heaping with an egg, a slice of meat, a helping of salad. But she was also

* Ludwig Kusche, *Heimliche Aufforderung zu Richard Strauss.*

† Harry Graf Kessler, *Tagebücher*, 1918-1937.

> irritatingly vulgar and tactless. She would have none of *Woyzeck* (Büchner's play, not the opera): How could she take an interest in the fate of a dirty little subaltern? How did that touch her ("her," she let us read between the lines, a general's daughter)? I said, "But *Carmen* is also the story of a subaltern." Pauline: "Yes, but romantic, Spanish, Merimée." I: "It seems to me that a German subaltern is no less consequential than a Spanish one. And anyway, I for one prefer Gretchen to Maria Stuart. . . ." I: "Ah well! I am just a plain democrat." Pauline: "You, a *Graf*, a democrat? Then you are befouling your own nest." I: "Beg pardon, *gnädige Frau*. Whether I befoul my own nest is a judgment which I must reserve for myself."
>
> Richard Strauss had become more and more uneasy. Now he broke into the conversation in order to terminate it, and explained to me that his wife knew nothing of politics. I was to pay no attention. . . .*

Hofmannsthal would hardly have enjoyed the company of such a woman. And since Pauline was always with Strauss, it was wiser to meet as seldom as possible. Even early in their relationship Strauss had to apologize for Pauline's behavior to Hofmannsthal. He wrote: "I hope you will come again to Berlin—and I promise you that my 'original' of a wife won't throw her keys into the room."† Obviously Pauline had been in a temper.

Aside from the incompatibility of temperaments of wives and husbands, Hofmannsthal must frequently have suffered under the knowledge that he was thought of as "merely" a librettist. In operatic history that is a secondary role, and no doubt Hofmannsthal's admirers, of whom there were a host, did not fail to point out to him that he was wasting his time. Strauss jokingly called him "his Da Ponte." He might better have called him "his Boïto," Hofmannsthal's contribution being as important as Boïto's was to Verdi. While his text had to be here and there "the obedient daughter of the music" (Mozart's definition), he did insist, and rightly, on the value of that text; there was no subservience in their collaboration.

Finally, we may adduce a mundane reason why the partnership endured: through Strauss, Hofmannsthal was able to augment his

* *Ibid.*, entry of January 29, 1926.

† Letter to Hofmannsthal, December 22, 1907.

income considerably. He was paid a good royalty (for example, 25 per cent of *Elektra*). This was important to him even before the inflation and before the influx of royalties in foreign currency. The poet who shut himself away from life did not disprize money. By no means.

Such was the man whom Strauss first met casually in Paris in 1900 and with whom he created six operas. Such was the man who, when he died in 1929, left a hole as wide as a church door in Strauss's life.

11

Elektra

It was Hofmannsthal who made the first approach. He sent Strauss a scenario for a ballet and asked whether Strauss was interested in setting it to music. After some consideration Strauss refused this, though with a courteous compliment to its "many moments of great poetic beauty." There was silence then on both sides until Strauss heard about the production of Hofmannsthal's adaptation of Sophocles' *Electra* (1903). Like *Salome*, this was staged by Reinhardt and again Eysoldt played the title role. She triumphed in this part too; even a staid professor of literature called it "one of the most magnificent portrayals of our generation."* Strauss went to see the play and was deeply impressed. He was well advanced with *Salome*—would *Elektra* not make an interesting sequel? This time it was he who took the first step: he approached Hofmannsthal and asked whether the poet would be willing to turn the play into an operatic text. Would he? He would indeed! The two men met, talked it over, and at the meeting Hofmannsthal suggested other operatic subjects. The idea of the collaboration was born.

Then Strauss began to vacillate. After *Salome* did he possess the force to tackle another subject as concentrated and emotionally charged? Was *Elektra* too similar to *Salome?* Would it be better to wait until he had put a sufficient distance between himself and

* Eduard Engel, *Geschichte der Deutschen Literatur,* Vol. II.

the *Salome* style? Had Hofmannsthal any other suggestions for him? Perhaps a subject from the Renaissance: "A really wild Cesare Borgia or a Savonarola would be the answer to my prayers."* What about a play dealing with that wicked Queen Semiramis which Hofmannsthal had mentioned? But Hofmannsthal said that he had nothing ready, and he urged Strauss to proceed with *Elektra*. He wrote that the two subjects differed in essentials. The colors of *Salome* were purple and violet, while *Elektra* "is a mixture of night and light, black and bright." The reasoning is specious: there is nothing bright in *Elektra* and the similarity between the two plays is patent, each being a one-act play dealing with the monomania of a woman. Fortunately, Strauss either did not see behind the argument or was sufficiently captivated by the play so that he agreed, and by the summer of 1906 he set to work. Once having decided, he began to compose enthusiastically, swallowing the text "skin and bones," even before the complete libretto was in his hands. He stopped only long enough to regulate the business arrangements, not only between him and Hofmannsthal but also with the publishers of the play. He wrote: "One does not need to be a businessman to wish to derive decent remuneration after sitting up with a long opera score night after night for two or three years. Once the pleasure of creation has passed, then the annoyance of performances and those dear criticisms begin, and only a good stipend can compensate one for that. Don't judge me as being too prosaic; I merely say out loud what other 'idealists' think to themselves."†

In her fine book, *The Greek Way*, Edith Hamilton gives us an analysis of the various treatments of the Electra tragedy by Aeschylus, Euripides, and Sophocles: "Aeschylus' Electra is gentle and loving and dutiful, driven on against her own nature by the duty so all-important in antiquity, to exact vengeance for a father's death." Euripides draws a character "in whom the lesser insults rankle as much as the great wrongs done her. . . . To Sophocles she is an embittered, stern, strong woman, who lives for one thing only, vengeance. . . . She is burning with resentment for every wrong that she has ever suffered."

Hofmannsthal's adaptation is close to Sophocles' portrayal: his

---

* Letter to Hofmannsthal, March 11, 1906.
† Letter to Hofmannsthal, June 5, 1906.

Elektra, burning with resentment, lives for one thing only, vengeance. But of course he shapes the ancient heritage with his own poetic gift. His treatment loses the antique nobility, he pries apart the frame that incases the turmoil, he screams where Sophocles speaks in measured tones, he narrows the Greek poet's wide and god-filled view to the observation of a clinical case. The fateful becomes less, the demented more, important. Hofmannsthal eliminates the role of the chorus, giving a few comments to the maids around the house, and suppresses as well the famous description of the chariot race in which Orestes was supposed to have been killed. He changes the end. After Aegisthus is slain, Elektra begins "a nameless dance" and then falls dead. In Sophocles, the play ends with a moan by the chorus on "this day's deed." Electra lives. Still, one could almost call the Hofmannsthal *Elektra* a translation or a transposition, a translation into twentieth-century idiom by a poet who had come in contact with Freud. Hofmannsthal had read *Studies in Hysteria* by Breuer and Freud.

As to the operatic adaptation, this was essentially a matter of condensing the play. Strauss took an active part in it from the start and Hofmannsthal gave Strauss what Strauss asked for, particularly "moments of rest" at one or two points, so that the composer could let the orchestra speak. Strauss worked at the complex score with a will, solving one problem after another with judicial calm. By June, 1908, he reported to Hofmannsthal: "The score is ready up to Orestes' entrance. Yesterday I began to compose from that point on. I am in an excellent vein, it appears."* While he was working, he kept asking Hofmannsthal for ideas for further operas, the appetite increasing by what it fed on.

As soon as it became known that Strauss was composing a new opera, various opera houses vied for it. Weingartner, who had succeeded Mahler as director of the Vienna Opera, made a strong bid to get the first performance, and offered the great singing actress, Anna Bahr-Mildenburg (wife of the author Hermann Bahr) as Elektra.† Hofmannsthal objected, being unwilling to become a prophet in his own country. He felt that Viennese audiences were so conservative and so swayed by outside opinion that the work

* Letter of June 22, 1908.

† She never did sing this role, but later sang Klytemnestra.

should not be given there until its success was confirmed. So it turned out that the première was again awarded to the faithful Schuch and Dresden (January 25, 1909). No difficulties of censorship intervened, because after all one dealt with a classic tragedy. The rehearsals were long, long and arduous, but Schuch was so expert a conductor that he prepared the opera in the prescribed time, Strauss lending a hand for the final rehearsals. The professional audience that attended the dress rehearsal remained silent, overwhelmed by the work, whereupon Strauss, misunderstanding the silence, said out loud, "Well, *I* liked it!"

In searching for the interpreter of the title role, Strauss had begged Schuch to find the most dramatic soprano possible. After several auditions, they settled on Annie Krull. The other roles were sung by Margarethe Siems as Chrysothemis—she later became the first Marschallin—Carl Perron as Orestes, and Ernestine Schumann-Heinck as Klytemnestra. Later Strauss stated that he was dissatisfied with Schumann-Heinck. Knowledgeable observers, however, testified to her excellent acting and singing in the difficult role. Possibly to get back at the composer, Schumann-Heinck said in a New York interview that she wouldn't sing the part again even if Mr. Hammerstein (impresario of the Manhattan Opera House) were to offer her $3,000 a performance. "And three thousand dollars is a lot of money for me, because as you know I have a heap of children." She then publicly called the opera a "horrible din."

She was not alone in that opinion. The grim music repelled as many as it attracted. To be sure, the opera was treated with respect and with full realization that Strauss had composed another important work, though opprobrious words like "decadent," "immoral," "music for flagellation" were strewn about.

Elektra enjoyed something less than a triumph at first, though it was not long before Strauss was able to tell Hofmannsthal that their work was playing to full audiences. In number of performances or in general popularity *Elektra* never did reach the level of *Salome*. An early critic wrote: "How beautiful *was* the Princess Salome!"* Of such quips there were aplenty: "though Strauss did not Elektra-fy the audience, he did Elektra-cute it." One cartoon

* The remark is attributed to Julius Korngold, the Viennese critic, father of the composer Erich Wolfgang Korngold.

showed the interior of the opera house, with the orchestra occupying the entire main floor (the score calls for an orchestra of 111) while the intensely suffering audience is relegated to the orchestra pit. There was a report that for his next score Strauss planned to augment the orchestra by four locomotives, ten jaguars, and a few rhinoceroses. It was said that at a Dresden performance, by some mistake, half the orchestra played the score of *Salome* and the other half *Elektra* but nobody noticed the difference.

The difference is that *Elektra* is a greater work than *Salome*. It is more difficult, pitiless in its demands on the audience, immersed in pitch-darkness, shrieking with dissonance, grim and graceless in its setting, unrelieved by erotic entertainment. In vain do we look for the love melodies we have come to expect from Strauss. This is as atypical of Strauss as the play is atypical of Hofmannsthal. There is but one moment where bitterness melts, hate dissolves into love, and Strauss lets us hear an old-fashioned cantilena: that is, in the Recognition Scene. Yet in the driving and punishing music of *Elektra,* Strauss reaches new heights. It pulsates with the blood of tragedy, setting before us with new force the old truth that hatred and thirst for revenge destroy not only the hated but those who hate. The tragedy, Greek locale or not, contains no Greek consolation. It is a twentieth-century work, important to us, a vital if brutal experience. It is like the *Guernica* of Picasso. When Strauss was chided that he made the music "needlessly ugly," he replied, "When a mother is slain on the stage, do they expect me to write a violin concerto?"

Three quarters of *Elektra* lies in the orchestra. Though Elektra herself is on the stage most of the time, the orchestra is there all the time. More than his other operas, *Elektra* is a tone poem. No wonder that it is a favorite of conductors and that it is frequently given in concert performances!

The opera grips us from the first—indeed, one of the finest passages, Elektra's monologue, is heard almost at the beginning—and we do not realize that all that does happen happens rather late in the evening. Orestes returns and Klytemnestra and Aegisthus are slain. All the preceding music serves character expression and portrayal, in monologues and duologues. *Elektra* contains no concerted numbers except the short scene of the servants, which serves as a prelude. To me the greatest scene is the interview between mother and daughter. Nothing like the figure of Klytemnestra appears in the three Greek plays. In both Euripides and Sophocles, Clytemnestra attempts to justify her deed on the grounds of Agamemnon's sacrifice of their daughter Iphigenia, and in Euripides particularly she is presented as a proud and eloquent queen. The stumbling, nightmare-ridden, ghastly wreck of a human being, with her "sallow, bloated face," is entirely the creation of Hofmannsthal. The fear which crawls over her at night—the nameless fear that covers her body and soul and cannot be exorcised unless it can be defined —is a motive that occurs several times in Hofmannsthal's writing:

And yet between night and day
when I lie with open eyes, something there is
that creeps over me, it is no word, it is
*no pain, it does not press, it does not strangle me.**

This is the worst kind of fear, and Strauss has expressed it with fearsome imagination: music that is as little anchored in tonality as Klytemnestra's sufferings are indefinite. The lapidary style of the opera here changes into a slimy softness. The scene is a work of genius. He rewrote the entire scene three times. In his old age he remarked that had he foreseen its consequences in "modern music," he would never have started "the mess."

As I have mentioned, Strauss treats the Recognition Scene, which has its counterpart in the Greek plays, as the lyrical kernel of the opera, dividing the preceding horror from the greater horror that is to come. The actual melody that pervades the scene is commonplace enough, but its dramatic use is superb, contrasting Elektra's cries of joy—"Orest! Orest!"—against the sweep of the orchestra. Once again it is the orchestra that tells us most: it reveals the quantity of love stored away in the soul of this harridan of hate. The recognition is followed by the scene in which Elektra remains alone while Orestes enters the palace. Her madness, which has been

* English translation from Hugo von Hofmannsthal, *Selected Plays and Libretti.*

foreshadowed in her first soliloquy, is here expressed almost solely by the orchestra, the voice being sparsely used. Like a caged animal she runs up and down. She has not been able to give her brother the ax that she had so carefully hidden away for this day. Then she hears the cry from Klytemnestra. "Strike once again!" Elektra screams. If we did not know differently, we would attribute these words to Hofmannsthal. They are Sophocles'.

Finally, after the deeds are done, the orchestra takes over once again in Elektra's dance. The dance is built of themes that have been heard previously, restated here with a pounding rhythm; it grows harsher and harsher, louder and louder—until Elektra's heart bursts. How different, how musically more potent, this great dance is from Salome's!

With all of our admiration for *Elektra,* we must note the defects. They are brought about by Strauss's lack of interest in the representative of normality, Chrysothemis, who wants to escape into life and "bear children." The Chrysothemis-Elektra scenes are too long, dull, and not convincing. She too screeches away, and when she pleads with her sister to let her escape from the dark house that is her prison, she falls into banality. In both *Salome* and *Elektra* Strauss was at his best when he set mania to music.

Can one feel indifferent about *Elektra?* I do not think so. One may be estranged by it, or one may concede it greatness, but it is as impossible to feel tepid about it as it is impossible to ignore a thunderstorm. Early in *Elektra's* career it stirred two men of prominence into public controversy. After Beecham gave the highly successful English première at Covent Garden in 1910, the critic Ernest Newman wrote:

> All but the Strauss fanatics will admit that, though he is undoubtedly the greatest living musician, there is a strong strain of foolishness and ugliness in him, that he is lacking in the sensitive feeling for the balance of a large work that some other great artists have, and that consequently there is not one large work of his, from *Don Quixote* onward, that is not marred by some folly or some foolery. If it were not for this strain of coarseness and thoughtlessness in him, he would never have taken up so crude a perversion of the old Greek story as that of Hugo von Hofmannsthal.

This stung Mr. George Bernard Shaw into eloquent fury. He asked in a letter to the *Nation,* in which Newman's first article appeared:

> SIR,—May I, as an old critic of music, and as a member of the public who has not yet heard *Elektra,* make an appeal to Mr. Ernest Newman to give us something about that work a little less ridiculous and idiotic than his article in your last issue?

From this point on the two men fought in long public letters which the *Nation* was delighted to print. The controversy sank to the level of style used in the *Eatonsville Gazette,* and Shaw and Newman slung Roman candles and sparklers at each other without shedding much real light on the work itself. Shaw wrote:

> Not even in the third scene of *Das Rheingold,* or in the Klingsor scenes in *Parsifal,* is there such an atmosphere of malignant and cancerous evil as we get here. And that the power with which it is done is not the power of the evil itself, but of the passion that detests and must and finally can destroy that evil, is what makes the work great, and makes us rejoice in its horror.
>
> Whoever understands this, however vaguely, will understand Strauss's music, and why on Saturday night the crowded house burst into frenzied shoutings, not merely of applause, but of strenuous assent and affirmation, as the curtain fell.

To this Newman replied:

> The spectacle of Mr. Shaw bringing up the opinion of a British audience on a point of art as a support for his own is delicious. Oh, Bernard, Bernard, has it come to this?

Four years later the controversy flamed up again. Newman's dour view of Strauss was confirmed by Strauss's new ballet, *The Legend of Joseph.* Listening to it was, he said, "like attending the funeral of a lost leader." Shaw answered that he proposed to contradict Newman flatly about "Strauss's next masterpiece" in advance, whatever it might be, and that "Mr. Newman's erroneousness is almost certain enough to be accepted as a law of nature; and his death-bed repentances may be as confidently looked forward to as the revivals of *Peter Pan.*" To him *Joseph* was a magnificent piece of work.

So it went on, and I am sure that both Mr. Newman and Mr. Shaw enjoyed themselves hugely.* In the end Newman changed his opinion about *Elektra*. He was intellectually honest enough to be able to change his mind. And to say so.

---

* The controversy is described in Ernest Newman, *Testament of Music: Essays and Papers*.

12

The Great Comedy

If it is darkest before dawn, it can also be lightest before dark. At least history can make it so. The few years during which Strauss passed from Greek tragedy to periwigged lightness, the years from about 1907 to 1912, were probably the happiest and seemingly the most carefree years that Europe had known since times forgotten. They were strutting and jockeying years, a joyously pushing era, with something remarkable being accomplished in almost every field of human endeavor, in industry and the arts, medicine and science, and most of all in the skill of living.

Edward VII, that puffy *bon vivant*, died in 1910, stuffed with fine French food. His funeral was one of the most sumptuous spectacles ever put on in England, attended by the heads of seventy nations all vying with one another in the splendor of their uniforms, the multiplicity of their medals, the gaudiness of the feathers in their shakos, the amount of gold in their braid, and, incidentally, the sharpness of their sabers. The Edwardian era coincided with *la belle époque* in France. That extrovert epoch put new wealth to conspicuous uses. The women of the *époque* rode in the new motorcars, brought fame to new Parisian couturiers, had themselves painted by Sargent or Boldini, and could be seen at night at London's Café Royal or the Pré Catalan in the Bois. It was a whirling world, at least for the favored.

No European country, at least no major country, was shut out from the general gaiety. The smile of Europe was ubiquitous, though it was not quite so broad in Moscow or in Budapest. But even there, in Hungary and the other polyglot nations of Austria, the ties to the Hapsburg monarchy still held strong: Kaiser Franz Joseph ruled with "careless tyranny," the whole country being run on the Austrian *schlampig* system. He never questioned the divine rights of any Hapsburg, were he ever so imbecilic, hated all modern inventions—he could not be persuaded to use a telephone—and even on his holidays arose at five A.M. to spin hazy plans for the future of Austria. Franz Joseph spent his summers in Bad Ischl, where he had built a summer palace for his mistress, the actress Katharine Schratt. Other people went to other spas—Baden-Baden, Karlsbad, Gastein, Montecatini—liver trouble being the fashionable disease.

La belle époque encouraged and took delight in new art, much of it gay. The Impressionists began to gather recognition and appreciation. Matisse, Braque, and Picasso were young. Nijinsky danced with the Ballet Russe, and Shaw wrote *Pygmalion* for Mrs. Patrick Campbell.

Germany participated in this vigorously elegant life, being more vigorous and less elegant than other countries, and contributing not only new music, serious and light,* but a theatrical skill hardly equaled since. Max Reinhardt spread the fame of the German theater abroad: his productions of Völlmöller's *The Miracle* in London and New York in 1912 were sensations. Before that he had enriched the theater with shining stagecraft, his repertoire ranging from Gorky's *The Lower Depths* to Ibsen's *Rosmersholm* to Euripides' *Medea*, and specializing in gay comedies, old and new, from Lessing's *Minna von Barnhelm* to Shaw's *Caesar and Cleopatra*, Shakespeare's *Twelfth Night* to Courteline's *Boubouroche;* Schnitzler, Aristophanes, Gogol, Nestroy, Kleist, Wilde—what did he not attempt and succeed in? Reinhardt was a difficult man. He slept all day and held his conferences all night with a break for lunch at two A.M. He was vain and capricious. He entertained as a laughing host one week and became a recluse the next. But he was a

* Most of the light stage works were imports from Vienna—for example, Oskar Straus's *The Chocolate Soldier* in 1908 and Lehár's *The Count of Luxembourg* in 1909.

genius of the theater who managed to gather about him a group of brilliant actors and fill the houses with an enthusiastic public.

It was a time for comedy. How was anyone to know that the round dance would come to a halt, that the comedy was to be cut off in the middle of a joke? Nonsense, the play would continue on a bright stage. Were we not civilized, at last? There was never going to be another war—so stated a widely read book published in 1910 (Norman Angell's *The Great Illusion*).

Germany enjoyed the greatest outward prosperity. That was not because, or was only partly because, industrialization had made such progress there, but because Germany kept piling up war machinery, which gave employment to hundreds of thousands and used as many tons of steel as it used men. The strikes engineered by the Socialists—and there were quite a few of such strikes—didn't really matter. Back to work—the army and the navy had to be built up because the fatherland needed "protection"!

The policy that Wilhelm had inaugurated had now engulfed him. He was the captor captured, the plotter outplotted. The real power had been taken away from him, the army having become the only significant force in German government. This is how one historian, L. C. B. Seaman, described the conditions:

> There was now no authority in Germany but that of the men of blood and iron, and they alone would make the great decisions of the day because nobody else was capable of making decisions. The Bismarckian system had been stood on its head. . . . The German authorities also differed from those of the other great powers in having fewer problems of internal morale to hamper them. It was only in Germany that there was any general feeling in favor of a policy of aggression before the war started. It is true that there were anti-militaristic groups in Germany, but to transform their pressure into effective restraint upon the government was impossible, since there was almost literally no government to restrain and only a shadow of a parliament by which to restrain it. Hence the only action by which the "good" Germans could stop war was by direct action —a general strike or a revolution. And what could not happen at the outset of war even in demoralized Russia or the racially divided Dual Monarchy could certainly not happen in Ger-

many. As it turned out, the moment war began the "good" Germans hastily dried their tears and got down to business.*

On and on went the building. In 1908, under the direction of Admiral von Tirpitz, three large battleships were launched—the *Nassau,* the *Blücher,* and the *Rheinland,* to be followed in 1909 by the cruiser *Invincible.* In September of that year Germany showed the world its first "improved dreadnought," the *Helgoland.* Only three months after, the seventh of these dreadnoughts, the *Thüringen,* slid from drydock into the sea. The use of this navy was rehearsed in 1911 by the landing of a gunboat in Agadir in Morocco, "to protect German interests." This surprising action caused a serious conflict with France. For a few days it looked like war. Then the conflict was arbitrated—it was not yet time to halt the comedy—and everybody went back to dancing and dining. Still, the drops of poison, the drops of political immorality, as yet largely untasted in the rich sauce of governmental gastronomy, accumulated until, in Churchill's phrase, "the vials of wrath were full."

People loved life, while a few power-possessed rulers prepared miching mallecho—that in brief describes the Europe of the first half of the second decade of the twentieth century.

What happened to Strauss during these years?

Success and more success. Six performances of *Salome* in Paris, led by him, in the winter of 1907. Appointment as guest conductor of the Philharmonic Orchestra of Vienna, a considerable honor considering how snobbish the Austrian orchestra felt toward a man from Berlin. An extensive European tour with the Berlin Philharmonic in 1908. Appointment as general music director of the Berlin Royal Opera House in the same year. (After a few months of backbreaking work in this post, he had to ask for a year's leave so that he might finish *Elektra.*) A first appearance as conductor at the Vienna Opera, conducting *Elektra* (June, 1910). Several entire "Strauss-Wochen" (Strauss Weeks) in various cities, Dresden, Frankfurt, and finally—hometown boy makes good—in Munich. The story was told that Strauss jumped into a cab, and when the cab driver asked him "Where to?" he answered, "It doesn't matter:

* *From Vienna to Versailles.*

I am in demand everywhere."* All this work he did, all this rushing to and fro he indulged in, even though, right after *Elektra,* he was already brooding over his next major work.

It was certain that this was to be a comedy. He put this condition clearly to Hofmannsthal. He had had enough of murder and perversion; it was necessary now, so to speak, to follow Death and Transfiguration with Eulenspiegel lightness. The poet suggested a comedy on a Casanova theme, which he had already half sketched out. Strauss was pleased with the preliminary scenario; but as Hofmannsthal developed it, it appeared that the comedy was too conversational and too slight for operatic use. Something sturdier was needed.

As it turned out, Hofmannsthal was persuaded by Reinhardt to shape the Casanova idea into a four-act comedy, entitled *Christinas Heimreise* (Christine's Homeward Journey). It was staged by Reinhardt and enjoyed a moderate success.

Strauss kept voicing his wish to make his next work "a Mozart opera." This was not immodesty on his part; he knew that he could not create another *Figaro.* He was trying to tell Hofmannsthal that he wanted a psychological comedy with both mischievous and sweet characters and, like Beaumarchais's play, containing round misunderstandings, love's complications, and disguises in which nobody recognizes anybody. For such a comedy he wanted to compose a melodious and "uncomplicated" score.†

In the winter of 1909, Hofmannsthal was visiting Harry Kessler in Weimar. The two men went for a walk, and Hofmannsthal discussed with him an idea for an operatic comedy. As Hofmannsthal warmed to his subject, the two men realized that it would fill Strauss's bill. They became excited and developed the idea in some detail. The creation of the plot seems to have been a give-and-take affair, with Kessler making a number of suggestions, though in later years he never made the slightest claim to being a co-author. Hofmannsthal dedicated the libretto of *Der Rosenkavalier* to him, which suggests that Kessler's role was more than that of a mere sounding board.

---

* I have heard the same story told about Herbert von Karajan. Musical jokes have a way of repeating themselves.

† In later years, Strauss said that the score turned out to be too complicated after all.

Hofmannsthal reported to Strauss on February 11, 1909, that he had completed on three peaceful afternoons a scenario for a *Spieloper*, "full of drastic comedy in its protagonists and situations, the action being colorful, lucid, and almost like a pantomime. Opportunities for lyricism, playfulness, humor, and even for a small ballet." The comedy contained two excellent roles, one for a baritone and one for a charming girl dressed as a man. The role would suit Farrar or Mary Garden.* The period was the Vienna of Maria Theresa.

Baron Ochs and Octavian—not a word was said of what in the end turned out to be the chief protagonist of the work, the Marschallin. It was to be a short work of merely two and a half hours, "that is, half the length of *Die Meistersinger*."

But as Hofmannsthal played with the task and then steeped himself in it with ever greater concentration, the work itself grew under his pen. It flooded over the shore of "drastic comedy"; it became, in part at least, serious and philosophical; the characters grew from burlesque types to individuals, and the original playing time of two and a half hours was enlarged, the final work being only a scant hour shorter than *Die Meistersinger*.

Borrowing here and there—a bit from Molière, an idea from an eighteenth-century French novel, a turn from a Viennese comedy by Haffner, an ingredient from *Don Pasquale* (or any other farce in which an old man wants to marry a young girl)—Hofmannsthal, that industrious comber of the beach of literature, produced a play that is original, theatrically effective, and yet fine and suave. To Strauss's momentary scruples that the libretto might be "a bit too fine-grained for the mob, " he replied, "I am not worried about your doubts that the work be too fine. The action itself is simple and

---

* Mary Garden, though she was a flaming Salome, never sang Octavian. Strauss did think of her for the part, if the anecdote which Mary Garden tells in her book (*Mary Garden's Story*) is true. She called on Strauss in Garmisch:

"I'm writing an opera for you."

"How exciting!" I said. "What's it to be called?"

"*Der Rosenkavalier*, and you're going to be a boy in it."

"How did you happen to think of me for the part?" I asked.

There was a glint of boyish mischief in Strauss's eyes. "My librettist, Hugo von Hofmannsthal, saw you in Paris and wrote me that you were just the wench to do it because you had such beautiful legs."

"Well, I never!" And we both roared with laughter. "Is the opera done?" I asked.

"Almost," Strauss replied. . . .

understandable even to the most naïve public: A fat, elderly, arrogant suitor, favored by the father of the bride, is bested by a young and handsome one—isn't that the *ne plus ultra* of simplicity? The treatment, however, must in my opinion remain as it is, that is, a turning away from the trivial and conventional. True and lasting success is brought about by the effect of a work on both the crass and the sensitive elements of the public. . . ."*

Strauss was all fire and flame. As one reads his letters to Hofmannsthal, written as soon as the crumbs of dialogue arrived and were gobbled by him, one can fairly see his eyes light up; one can see him seizing his pen and going to work with a smile on his face. Indeed, he annotated the first typescript of the libretto with a number of musical themes that occurred to him as he was reading. He could not thank Hofmannsthal enough. "The first scene is charming and will set itself to music like oil and butter. I am already hatching. You are Da Ponte and Scribe in one."† "I received the first act yesterday and I am simply enchanted. It is charming beyond measure. . . . The final scene is glorious. . . . I fooled around with it today. . . . The close of the act is delicious. In short, you are a great fellow. When do I get the rest?"‡ Strauss seemed to compose the complex score faster than Hofmannsthal could write the words.

But with the second act the barometer dropped; there was heavy weather. Hofmannsthal's original text of the second act has been preserved and published, and we therefore have an opportunity to see how the act was revised and what part Strauss took in this revision. Hofmannsthal's original second act contained no dramatic climax, no duel, no uproar after the duel, but instead lost itself in a lengthy and rather lame discussion between Sophie and Octavian on the nature of marriage. Octavian, when discovered by the two Italian intriguers, pulls out a purse, the coins clink, and the two turncoats now go over to Octavian's side to plot with him against the Baron, thus unnecessarily anticipating some of the third act. There are other differences, but these will suffice to show how much Strauss himself contributed to the drama.

---

* Letter of May 12, 1909.
† Letter of April 21, 1909.
‡ Letter of May 4, 1909.

Strauss wrote Hofmannsthal a letter, which is worth quoting because it demonstrates Strauss's instinct for the theater, an instinct that operated at its best when the problem was one congenial to him:*

> Three days of snow, rain and fog have made me come to a decision today which I don't want to keep from you any longer. Please don't get angry, but think over calmly all I'm going to say to you. Even on my first reading of Act II I felt that there was something wrong with it, that it lacked the right dramatic climaxes. Now today I know approximately what's wrong. The first act with its contemplative ending is excellent as an exposition. But Act II lacks the necessary clash and climax: these can't possibly all be left to Act III. Act III must overtrump the climax of Act II, but the audience can't wait as long as that: if Act II falls flat the opera is lost. Even a good third act can't save it then.
>
> Now let me tell you how I picture the second act. If you can think of something better still, *tant mieux.*
>
> Well then, up to the Baron's entrance everything is fine. But from there onward it's got to be changed.
>
> The Baron's two scenes with Sophie are wrongly disposed. Everything of importance in these two scenes must go straight into the first scene, when the Baron must at once become so distasteful to Sophie that she resolves never to marry him. Octavian must remain a witness to the *whole* scene, quietly getting more and more furious as the Baron, not in the least embarrassed by his presence but on the contrary treating him as a young buck and bragging to him about his successes with women, performs his capers with Sophie. Then the Baron's exit, to sign the marriage contract, and his parting words to Octavian, advising him to 'thaw Sophie out a bit.' Then the declaration of love between Octavian and Sophie, together with the highly dramatic effect of the couple being surprised by the two Italians.
>
> *But from here onward:* Attracted by the shouting of the Italians, the Baron himself enters, and the Italians tell him everything. The Baron, at first amused rather than angry, to Octavian: "Well, my lad, it didn't take you long to learn from me." The argument between Octavian and the Baron becomes increasingly heated; they fight a duel and Octavian wounds the Baron in the arm. At the Baron's scream "He has murdered

* Letter of July 9, 1909. Quoted from *A Working Friendship: Correspondence.*

me" everybody rushes in. Grand tableau. Scandal: "The Rose Bearer has wounded the bridegroom!" Faninal horrified. The Baron's servants bandage their master. Sophie declares she will never marry the Baron. Here Faninal's part could be a little stronger: he shows Octavian the door, informs Sophie that the marriage contract has been signed, sealed and delivered, and that he'll send her to a convent if she won't have the Baron. Exit Octavian, furious; to the Baron: "We shall meet again." Sophie is carried off in a faint. The Baron remains alone, this time still the victor. Short monologue, partly cursing Octavian, partly bemoaning his wound, and partly rejoicing in the luck of the Lerchenaus. The Italians creep in and hand him Mariandel's invitation to a tête-à-tête. This can be left as an effective surprise for the audience. No leading up to it. The end of the act remains as before, except that one might work in the point that the Baron does not tip them. The later scene, which you have sent me, is not necessary.

The arrangement between Octavian and the Italians can be brought up briefly at the beginning of Act III, just before Valzacchi hands the lady's maid over to the Baron. As the Baron catches sight of Mariandel he exclaims again: "The resemblance!" And this pretty theme can then recur repeatedly during the scenes between Mariandel and the Baron. The Baron in tête-à-tête with his right arm bandaged is also a comical situation.

What do you think of it? Don't be too anxious about motivating the Italians' change of sides. Perhaps you'll even find an opportunity to work in the little scene of Octavian's outbidding the Baron with the Italians, somewhere during the confusion of the scandal ensemble with its choruses. The audience *does not need it.* They'll tumble to it all right. The more mischievous Octavian is the better. At all events the clash must come in Act II: the fade-out ending will then be the most effective. At present it isn't effective because the climax preceding it is too weak. Have I made myself clear? Do please think it over. If you like I could come to Aussee to consult with you. As it now stands I can't possibly use the second act. It is not well planned and is flat. Believe me: my instinct does not deceive me. The song "Mit dir, mit dir keine Nacht mir zu lang" can be introduced in the first, and only, scene between the Baron and Sophie. It'll then be most effective just before the curtain, as a reminiscence. I can also see a lot of comedy in the third act when the Baron, caressing Mariandel, is time and again reminded of that scoundrel of a Rose Bearer and works himself into a rage. That, as I see it, should be great fun. He thus fluctuates between amorousness and fury over the resemblance with those cursed features. A good comedy theme, I think.

Well, now, I hope you won't be angry with me. But I feel that, as it now stands, I can't do anything with the second act. It's too much on one level. I must have a great dramatic construction if I want to keep myself interested for so long in a particular setting. Alternatively, Octavian might declare immediately after the duel that he too is willing to marry Sophie. Octavian could be a Baron and Lerchenau a Count; Faninal, a comical title-hunting character, wavers between the Baron and the Count, and eventually prefers the Count.

It's only an idea.

It is certainly right that in Act II Octavian should be defeated and Lerchenau, though winged, emerge victorious, until, in the third act, he is utterly and completely licked.

A possibly good way of introducing the Marschallin into Act III would be if she had already, by way of gossip, learned of the events at Faninal's house. As you see, a wealth of themes; all that's wanted is the poet who could draw it all together and clothe it in graceful words, and that's you. Please don't let me down!

Shall I come to Aussee? Or do you get my point? Have I expressed myself clearly enough? No ill feelings. I've started on the draft of Act II and shall compose it, for the time being, as far as Lerchenau's entrance.

He could not wait for Hofmannsthal's answer, and the next day followed up this letter with another: his proposal, he was convinced, served the "architecture and development of the act" better than the original scheme. "It must happen to you, as it happens so often to me, that one is dissatisfied with something, yet one is not fully conscious of that dissatisfaction until another person lays his finger on the sore spot. . . . Please do not be angry that I apply the spurs to your Pegasus. But I want this opera to be first-class. And as I told you, the second act is not up to what I expected and what you are capable of delivering."*

Hofmannsthal, fortunately, was amenable, more amenable now, when his talent was at floodtide, than later, when it began to ebb.

---

* Letter of July 10, 1909.

He reshaped the act into the form in which we know it. Later Strauss wanted a real love duet for Octavian and Sophie. The first sketch was "too tame, too affected, too timid, too lyrical." Very well. Hofmannsthal gave him a love duet, though not a passionate one. As he pointed out, "I do not want to force these two young naïve creatures, who are so little like those of the *Walküre* or *Tristan*, to yell at each other erotically à la Wagner."*

So it went on in good humor, with respect and admiration on both sides. When, after about a year's work, Hofmannsthal wrote to Strauss that he had found the task so sympathetic "that I am almost sad to have to write Curtain," he meant what he said.†

What are the characteristics that make *Der Rosenkavalier* Hofmannsthal's masterpiece? The plot, while not highly original, is serviceable: it contains enough to let us concentrate on atmosphere, diction, and character. The atmosphere is light, perfumed, and amorous. What better setting for a comedy created by an Austrian poet than this Vienna of the eighteenth century, this rich city of easy morals and easy manners, with a smile in every boudoir and every *bistro?* Hofmannsthal adumbrated the main action with incidental characters, whose function it is to help create atmosphere: the little Negro page, Sophie's duenna, the two Italian intriguers (who are more than incidental and do further the plot), the loyal but stupid policeman, the lackey of the Baron ("a child of my caprice"), the unsavory innkeeper, and all that crowd who appear briefly in the levee scene. Hofmannsthal took the levee scene from Hogarth's painting in the *Marriage à la Mode* series.‡ They are all there: the chef who, aided by an assistant, hands the Marschallin the choice of the day's menu; the French milliner; the animal vendor; the scholar with his folio; the notary; the hairdresser and his assistant; the singer and the flutist, who are sent by a friend to serenade the mistress of the house; the usual alms seekers, here the old mother and her "three poor aristocratic orphans."§ The atmosphere

---

* Letter of September 7, 1909.

† Letter of June 10, 1910.

‡ To be seen at the National Gallery, London. Reinhardt may have suggested the scene to Hofmannsthal.

§ Their tawdry melody echoes in the Marschallin's mind when she thinks of growing old.

is aided as well by the two masquerades—Octavian as Mariandel, Annina as the Baron's wife. What would Vienna be without a masquerade?

The language of *Der Rosenkavalier* is made-up language, an eighteenth-century German invented by Hofmannsthal; rather it is several kinds of German, each character expressing himself in a way consistent with his social status. The Marschallin speaks a mixture of *Hochdeutsch* (standard German) and the graceful, *schlampig* Viennese dialect that perhaps *was* spoken at the court of Maria Theresa. She uses French phrases—she seems to be bilingual—and at the same time picks up phrases that were lying around in the streets of Vienna and not in the First District alone. The Marschallin is adept at making fine distinctions in the way she addresses another person, using three forms, the polite *Sie*, the familiar *du*, and the *er*, third person singular, which was characteristic of eighteenth-century usage.* Baron Ochs can do all this too, except that he wears his grammar with a difference—still aristocratic, shot through with French, but containing many grammatical errors (such as the double negative) and country-bumpkin expressions. Octavian speaks an even more cultivated German than the Marschallin, but when he acts Mariandel he uses servant-girl Viennese. Faninal's language is affected, and Sophie inherits her father's *nouveau riche* mannerisms. Except when she is moved, then she speaks simply and sweetly. The two Italians spout a horrible mixture of Italian and German.

Hofmannsthal's libretto is without peer in linguistic skill. That skill goes to waste in performances of *Der Rosenkavalier* in non-German-speaking countries, where the words are not understood and the gradations of social standing, the local gossip, and the Viennese allusions mean little. Hofmannsthal believed, shortly after the successful première of *Der Rosenkavalier*, that the work would retain its place on the stage for several, perhaps for many, decades. At least, that is, on the German stage; the reception of *Der Rosenkavalier* at La Scala had been anything but encouraging. "It is true," wrote Hofmannsthal, "that my libretto contains the *heavy*

* When they are alone, the Marschallin calls Octavian "*du*." When she teases him or is annoyed by him, she uses "*er*." When she needs to be formal, it is "Rofrano" or "*Der Herr Graf*."

defect that much which goes to make up its individuality and its charm disappears in translation."*

Yes, a part of the opera's fun is verbal. For example, Ochs's recital of his amatory prowess in Act I is only lightly punctuated by music. Faninal's rage after the Baron is pinked is a verbal outburst, the music taking second place to the text. Not only the wit, but the thought content that gives this text its body and flavor, makes it necessary that we understand the words. The philosophy of the Marschallin, her animadversions on the passage of life, the inconstancy of feeling, and the sadness of growing old, lose a part of their musical savor if the words remain incomprehensible.

Logic would therefore lead us to believe that *Der Rosenkavalier* is not an opera that would appeal to non-German audiences. But logic is a nearsighted guide on the road of art. What Hofmannsthal thought to be a heavy defect turned out to be no defect at all. *Der Rosenkavalier* is the most "international" opera of the twentieth century.

There are two reasons for this. First, Hofmannsthal populated the comedy with extraordinarily vivid characters: they are among the most "real" in operatic comedy—like Figaro and Falstaff and Alicia Ford and Hans Sachs and Rosina. Second, Strauss's music makes these characters come alive; music is the medium through which the characters transmit their *joie de vivre* to us, and music makes them international. It works—in Cleveland as in Vienna.

When Hofmannsthal and Strauss began the opera, they conceived as the central character that tourist from the hinterland, the big, bad, bouncing Baron Ochs of Lerchenau. In the beginning the other protagonists were subordinated to the fat provincial whose visit to Vienna and *mariage de convenance* were to constitute the main action. Hofmannsthal and Strauss wanted to create another Falstaff; at least, Falstaff's name crops up in the correspondence. Hofmannsthal worried about the casting of the part, protesting that if the role were to be played by a thin, "specterlike" actor instead of an expansive, "comfortable" interpreter, it would mean the death of the opera. He wanted it done in *buffo* style, and, if need be, a foreigner, an Italian, was to sing it. (Hofmannsthal men-

---

* Letter of March 20, 1911.

tioned Antonio Pini-Corsi, a surprising choice, for how could an Italian have handled the Austrian dialect? Carl Perron, a German, played the role at the Dresden première in 1911. He was not entirely satisfactory, particularly since he labored under the handicap of a cold. The singing actor whom Hofmannsthal and Strauss really wanted was Richard Mayr. But Mayr was unavailable for the première, being occupied in Vienna. Later he did play the part, and played it so superbly that Strauss said that he *was* Ochs. Mayr replied that he wasn't quite sure whether that could be considered a compliment.)

Ochs is of course no Falstaff. He is not only not that witty in himself but does not produce that much wit in other men. Still, he is a uniquely funny creation, being a double spoofing of the chaser who thinks himself irresistible and the boor who thinks himself a diplomat. He turns out to be one of those "villains" of the theater whom, though he combines in himself a list of traits we dislike, we end up liking. He is, as Octavian describes him (though in a moment of fury), "a *filou,* a dowry hunter, an out-and-out liar, a dirty peasant, a fellow without decency or honor." Octavian might add that he is a coward, stingy, a snob, and, like most snobs, subservient to those who outrank him. He comes from "up north," presumably near Bohemia. That is a local Austrian joke: the ignoramuses hail from Bohemia. So Ochs is the hayseed who is shown up in the big city, with his airs, his ignorance, his stilted German, and his worse French. Yet he is so expansively and rotundly drawn that we laugh at him with easy tolerance. He even shows one good trait: he is something of a good fellow; as he says, he is "no spoilsport never." We are not at all sorry that he loses his bride but wouldn't have minded if he had captured her dowry.

Octavian, with his seventeen years and two months, is the dashing hero of the opera, dashing from his white wig to his satin shoes, carrying with him in well-born poise all the attractiveness that only unprincipled youth can embody. Octavian is modeled on Cherubino. Hofmannsthal said so. But he is not Cherubino. He lacks Cherubino's mystery; he lacks the aura of awakening, the combination of being bold with love and being afraid of it. Octavian is not mysterious. All the same, he is a most attractive creation. Not only to Sophie and the Marschallin but even to the audience that attraction is largely a physical one. Octavian does not say anything very witty or profound. He bears a light heart in a lithe body—that is enough. He makes love well, differently to the older than to the younger woman; Hofmannsthal writes these scenes with a delicate difference. Octavian is courageous, as he has been brought up to be. He is headstrong; that is to be expected from somebody who must have been everybody's favorite. The poet named him Rofrano and tells us that the Rofranos were a very noble family. It is not a Viennese name,* and, I believe, Hofmannsthal meant to suggest that in Octavian's character some volatile Italian traits can be found. At any rate, he acts impulsively—and loves playacting. He does the part of Mariandel to perfection, and we can guess that the elaborate scenario in the inn was his idea.

Sophie is a product of the eighteenth-century equivalent of a finishing school for young ladies: she comes "fresh from the convent." But she is not just the stock ingénue, the goody-goody virgin. Her innocence is relieved by a certain amount of spunk. She stands up for herself, convent or no convent. Confronted with her intended, that pockmarked "horse trader," she learns soon enough how to help herself. The playwright Hermann Bahr criticized "the ordinariness" of Sophie's speech. Hofmannsthal replied that her way of expressing herself—a mixture of what she had learned in the convent and the jargon of her father—is consistent with her character, a girl like a dozen others. In that lies the irony of the situation: Octavian falls for the first "nice" girl of his own age who comes along. Sophie has to be as she is, says Hofmannsthal, if she is not to detract from the dominating figure of the Marschallin.

Faninal is a Viennese Jourdain. He is a small-scale snob. His "von" dates from yesterday; he has a holy respect for all truly titled people he meets, the Baron and Rofrano and of course the Marschallin herself. But he is not a bad fellow and proves himself in the end a softhearted father.

Marie Therese, Princess of Werdenberg, wife of the Field Marshal of the Imperial Austrian Army, grew to be the central character

---

* Ilsa Barea in her book "*Vienna*" points out that a Rofrano did live in the Vienna of the eighteenth century. He was Geronimo Marchese di Rofrano, Imperial Privy Councillor and member of the Supreme Spanish Council. (Miss Barea perceptively discusses Hofmannsthal as a representative of the Viennese spirit.)

of the opera as the work progressed. I mentioned that it was not so planned; but even fairly late in the development of the scheme we find her still merely one of the protagonists, not the unique personality she was to become. She became central and dominant almost by accident, as if she had a life of her own that pressed and enlarged the boundary of the poet's and the composer's imaginations. (This is not a unique phenomenon in art, though it is usually the work itself, not just one character, that grows beyond the plan. Thomas Mann's *The Magic Mountain* was planned as a short story. *Die Meistersinger* began as a "short, light opera.") However it happened, it finally dawned on Hofmannsthal that it was the Marschallin who was the unique creation in the comedy. Almost at the last moment he recast the final scene, treating it at greater length because, as he told Strauss, "It is she whom the public, and especially the women, will regard as the leading personality." As Ernest Newman puts it, "There can seldom have been a more curious example in literature of a character gradually taking such possession of its creator that it evolves silently on lines of its own until he is surprised to find that it has turned out something quite different from what he intended it to be in the first place."* The Marschallin has offered a never-ending challenge to a score of singing actresses (in this role of all roles the acting is as important as the singing), a challenge which none but Lotte Lehmann has fully met.

It is easy to become sentimental about the Marschallin, to call her, as several critics have done, the female Hans Sachs. Hofmannsthal himself made the comparison. We need no such fulsome comparison. She is an experienced, wise, and understanding woman, but she is certainly not all-wise, devoid of foible or vanity. More important, she is certainly not beyond the pale of life, beyond error and passion, looking back from a vantage point of tranquillity. Strauss himself has told us that the Marschallin should be "a pretty young woman, no older than thirty-two years. True enough, in a bad humor she calls herself an 'old woman' in comparison to the seventeen-year-old Octavian, but surely she is not David's Magdalena—who, by the way, is likewise portrayed too old. Octavian is neither the first nor the last lover of the beautiful Marschallin, and she

* *More Stories of Famous Operas.*

must not act the closing of the first act too sentimentally, as tragic farewell to her life, but must retain some measure of Viennese grace and lightness, with one mournful and one joyous eye."*

These "thirty-two years" we must take in eighteenth-century terms (see Jane Austen, where a woman of thirty is considered almost beyond marriageable age), not in terms of a twentieth-century life span. At thirty-two, which might be the modern equivalent of forty or forty-five, she has learned her lesson that time cannot stand still, nor can love. She knows that Octavian must be passed on to one who is "younger and prettier." Undiplomatically she tells him so, though he chases the thought away, only to make it come true a day later. She has clear eyes and she knows "when a thing has come to an end." She isn't going to spoil those eyes by weeping, however. Even when she is sad she refuses to become lachrymose. One tear, perhaps, and then on to the next experience. It is her humor, her sense of life played as a game—serious now and then but still a game—that endears her to us. If we are not quite dealing with a Viennese masquerade, as the Marschallin calls the affair in the last act, neither are we dealing with a triangle in which she becomes a point of tragedy.

What other traits can we discern which account for the Marschallin's having so strong a hold on the audience that the comedy, originally entitled *Ochs*, could in the end be entitled *Marie Therese*—and this in spite of the fact that she is absent for one whole act and half another? She belongs to the loftiest aristocracy, the Field Marshal's office being one of the highest in the realm. But she takes her social position for granted. She possesses the elegance of simplicity; she is naturally gracious in all she says and does, equally at ease with the bourgeois Faninal and the suburban policeman. We can be sure that her staff of servants is devoted to her. Her genuine kindness is part of her elegance.

So far we have spoken only of the text. What wonderful music is there in the opera! As in *Till*, Strauss's comic vein comes to the fore, and the magician from Munich, now operating in Vienna in three-quarter time, is at his most ebullient. There is melody everywhere, singing away, blooming, luxuriating, flourishing, and inun-

---

* Willi Schuh (Ed.), *Richard Strauss: Betrachtungen und Erinnerungen.*

dating the listener with its glow. Strauss was forty-five years old when he began to write this music, but of middle age there is no trace.

The waltzes? To be sure, they are anachronistic, for the waltz was unknown in the eighteenth century. To put them in was Hofmannsthal's suggestion. He wrote: "For the last act, think of an old-fashioned Viennese waltz, partly sweet, partly impudent. It must permeate the whole act."* Famous as these waltzes are, they do not, in my opinion, constitute the most endearing part of the music, though they undoubtedly have helped give the opera its popularity. Obviously, they do help to make the score Viennese. *Der Rosenkavalier* is often so Viennese that it is like a walk on the Ringstrasse or a promenade in the Prater. Like the Marschallin herself, who is "half sad, half merry," the music alternates between melancholy and gaiety, between philosophy and superficiality, between introspection and parade; such alternation marks the Viennese character.

A mere listing of the high points of the score reminds us how high are the peaks. The opening scene, followed by the charming breakfast scene; then the moment at which the Marschallin realizes that the intruding visitor is not her husband; the little Trio of the Marschallin, Ochs, and Mariandel; during the levee, the Italian tenor aria, where Strauss seems to say to us that if he sets out to write an Italian tenor aria he can make it just as Italian and as tenorish as anybody; the two monologues of the Marschallin, in which Strauss lifts what may be middling wisdom to the realm of pure truth; the Octavian-Marschallin scene, where Strauss expresses, by means more subtle than those usually employed by the operatic composer, the tenuous perils of a love relationship; finally, the beautiful quiet close of the first act.

The second act is perhaps less endowed with purely musical beauty; but there is the excitement of Rofrano's entrance, the silver sound of the presentation of the rose, the delicacy and sweetness of the first duet, in which Octavian and Sophie soar to a never-never land of happiness, and the lush and slightly tipsy waltz that closes the act.

---

* Letter of April 24, 1909.

The greatest music of the opera is to be found in the third act, from the entrance of the Marschallin to the end of the opera. Hofmannsthal feared that the dramatic interest flattened after the exit of the Baron. Strauss told him not to worry—if Hofmannsthal would take the responsibility for the beginning of the act, he himself would take the responsibility for everything that followed.

He was as good as his word: all that follows is composed with winged inspiration. The wonderfully suggestive recitatives, those whispered exchanges, those broken phrases, reveal the unhappiness in the Marschallin's heart, though even in this scene of renunciation she remains worldly wise, a figure of comedy, not of tragedy. Octavian, now nothing but an awkward boy, stammers with embarrassment and is torn between the two women, while Sophie spouts in frightened volubility. All this leads to the musical climax of the opera, the incomparable Trio, which in its exaltation reaches the height of the Quintet of *Die Meistersinger.*

The Marschallin having taken her leave with one of the finest exit lines in the theater—"*Ja, ja*"—Strauss now concentrates on the two young people and gives them an "old-fashioned" Bellinian duet, drenched in starlight from a cloudless sky. The episode in which the Page looks for Sophie's handkerchief is the final exclamation point at the end of a long love letter.

The faults of the work are minor, though faults there are. I can point them out as well as the next man—some inordinate lengths, the poor musical inspiration of Baron Ochs's first-act narrative, the touches of banality here and there, particularly in the second act, the lack of witty music in the Rehearsal Scene of the third act. Does it matter? With its faults *Der Rosenkavalier* remains a romantic and melodious delight, a comedy that not only smiles and laughs but also has a brain and a heart. It belongs among the half-dozen most exhilarating comedies of the lyric stage.

Bringing the work to the stage proved almost more difficult than creating it. Once again Germany's leading opera houses competed for the latest sensation. Once again, after due consideration, Strauss awarded the opera to Dresden, and that again for the reason that Schuch was still there, ready to put all the resources of the opera house at Strauss's disposal. Even so, Strauss did not make it easy for Dresden to accept. His demands this time were not only financial and artistic; he asked for what in American legal parlance is called a "block-booking" contract. Dresden could get *Der Rosenkavalier* only if they would pledge themselves to a minimum number of performances of *Feuersnot* and *Elektra* (Strauss did not worry about *Salome*) over a certain number of seasons. At this the intendant of the opera house reared up decisively, feeling that his independence was threatened. The other opera houses closed ranks. If Strauss had his way, no impresario could make plans for a free balanced repertoire. They weren't going to let any composer, no matter how prominent, dictate to them.

When the facts became known, there was a great to-do in musical circles. Strauss came in for some sharp rebukes, which he attempted to answer. He argued that the author of a work had nothing to say about its future fate, its staging, distribution of the roles, the conductor, and so on, and that it was in the power of any management of any opera house to put a strong cast together for the first performance of a new work only to substitute artists of doubtful quality for subsequent performances. An opera was delivered into the merciless hands of the impresario. Strauss's motives in exacting a guarantee for performances of his *Salome* and *Elektra* (in his public reply he changed *Feuersnot* to *Salome*) for ten years were first, to exercise some control over the quality of performances and second, to assure his works continuity so that the younger generation could decide for themselves whether they liked or did not like the operas. Spurious reasoning indeed. A composer could withdraw a work from an opera house if he didn't approve of what was done to it, and no impresario would withhold an opera from "the younger generation" if interest existed. Strauss had to give in; the combination contract was vetoed.

In matters of casting and staging Strauss and Hofmannsthal got their way. They decided that not only the Dresden première but subsequent performances in other opera houses were to be given with the scenery by Alfred Roller, a brilliant stage designer who had worked with Mahler at the Vienna opera, one of the first designers to relegate to the storeroom the netted trees, papier-mâché mountains, and fussy interiors of the nineteenth century. Roller had also done work for Reinhardt; what he produced for *Der Rosenkavalier* was so good that it still serves, more or less, current productions.

The casting gave them little difficulty, except for the part of the Baron. Margarethe Siems, who was the Chrysothemis of *Elektra*, was the first Marschallin, and Eva von der Osten was chosen for Octavian. It is significant that she was a soprano, in view of the fact that the part is usually taken by a mezzo. As a matter of fact, Hofmannsthal wanted Gutheil-Schoder, not because she was a mezzo but because he felt that in figure and acting ability she was the ideal choice. Gutheil-Schoder later became one of the great Octavians. On the other hand, so did Jeritza, who was a soprano.

We have seen that Strauss wanted Mayr for the Baron and could not get him and that he finally chose Carl Perron, a fine singing actor and his first Jokanaan, but a tall, thin man who, according to Hofmannsthal, lacked the elements of the "buffo-like, the Falstaffian, the comfortable, that which wakens a smile."*

Strauss soon realized that this comedy could not be staged by the usual operatic stage director, that a new light and winged style had to be taught to the singers, that they needed to be shown how to comport themselves in the boudoir and town house of eighteenth-century Vienna. He felt that the stage director at Dresden, Georg Toller, who had done very well with *Elektra*, was inadequate for *Der Rosenkavalier*. So Strauss took two steps. He begged Hofmannsthal to come to Dresden and supervise the acting rehearsals, giving him full authority to cancel or postpone the première should he be dissatisfied. His second step was to invite Reinhardt to take over the direction. This was, of course, a slap in the face to Toller, who, to make the insult worse, did not learn of the step until he read the news in the morning paper. To Toller's protests Strauss answered somewhat petulantly that he could not understand why Toller would not be glad to have the help of a Reinhardt. To smooth matters over, Reinhardt was called a "consultant." On the first day Reinhardt did not go up on the stage, but conferred with the actors in the auditorium. He took them one by one into a remote corner of the auditorium and explained and mimed each part.†

* Letter to Strauss, January 2, 1911.

† Some claim that Reinhardt was at first not allowed to go on the stage because he was a Jew, Dresden being particularly anti-Semitic. There is no real evidence one way or the other on this point.

He wrought his usual miracle. He caused the Marschallin to spring to life exactly as the two partners had envisioned the figure. He showed the plump Octavian how to behave like a boy of seventeen. He filled the comedy with bits of amusing business. He staged the levee scene reproducing the figures from the Hogarth painting. He even overcame the lack of humor in Perron, who had been used to singing the Dutchman and Wotan. From the second day on, he was on the stage, no longer "consultant" but the stage director, inspired and inspiring, with the infinite capacity for taking up each detail.

Before the public dress rehearsal, Perron became ill and was able merely to walk through his part. A very nervous Strauss apologized to the audience, but it was clear that even with a Baron with a head cold the work was going to be a success. That success proved to outrank any of the previous successes Strauss had experienced. It was clamorous, warm, growing from scene to scene, act to act, reaching one climax at the end of the second act, another and stronger climax at the end of the Trio, and breaking out in shouts, bravos, and hurrays at the fall of the curtain. Strauss grinned from ear to ear, was mobbed by admirers, and graciously gave much of the credit not only to Reinhardt but to Schuch, "who washed away all the usual operatic junk and produced a true comedy for music.* Hofmannsthal, for once smiling as well, occupied himself with repeatedly shaking Reinhardt's hand.

Der Rosenkavalier had created so much advance interest that other opera houses did not wait for the Dresden success to bring it forth on their own stages. One day after the Dresden première (January 26, 1911) came Nuremberg. After that, in short order, Munich, Basel, and Hamburg (where the part of Sophie was first sung by Elisabeth Schumann and where Lotte Lehmann was a beginning singer), Milan, Prague, Vienna on April 8 (for the first time with Mayr), Budapest and Amsterdam in November, where Strauss conducted his own opera for the first time.

Berlin had hesitated, presumably because of opposition from the royal house to the "sexual character" of the comedy. The intendant, Georg Hülsen, watched with envy the Dresden success—fifty

* *Wiener Neue Freie Presse*, January 25, 1911. Later Strauss wasn't quite so enthusiastic about Schuch because Schuch insisted on making cuts.

sold-out performances were given within one year and a special clerk had to be hired by the post office to handle the mail orders. When Berlin hesitated, an enterprising tourist agency arranged for special "Rosenkavalier trains" to be run between Berlin and Dresden, round trip 16.50 marks, second class on the train and a seat in the orchestra.

Herr Hülsen mumbled to Strauss that perhaps if some trifling changes were to be made in the text, a Berlin performance could be arranged. Strauss replied that Hülsen need not bother to fight the good fight for him and to let himself be caught between his duty toward the Prussian court and his feeling of friendship for Strauss. As far as Strauss was concerned, Hülsen was quite at liberty not to perform *Der Rosenkavalier* in Berlin. Changes in the text? Strauss was sure that Hofmannsthal would refuse to make any, but, said Strauss to Hülsen, "Why bother Hofmannsthal? Why do you not, with your great poetic gifts, attempt the corrections yourself?" Even such sarcasm did not stop Hülsen. He persisted and finally got his way with Strauss and Hofmannsthal, both of them knowing full well how important a Berlin performance was to them. *Der Rosenkavalier* was given in Berlin in a bowdlerized version. Hülsen could not help showing the bed on the stage in the opening scene—though it was shown discreetly unoccupied and well to the back of the stage—but the word "bed" seems to have been placed on the "forbidden" index, so that the Marschallin's admonition to Octavian, "Throw your rapier behind the bed," became "Throw your rapier behind the screen," and even poor Sophie could not take her almanac of the Austrian nobility "to bed with her," but read it "quietly in the evening." Needless to say, Baron Ochs's narrative in the first act was reduced to a stump. The first Berlin Marschallin was Frieda Hempel. She was the finest Marie Therese before Lotte Lehmann and sang the part at the United States première at the Metropolitan Opera House December 9, 1913, Alfred Hertz conducting.

It was a gala event at the Metropolitan,* though with the New

* There is a small mystery connected with this first performance. One of the services supplying news pictures has in its file a picture of Strauss, Gatti-Casazza and Alfred Hertz. A note on the back indicates that it was taken while Strauss was in America for the first performance of *Der Rosenkavalier*. Inquiry reveals that Strauss was not in America in 1913. This fact is confirmed both by his son, Franz Strauss, and by

York critics, the opera was "not the unequivocal success that its later popularity might have indicated."*

At the Milan première occurred one of those typical Italian operatic squalls, which turned into a fair breeze at the last moment. Pavel Ludikar, who sang Ochs, has left us a vivid account of the matter.† The younger element in the audience, who had seen in the Strauss of *Elektra* the apostle of modernism, was disappointed in *Der Rosenkavalier*, since the composer had the effrontery to fill it full of tunes. The traditional La Scala operagoers felt that Viennese waltzes could, if need be, be tolerated in a ballet, but hardly in a grand opera production. Neither side was pleased. A rain of leaflets showered from the gallery in which Strauss was dubbed a traitor to the future of music. When Mariandel sang of the "pretty music" to be heard at the inn, some yelled, "What pretty music?" Tullio Serafin, who was conducting, kept on, though Lucrezia Bori, who sang Octavian, could hardly make herself heard. Miraculously, at the Trio, the audience's mood veered from the inimical to the receptive —perhaps because the Trio was the kind of operatic number to which they could respond—and both young and old were satisfied.

The copious newspaper articles ranged from the extravagantly laudatory—in one of them the opera was called the greatest comedy since *Figaro*—to deep damnation. The Leipzig critic, F. A. Geissler, declared, with a clairvoyance that only a critic can summon, that the opera represented "so deep a nadir that one must henceforth bury all hope for Strauss as a musical dramatist." Up among Mozartean stars or down into the drink—the public, as usual, made up its own mind. The world over, it began to love *Der Rosenkavalier's* warmth, its humanity, its charm, its excitement, and the fullness of its melodies, including the waltzes.

In 1945, the troops of the Allies began to occupy Germany. The Americans reached Munich and searched for billeting quarters

Anna Case, who sang Sophie in the first production. Nobody, however, seems to know how or where the photograph was taken. The three men must have met someplace in Europe, unlikely though that seems. The puzzle is complicated by the fact that the photograph was taken by a New York photographer. It might possibly have been taken in 1922 when Strauss was here, except that Hertz was no longer with the Metropolitan; he was conductor of the San Francisco Symphony.

* Irving Kolodin, *The Story of the Metropolitan Opera.*

† Article in *Die Schweizenrische Musik Zeitung,* Vol. 90-8, 9.

around Munich. A Captain Kramer (that is the name that Franz Strauss remembers) came to the house in Garmisch. An old man slowly walked to the door. He said, "I am Richard Strauss, the composer of *Der Rosenkavalier.*"

13

Ariadne

The composition of *Der Rosenkavalier* had flowed so smoothly, the text had proved so satisfying to Strauss, the poet had demonstrated so nimble a sympathy for the problems of music, and, most important, the success of the collaboration promised to remain so enduring, that a subtle change now began to take place in the Strauss-Hofmannsthal relationship. Nothing was said, but reading between the lines one perceives that the scales, hitherto balanced, now swung slightly, the poet's side registering more weight. At least temporarily he became the guiding spirit, taking Strauss by the hand and leading him—though surely without arrogance and without any smaller appreciation of the composer's contribution—toward those subjects, those themes, those ideas, which best suited Hofmannsthal. Had not the idea of eighteenth-century Vienna, Hofmannsthal's idea, proved splendid? Let Strauss now accept Hofmannsthal's invitation to enter new regions of the imagination in which the poet dwelt comfortably.

Hofmannsthal led Strauss partly up the garden path. As the years passed, Hofmannsthal became increasingly enamored of poetic conceits and became less interested in plot and people, both vital to the operatic composer. To put it simply (perhaps too simply), he was no longer content to tell a story, tragic or charming; he needed to be allusive and revelatory. He began to operate with "symbols," those willing servants of the playwright which substitute for characters—but never substitute well.

As invention came less readily to him, he began to dig to try to find the hidden waters that feed the ground on which we tread. But he discovered no more than a trickle. He used it to moisten complicated clay figures. Strauss saw this—and yet did not. He knew perfectly well that he needed words, situations, protagonists, which could help him compose music of rage or rapture. What use had he for abstractions, for symbols? Yet, because Hofmannsthal was necessary to him, Strauss accepted them in the end. That he did accept them indicates an imbalance.

As yet there were few signs of weakness, though it is clear that their next project was to give the poet the greater role. Hofmannsthal suggested a literary project, with—more or less—incidental music.

Strauss wanted something to work on immediately. Six weeks after the première of *Der Rosenkavalier* he wrote to Hofmannsthal, "I am extremely curious about what you have to tell about *The Stone Heart* and that little Molière thing. Don't forget, I have nothing with which to work during the summer. I no longer take the least pleasure in writing symphonies."*

The Stone Heart was suggested by a fairy story by the nineteenth-century author Wilhelm Hauff, but Hofmannsthal soon dropped the idea. "That little Molière thing" was to be an adaptation by Hofmannsthal of *Le Bourgeois Gentilhomme*. He thought it would be charming if Strauss were to write some incidental music for this adaptation. But there was more to it. Molière ends the play with a "Turkish ceremony," an entertainment Jourdain presents for Count Dorante and the Marquise Dorimène. Hofmannsthal proposed that the Turkish ceremony be dropped and that instead a tiny chamber opera, some thirty minutes long, be served up as the entertainment, in addition to the incidental music occurring within the play. In the little opera Hofmannsthal wished to contrast "heroic mythological figures in eighteenth-century costumes, dressed in crinolines and ostrich feathers, with figures from the *commedia dell' arte*, Harlequins and Scaramouches."† The chamber opera was to be called *Ariadne*. All this—adaptation, incidental music and chamber opera—was destined for Reinhardt, who was interested in

---

* Letter of March 17, 1911.
† Letter to Strauss, March 20, 1911.

producing the Molière play in his Deutsches Theater in Berlin. It was by nature of a thank offering, both partners feeling a deep sense of gratitude for the contribution Reinhardt had made to *Der Rosenkavalier.*

In the same letter in which Hofmannsthal proposed *Ariadne,* he spoke of a major subject that thoroughly fascinated him, whether "as an opera or as a play with accompanying music." This was "a magic fairy tale" juxtaposing the fate of two couples. "For one of the women your wife could serve as a model, though discreetly. This is just between ourselves, and not of great importance. She is a bizarre woman, a good soul deep down, but incomprehensible, moody, domineering and yet sympathetic." This was the first mention of *Die Frau ohne Schatten.* Hofmannsthal put the subject aside to concentrate on Molière and *Ariadne.*

Strauss was at first less than captivated by the *Ariadne* proposal. He did not warm up to the "types" that the opera seemed to present. Zerbinetta as a main character did not as yet exist—she was merely a conventional *commedia dell' arte* figure—nor did the character of the Composer. Strauss was more intrigued by *Die Frau ohne Schatten,* but he seems to have realized that Hofmannsthal would need a long time to develop the theme. Indeed, Strauss became worried about being unemployed and got in touch with D'Annunzio—whom he had met in Milan at the première of *Der Rosenkavalier*—and asked him for a libretto on a modern subject, "very intimate and highly neurotic in psychology."* Though he was willing to knock on any door, he had little hope that D'Annunzio would come through. So Strauss continued to implore Hofmannsthal to get to work: it was up to him. He was sitting around waiting for the poet "with greatest longing."

Hofmannsthal now suggested that the divertissement offered by M. Jourdain to his guests could be logically connected to the spoken play instead of being just a postlude. The Composer of the opera—the "Maître de Musique" in Molière's play—was to propose *Ariadne* as musical after-dinner entertainment, and Jourdain was to be seized by the whim of giving a serious opera and a harle-

* Strauss told Hofmannsthal that D'Annunzio had approached him. The reverse is more probable.

quinade, not one following the other but *both together.* Jourdain's guests were to take their places in comfortable *fauteuils,* the orchestra, visible on the stage, was to tune up, Zerbinetta was to try a few roulades, and then both spectacles were to begin.

When Hofmannsthal sent the sketch to Strauss in May, 1911, Strauss found it promising but a bit thin. It was Strauss's own idea to make Zerbinetta a leading character and to turn her part into a "show-off" role, envisaging for the part a Selma Kurz, a Frieda Hempel, or a Tetrazzini. Strauss also pointed out that it was quite impossible to have the orchestra visible on the stage, as first-class musicians from the Berlin Court Opera would refuse to appear in costume and to "act."

Hofmannsthal was astonished that Zerbinetta, an old-fashioned coloratura character, should capture Strauss's imagination. But he acquiesced, replying at the same time that a star of Tetrazzini's fame would be far too costly, that at any rate he was tired of working with "prima donnas who have not the slightest talent for acting," and that some new exotic talent, a charming American girl, or Danish or Italian, with an exquisite but not necessarily large voice, a Farrar or Mary Garden, ought to be found. To which Strauss replied, "Where is one to find such talent?" (In point of fact, Kurz did sing Zerbinetta later in the Vienna première of the second version of the opera and made the part into one of her famous achievements.)

While the correspondence about the libretto was going on, Strauss set to work composing the incidental music for the play. Hofmannsthal kept filing and polishing, at the same time producing a thoughtful text for a bravura aria for Zerbinetta, because, he said, "When two people like ourselves set out to create something playful, it has to become seriously playful." It was not until July that he sent the last pages of the text. Strauss received it with something less than full enthusiasm. His words to the poet were "sparse and cool." "Quite good," wrote Strauss, "except the end." Hofmannsthal was hurt, and protesting that he valued unvarnished honesty in their relationship, he yet smarted over this lack of approbation. In the middle of July he wrote Strauss a long letter, explaining the inner and mystic meaning of *Ariadne*:

> What it is about is one of the straightforward and stupendous problems of life: fidelity; whether to hold fast to that which is lost, to cling to it even unto death—or to live, to live on, to get over it, to transform oneself, to sacrifice the integrity of the soul and yet in this transmutation to preserve one's essence, to remain a human being and not to sink to the level of the beast, which is without recollection. It is the fundamental theme of *Elektra*, the voice of Elektra opposed to the voice of Chrysothemis, the heroic voice against the human. In the present case we have the group of heroes, demi-gods, gods—Ariadne, Bacchus (Theseus)—facing the human, the merely human group consisting of the frivolous Zerbinetta and her companions, all of them base figures in life's masquerade. Zerbinetta is in her element drifting out of the arms of one man into the arms of another; Ariadne could be the wife or mistress of *one* man only, just as she can be only *one* man's widow, can be forsaken only by *one* man. One thing, however, is still left even for her: the miracle, the God. To him she gives herself, for she believes him to be Death: he is both Death and Life at once; he it is who reveals to her the immeasurable depths in her own nature, who makes of her an enchantress, the sorceress who herself transforms the poor little Ariadne; he it is who conjures up for her in this world another world beyond, who preserves her for us and at the same time transforms her.
>
> But what to divine souls is a real miracle, is to the earthbound nature of Zerbinetta just an everyday love-affair. She sees in Ariadne's experience the only thing she *can* see: the exchange of an old lover for a new one. And so these two spiritual worlds are in the end ironically brought together in the only way in which they can be brought together: in non-comprehension.*

And so on at greater length.

Strauss soberly replied that if *he* did not fully understand the meaning of the work, how did Hofmannsthal expect the public, and even worse the critics, to comprehend these arcane themes? If he failed to get the drift, could the ordinary spectator be expected to unravel the clues? He was sorry to be critical; he could be wrong: perhaps he was in a bad mood. His family was away and his doctor had forbidden him to smoke cigarettes. But all the same . . .

* Letter written in July, 1911. From Richard Strauss and Hugo von Hofmannsthal, *A Working Friendship: Correspondence.*

Hofmannsthal replied with an even longer letter in which he expounded his conviction that only that which was a "smooth anecdote" was immediately comprehensible. *Tosca* or a *Madama Butterfly* could be understood at once. But the content of a truly poetic work of art needed time to surface from the depth; it could not be at once clear to the casual listener. However, as to making the symbolism a bit clearer, he had a suggestion—would it help? When Jourdain conceives the notion to telescope the two works into one, Zerbinetta is sent for, the meaning of the heroic opera is explained to her, the character of Ariadne is elucidated, and she is charged with the task of intervening in the action without causing undue disturbance. "This offers us the opportunity of stating quite plainly, under cover of a joke, the symbolic meaning of the antithesis between the two women."* What did Strauss think of this?

Strauss thought it a good solution. An even better one, he remarked wryly, might be to read aloud Hofmannsthal's last explanatory letter. (At Strauss's suggestion, the letter was expanded into an essay and was later published by Hofmannsthal.) But, Strauss wrote, he still wanted more palpable characters. He felt that the Composer and the Dancing Master were two characters capable of further development. Here, in creating the figure of a young composer, was a heaven-sent opportunity for Hofmannsthal to demonstrate wit and irony, a little guying of oneself, a little self-persiflage, a few truths about the artist's relation to the public and the critics. "Let go everything that you have on your soul: you will never find a better opportunity. But is there enough malice in you? If not, hire a collaborator."† Yes, the explanatory scene before the opera ought to become the core of the piece, and he gave Hofmannsthal permission to let Zerbinetta have an affair with the Composer, "provided that he does not become too lifelike a portrait of me." This suggestion, the development of the character of the Composer and his relation to Zerbinetta, was carried through in the second version and accounts for much of the charm of the Prologue of the later *Ariadne*. Strauss must be given full credit for the idea.

Strauss, then, kept pulling away from the symbolism, from the mystic analysis of "fidelity," from the concept of Bacchus the god

* Letter of July 23, 1911.
† Letter of July 24, 1911.

as "both Death and Life at once," and he kept steering toward people and their relationships. Yet he had something to build on: the juxtaposing of the serious and the frivolous and the intertwining of one with the other—that was Hofmannsthal's idea. It proved finally to be a most attractive notion.

It soon appeared that it was physically impossible for the Deutsches Theater in Berlin to mount a production which in two acts would present a spoken play (Hofmannsthal had reduced Molière's five-act comedy to two acts) and then give a one-act opera with an orchestra of thirty. Strauss, by that time immersed in *Ariadne*, began to look toward other stages where such a hybrid evening might be encompassed.

Hofmannsthal was thunderstruck. In an epistle that covers many, many pages* he stormed at Strauss. How could the composer even consider taking the work away from the Deutsches Theater? Only Reinhardt could do justice to this difficult piece. If anybody else were to attempt it, it was bound to fail. Only for Reinhardt's stage was this unique creation invented. Only he would know what to do with the sophisticated mixture of styles, with the deep meaning hidden behind casual playacting, with the figure of Jourdain, which stands as a symbol for the public. Hofmannsthal treasured this work above anything else that he had done, and Strauss would hurt him beyond the possibility of repair if he did not accede to his wishes. Strauss owed him this. How many sacrifices had he not made, and made willingly and with joy, to give Strauss texts for his operas! No doubt, should they now part, Strauss could find both in Germany and abroad men of talent and quality to write librettos for him. But their collaboration, this unique working together, would be forever ended. What was needed for *Ariadne* was love above all, enthusiasm, a superhuman effort by somebody who would risk everything to make it come to life. Reinhardt was the only man.

The tone of the letter is almost hysterical. It reflects not only the grievance that Hofmannsthal must have felt over what he thought was Strauss's lack of understanding for the poet's delicate brainchild but deep down within himself his own uncertainty about the

* Letter of December 18, 1911.

dramatic strength of the work. Would he have acted so defensively had he been quite sure?

Strauss replied to the effect: "Why do you carry on so?" He had not the slightest intention of taking the production away from Reinhardt, being quite as sensible of the value of Reinhardt's contribution as the poet. But the theater in Berlin was impossible. That was an incontrovertible fact, and they would now have to look around to find what theater could serve both a play and an intimate opera.

After much trouble, Strauss finally settled on Stuttgart. He persuaded the intendant of the little Court Opera to accept the world première. He had to persuade him, because Stuttgart was a parochial nest and it did not willingly accept a stranger in its midst. But it finally consented to open the door to Reinhardt and his Berlin company.

The Stuttgart management, beset with ignorant small-town bureaucrats, didn't make things easy. All kinds of chicanery were brought to play: Reinhardt couldn't get enough time for rehearsals; on the day of the dress rehearsal most of the technical staff of the theater had been pre-empted to work at another theater in town; and so on. Reinhardt and Strauss persevered stubbornly and succeeded in setting a superb performance before an audience of eight hundred. Strauss conducted. For the part of Ariadne Strauss had engaged a young soprano whom he had seen in a production of Offenbach's *La Belle Hélène,* a stunning tall blond girl by the name of Mizzi Jeritza. When she made the transition from operetta to opera, Mizzi became Maria. The Zerbinetta was Margarethe Siems. How often since has a Marschallin sung Zerbinetta?

For the first time since he had become famous, Strauss tasted failure. The audience was bored. Boredom was something Strauss had not encountered before: he had not experienced that pale politeness which spreads a deadlier pall than dislike. Strauss blamed the failure on the fact that King Wilhelm of Württemberg held a diplomatic reception in the interval between the play and the opera, so that the interval lasted three quarters of an hour. The spoken Molière play took an hour and a half, then the interval, and then the opera *Ariadne,* which lasted an hour and a half. Very wearying to the audience!

Strauss understood later that there was another reason why this double entertainment did not entertain: the public that went to hear the play did not necessarily want to hear an opera, and vice versa. Nor was this project practical as theater. Few theaters, even in Germany, could command a first-class cast of speaking actors as well as the skilled singers required to essay such difficult parts as Zerbinetta and Ariadne.

All the same, the work was given in several opera houses during the next years, notably in London under Beecham, where Somerset Maugham made an excellent translation of the play and Herbert Tree played Jourdain. Beecham was very fond of the work: "In this, the earlier version of *Ariadne,* I have always considered that the musical accomplishment of Strauss attained its highest reach, yielding a greater spontaneity and variety of invention, together with a subtler and riper style, than anything that his pen had yet given to the stage."* Nevertheless, and with due deference to so eminent an authority as Beecham, the second version has proved to be very much preferable.

Strauss and Hofmannsthal were discussing a second version shortly after the première of the first. And there is some evidence that Strauss had thought of this possibility even earlier.

In the second, they agreed, the Molière comedy would be eliminated, and there would be substituted instead a Prologue, which would take the audience backstage to observe the actors getting ready. The Composer now became the leading character of the Prologue, as Strauss had originally proposed. But now Strauss hesitated, being tired of the subject altogether and feeling instinctive antipathy toward a plot involving a musician; he thought it an inside joke. Later he discussed the Prologue with the conductor Leo Blech, who suggested that the Composer be cast as a soprano part. That suggestion immediately rekindled Strauss's interest. Here was another opportunity to create an Octavian-like figure. Hofmannsthal was not so sure. Strauss managed to persuade him, saying that the prospect of having a tenor sing the part made him shudder, and the baritone voice would not be suitable for a young composer.

The text of the Prologue was based on a scene of the first version,

---

* *A Mingled Chime.*

although the locale was changed from Paris to the house of "the richest man in Vienna," a Faninal who never appears and is represented by the fatuous Majordomo. The episode of Zerbinetta's flirting with the Composer—and more than a flirtation is involved; for a brief moment she is genuinely attracted to him—was new, Hofmannsthal writing it with lambent delicacy and grace. The ironic comments about the composer's lot as well as the tribute to music—all these were developed by the poet according to Strauss's original suggestions. Hofmannsthal never wrote anything finer than this Prologue. Once again we may observe a true collaboration, as in the second act of *Der Rosenkavalier*.

After a three-and-a-half year interruption, Strauss again took up the work. No doubt that his ideas had been long thought out; no doubt that they belonged to the clearer time of comedy, though the committing to paper of the second *Ariadne* was done in the summers of 1915 and 1916.

It took Strauss seven weeks in all to finish the revised version, a period so short as to indicate further that the music was ready in his head. A few cuts were made in the opera itself, and the ending was abbreviated: instead of a closing song and dance for Zerbinetta, there is merely a brief ironic reprise of her view of life, or rather of her view of men.

In summary, then, Strauss's work for the *Bourgeois-Ariadne* project includes the following:

1. The incidental music to the *Bourgeois Gentilhomme* play, plus the one-act opera *Ariadne auf Naxos* in the first version as given in Stuttgart.
2. Additional incidental music composed when Reinhardt gave *Le Bourgeois Gentilhomme*, without *Ariadne*, as a three-act play in a new production in Berlin in 1918. This production ended with the Turkish ceremony as in Molière, and for it Strauss composed ten additional numbers, seventeen in all. This version was also given in Vienna in the Redoutensaal in 1924, Strauss conducting.*
3. From the incidental music Strauss formed an orchestral suite,

* It was performed (with a narration) by the Boston Symphony, Erich Leinsdorf conducting, on the occasion of the centenary of Strauss's birth (1964).

"Le Bourgeois Gentilhomme Suite," a thoroughly delightful piece of nine numbers, witty, ingratiating, sentimental. (It was premièred in Vienna in 1920, Strauss conducting.) The composer used some of the original themes Lully wrote for Molière, as well as those of his own invention, scored it all for an orchestra of forty, and obviously enjoyed himself—as do the audiences that hear the Suite.

4. *Ariadne*, second version, with the Prologue as Act I, which is the work in currency.

This *Ariadne* is a joy. That is, three quarters of the work is a joy. The Prologue, scored for a chamber orchestra, is a beautiful amalgam of the old and the new, of the old *commedia* and of modern skepticism, of sentiment and irony, practical wisdom and impractical idealism, flirtation and sincerity, all welded into an entity of music and poetry that glows and glitters and dazzles.

The Prologue is so designed as to invite us into a sparsely furnished backstage; it begins dryly, and only gradually does the music take on a richer hue, until it progresses to the two climaxes: the moment—the *Augenblick*—which Zerbinetta and the Composer have together, in which they forget the world around them; and then, shortly after, the Composer's apostrophe to music, "Music is a holy art," which is as worthy of music as Schubert's "An die Musik." We must understand the words—and they must be given in German, for translations of this Prologue are impossible, so closely are words and music paired—if we are to hear the music aright. Then the Prologue becomes irresistible.

The opera is rich in melodies. One by one they pass: the siren song that the three attendants of Ariadne sing, Ariadne's recollection of her love for Theseus, Harlequin's consoling serenade to Ariadne, then Ariadne's noble aria in which her mind runs on thoughts of death and release from a life she can no longer bear, followed by the *commedia dell' arte* quartet—until we arrive at that delightful feat of legerdemain, Zerbinetta's famous "Grossmächtige Prinzessin." We have seen that Strauss suggested that an old-fashioned coloratura aria be inserted into the score, and he urged Hofmannsthal to become familiar with the "Caro nome" and the mad scenes of "*Lucia* et al." Hofmannsthal never quite approved of the idea; yet his doubts did not prevent him from giving Strauss exactly what the composer needed. It is worth noting that Hofmannsthal's words, which usually cannot be understood in performance, are superb, expounding as they do Zerbinetta's philosophy, her definition of fidelity to one man at a time, her belief that each new lover is a god—as Theseus was a god to Ariadne, and Bacchus will be.

Unfortunately, the opera begins to go to pieces with the arrival of Bacchus. From here to the end we are in a German Olympus, and a mighty noisy one. Strauss turns Wagnerian, and that fatal *Tristan* chord makes its appearance. The young god turns out to be a *Heldentenor.* The upwelling at the end, Ariadne's and Bacchus' apotheosis, is meant to be mystically soaring, but lands flatfooted in bombast.* Hofmannsthal failed too. The poetry is so bad, compared to the rest of the opera, that it could have been written by a substitute.

This flaw of the last quarter of an hour sends the audience home dissatisfied; that may be one reason why *Ariadne* is not so popular as it should be. We have to accept it as an "unfinished" masterpiece. But a delectable small masterpiece it is. It was not created with ease, as *Der Rosenkavalier* was, having been revised and fussed over, loved by its parents and then disliked—"A curse on all reworkings!" exclaimed the irritated Hofmannsthal—then loved again, a failure at first, only gradually a success.

That success—though it fell short of the success of *Der Rosenkavalier* or *Salome*—began with the second version. It was given at the Vienna Royal Opera House on October 4, 1916. Hans Gregor was then the director of the opera house. Maria Jeritza, now famous, was cast as Ariadne; Selma Kurz, Strauss's favorite coloratura, whom he had been unable to get for the Dresden performance, was Zerbinetta. Maria Gutheil-Schoder was to have been the Composer. Hans Gregor, for reasons of his own, probably because he wanted to develop new artists, had a different idea: a new soprano had just arrived from Hamburg, and he believed that a brilliant future lay before her. Without saying anything to Strauss, he had Lotte Lehmann coached as understudy. When it came time for

* Romain Rolland suggested that Strauss change the end to a septet for the principals. It might have been better!

the first rehearsal, Gutheil-Schoder did not show up. That happens with prima donnas. Gregor seized the opportunity and suggested to Franz Schalk, the conductor, and to Strauss that the understudy, who "happened" to be in the house for a rehearsal of *Lohengrin,* should sing through the part. Lehmann had hardly sung a dozen notes before Strauss began to take the keenest interest in her. The next day Gutheil-Schoder again excused herself, again Lehmann sang, and now Strauss decided that it must be she who should be chosen for the première. Gutheil-Schoder never forgave Gregor, and Lehmann overnight became the idol of Vienna.

It was only in Strauss's operas that Lehmann and Jeritza appeared together,* for there existed the liveliest kind of jealousy between those two. I heard *Ariadne* with this cast, and I still remember the humor of Jeritza as the Prima Donna, the sweet sincerity of Lehmann, the bravura of Kurz.

Perhaps it is because *Ariadne* is connected with my boyhood that I treasure it so highly. Still, judging it as objectively as I can, I believe that the double work, so deftly fitted together, is like a little casket by Fabergé with secret compartments—the more intriguing the more one plays with it.

---

* An exception: Jeritza as Carmen, Lehmann as Micaëla.

14

The War and *Die Frau ohne Schatten*

The early summer of 1914 was a particularly sunny and pleasant one. People were basking on the Lido, climbing the Bavarian Alps, taking long walks in the Schwarzwald; those who had money were repeating a visit to their favorite spas in the hope of correcting in one month a year's overeating. On July 27 they were enjoying themselves; the next day Austria declared war.

I remember how as children we all ran out into the streets when the Austrian soldiers, looking trim and jaunty, their bonnets decorated with summer flowers, passed the house where we lived in suburban Vienna. If by luck they halted, we gave them *Honigbrot,* a dark bread thickly smeared with fresh butter and honey. It was a lark.

The war was to be a short one, really nothing more than a maneuver half in earnest. Kaiser Wilhelm promised that the boys would be back home before the turn of the leaves.

Shortly before the war broke out, Schuch had died (May 10), but Strauss could not go to the funeral because he was in Paris, preparing the première of his new ballet, *Josephslegende.* In June he conducted in London and then went for a holiday to Italy. There the declaration of war surpised him; he hurried home. Some time after, a part of his fortune,* invested in England, was seized. It was a hard blow.

---

* Franz Strauss estimates it at £50,000 (the equivalent of $250,000 in 1914), though some estimates run higher.

Strauss was fifty in 1914. Honors were heaped on him for his birthday, such as the naming of a Munich street after him and the bestowal of an honorary degree upon him by Oxford University (which it had awarded to Haydn long before). As some successful men do, he had become more handsome in middle age than he was in his thirties. His person carried an aura of distinction; the eyes were clear and blue, his glance now veiled now intense, his face very pale, his forehead domed and enormous, framed by finely curled hair now receding and turning gray. (See the lithograph by Max Liebermann in the illustration section.) He was as conservatively dressed as an ambassador, dark suit and restrained tie, his appearance consciously belying any trace of Bohemianism. He spoke in a diplomat's voice the soft fat dialect of his Bavaria. He moved in a springy gait, but deliberately. His demeanor was even-tempered, although there were times—not many—when he lost this placid air; then a fierce rage would shake him and turn his pale face red, only to subside as quickly as it had erupted.

This man of middle age was engaged in composing the first act of what he sometimes called his "most important opera," sometimes his "child of sorrow," sometimes a work "not free of nervous exaggeration," sometimes "a beautiful allegory." Most of these judgments are judgments in retrospect. But even as he was setting the notes on paper, he vacillated between respectful enthusiasm—respectful toward the ceremonial seriousness of the text—and a queasy doubt as to what he was doing with that much literary mysticism. The length of time required for the composition gives an indication of the struggle: it took Strauss more than three years to compose *Die Frau ohne Schatten,* as against seventeen months for *Der Rosenkavalier.*

Part of this protraction is accounted for by Hofmannsthal's being otherwise engaged and difficult to reach, part by Strauss's decision to return to orchestral music and to compose the *Alpensinfonie* (Alpine Symphony), part by his revision of *Ariadne.* Still, knowing how fast Strauss worked when he was in the vein, one deduces that he groped and grappled.

The first act was unfinished when war broke out. A day or two later, Strauss learned that Hofmannsthal had left Vienna and joined the military forces. Strauss was "disturbed to the highest degree." Did Hofmannsthal *have* to be actively engaged in the fighting? "Really, poets ought to be permitted to stay at home. There is plenty of cannon fodder available: critics, stage producers who have their own ideas, actors who act Molière, etc."* This is what he wrote to Hofmannsthal's wife, begging her to tell him where her husband was and whether he was in a danger zone. He went on to say, "I am absolutely convinced that there will be no world war, that the little altercation with Serbia will soon be over, and that I will receive the third act of my *Frau ohne Schatten.* May the Devil take the damned Serbs!"

When he could no longer doubt that there was going to be a war, he at first marched along with the general bellicose enthusiasm. How could he help it when the trumpets sounded as loud as they do in *Ein Heldenleben?* Finishing the draft of the first act of *Die Frau ohne Schatten,* he wrote in the manuscript: "Completed August 20, 1914, on the day of the victory of Saarburg. Hail to our excellent and courageous troops, hail to our German fatherland!"

Three weeks after the above letter to Gerty Hofmannsthal, he wrote her again, expressing his relief at hearing the news that Hofmannsthal was out of danger and stationed in a safe post. (Hofmannsthal was employed as a war correspondent and propagandist.) He spoke to her then of a different state of mind, of the depression he had experienced in the first days of the war. But now that the news was so good, now that Germany was winning victories all around, he had got over the depression and had plunged himself into incessant work. In a joking vein he wrote, "Hugo has the damned duty not to die for the fatherland before I get the third act, which, I hope, will earn him more honor than a fine obituary in the *Neue Freie Presse.* But joking aside—these are great and glorious times, and both of our peoples have shown themselves as magnificent; one is now ashamed of the nasty critical words which one has uttered about the brave, strong German nation. One feels exalted, knowing that this land and this people stand at the beginning of a great development, that they must and will assume the leadership [*Hegemonie*] of Europe."†

As the war continued, as difficulties to his own work arose,

* Letter to Gerty Hofmannsthal, July 31, 1914.
† Letter of August 22, 1914.

Strauss became not quite so firm in his enthusiasm. He occasionally gave the impression that he believed the war was conceived as a private plot against him, robbing him of access to his librettist and of performances of his works outside Germany. At other times he veered again toward patriotism, regurgitating the propaganda-fed belief that the German people were superior to other nations, braver and finer. This certainty was again blown away by doubt. He wrote to Hofmannsthal:

> Amidst all the unpleasant things which this war brings with it—except the brilliant feats of our army—hard work is the only salvation. Otherwise the incompetence of our diplomacy, our press, the Kaiser's apologetic telegram to Wilson, and all the other undignified acts that are being committed would be enough to drive a man to distraction. And how are the artists treated? The Kaiser reduces the salaries at the Court Theater, the Duchess of Meiningen turns her orchestra out into the street, Reinhardt stages Shakespeare, the Frankfurt theater performs *Carmen, Mignon, The Tales of Hoffmann*—who will ever understand this German nation, this mixture of mediocrity and genius, of heroism and obsequiousness?*

Here we have the spectacle of a man who believed himself to be an "international artist" objecting to Shakespeare and Bizet because they were born among the ranks of the enemy nations. (At that Strauss's view was no narrower than the view of those on the other side who boycotted German opera.)

In the same letter he says, "We are bound to win, of course—but after that, everything will be bungled." In the winter of 1914-15 he wrote to Hofmannsthal saying that somebody had told him that the poet was unwell, that he was overcome with grief for the dying Austria. "Was that so? Shouldn't we hold fast to the hope that the German *Kulturland* would save Austria and lead it toward a new, more beautiful future? As to all the rest, let that go where it really belongs, to savage Asia."† He had not lost his hope for a better mankind. Perhaps it would come when Christianity had perished from the earth. He continued: "My sister's servant writes from the

---

* Letter of October 8, 1914. Quoted in Strauss and Hofmannsthal, *A Working Friendship: Correspondence.*

† Letter of January 16, 1915.

front: 'Honored Frau General, I really have had enough!' Those are my sentiments as well. But who can foresee the end? Shall we never again see the Louvre, never again the National Gallery? And Italy? In April I am supposed to go to Rome, where a short while ago *Ein Heldenleben* was performed with extraordinary success. I am supposed to conduct two concerts. As yet they have not been canceled. . . ."

Though positive alternated with negative, though patriotism would be spelled by perplexity, Strauss never once evinced a sign that he felt a twinge of guilt, that he as a German felt culpable for the army's savagery, that he pitied or was ashamed, that he realized that Germany's aggression had degraded human beings to the level of earthworms in trenches. He must have known of the Pan-German League, the powerful aggregation of Nationalists with their hatred of democracy, of the Jews, and of the Socialists. He must have known of the two manifestoes (1915) which clearly stated Germany's war aims.

> In one of these, the six most powerful German business associations called for the complete annexation of Belgium, a strip of the French coast reaching to the Somme, the iron ore of Longwy and Briey, and coal mines in some French departments. To balance this gain in industrial power, "an equivalent agricultural area to be acquired in the east" was considered necessary.
>
> The second memorandum, nearly topping the first in its demands, was signed by German university professors and civil servants. They advised making maximum demands. France was to be ruthlessly subjugated politically and economically, and forced without mercy to pay the highest war indemnities. Belgium's annexation was demanded "by the most immaculate concept of honor." No demand for reparations could be high enough for England, that "nation of shopkeepers." Russia was to cede land expropriated from previous owners. Quite a few other phantasies adorned this memorandum.*

At the beginning of 1915, England's fortunes were at their nadir. Its army was ridiculously ill-trained, its leadership maladroit, the losses of men fantastically high. In the same month in which

---

* Hannah Vogt, *The Burden of Guilt: A Short History of Germany 1914-45.*

Strauss wrote the letter quoted above, Rupert Brooke wrote to John Drinkwater: "Come and die—it will be great fun."

At such moments as Strauss deplored the war, he did so because he would have liked to travel again, to see paintings he loved, or to assist at performances of his works. He did not, so far as I know, offer to help the war effort (by, for example, conducting benefit concerts), yet he did not cease being a Teuton. His cosmopolitanism was not even skin-deep. It fell away from him when the cry of "*Deutschland über Alles*" sounded. One contributory cause to Strauss's Teutonism at the time—though I am not sure how important a cause—was his dislike of the French. This was in the best German tradition, as satirized by Goethe in *Faust:*

> Ein echter deutscher Mann mag keinen Franzen leiden,
> Doch ihre Weine trinkt er gern.
>
> (*A true German can never like a Frenchman,*
> *But he loves to imbibe their wines.*)

Josephslegende had been wildly successful in Paris. This was a ballet on a scenario by Hofmannsthal and Harry Kessler. It was commissioned by Diaghilev as a stellar vehicle for Nijinsky, though as it turned out Nijinsky did not dance it, Joseph being interpreted by the young, resplendent Massine to choreography by Michel Fokine. Strauss was not very comfortable with the Biblical subject nor the virginal Joseph, and the ballet is one of Strauss's weakest scores. But Paris loved it. Seven years before that, Paris had responded to the performances of *Salome* conducted by Strauss himself. Even then Strauss showed his antipathy toward the French. Romain Rolland described Strauss's Parisian sojourn in a letter to his Italian friend Sofia Bertolini Guerrieri-Gonzaga:

> Strauss is a Shakespearean barbarian: his art is torrential, producing, at one and the same time, gold, sand, stone, and rubbish: he has almost no taste at all, but a violence of feelings which borders on madness. Of the three* he is, despite all his faults, the one I love the most because he is the most vital. And he himself is greater than his works: sincere, loyal, and absolutely open. He is a good judge of himself and he has a regard

* Strauss, Debussy, Rimski-Korsakov.

> and a friendship for me because I have never spared him criticism. Unfortunately he has a terrible wife who has done him great harm here. She is the daughter of a general and a woman in a sick state of nerves. In Germany her transports of anger are well known; in France people don't greatly care for these displays of hers. Would you believe that this foolish woman went about saying in Paris society that there was only one way of getting the French to do something, and that was with fixed bayonets! Strauss himself has shown a deplorable clumsiness of speech, slinging abuse at the Republic and bitterly criticizing Paris. In a word, people have come to hate them.*

Was the bayonet talk merely an irritated expletive caused by the custom of French orchestras of sending substitutes to rehearsals? Probably—but what a thing to say! Rolland's letter is corroborated by Gide, who quotes Pauline Strauss as saying at a rehearsal, "Allons, il est temps de revenir ici avec les baïonnettes." Jean Cocteau is supposed to have replied, "Non, madame, les rasoirs suffisent." (*Rasoirs* means razors, but in slang it means "bores.")

So France was the chief enemy and bayonets were useful tools. Yet Strauss was too intelligent not to be offended by some of the war's humbug. In February, 1915, he wrote to Hofmannsthal saying that he was disgusted by the twaddle he read in the newspapers about the regeneration of German art, and how "Young Germany is to emerge cleansed and purified from this 'glorious war,' when in fact one must be thankful if the poor blighters are at least cleansed of their lice and bedbugs, cured of their infections and once more weaned from murder!" But he still felt that Germany was going to win the war. "There is unbelievable confidence in our navy. The Russians will soon cave in, and popular sentiment in England is already said to be very lukewarm."†

When in February, 1917, Germany made the decision of unrestricted submarine warfare and the United States entered the conflict, starvation within Germany began. Food rationing produced a black market within the beleaguered camp of 60,000,000 people. There followed the horrible "winter of turnips."

1917, 1918. The hell continued, the fires burned, the cries of pain

---

* Letter of May 31, 1907, quoted in Edward Lockspeiser, *Debussy: His Life and Mind.*

† Letter written in February 1915.

increased, and no one knew how to stop them. When the many-headed monster was finally made impotent, it was not encaged through victory but through exhaustion. No one had won the war. All had lost it. We can never know or measure its exact toll: a low estimate of its deaths is 12,000,000.

Strauss did not actually suffer from the war. He was rich enough to get food, though that was particularly difficult in Berlin. In Garmisch he could get it from the farms all around him. He saw, he must have seen, the suffering as he walked the streets of Berlin or looked out of the windows of his villa. He withdrew himself from the life around him. He withdrew not only into the world of music but into a kind of music particularly removed, so to speak, from all contact with reality, that is, the tone-painting of a landscape and a philosophical fairy tale.

In his correspondence with Hofmannsthal from 1915 on, the war was hardly ever mentioned. A voice to say "Stop!" was desperately needed. Strauss's voice, which would have been listened to in Germany, was not raised. It is all very well to say that he was a musician and politics was not his business. Yet his utter silence indicates a purposeful isolation, a desire to crawl into a shell, a weakness. And that weakness seeped into his work.

It is my belief that though he did not suffer, the war and all that followed after—the inflation, the disappearance of the German middle class, the unstable governments, the threat of no government at all, the unemployment, the nightmares of despair and false hopes that buffeted the life of Germany and Austria until the worst arrived in 1933—profoundly influenced Strauss the artist. He lost not one ounce of his will to work. His appetite for accomplishment was as keen as ever. What he did lose was strength, freshness, humanity. With the sinking of the German civilization Strauss's brain and heart declined. He was so deeply rooted in German romanticism, in the long tradition that had produced Brahms and Wagner, that when romanticism was slashed by the bayonets, when its roots were blown up by the mortar shells, Strauss lost his roots. He could no longer grow and flourish. He began to "reminisce," singing the same song over again to a more stilted accompaniment and in a feebler voice. This enfeeblement is not synonymous with "having written himself out." He composed a great deal after 1918. He did not lack ideas. But the ideas were all too often forced and shoddy.

After the war, he was no longer a "modernist." A harsher music was needed, perhaps. At the beginning of the war, Bartók was thirty-three, Alban Berg was twenty-nine, Prokofiev was twenty-three, Schönberg, the oldest, was forty, Stravinsky was thirty-two. These were the men who took over.

Hofmannsthal too was affected by the war, though in a very different way. He suffered and pitied and wept for the wounded. "What should we Austrian authors now do?" he cried, and he answered himself, "Die!" He fell into a lassitude of despair. He saw himself as a stranger in a new world; what he had to say no longer mattered.

Though the war weakened Hofmannsthal, he had strength enough to carry through a plan he had helped to formulate, a plan that was to have great significance for his native country. He, along with other high-minded artists, wished to turn beautiful Salzburg, Mozart's birthplace, into a city devoted to the arts. The idea was slow a-borning and met with many bureaucratic difficulties; it was further hampered by local jealousies and the incompetence of dilettante well-wishers. But Reinhardt believed in it and he was spurred on by Hofmannsthal. In 1917 the "Salzburg Festival-House Society" was formed. Franz Schalk, the eminent conductor of the Vienna Opera, was one of the moving spirits of the enterprise. But it took another three years, and war's end, for the artistic leadership to be agreed upon. This first "Art Council" was a triumvirate consisting of Reinhardt, Schalk and Strauss, who had been persuaded by Schalk to join. Hofmannsthal joined later, devoting much care and love to Salzburg. His *Jedermann,* an adaptation of the old morality play, which he wrote in 1911, was eventually given in model performances in front of the cathedral. No one who saw these performances with Moissi can forget them. For Salzburg he wrote a special play, *Das Salzburger grosse Welttheater.* In 1922 the musical part of the Salzburg Festival was inaugurated with performances of four Mozart operas, of which Strauss conducted two.

Strauss was then offered the presidency of the Festival-House Society. He wrote to Hofmannsthal that he wished to decline it, for by rights the post should go to Reinhardt, "the creator of the festival idea." Hofmannsthal replied that "those Philistines will never accept Reinhardt as president; they hate him for three or four reasons, as a Jew, as the owner of a castle,* as an artist and as a lonely, shy man whom they cannot understand."† Strauss then accepted the presidency; until his death he was often and intimately connected with Salzburg.

To turn to Strauss's creative output during the war years, there were two major works: a long symphony and a long opera. Because Hofmannsthal could not deliver the text of *Die Frau ohne Schatten* quickly enough, Strauss composed the *Alpensinfonie*.‡ (That, at least, is the reason Strauss gave for returning to symphonic music.) It is a mountain of a symphony, but thin in inspiration though enormously fat in orchestration. He needed for it a huge orchestra, to which he added an organ, a wind machine, a thunder machine, and cowbells. "Finally I have learned how to orchestrate," he said after the dress rehearsal. Erich Leinsdorf has described this symphony as one "which I still consider one of the happier inventions of Strauss except that it is too long and requires too large an orchestra to have a complete unity of purpose. It is as if a speaker who had a small topic came with a huge manuscript of ten or fifteeen thousand words and delivered a light after-dinner speech in stentorian tones."§

As to *Die Frau ohne Schatten,* this is the opera about which opinions differ more sharply than about any other of Strauss's major works.

To point this difference, let me quote two recent opinions which I have chosen purposely from non-German critics.|| One is by William Mann, critic of the London *Times:*

> The grandeur and subtlety of the orchestral colours, the masterly control of symphonic technique (unequalled even in *Don Quixote* or *Der Rosenkavalier*), and the vocal characterization summon an admiration that one may, given full understanding, be tempted to express about no other Strauss opera. . . .

---

* Leopoldskron in Salzburg, a sumptuous castle, which was Reinhardt's residence.

† Letter of September 4, 1922.

‡ He called it at first, the "Anti-Christ" Symphony! It is an inexplicable title.

§ The *Atlantic,* August, 1965.

|| A German critic, George Bittner, wrote: "A great work of music has been born. Perhaps it is the greatest our stage has seen since the death of Richard Wagner." But this was right after the première.

> Strauss, in *Die Frau ohne Schatten,* found the inspiration for his masterpiece.*

The other is by Alan Rich of the New York *Herald-Tribune:*

> If this is a masterpiece of music drama, the word "pretentious" might as well be stricken from the language. What Strauss has created in this extended discourse on matrimonial responsibility, human frailty and inhuman greed is a grotesque pomposity, at times ugly beyond belief, at times sentimental and saccharine to the point where one's teeth begin to ache, and artistically meretricious.

I find *Die Frau ohne Schatten* a peculiarly irritating opera, and not because its music is totally disappointing but because it is disappointing for long stretches, and just as one has given up hope, the music becomes valuable again and one hears something that is beautiful and exalted. It is an opera that anybody interested in twentieth-century music cannot ignore. But it is an opera difficult to enjoy. It seems to last forever. It goes on and on. So there one sits, watching the symbolisms lumber by and hearing all too rarely the voice of a great opera composer.

Hofmannsthal's libretto, which one German critic has placed "among the most beautiful poetry of our time," has to me few redeeming features. Hofmannsthal wears the necromancer's hat and walks the paths of Baghdad. The role does not suit him. He is not good as the Oriental "Teacher." The tale he tells is so contorted that it proves a murky maze even to the thoughtful reader. If the reader does find his way among the bloodless symbols, he discovers that the philosophy is but pseudo-profound and the ethics elementary. As to the language, it is an Arabian-Nights German, mannered, excogitated, stilted. Hofmannsthal first wrote the libretto and then turned it into a long novella. The prose version is better, but not nearly so good as several of his earlier stories.

Like that of *The Magic Flute,* the theme is one of purification by trial. Its central character is the Empress, a being of the spirit world, daughter of a god and an earthly mother. The Empress loves the Emperor, who, hunting one day in the forest, captured her in

---

* *Richard Strauss: A Critical Study of the Operas.*

the shape of a gazelle. She has now lost some of her supernatural powers, and to her horror she learns that unless she acquires a shadow—she does not possess one, being "transparent as glass"—her beloved will turn to stone. The shadow stands as a double symbol: a woman with a shadow is a woman who may bear children, whose womb is fertile; but the shadow also stands for pity, for understanding and tenderness, for the capacity to feel.

When the Empress learns the fate that is to befall the Emperor, she forces her Nurse—a mysterious creature, a Kundry who obviously has visited Dr. Freud once or twice—to take her to the world of men. They penetrate into the house of the poor Dyer, Barak by name (he is the only character in the opera who has a name). They persuade Barak's Wife to sell her shadow, her reward being the delights of the world, wealth, and a handsome young lover. The wife is a cantankerous, carping, strident creature, unfulfilled because she has no children. For two of the three acts she whines away, Strauss setting her lines to music that is ugly and ungrateful. Listening to her, one is inclined to tell Barak, the personification of goodness, "For God's sake, slap the woman!" Barak has three brothers, who are less interesting than Ping, Pang, and Pong in *Turandot,* and who also yap incessantly.

Eventually the Dyer's Wife comes to understand how good a human being Barak is. She realizes that she loves him, has always loved him. Barak in turn reproaches himself for not sufficiently protecting and helping her. Banished to a mysterious dark vault, they grope for each other and cannot find each other. At the final moment, the Empress refuses to accept the shadow from the Dyer's Wife. There is blood on it. Rather be condemned to eternal coldness, rather see her Emperor turn to stone, than to do injustice to one human being. So she too learns wisdom; she too arrives at understanding. And in the triumphant final scene, where Barak and his wife do find each other, she and the Emperor are pardoned. The Empress throws a shadow, which forms a golden bridge across which the two happy couples meet.

The theme of the human being who sells his shadow occurs not only in Scandinavian legend and in Oriental tales but in a famous story by the nineteenth-century German writer, Adelbert von Chamisso, *The Strange Tale of Peter Schlemihl.* Peter sells his shadow as Faust does his soul. But the shadow is only one of the many symbols Hofmannsthal uses. He throws in everything—a magic fountain, a gazelle, a falcon, a mysterious messenger, a supreme Oriental deity, everything including the kitchen stove. On that stove little fishes are frying, the little fishes being the symbols of the unborn children—surely a remarkably tasteless bit of imagery for a poet as tasteful as Hofmannsthal.

The music, as I have said, is an extraordinary mixture of the sublime and the boring, ugly *Sprechgesang* and warm melodies. The orchestral apparatus is larger than that of *Der Rosenkavalier* (107 musicians against 93), the earthly scenes being set to a full orchestra, the scenes in the spirit world to a chamber orchestra. Some of the orchestral interludes are superb, of great thrust and power. But the finest music occurs in Act III, Scene 1, a touching monologue by the Dyer's Wife followed by Barak's soliloquy ("Mir anvertraut"), the two then uniting in a duet ending with Barak's words "If I might see her once again and say to her, 'Do not be afraid!' " Here one hears the Strauss who wrote "Traum durch die Dämmerung."

When the opera was finished, the war was still raging, and both Hofmannsthal and Strauss felt that the conditions then prevailing in the German opera houses did not favor a production of so elaborate a work. Accordingly, they waited two years. By that time Strauss had formed a connection with the Vienna Opera—of that more in the next chapter—and the première was given in Vienna on October 10, 1919, Schalk conducting, scenery designed by Alfred Roller. Once again Strauss was able by great diplomacy to have both Jeritza and Lehmann in the same opera, Jeritza singing the Empress and Lehmann the Dyer's Wife. Mayr was Barak; Oestvig, a handsome Norwegian tenor, the Emperor; and Lucy Weidt the Nurse. In spite of high anticipation and the enormous publicity that preceded the première, the work was not a success. Julius Korngold—a spiteful critic, to be sure—wrote: "*Die Frau ohne Schatten* has her shady side: the libretto."

Because the opera does contain some fine music, because it offers several imposing roles, and because it presents an interesting challenge to scenic designer and stage director, *Die Frau ohne Schatten* is occasionally revived. Once in a while it even scores a success, and not in Germany alone. But such success is transitory, and one comes to the conclusion that the Emperor who almost turns to stone was created by a composer who was beginning to turn to stone.*

* P.S. Since this chapter was written the Metropolitan Opera revived *Die Frau ohne Schatten* as part of its opening season (1966–67) in its new home in Lincoln Center. The production, with its sets by Robert O'Hearn, its direction by Nathaniel Merrill and the sensitive conducting by Karl Böhm, is superb. If anything can aid this curious opera the Metropolitan presentation will do so. Harold C. Schonberg, writing in *The New York Times* October 4, 1966, said: "The second scene of Act II is one of the most poetic and moving things Strauss ever composed, and some of Barak's music ranks with anything in Strauss for intensity and depth. Even with the unfortunate last scene, *Die Frau ohne Schatten* must rank with *Der Rosenkavalier*, *Elektra* and *Salome* as a great opera." Just the same, my opinion remains unchanged. The unevenness of the opera, its many pages of forced inspiration and, worse still, of no inspiration at all, indicate the decline in Strauss's creative powers.

15

The Vienna Opera

How many Parisians have never been inside the Louvre? Many thousands, no doubt. Yet I dare say all of them know that there is in the Louvre a painting called the *Mona Lisa.* How many Viennese have never been inside the Vienna Opera House? Many thousands, no doubt. Yet I dare say that all of them feel the liveliest concern with what is going on within the walls of that ill-proportioned building, which, standing at the very center of the city, serves as a symbol as recognizable as the giant Ferris wheel in the Prater or the Gothic spire of the St. Stephan's Church or the *Heurigen* wine at Grinzing.

Glorious music has been made there. It has nurtured many fine artists. It has introduced new ideas in stagecraft. It was, and is today, a magnet for music lovers of all nations. So the Viennese feel a legitimate pride in *unsere Oper.*

They feel an illegitimate pride as well. To them the opera house represents not only an art institution but a sports arena in which one singer is pitted against another, one conductor against the next gladiator with a baton, one prima ballerina against or with her latest lover. The opera is, as well, a mill grinding out a continuous supply of grain for gossip. That gossip is chewed over from morning to night, beginning with the *Kipfel* and the coffee. The newspapers devote a great deal of space not only to reviewing performances but to speculating on the feuds between singers and to coming changes in the management—changes in management are forever imminent—and to acidulous criticism of repertoire policy. Whatever is played is not right. Why can't we have—? they complain, reciting a long list of unperformed operas. The waiter at Sacher's or the conductor of a streetcar named D—which along with many others passes the opera house at a respectfully slow pace—is an expert on how badly "his" money is being spent in "his" opera house. Practically every Viennese of education has a pet plan as to how things can be improved.

I have called the building ill-proportioned. Its outside is that. Its interior exhales the echoes of applause, the shock waves of past bravos. It does so even in its rebuilt version, which was constructed after the interior had been destroyed during World War II. There is a light to it and a smile to it and a smell to it, a good, traditional smell compounded of perfume, people, greasepaint, rosin, and draughts of night air. Its stage apparatus, the hydraulic platforms, the revolving stage, the dressing rooms, the lighting equipment—all these are exemplary. Yet even the inside of the original building was imperfect, so imperfect indeed that the architect committed suicide after completing it. In the third and the fourth galleries there were large sections from which only a corner of the stage could be seen. The standing room downstairs was (and still is) a suffocating compound into which young people were herded after they had stood in line on the street for hours. It didn't and doesn't matter. Not to the enthusiastic young opera lovers.

There are two other characteristics of the Vienna Opera that are significant. The first is that it seeks great men to lead it, and having obtained them, it promptly begins to dig a hole under the ground on which they stand. Men of high artistic standards are of course uncomfortable to have around. Vienna wants such men, woos them, wins them—and then repudiates them. Gustav Mahler, who endowed the Vienna Opera with performances of fabulous excitement, was chased out of Vienna. Felix Weingartner, though a less uncompromising musician and a less admirable character, was similarly ill-treated. Recently we had before our eyes the example of Karajan. It happens again and again. Paul Stefan, writing the history of the Vienna Opera, said, "Vienna has hounded its best men into bitterness if not worse."*

---

* Paul Stefan, *Die Wiener Oper*.

The second characteristic of Viennese operatic life is this: that it has often been at its best when times were at their worst. Making music has served as an antidote to misery.

How great was the misery at the end of World War I! A dark slush covered body and soul. There was famine lasting for some months even after the war had ceased. My mother used to stand in line to get a loaf of bread for her four children. That loaf was adulterated with wood shavings and had to be soaked overnight in water and then rebaked to make it halfway edible. The only meat available was a low-grade Argentine corned beef, practically inedible. Money became worthless, wiping out the middle class. Teachers, doctors, lawyers, government officials found themselves reduced almost to beggary. A terrible epidemic of grippe swept the city, taking its toll of the undernourished children. Some of the children were sent to families in the neutral countries, Switzerland and Scandinavia, where they could be fed.

Yet with all that, the Vienna Opera functioned, and functioned ambitiously. Franz Schalk, a superb conductor, was appointed director on October 15, 1918, and Strauss was to follow shortly to share the task.

What was it like to go to the opera in those febrile and frazzled days? Let Stefan Zweig tell us:

> I shall never forget any of the opera performances in those days of dire need. One groped through half-lighted streets; illumination had to be limited because of lack of coal. One paid for a ticket in the gallery with a roll of bank notes which in former years would have been sufficient to buy a season's subscription in a deluxe loge. One sat in one's overcoat because the hall was not heated and one huddled against one's neighbor in order to get warm. How sad, how gray was the hall which once shone with uniforms and costly outfits! No one knew whether it would be possible to continue the opera the following week, if the devaluation of the money were to roll on or the delivery of coal were to stop even for one week. The despair seemed twice as great in this house of luxury and royal splendor. The men of the Philharmonic sat at their desks, they too gray shadows, in their old threadbare full-dress suits, emaciated and exhausted by their deprivations, like ghosts in a house which in itself had become ghostly. But then the conductor raised his baton, the curtain parted, and it was as glorious as ever before. Every

> singer, every musician gave his all; for all felt that perhaps this was the last time in the house they loved. And we heard and listened, receptive as never before, because perhaps it was the last time. Thus did we all live, we thousands and hundred thousands; every one of us summoned all his strength in those weeks and months and years, a hairsbreadth removed from the abyss. I have never felt in a people or in myself as strongly as I did then the will to live — then when it was a question of sheer holding on.*

History repeated itself after World War II. There was no opera house then, and the performances took place in the small Theater an der Wien, the old theater near the market where *Fidelio* had first been performed. Once again Vienna was desolate, a city split into zones administered by the Americans, the Russians, the British, and the French. Once again it was a center of lawlessness, smuggling, and East-West intrigue. But the performances at the Theater an der Wien were great performances, inspired by conductors such as Herbert von Karajan, Josef Krips, and Karl Böhm, with a group of singers who worked together with unparalleled enthusiasm and spirit, who took fire from one another. George London told me that never since has he worked under such inspiring conditions.†

And then—then, around 1950, as things began to get better, as Vienna rose from the doldrums, as industry restarted and tourism flourished—the bickering and baiting began once again. The school for scandal was once more in session. Vienna seems to need what the Viennese call a *Hetz'*, a mud-slinging chase. Today Vienna is extraordinarily prosperous. And the Opera? The Opera is a mediocre institution, unimportant as a creative force though praised by

---

* *Die Welt von Gestern.*

† George London writes: "A classic example of Viennese ingratitude and intrigue concerns Josef Krips, the conductor, and Egon Hilbert, who directed the Austrian state theaters in the postwar period. Krips was the General Music Director of the Opera who, from nothing in 1945, built the famous Mozart Ensemble of the Vienna Opera and was its guiding artistic spirit for almost a decade thereafter. Hilbert, defying the authorities, started playing opera in the Theater an der Wien practically from the moment the last shot was fired in 1945. In time Krips's situation was made untenable by various and persistent intrigues, and Hilbert was hounded out of office by a reactionary and jealous Minister of Culture. In 1955, at the ceremonies celebrating the rebuilt opera house on the Ring, neither Krips nor Hilbert was present. They had not been invited."

tourists who are seduced into liking performances by the very fact that they are on a holiday. Once in a while the house delivers a fine performance, but most of the time it puts before uncritical audiences performances that go on without rehearsals and are scraped together from an international cast of singers who arrive at the last possible moment and leave at the earliest possible moment.

Why should Strauss have wanted to shoulder that pack of executive troubles and picayune annoyances which the director of an opera house must carry? And at a moment when conditions were inauspicious? It was a challenge. It was the old restlessness. It was the marshal instinct, so strong in him.

Before the war's end, in the summer of 1918, Strauss conducted a week of his own works, *Elektra, Der Rosenkavalier,* and *Ariadne,* at the Vienna Opera. His personal success was great. In addition, *Salome* had finally been declared safe enough to shed her seven veils in the house on the Ringstrasse. Observing all this, the intendant of the opera, Leopold Andrian, conceived the idea of inviting Strauss to share the administration with Schalk. When Hofmannsthal heard of the plan, he was amazed and worried. He dashed off a long, perturbed letter to his partner. Yes, he wrote, fifteen years ago Strauss would have been "the ideal person to bring about the urgently needed renaissance of the Vienna Opera, but I don't believe you are that today." Today Strauss would be hampered "by your own personal convenience and the egotism of the creative musician." He said with remarkable candor: "I believe, when it came to engaging artists, making enemies, friends, etc., in short in handling the policy of the theater, the advantage to your own works would be uppermost in your mind and not the advantage to the institution."*

Strauss took such frankness placidly. He brought forth all sorts of counterarguments—that it had been his dream for thirty years to assume the "de facto supreme direction of a big Court Opera House," that he composed only in the summer, that he knew he was capable of reorganizing the institution, that he could by conducting and restaging not only infuse new vitality into perform-

* Letter of August 1, 1918.

ances of Mozart and Wagner, Gluck and Weber, but also support what new works seemed worthy to him, and that his wife loved Vienna and wanted to go there "à tout prix"—all of which demonstrated that he had quite made up his mind.

Overtures were made to Strauss from the Berlin Opera as well, Berlin wishing to retain him in some capacity. Strauss put forth in all earnestness the suggestion that he become the head of *both* opera houses! Even he saw after a while that such a plan would not be quite feasible. So he finally decided on Vienna.

Negotiations were kept secret. When the contract had been signed, Strauss issued a preliminary program in which he called for a "thoroughgoing reform of the opera house, now or never," a new look at all departments, and a pensioning off or simply getting rid of the superannuated singers. And that "radically"! As to the repertoire: "It is not necessary to give *Traviata, Masked Ball, Mignon, Faust* every week. That's why I am coming to Vienna, to make a new modest try at a repertoire which is lofty and German."* The singers' fees were too high, with the exception of Slezak and Kurz. Indispensable were Jeritza, Lehmann, Gutheil-Schoder, Weidt, Kiurina, Oestvig, Mayr, Duhan, Schipper, Schmedes, and Tauber—all others unimportant. Away with them, if need be.

So intransigent a plan, so strongly stated, could not have endeared the new director to the conservative and sentimental Viennese. What was this Bavarian panjandrum planning for *unsere Oper?*

When the appointment was announced, the reaction of part of the press, part of the public, and virtually all of the personnel of the opera house was as violent as if it had been decided that Frank Lloyd Wright were to rebuild St. Stephan's steeple. The pro and contra factions threatened to become as bitter against each other as the Guelphs and the Ghibellines. In a Vienna "a hairsbreadth removed from the abyss," no question seemed more burning than whether it was right to have Strauss. In short, it was a Viennese *Hetz'*. It culminated in a revolt by the personnel of the opera house. A resolution was drawn up and signed by practically all the singers, musicians, ballet members, and technical staff, which peti-

* Letter to Franz Schalk, December 18, 1918.

tioned management as well as Schalk, who acted as provisionary manager, to declare the contract void. Only Jeritza and Kurz refused to sign the petition. Schalk, by virtue of his position, kept aloof from the turmoil, but finally came out for Strauss, declaring publicly that he was convinced that anybody who had but the faintest connection with the musical life and death of Vienna must be for Strauss.

Why such heat, why the battle, what were the arguments against Strauss's appointment? First, that Strauss was a composer and had neither the experience nor the qualifications necessary to head an opera house. Second, that it would be impossible with his international fame to make him sit still long enough in Vienna. Third, that he would favor his own works—he was bound to. Fourth, that his salary of 80,000 kronen was too high. (It soon was apparent that this stipend, high as it was, actually represented a financial sacrifice for Strauss, because he could earn more free-lancing as a conductor. At any rate, with the inflation continuing, any amount of kronen became meaningless.) Fifth, it was rumored that Strauss planned a series of concerts with the Vienna Philharmonic to be given in the opera house. But the Vienna Philharmonic had an agreement with Weingartner for a number of concerts; Strauss's plan would interfere, the more so as there was no love lost between Weingartner and Strauss. Sixth, any double administration was dubious. What was wrong with Schalk alone? Such were the arguments—but they all came down to a fear that Strauss would sweep with too stiff a broom, and that some members were going to lose their jobs.

As soon as the contra-Strauss group had had its say, the adherents raised their voices. Among them were some of the foremost intellectuals of the city, who sent an open telegram to Strauss. The telegram was signed by such men and women as Julius Bittner, Alma Mahler, Dr. Halban (Vienna's leading obstetrician and Selma Kurz's husband), Hofmannsthal, Felix Salten, Arthur Schnitzler, Sil Vara, the critic Richard Specht, Georg Szell, Jakob Wassermann, and Stefan Zweig.

This was followed by a decided swing in sentiment on the part of an important and vociferous element of the opera public, the habitués of the standing room downstairs, as well as the claque, who operated mostly in the third and fourth galleries. At a performance of *Parsifal,* as the house darkened and the conductor, Leopold Reichwein, raised his baton, an organized "spontaneous" demonstration took place: the standees on the orchestra floor shouted "Strauss," and these calls were echoed by the galleries, for some minutes preventing the performance from beginning. Richard Specht gave a public lecture in which, with much heat and passion, he castigated the personnel of the opera house. Soon the Opera Committee met again and decided to withdraw their official objection to Strauss.

The one who acted sensibly was Strauss himself. He stayed away from Vienna, he refused interviews, he issued no statements. Only when it was all over and the contract had been newly ratified did he reassert his willingness to come and "earn the confidence of my dear friends." He was quite willing to withdraw the planned première of *Die Frau ohne Schatten* if the slightest suspicion was abroad that he was using his appointment as a means to further his own works. In making such an offer, he was of course quite safe, as he knew very well that the première of a new Strauss opera was a desirable plum for any opera house to pluck.

In the fall of 1919, then, he began his co-directorship. He held the post for five years. He threw himself into the regenerative work with his utmost energy. The very first season he himself conducted restudied performances of *Fidelio, Tristan,* and *Die Zauberflöte,* in addition to his own *Ariadne* and *Rosenkavalier.* The performances were superb—I heard many of them.

He accomplished remarkable things, such as a new staging of *Lohengrin,* conceived musically as a lyrical work, free of the usual Wagnerian barking; a new Ring cycle; *Der Freischütz* with Lotte Lehmann as Agathe, Elisabeth Schumann as Ännchen, and Michael Bohnen as Kaspar. *Carmen,* which as a repertoire piece had become lax and *schlampig,* he restudied from the ground up, teaching the part to Jeritza, with Lehmann as Micaëla. For his favorite *Così fan tutte* he acted as both conductor and stage director. He and Schalk inaugurated (in 1920) the first of the Vienna Festival Weeks. To *Don Giovanni* he restored the final Sextet and presented Alfred Jerger in the title role. Jerger was a superb actor, though not a mellifluous singer. Strauss's opinion of him was "Forget about *bel canto* and watch him get inside a role." The charming little Redoutensaal was opened for such works as *Figaro, Così,* and *The Barber of Seville.* One of his greatest performances was a *Tannhäuser* with Leo Slezak, Lotte Lehmann, and Gertrud Kapell.

The community of Vienna expressed its gratitude by awarding Strauss a somewhat qualified gift. Near the beautiful baroque palace of the Belvedere there lies the small and peaceful Jacquingasse. A plot of ground there, formerly a part of the Botanical Gardens, was loaned to Strauss for a period of several decades with the understanding that a house was to be built according to his own plans and wishes. This "little castle" was to harmonize in style with the surroundings. The house was completed in 1924, and Strauss lived there with his family off and on for many years. It was furnished with antique furniture, with an excellent Gobelin tapestry, a grand piano, and indeed all the comfort a prince could want. The furniture as well as the house itself was supplied by the community, in return for which Strauss agreed to a certain number of additional conducting engagements with the Vienna orchestra. He presented the community with the manuscript of *Der Rosenkavalier;* it is now in the Austrian National Library.

Yet in spite of all Strauss's accomplishments, Vienna was not satisfied. Soon enough discord and doubt began to be raised. The newspapers spoke of "the glorious era of Gustav Mahler." The initial accusation—that Strauss was using the Vienna Opera for the promotion of his own works—was heard again. Looking at the statistics of the five years of his tenure and particularly at the works he himself conducted, one might conclude that there was some substance to the rebuke. Perhaps if Strauss had not been there, the *Josephslegende* would not have been given nineteen times in five years, *Feuersnot* seven times (in one season), and *Die Frau* twelve times. On the other hand, *Der Rosenkavalier* (thirteen performances), *Salome* (sixteen), and *Ariadne* (thirteen) enjoyed no more performances under Strauss than they would have normally had without him. It was perfectly natural that his own works be emphasized under his own baton. However, his new works did not fare well. It was said that the Viennese would much prefer a *Frau mit Schaten* (firewood). As to *Josephslegende,* the quotation from the Bible "And the Lord was with Joseph" was supplemented by "But he definitely was not with the *Josephslegende.*"

The Viennese complained that he was frequently absent. He and Schalk took the Vienna Philharmonic and part of the Opera ensemble to South America from August to November, 1920. Again, in 1923, he journeyed, though without Schalk, to that continent. He raised a good deal of money for the Vienna Opera—but the Viennese didn't like the hiatus.

Independently Strauss kept up his guest conducting, in Berlin, Budapest, Bucharest, and, in an extended tour, his second and last, in the United States. (Of this a few words later on.)

The Vienna public felt aggrieved. Strauss did not belong to them completely.

The double direction did not work. A double direction hardly ever does. Schalk was a dour and pessimistic man. Strauss said that his favorite motto was "It cannot be done." Schalk claimed that he had a budget to meet to which Strauss did not pay the least attention. Confronted with the figures, which showed huge losses, Strauss replied, "I am here to lose money."

Schalk, I believe, did not personally like Strauss and may have been jealous of him as a conductor. He took every opportunity to point out that it was impossible for him to discharge his duties if another man could make decisions about the repertoire. The organizational responsibilities were not sharply enough defined. What happens in business organizations can also happen in artistic institutions. In either case the result is confusion.

Relations between the two men steadily worsened*; things

---

* On February 4, 1924, before the conflict came to a head, Strauss wrote Schalk a conciliatory letter, a sort of last appeal, in which he addressed him as "Dear and honored friend" and in which he pointed out that without the necessary funds Strauss's function had become a meaningless farce, that for four long years he had tried to preserve the high standards that Schalk had helped to attain, that now he hears that everybody is dissatisfied, that there is talk of "bankruptcy of the *Staatsoper* (was it ever solvent?)," that Strauss is being censured for taking a holiday in mid-season, etc.

He intends to make one further try at arriving at an understanding with the government officials. But he has only slight hope. He warns Schalk that a diminution of funds—which he hears has already been decided—may harm Schalk's work and quotes *Fidelio* at him: "Be on your guard and seek your own safety; mount to the top of the tower, take a trumpeter with you!"

Strauss concludes: "Even if I become the ex-director I'll remain in Vienna: you and I can then play piano four hands or play chess. Poor *Oper!* It is really sad."

The letter is not inimical, just disillusioned. (The original is in the Austrian National Library.)

finally got so bad that Schalk and Strauss no longer spoke to each other but communicated the necessary instructions through a third person, the chief stage manager, Josef Turnau. Strauss finally put it as a condition that if he were to continue to work in Vienna, Schalk would have to resign as co-director, though he would be welcome to stay on as conductor. Andrian, the intendant, did not comply with this demand. Strauss, who happened to be in Dresden for the first performance of *Intermezzo,* learned there that Schalk's contract was going to be renewed. Strauss sent in his resignation.

The rupture excited all of Vienna. The debate raged in the press. One enterprising newspaper organized a plebiscite, and for three weeks collected votes, signatures, and opinions from citizens. Strauss behaved himself with his usual aloof composure. After his resignation he gave an interview in which he reviewed the achievements of his directorship and concluded that he was neither "angry nor bitter, and that I will forever remember with pleasure the hours I have devoted to the Vienna Opera."*

Such was his official statement. Yet the blow to his pride must have been a galling one. When he took leave of Andrian, he looked at him coldly and said, "Richard must go, the Minister stays," referring to Wagner's troubles in Munich. (Hugo Burghauser, who was a member of the orchestra, overheard this and told me the story.)

The letter he wrote Hofmannsthal imparting the news no longer exists, but Hofmannsthal's reply does. It is to Hofmannsthal's credit that he did not say "I told you so." He wrote Strauss that he understood the reason for his resigning. He urged on him, however, the desirability of maintaining reasonably good relations with Vienna. There was, to be sure, no danger that their works would be thrown out of the repertoire. But there was a wide cleavage between "throwing them out" and "lovingly keeping them alive." Looking at the situation practically and coldly, he said, the advantages that the house in Vienna offered—such as the scenery by Roller, the stage equipment, and the orchestra itself—made it seem desirable not to break with Vienna irrevocably.† (It sounds a bit as if the poet was looking out for his own income.)

---

* *Neues Wiener Journal,* November 14, 1924.

† Letter of November 29, 1924.

Heeding Hofmannsthal, Strauss avoided an open break. But it was a full two years before Strauss forgave Vienna. He returned then—that is, in December, 1926—to conduct *Elektra* and to be feted and applauded to the echo. He did retain the house in the Jacquingasse, and it was in Vienna that the marriage of his son Franz was celebrated (January 15, 1924).* He married the daughter of a well-to-do Jewish merchant, Alice Grab. She was a blond, pretty, and highly intelligent girl, and over the years Strauss became very fond of her. She was one of the few he really loved. (She is still married to Franz, and now acts as the hostess of the Strauss villa in Garmisch.)

No doubt she contributed to Strauss's losing the anti-Semitic prejudice instilled in him by his father, and by Ritter and Bülow. But in truth he had lost most of this prejudice with maturing age; several of the men who served him and with whom he had formed business or artistic connections were Jewish. For example, Willy Levin, the banker and art collector who looked after his financial interests; the Fürstner family, his publishers; Selma Kurz; Max Reinhardt; Otto Kahn. Once in a while in his old age the stupid racial bias broke through, but only briefly. Elisabeth Schumann,† who made an American concert tour with him and his son, noted in a diary she kept that actually Strauss seemed unprejudiced and tolerant.

Indeed, Schumann reminisced about him with much affection. She found him attractive as a man. Perhaps just because he was working so hard, he was gay and in constant good humor. He felt triumphant because he had smuggled cigarettes into the United States. While traveling, he could not get a skat party together, but he managed to have constant poker games lasting until the early hours of the morning. He told Schumann, "I am a tolerable composer, a pretty good theater director, but an excellent tour organizer." He mislaid the notes for one of his songs she was to sing, but reassured her that he knew the accompaniment by heart. He then proceeded to make a mess of it.

In addition to accompanying Schumann, he conducted the New

---

* For the wedding Strauss composed a charming little "Marriage Preludium" for two harmoniums.

† She was married to Karl Alwin, the conductor. He too was a Jew.

York Philharmonic and the Philadelphia orchestras. Strauss was properly appreciative of the two superb orchestras. Richard Aldrich, writing in *The New York Times,* said: "And when each piece was finished anybody could see that Dr. Strauss's first demonstration was one of cordial and eager approval to the orchestra in front of him. He clapped and nodded and smiled almost humanly at its members—and not till then did he turn with punctilious formality and perfectly clicked heels to bow impassively, inexpressively and just deeply enough to the public."

The final concert was given in the Hippodrome in New York (a building hardly suitable to music but one accommodating a huge audience) on New Year's Eve, 1921. Aldrich reported: "Dr. Strauss ended his visit to the United States a week ago last night to the enthusiastic manifestations of a crowded Hippodrome. It has been from his point of view, as well as from others, highly successful. He is supposed to be taking home with him $50,000 of his own, which makes a magnificent sum when translated into German marks and a much more magnificent one when translated into Austrian kroners. (*sic*)

"He also hopes to take back with him $500 for the musicians of Central Europe still suffering from the effects of the war. This he has collected from musicians of the orchestras here and elsewhere that have played under his direction."

Only $500? Was Aldrich being sarcastic when he continued: "All will commend the eminent composer's disinterested thoughtfulness in raising this sum . . . "?*

* Richard Aldrich, *Concert Life in New York, 1902-23,* review of January 8, 1922.

16

Intermezzo, Helena, Arabella, and the Death of Hofmannsthal

Whether Strauss accepted the Herculean labor of the Viennese stable because he felt in himself a postwar creative weakness—if he did, this feeling was a subconscious one—or whether the chapter was merely coincidental, is difficult to say. How much should one ascribe to accident in the life of a talent? Whatever the reason, he did not compose much while he was enclaved at the *Oper*, the only major work, if major it is, of this period being a two-act comedy, *Intermezzo.*

After the heavy load of *Die Frau ohne Schatten,* Strauss searched for something light, diverting and simple. He had once or twice expressed to Hofmannsthal his wish to "become the Offenbach of the twentieth century." He remembered an incident in his life, long ago, which had caused him no end of domestic embarrassment. In 1903 an Italian opera company was giving a season in Berlin. The conductors were Josef Stransky and Arturo Vigna. One evening Stransky and the company's leading tenor, de Marchi, and the impresario Edgar Strakosch were having a drink at the Hotel Bristol. They were conversing in Italian, when Marchi and Strakosch were approached by the kind of young girl who approaches artists in a public place. She had heard the Italian conversation, guessed that they were members of an opera group, and forthwith asked for a free ticket. Marchi told her to address her request to the conductor Stransky, whose name he consistently mispronounced as *Straussky.* Stransky or Straussky joshed the girl and carried on a flirtation with her, but promptly forgot the incident. The girl, who was nothing if not enterprising, looked up the name of Straussky in the telephone directory, found a listing under Hofkapellmeister Richard Strauss, and sent him a note: "Dear Sweetheart: Do bring me the ticket. Your faithful Mitzi. My address: Mitzi Mücke, Lüneburger Strasse, 5." This letter arrived while Strauss was absent from home. Pauline opened it—Pauline would—gave her husband no benefit of doubt, immediately assumed flagrant infidelity, and consulted a lawyer with a view to getting a divorce. Strauss was completely baffled when, on returning home, he faced Pauline's accusations, which no doubt were uttered in a stentorian fortissimo. After painful days, a friend of Strauss's, Friedrich Rösch, managed to get at the truth and, what was more difficult, to convince Pauline that her husband had been a victim of mistaken identity.

This incident he proposed to Hofmannsthal for a possible comic opera. Hofmannsthal was not interested. The poet suggested that the playwright Hermann Bahr, who was a great admirer of Strauss's, and whose comedy *The Concert* was a favorite of the composer's, might like to develop the subject. Bahr consented and drafted a sketch. Strauss was not entirely happy with it; neither was Bahr. He agreed to try again. He asked Strauss to jot down his ideas for suitable scenes. Strauss did so, to Bahr's wholehearted approval. Indeed, he advised Strauss to proceed on his own: this libretto, which needed simple diction and was so entirely Strauss's idea, required no collaborator. The composer accepted this suggestion, and during a week's stay at a sanatorium he wrote the entire play. Strauss paralleled the marital misunderstanding with another autobiographical incident. His wife had once met a shy young man who later turned out to be a bit of a confidence trickster and attempted to borrow money from Pauline (needless to say, unsuccessfully).

What Strauss was striving for was the expression of the everyday in operatic terms, a prose dialogue that was now spoken, now sung, while the music pirouetted around the words with the lightest steps. The style bears a certain affinity to that of the *Ariadne* Prologue.

When he had completed the little opera—because of his commitments the composition took the better part of five years—

Strauss wrote a learned foreword to it in which he explained his purpose and traced *Intermezzo* back to the old German *Singspiel.*

But there is nothing pedantic about this *opera domestica.* One may question its taste, for Strauss pictured himself—he is now Kapellmeister Robert Storch and his wife is Christine—as an altogether exemplary fellow, of a nature so sweet and kind as to call forth a sighing protest from Christine: "That eternal good disposition!" Christine is the main character, by turns a termagant (in the first scene, where she complains about her life, rails against the fate of being the wife of a famous man, and bemoans the fact that he is always at home when "normal" men go to the office); a woman susceptible to flattery (the flattery being laid on by the dubious young man she meets, Baron Lummer); a carping *maîtresse de maison,* for whom the house is never clean enough and who cannot keep servants; a teary mother; a woman scorned that Hell hath no fury like; a loving wife who refuses to show her love; and in the final scene of reconciliation the companion who melts into the arms of the returned Herr Kapellmeister and murmurs, "Ours is a happy marriage!" She has as many moods as has the Hero's companion in *Ein Heldenleben.*

Though we need not take this "harmless little slice of life," as Strauss himself called it, seriously, it does serve to illustrate the curious attachment Strauss felt for his wife, an attachment that went beyond that of "a happy marriage." He saw her clearly. He makes fun of her. In the first scene, among all the complaints she sounds against him, he includes her saying that she comes from a better family than he does. In the scene where Storch plays skat with his friends, the friends talk about her in the most unflattering terms (Strauss here pictured some of his card-playing cronies), calling her "a horror, simply dreadful!"* How did Pauline like that?

All the same, he was enthralled by her and, as I have suggested earlier, did indeed enjoy his thralldom. "One could make ten plays out of my wife," he wrote to Hermann Bahr. Like Hofmannsthal, but on a much earthier plane, Strauss was absorbed by the problem of fidelity. *Ariadne, Die Frau ohne Schatten,* the *Egyptian Helena,*

* The skat party is a famous scene and has been called "true to life." Only non-cardplayers would call it that, for real cardplayers know that gossip about women would be impossible during a serious card game.

and *Arabella* all revolve around the theme of fidelity. So does *Intermezzo.*

Strauss's autobiographical opera is faintly embarrassing if we overemphasize its autobiographical content. If we can remove ourselves a sufficient distance—time may do this for us—we see that it is amusing and witty. It is also often beautiful, its charm being chiefly contained in the orchestral interludes that separate the short scenes. They are tiny tone poems. When the Herr Kapellmeister leaves, the orchestra describes his *Reisefieber* (an expressive German word meaning the nervousness one feels prior to a voyage). When Christine meets the Baron, they go dancing to a good waltz and a Bavarian *Ländler.* There is a *Träumerei* at the hearth, and a stormy interlude while the desperate Storch is pacing back and forth in the Prater. The last scene ends in a quiet close in Strauss's best vein. It glows a little like the end of *Der Rosenkavalier,* but in a weaker color.

Intermezzo is certainly no masterpiece and lies several steps down from the level of *Ariadne.* Still, given the right tempo—Strauss wanted it played as if the whole thing were "shot from a pistol" and he obviously tried to set the conversation in such a way that every word would be understood, exhorting the singers to be "good actors, to sing at half voice, and to pronounce clearly"—and given a cast of good-looking singing actors, the opera plays well and is a stimulating evening in the theater. Reinhardt considered it so, and said that it could be acted as a spoken play. Quite a compliment!

Strauss completed the composition while he was in Buenos Aires in 1923. Vienna would have been the logical place in which to produce it, but because of his strained relations with the Opera management, Strauss turned once again to Dresden. Fritz Busch, now in command, was a guarantee that *Intermezzo* would be given a fine performance; under his direction the standards of Dresden had again become as high as in the days of Schuch. The première took place November 4, 1924. Busch was perceptive enough to engage Lotte Lehmann for the part of Christine, and she managed to endow the role with more sympathy than it inherently possesses.

Only one other work of the Vienna period needs to be mentioned. This is a ballet entitled *Schlagobers.* No prosperous Viennese would drink his afternoon coffee in pre-dieting days without

Schlagobers, whipped cream. Even today it is ladled out in big gobs at Demel's at *Jause* time. Strauss wrote his own scenario for the ballet. The music seems concocted with ersatz whipped cream; with the exception of an attractive Nocturne (the Dance of Prince Coffee), it is difficult to believe that Strauss could have squeezed out a score so saccharine.

Once Strauss had run through the first excitement of being an opera director, once he sensed which way the Vienna wind was blowing, he turned again to Hofmannsthal. From aboard ship, on the way home from Buenos Aires, he wrote him that he would soon be back and "without work." Quoting *Parsifal,* he exhorted Hofmannsthal: "*Auf Kundry—ans Werk!*"

Poor Kundry! Poor poet! He was passing through a bad period, adding to general misery his own special one. "To work here," he wrote to Strauss in 1919, "in rooms which are hardly heated, with the stoppage of gas and the almost complete stoppage of electricity, is as good as impossible."* More than a year later: "I am almost unable even to read and suffer a constant nervous depression. The slightest change of weather, a short letter such as this one, a short conversation—everything strains me unbelievably. . . . Now in March I must take care of myself especially, March being my critical month. I fell ill in March 1917, 18, and 19, and I shall certainly die in March as my mother did."† (He didn't; he died in the month of July.)

Even two years later, when times had improved, Hofmannsthal had not. "Our relationship, which at one time was so special and meaningful, is now a more difficult one. . . . We live nowadays like little people whose goal can only be just to exist halfway *decently and cleanly.*"‡

As late as the beginning of 1923, he was still an author in search of a character. "Isn't it curious that formerly I could find a suitable subject so easily? Today it is much more difficult. Were you to espy me late at night through my window, you would see me assiduous

* Letter of January 4, 1919.
† Letter of March 10, 1920.
‡ Letter to Strauss, April 15, 1922.

and willing, leafing through Lucian, reading old stories by Stendhal and Musset, perusing Scribe's librettos!"*

The idea of writing "mythological operas, the truest kind that exist," and specifically the idea of an opera on the ever-fresh Helen theme, lay in Hofmannsthal's mind for some time, though it was not until April, 1923, that he proposed *Die Ägyptische Helena.* As was his wont, he dipped into other sources for his inspiration. He turned to Herodotus, who was the first to twist Homer's tale into an interpretation of his own, which was that Helen never reached Troy but landed with Paris in Egypt. There King Proteus forced Paris to journey alone toward Troy while he held Helen captive to take her back to her rightful husband after the end of the Trojan War. A phantom substituted for her. The Sicilian poet Tisias took the opposite view, and, according to legend, he was punished by the gods with blindness for having defamed Helen's character. He then accommodatingly wrote a version similar to Herodotus'. Euripides as well, in *Helen,* let the heroine exist peacefully in Egypt.

Hofmannsthal's version attempts to weave into the story psychological motives dealing in modern terms with problems of marriage. After the fall of Troy, Menelaus brings Helen back. On the ship he determines to kill her. She must die, and die by his own hand, as a sacrifice to the unnumbered dead who fell in the war. The nymph Aithra, daughter of an Egyptian king and necromancer, and no mean magician herself, observes Menelaus about to carry out the deed. She causes a storm to spring up, the ship is wrecked, Menelaus saves Helen from the flood, and both are spirited to Aithra's palace. Here Menelaus draws the very sword with which he killed Paris. Through the working of Aithra's magic he becomes confused and believes that Paris, still alive, is outside the palace. He rushes away, and the two women, Aithra and Helen—she beautiful and self-confident as ever—are left alone. Aithra gives her a potion, which will bring peace and forgetfulness. Helen falls asleep. On Menelaus' return Aithra tells him that the true Helen has all this time remained safe, inviolate and unaged, in the palace and the Helen he and all the Greeks knew was a phantom. To him also she

* Letter to Strauss, February 4, 1923.

gives a pacifying draught. He goes to Helen—for a second bridal night.

The magic has worked but imperfectly. Helen has won back a doubting and uncertain husband. He no longer knows which is the real person, which the phantom.

A resplendent desert Sheik appears, followed by his retinue and his young son. Both father and son fall passionately in love with Helen. History threatens to repeat itself. They plan to carry Helen off. Menelaus must again avenge his honor. He kills Da'ud, the Sheik's son.

Helen, with great courage, determines to release Menelaus from his trance. She tells him the truth. Once again he raises his sword. Once again he lets it fall. He cannot kill her. He cannot leave her. Nothing can separate him from Helen, unfaithful or not, for man and wife are one. Helen's daughter, Hermione, is summoned by Aithra. Menelaus, gazing at his wife, speaks to the child. "See, child," he says, "what a mother I bring you."

This is the best I can do in giving the main lines of a libretto the meaning of which is so obfuscated that only its author could explain it, and perhaps not even he. Obscurantism abounds. The magical-psychological potions brewed by Isolde's mother have become so numerous that Aithra seems a walking apothecary and the frequent ministering of draughts for forgetting and remembering borders on the ludicrous. None of the characters has any substance, none trenchant traits, Menelaus in particular being a fractious creation. Theatrically the work is long and ineffective. There is an "All-knowing Sea Shell" (contralto) who reports to Aithra like a radio loudspeaker. There are three Elves, for no particularly good reason. It is perhaps unnecessary to add that Hofmannsthal thought, "I believe and hope that considered as a work for music, as an opera, it is the best thing I have created." *

But Strauss's part of the work is equally weak. He did manage to inject a little luscious sex into the score, particularly in Helena's aria as she awakes from her second wedding night ("Zweite Brautnacht"). But during most of the opera the Straussian formulas are repeated, and often Strauss wears the Wagnerian breastplate.

* Letter to Strauss, February 14, 1924.

What melodies there are are facile. When Strauss played the score for Fritz Busch and asked him for his frank opinion, Busch volunteered that he thought Da'ud's song " a cheap invention." Strauss replied, "That is required for the servant girls. Believe me, my dear Busch, people would not go to *Tannhäuser* if the 'Evening Star' were not in it. Or to the *Walküre* without the *Winterstürme*."* This is so cynical a remark that we ought to doubt Strauss ever made it, did we not know Busch as a truthful man. Neither the remark nor the correspondence with Hofmannsthal shows any great conviction on the part of the composer.

However, when the *Egyptian Helena* failed at the first performance, Strauss tried twice to revise it (after Hofmannsthal's death). There exist three versions of this feeble fable: the original one, a Viennese version given in Salzburg in 1933 and a 1940 Munich version, prepared with the help of Rudolf Hartmann and Clemens Krauss.

The première, which Fritz Busch conducted in Dresden (June 6, 1928)—Strauss had promised it to Busch in gratitude for what Busch had done for *Intermezzo*—had Elisabeth Rethberg in the title role, though from the very first both authors had conceived the part for Jeritza. When it came down to it, Jeritza, who by this time had made a spectacular success at the Metropolitan as Tosca and in other roles as well, asked for a fee that Dresden thought exorbitant. So did Strauss. Remembering Rethberg's magnificent singing in a Dresden performance of *Die Frau ohne Schatten*, he suggested her. Hofmannsthal was furious: he thought Rethberg too amply proportioned and unglamorous. He was somewhat mollified when, five days after the Dresden première, Vienna gave the opera with Jeritza, Strauss conducting. Speaking of fees, it was reported that Strauss sold the rights to the opera to his publisher outright for $50,000, the highest fee ever paid for an opera.

The Metropolitan produced *Die Ägyptische Helena* in November of the same year. I remember the preliminary excitement surrounding this event—the Metropolitan had raised the prices of orchestra seats to what was then a new high: I think it was eleven dollars—and though I could ill afford it, I bought two tickets. I

---

* Fritz Busch, *Aus dem Leben eines Musikers.*

remember that Jeritza was magnificent, as near to the realization of famed Helen as a mortal actress could be. I remember too the letdown as the opera progressed, the audience being totally apathetic.

Though I have no wish to kick a dead opera, I do want to quote portions of Lawrence Gilman's review in the New York *Herald Tribune*, if only to show what felicitous, well-turned musical criticism can be like and to regret that such writing can no longer be read with our morning coffee:

> It would, alas, have needed more puissant creative wills than those of Hugo von Hofmannsthal and the aging Richard Strauss to provide our lyric theater with an adequate operatic setting of any phase of the Helen legend which would set that immortal wanton sustainedly before us. Even the lucent Jeritza might well have despaired of evoking for us more than Helen's silent image when she saw what Strauss and his librettist had contrived for her. The Helen of incomparable tradition worshipped in such poetry as that which clad her fairness in the beauty of a thousand stars and spread her loveliness upon the evening air, would scarcely consider herself fitly honored by anything that von Hofmannsthal invites her to say or Strauss to sing. For the quality that one vainly seeks in the text and music of this opera is that note of high and magical beauty which should sweep through its irony and its melodrama and its fantasy like a horn call on the wind, and take us by the throat. . . .
>
> There is almost everything here that is requisite—everything but distinguished and pregnant music. . . .
>
> These swelling, full-throated melodies that sweep with so grandiose a rhetoric from the lips of his singers are poor and platitudinous music, suggesting models not always of the worthiest. One of the principal themes is but a variant of the song of the Hindoo Merchant from Rimsky-Korsakoff's "Sadko." These sumptuous harmonies, that richly fibered counterpoint woven by Strauss's glowing orchestra, have neither salience nor life. Hollow and unkindled, they depress us by the emptiness of their rhetoric, the triteness of their musical speech. The power and pungency of the greater Strauss of former days are missing from this splendidly vacuous score. At best he can only borrow from himself, at worst he can but remember his inferiors. . . .*

* Review of November 7, 1928.

The whole Helena project reminds me of two aging German professors who long to escape to sunlit Grecian fields but can get no farther than the Hotel Adlon in Berlin. The entire opera is a less youthful tribute to Helen than a few paragraphs by Nikos Kazantzakis (in *Report to Greco*), who summons her "oft-kissed farroving body."

But for their next project, Hofmannsthal and Strauss seemed to borrow new youth. Each of them dipped into existing and remembered material, Hofmannsthal for the story, Strauss for the musical style. If their product, *Arabella,* is not a great opera, if indeed it shows some irritating weaknesses, it is at least an opera to which one can frequently listen with pleasure and which in isolated scenes and one extended portion—the last half of the third act—shows that Strauss could still compose like the genius of romanticism he once had been. The Viennese epigram that *Arabella* is the *Sklerosenkavalier* (The Sclerosis Cavalier) is not altogether just, though the similarities to the greater work are patent.

Strauss wanted Hofmannsthal to give him another *Rosenkavalier.* Even when he was considering *Helena* he told him: "Most of all I would like a second *Rosenkavalier* without its mistakes and lengths! *You must write this for me still!* I have not yet said my last word in this vein."*

In due course Hofmannsthal bethought himself of a novella he had written in 1910 called *Lucidor—Characters for an Unwritten Comedy.* It is a charming little work, poetic and humorous, dealing with two young girls, Arabella and Lucile (Zdenka in the opera). The mother, an eccentric lady, chooses to present Lucile as a boy. As Lucidor she falls in love with one of Arabella's admirers, Wladimir, and—since Arabella cares not two straws about him—she begins to console him by writing him love letters, forging Arabella's handwriting. Eventually she welcomes him at night to her room under cover of darkness. Wladimir, under the illusion of having been granted Arabella's favors, betrays the affair. The ensuing scan-

---

* Letter of September 8, 1923.

dal is resolved happily, Lucile getting her beloved as a legitimate girl.

The two men met in the winter of 1927, and Hofmannsthal told Strauss the story of *Arabella*. He added to the original novella the character of Mandryka, the fabulously rich landowner, who is in love with Arabella. Zdenka is in love with Matteo, a young officer, who longs for Arabella. Pretending to be Arabella, Zdenka spends the night with Matteo. Misunderstanding the situation, Mandryka is stung into a jealous fury—until in the end the truth emerges. Hofmannsthal set the second act at a coachman's ball, for no more cogent a reason than to introduce Fiakermilli, queen of the ball, a coloratura. Strauss liked the whole scheme. "But," he wrote almost immediately, "I would like to weave into the material some more serious conflicts for the soul, which would raise it above the usual comic complications and make the participation of music truly necessary."*

So began the working out of the libretto, with Strauss collaborating to the hilt, often with perceptive and practical suggestions, sometimes with outrageously tasteless ones, so that when Strauss accused himself of indulging in *Kitsch* (cheap artistic junk), Hofmannsthal did not contradict him.

Never had the composer been more exigent. It was almost as if he were trying to make up for his easygoing attitude during *Helena*. "Don't be angry with me if I have to be critical once again," he writes. And then he lays about him, sometimes diplomatically and sometimes brutally.

Hofmannsthal had suggested a simple ceremony of Arabella's handing her betrothed a glass of pure water. Strauss worried over that: there had been too much to drink, too many potions, in the preceding *Helena*. Hofmannsthal replied: "That because of the magic potions in *Helena* one is not permitted to hand out a glass of water—that I cannot get through my head."† How would it be, Strauss proposed unexpectedly, if Mandryka, at the moment that he is convinced of her infidelity, were to shoot himself, and Arabella handed the dying man a glass of water? After all, the play need not be a comedy. Was the subject not essentially tragic? So it

* Letter to Hofmannsthal, December 18, 1927.
† Letter to Strauss, August 5, 1928.

went on and on, with pages and pages of letters passing between them.

And Hofmannsthal? With remarkable compliance he labored, wrote and rewrote, attempting to give Strauss all he wanted, though without sacrificing his own integrity. Only once did he cry out: "The thought comes to me that perhaps, quite without willing it, indeed without being conscious of it, something has entered our relationship similar to what occurs in marriages from time to time after fifteen years or so and against which both partners are helpless; that is, an inner fatigue, a coldness."* At other times he merely begged Strauss "to have confidence in his old but still quite lively librettist," and he passed on to him the usual compliments of his admirers, which included one opinion that *Arabella* was better constructed than *Der Rosenkavalier*. Both Werfel and Wassermann had praised it.

If what the two finally produced was not so good as it ought to have been, the fault lay, at least partly, in the postwar debility which sapped much of Europe's strength, an atony that engulfed Germany and Austria particularly, a declension affecting two talents that were remainders of another era. The *Zeitgeist* was a leech that thinned their blood.

The partnership came to an end with horrible and dramatic suddenness. In April, 1929, Strauss had fallen ill. To recuperate, he went to his beloved Italy in May, and then to Karlsbad to take the cure. Returning to Garmisch, he kept up his demands for revisions of Act I. On July 10 Hofmannsthal sent him still another version, of which he said that he had done his very best to transform the act, particularly the scene between the sisters and Arabella's final monologue, into "the lyrical." Strauss took three days to read the new draft, and on the evening of July 14 he sent his collaborator a telegram that read: FIRST ACT EXCELLENT. HEARTFELT THANKS AND CONGRATULATIONS. FAITHFULLY YOURS. The telegram arrived on the fifteenth. Hofmannsthal never opened it.

It was the day of the funeral of his eldest son, Franz, who had taken his own life two days before. (What made him do this remains a mystery. I have been unable to find facts; the guesses range

* Letter of November 19, 1928.

from the suicide's being the result of his having contracted a disease to the theory that the son of the famous father, being untalented, could no longer face a life of mediocrity.)

The father was in deepest mourning. He did not cry out but sat in his study in silent grief. He attempted to muster all his aristocratic strength not to give way or break down. He insisted on wanting to accompany the body of his son. On the morning of the funeral, Hofmannsthal started to dress himself and bent down to reach for his hat. Suddenly he mumbled to his wife, "I am not feeling well." He spoke with a thick tongue, his speech being almost incomprehensible, his face distorted. Gerty realized at once that something was seriously amiss. She looked at him and he stammered, "Why do you look at me?" But he did not go to the mirror. They loosened his collar and made him as comfortable as they could on the couch. He died from a stroke almost immediately and without ever recovering full consciousness. On July 18 he was buried in the little Pfarrkirche in Rodaun. The church overflowed with people and flowers; "all the rosebushes of Vienna must have been plucked," wrote Kessler. But Strauss could not be there.

Strauss wrote his widow:

> After yesterday's terrible news of the death of your unfortunate son, now this frightful blow to yourself, to your children, to me, and the entire world of art. I still cannot comprehend it or lend words to my grief. It is too terrible!
>
> This genius, this great poet, this sensitive collaborator, this kind friend, this unique talent! No musician ever found such a helper and supporter. No one will ever replace him for me or the world of music! Posterity will set up to him a monument that is worthy of him and which he has always possessed in my heart—ineffaceable gratitude in the heart of his truest friend will be the feeling that I shall preserve for him in admiration to the end of my days. The wonderful libretto which he sent me so shortly before his tragic end, and for which in my supreme happiness I was only able to thank him in a brief telegram, will remain a last glorious page in the work of this noble, pure, high-minded man. I am profoundly shocked, and moreover still indisposed, so that I cannot even see my unforgettable friend to his last rest. We have not even been able so far to learn the date and time of the interment. My son and Alice are hurrying to Vienna! If they manage to arrive in time they will represent

my wife and me at the bier of him whom I shall never forget. Pauline joins me in conveying to you her sincerest participation in your grief! To you and the children all good wishes in profoundest sympathy,

Yours, most deeply moved,
DR. RICHARD STRAUSS*

Gerty told Kessler that the death of the son was *not* responsible for the death of the father: in fact, three years earlier the doctors had diagnosed a serious hardening of the arteries. After Franz's suicide Hugo had continued his activities, written letters, had spoken of death in long, wonderful conversations, though he had also wept, much and bitterly.

When Strauss had recovered a little from his deep grief, he had to face the problem of what to do with the text of *Arabella*. Should he abandon the opera? Should he proceed with the work? Knowing that the libretto was not as yet totally satisfactory, should he call in another writer? Should he attempt to write his own emendations? He finally decided to leave the text exactly as it was and to proceed with the composition.

He took time with it, over three years, finishing the score on October 12, 1932. He remarked that he would be an old man of seventy before *Arabella* was ready. He bettered his timetable by two years.

"Uneven" is the word for *Arabella*. It is uneven in inspiration, uneven in dramatic tension, uneven in the skill with which the characters are musically fulfilled. Strauss had nothing very new to say; yet often, when he couched old thoughts in new melodies, the result was beautiful. Typical of this unevenness is the opening, where a dull scene with a fortune-teller is followed by a dull scene between Zdenka and Matteo, to be followed by a sensitive and exquisite duet between the two sisters, with Arabella's confession, "Er ist der Richtige nicht für mich! (He is not the right one for me.)" The two girls, one surer of herself than the other but both looking at the future with expectant eyes, both questioning fate with curiosity, are portrayed with delicacy and wisdom. The confrontation between Mandryka and Arabella's father I find crude,

* Letter of July 16, 1929. Quoted from Strauss and Hofmannsthal, *A Working Friendship: Correspondence.*

but then the close of the act, with which Strauss took such trouble, is composed in his best romantic manner, with Arabella musing on men, a young girl's conventional thoughts lifted by music to importance.

Most of the second act, which is supposed to be gay, is dreary, barring a fine duet between Arabella and Mandryka. The whole Fiakermilli scene is dreadful. Her aria is obviously another attempt to create a Zerbinetta coloratura piece, but what a difference between this and the earlier creation!

Arabella's third act contains the best music, even though here and there the similarity to the sounds of *Der Rosenkavalier* is all too obvious. The end is the finest portion of the work: it is characteristic of Strauss that even in his weaker works he manages to summon inspiration for the final scene (*Ariadne*'s final scene being an exception). Here too Hofmannsthal rose to his former mastery, giving Strauss words and phrases that are simple, uncluttered, and heartfelt. The glass of water is clear.

But altogether the work is a disappointment, with a plethora of uninspired pages. We must repeat: uneven. Yet it has its adherents; Robert Sabin, reviewing a recent recording of the opera in *The American Record Guide*, August, 1964, calls it one of Strauss's greatest: "In *Arabella* Strauss is saying eternal things of the greatest human importance (as Verdi did in *Falstaff*), through the mask of naïveté and spontaneity." "Eternal things" come at a discount these days.

Strauss had destined the work for Dresden, and dedicated the score to both Alfred Reucker, the intendant of Dresden, and to Fritz Busch. But before these two could begin the work, Adolf Hitler had come to power, and both of them were promptly dismissed from their posts. Strauss, at first disturbed, withdrew the score. But the new management of the Dresden Opera insisted that the contract be fulfilled, and Strauss, perhaps feeling that just then consent was the better part of valor, proceeded, specifying that he personally was to approve all the artists.

The première took place on July 1, 1933, as part of an opera festival. A considerable number of Brownshirts and of Nazi bigwigs were to be seen in the audience. Clemens Krauss conducted and Viorica Ursuleac, later Krauss's second wife, sang Arabella. Krauss had come from Vienna at Strauss's demand. So had the Mandryka, Alfred Jerger. Even the scenic designer was imported from Vienna, Leonhard Fanto. In those early days of Nazism, Strauss could still command what he wanted.

The opera scored a polite success in Dresden, no more than polite. It was far more successful at its Vienna première, which followed shortly after, because Lotte Lehmann sang Arabella. It was not given at the Metropolitan until 1956. It enjoys a fitful existence in the world's opera houses when a consummate artist such as Lisa della Casa fills the title role. *Arabella* depends on the charm of the Arabella. As a stage work, it has not proved itself a potent product.

17

Strauss and the Nazis

Strauss was not a Nazi. He was not an anti-Nazi. He was one of those who let it happen. He was one of those who played along. He was one of those who thought, "Well, they won't practice as viciously as they preach." He thought so until the hoodlums touched him personally.

That Strauss was politically naïve, that indeed he was politically illiterate, being unable to read the handwriting on the German wall, has been attested even by several of his admirers. Hermann Bahr noted in his diary: "Strauss asseverates that he comes from peasant origin, that he had risen by his own efforts, and whatever he achieved he is willing to defend against others who have not succeeded. In general, and politically, he asserts the right of the strong. He is opposed to universal suffrage, wants a true aristocracy, a selection of the strong—believing that everyone can be strong if he disciplines himself. . . ."*

Similarly, Harry Kessler noted, on the occasion of being with Strauss in Hofmannsthal's house: "Among other things, Strauss gave forth his droll political views, the necessity of a dictatorship, etc. Nobody took it seriously."† A later entry recalled the incident: "Strauss talked such nonsense that Hofmannsthal apologized to me in a letter."‡

---

* Written in November, 1915. Quoted in Walter Panofsky, *Richard Strauss: Partitur eines Lebens*.

† Harry Graf Kessler, *Tagebücher*, entry of June 14, 1928.

‡ *Ibid.*, entry of July 18, 1929.

But there is a great difference between political naïveté and the acquiescence to dictatorship by perverts. Millions of words have been spoken, hundreds of books have been written, which grapple with the question of how it could happen that a nation which produced a Richard Strauss and a Thomas Mann and an Albert Einstein could be induced not only to bray "*Sieg Heil!*" to an Adolf Hitler but to honor a Himmler, who when he was nineteen was accused of murdering the prostitute who supported him (he was acquitted for lack of evidence); or to genuflect before a Kaltenbrunner, "nearly seven feet tall . . . with small, delicate hands nevertheless capable of immense feats of strength . . . consuming 100 cigarettes a day and, like many of his colleagues, an incorrigible alcoholic, drinking from early morning, champagne, brandy and various spirits . . . arriving in excellent humor at a camp where various methods of execution were demonstrated."* The phenomenon of National Socialism has been analyzed politically, economically, historically, psychologically, truculently, and apologetically. Yet who can ever understand it? The insane dichotomy of a great nation could be symbolized by the Gestapo's Heydrich, a pervert who enjoyed two great pleasures in life: one was to kill human beings, the other was to play chamber music. He excelled at both.

Strauss may not have known these particular men personally. But he was too prominent a personality not to have been exposed to the leaders of the Nazi party or been ignorant of their aims, methods, and precepts. Their inhumanity was not, and could not have been, unknown to him.

At the very beginning, Strauss accepted Hitler. No, more than that; he welcomed him with high hopes. He swallowed the fable that the new regime would "uplift German art" and expunge "the decadent." (That did *not* mean *Salome!*) He met several times with Hitler, Göring, and Goebbels, who accorded him interviews since they were trying to get this international figure on their side. On November 15, 1933, he accepted his election as president of the Reichsmusikkammer (the Government Bureau which had jurisdiction over all musical matters). He felt that "through the good intention of the new German government to support music and the the-

---

* Jacques Delarue, *The Gestapo: A History of Horror*.

ater something really beneficial could be accomplished."* On February 13, 1934, he made a public address, opening the first meeting of this official body. He thanked Hitler and Goebbels and said, "After the assumption of power by Adolf Hitler, much has been changed in Germany, not only politically but also in the realm of culture. Already, after a few months of the National Socialist government, it has been able to call into being a body such as the Reichsmusikkammer. This proves that the new Germany is unwilling to let artistic matters slide, as it did more or less up to now. It proves that new ways and means are determinedly sought to make possible a new vigor in our musical life." This speech was followed by one orated by a Dr. Friedrich Mahling, Press Chief of the Reichsmusikkammer, and the speeches were followed by a "*Sieg Heil*" in a triple shout, hailing the Führer as "champion and creator of the work of national culture." The singing of the Horst Wessel song closed the meeting.†

He willingly accepted honors tendered to him. On his seventieth birthday, in June, 1934, he was presented with two silver-framed photographs, one of Hitler, inscribed "To the great German composer, with sincere homage," and one of Goebbels, "To the great tonal master, in grateful homage."

Strauss knew perfectly well what was going on. He not only read about the burning of the Reichstag and the subsequent trial, which made a mockery of court procedure; he also saw and heard the parade of Bavarian Brownshirts who roamed the streets of Munich with noisy rowdyism, looking, in their short pants, knobby knees, and paunches, like boy scouts gone berserk. He witnessed the vandalism of Jewish property. He could not have escaped the news of the infamous "Crystal Night" (November 9, 1938). Close to home he learned what was happening to fellow musicians. Bestiality was all around the man who had set to music the words "Music is a holy art." When Goebbels attacked Hindemith—and Furtwaengler, who had taken Hindemith's part—Strauss is said to have sent Goebbels an approving telegram.

---

* Quoted in Panofsky, *op. cit.*

† The documents relating to this meeting and to other musical affairs during the Nazi regime are given in *Musik im Dritten Reich*, edited by Joseph Wulf. It makes incredible reading!

He knew about the incident at Dresden: at a performance of *Il Trovatore* (March 7, 1933), Fritz Busch,* who was to conduct, was received by filthy catcalls, the demonstration being organized by half-drunk SA men. Busch had to leave the house in which he had worked for twelve years. Bruno Walter, a Jew, was to conduct at Philharmonic Hall in Berlin. Threats were made, and on inquiring about the official position of the Ministry, Walter was told by Dr. Funk (later the president of the Reichsbank), "We don't wish to prohibit the concert, for we are not interested in getting you out of an awkward predicament, let alone in relieving you of your obligation to pay the orchestra. But if you insist on giving the concert, you may be sure that everything in the hall will be smashed to pieces."† Strauss consented to substitute for Bruno Walter. He said later that he did it to help the orchestra. He did contribute his fee (1,500 marks) to the men of the orchestra. Fritz Stege, the critic of the *Völkischer Beobachter,* complimented Strauss because "he refused to be intimidated by threatening letters from an America incited by the Jews."‡

From America came a cablegram to Hitler (April 1, 1933) protesting against the treatment of Jewish musicians. The cable was signed by Arturo Toscanini, Walter Damrosch, Frank Damrosch, Serge Koussevitzky, Artur Bodanzky, Harold Bauer, Ossip Gabrilowitsch, Alfred Hertz, Charles Marin Loeffler, Fritz Reiner, Rubin Goldmark. It was not to be expected that the Nazis would heed an appeal by a group of musicians, however prominent, some of whom were Jews. But Strauss kept quiet.

Toscanini was supposed to conduct *Parsifal* and *Die Meistersinger* in Bayreuth that summer: to get him was considered a musical scoop of the greatest importance, and all sorts of honors had been prepared for him by Winifred Wagner and the town of Bayreuth. On June 5 Toscanini canceled. He did so after a long mental struggle, because of "painful events which have wounded my feelings as a man and as an artist." Toscanini's message to Winifred Wagner became public knowledge in Germany. *The New York Times* reported:

---

* His brother Adolf, the violinist, had come out against the Nazis.

† Bruno Walter, *Theme and Variations: An Autobiography.*

‡ *Zeitschrift für Musik,* May, 1933.

> News of this has crept through the defensive propaganda of the government and brought home to the music-loving German masses the full weight of world condemnation of certain Nazi practices. For once no attempt has been made even to attack a critic of Hitlerism or to ascribe his action to Jewish machinations.
>
> On the contrary, Signor Toscanini's high standing as an artist and his great services to Bayreuth are fully acknowledged, and it was revealed today that the official radio ban placed on his works [recordings] as a punishment for his heading a cabled protest to Chancellor Hitler against the persecution of fellow-artists has been revoked on the ground that it had been caused by a "mistake."*

Strauss replaced Toscanini. He conducted the opening *Parsifal.* He said later that he did it to save Bayreuth. (Karl Elmendorff was entrusted with *Die Meistersinger.*) There was of course no necessity to "save Bayreuth." It was quite safe under Hitler.

On the occasion of the fiftieth anniversary of Wagner's death, Thomas Mann gave a lecture in Belgium that was later published as his essay "Sufferings and Greatness of Richard Wagner." It was one of the most perceptive commentaries on that much commented-upon composer. To the Nazis, however, it was insufficiently adulatory, a case of *lèse majesté.* Hitler's newspaper, *Völkischer Beobachter,* called Thomas Mann a "semi-Bolshevik." Several German artists chimed in and signed an open letter vilifying Mann. Strauss was one of the signatories.

Strauss never contemplated leaving his native land, though as a musician it would have been easier for him to do so and find welcome abroad than it was for a German author or a German actor. While Strauss was being feted, Mann left Germany, leaving his possessions behind. As early as May 15, 1933, Mann wrote a letter to Albert Einstein which deserves to be reread after all these years:

> HONORED HERR PROFESSOR:
>
> My frequent change of domicile is the reason I have delayed thanking you for your kind letter.

---

* Wireless to *The New York Times* from Berlin, June 7, 1933.

> It represented the greatest honor tendered to me not only in these frightful months, but perhaps in all my life. Still, you praise me for an action which came naturally to me and therefore does not deserve praise. Not so natural is the situation in which I now find myself: at bottom I am much too good a German not to be heavily oppressed by the thought of permanent exile. The break with my country, a break which is almost inevitable, weighs on me and frightens me—a sign that my action does not fit my character, which is shaped by elements of a tradition going back to Goethe and is not truly suited to martyrdom. To force this role on me, things false and evil had to happen. False and evil is this entire "German Revolution," according to my deepest conviction. It lacks all those traits which have won the sympathy of the world for true revolutions, however bloody. Its essence is not "exaltation," whatever its supporters may say or bellow, but hatred, revenge, common killer-instinct, puny chicanery of the soul. Nothing good can come of it, never will I believe it, neither for Germany nor for the world. To have uttered to the best of our ability a warning against the moral and mental misery which these forces have brought about—that will some day earn us a degree of honor, even though we may perish in the meantime.*

Strauss's position was that he had been a German composer under the Kaiser, that he had been one under the Weimar Republic, that now under Nazism he was president of the Reichsmusikkammer, and that were Communism to come to Germany, he should become a Commissar. It made no difference to him. He wrote to Stefan Zweig: "I am well. I am at work, just as I was eight days after the outbreak of the famous World War."†

Indifference invaded, opportunism guided, Strauss. In 1932, when Hitlerism was as yet merely threatening, Otto Klemperer called on Strauss. At tea the conversation turned to recent political developments. Pauline said—"rather vehemently, as was her nature"—that if the Nazis were to cause Klemperer any trouble he should send them to her, and she would fix them! Whereupon Strauss smilingly replied, "This would be a fine moment to stand up for a Jew!" Klemperer's daughter Lotte comments: "This opportunism was so

* Erika Mann (Ed.), *Thomas Mann Briefe 1889-1936*.

† Letter of April 4, 1933.

blunt, so naked in its total amorality, that my father to this day feels more amused than offended by the incident."*

Strauss said in after years that the reason he showed compliance with the Nazi regime was his fear for Alice and his two grandchildren, one of whom was then (1933) five years old and the other a baby of one. Undoubtedly there is truth in this. And it is a proof of how badly the Nazis needed Strauss as a representational symbol that even after he had become *persona non grata,* Alice and the grandchildren were never threatened, though they were confined as much as possible to the house in Garmisch. Much later, when Strauss went to Vienna with his family (1942-43), he made a "deal" with Baldur von Schirach, the *Gauleiter* of Vienna, that he, Strauss, was not to make any public utterances against the regime and in turn Alice was not to be molested. Schirach kept his word. Strauss agreed to compose music to honor the Japanese royal family (*Japanische Festmusik,* 1940) under the condition that Alice and her sons were to be left alone. All the same, the two little boys suffered frequent humiliation: their schoolmates spat at them on the way to school. Pauline spoke her mind. Neither the *Gauleiter* nor the Gestapo could frighten *her!* Once at an official reception she turned to Schirach and said, "Well, when the war is lost and you'll be runnning away, Herr Schirach, we'll always have a little place of refuge for you in our house in Garmisch. But as for the rest of the mob—"† Richard was sweating visibly.

Neither Strauss's acquiescence nor his optimism, if in truth he felt any optimism, lasted long. First came the matter of the Salzburg *Festspiele* in 1934, where Strauss was scheduled to conduct *Fidelio* and an orchestral concert. His appearance was canceled; the Nazis did not look with favor on cooperation with the then inimical Austria. Then he became disillusioned with the Reichsmusikkammer itself. He wrote to a trusted colleague, Dr. Julius Kopsch, a conductor:‡ "Nothing is accomplished by these meetings. I hear that the Aryan law is to be sharpened and that *Carmen* will be forbidden. I have no wish actively to participate in such embarrassing blunders. . . . My extensive and serious proposals for reform were

---

* Letter to the author, January 24, 1966.

† Quoted in Walter Panofsky, *op. cit.*

‡ Later president of the International Strauss Society.

declined by the Minister. . . . Time is too precious to me for me to participate further in such amateurish mischief [*Dilletantenunfug*]."* He preserved some of his humor. He was sent a questionnaire asking whether he was an Aryan artist and demanding that he name two witnesses to his ability in his chosen profession. The two he cited were "Mozart and Richard Wagner."†

He really did not become angry until his work was hindered, until he saw the threat to his new collaborator, Stefan Zweig, until the episode before the première of their first and what was to be their only opera, *Die schweigsame Frau* (The Silent Woman). After Hofmannsthal's death, Strauss felt that he was never again going to write an opera. Where was the partner with whom he could work? Was he, still so replete with the desire to compose, condemned to the life of a "well-to-do lazy pensioner"? One day in 1931, Zweig's publisher, Anton Kippenberg, director of the Inselverlag, was visiting Strauss on his way to see Zweig. Strauss, though he did not know Zweig personally, suggested casually that Kippenberg might ask the famous author if he had any ideas suitable for an opera. Zweig had for years been an ardent admirer of the composer's, and, being an unusually modest man, he had not dared to seek his acquaintance. He responded at once by sending Strauss a facsimile of a Mozart letter from Zweig's rich collection of manuscripts, telling Strauss that he would like nothing better than to submit a "musical plan" to him. He had not done so before because "when he worshiped he was ill at ease." The two men met in Munich, and Zweig suggested the subject of *The Silent Woman*, based on Ben Jonson's *Epicoene*.

The collaboration began, and many letters went to and fro. Strauss was overjoyed. Zweig seemed sent from heaven. The scenario was "the born comic opera . . . better suited to music than *Figaro* or the *Barber*." Here was a new lien on youth, the chance to begin again. The collaboration turned out to be pure pleasure, easy and lighthearted, with Zweig being throughout accommodating to and almost humble before the composer. Even before the first libretto was finished, Strauss was firing away at further projects with his new collaborator, reviving the old idea of *Semiramis*, or any-

* Letter to Julius Kopsch, October 4, 1934.
† Questionnaire dated December 12, 1935.

thing else, "prince or confidence man, but no virtuous namby-pamby or martyr."

Then came the edict against the Jews, and Zweig—prominent representative of his religion that he was and author of the Biblical drama *Jeremias**—knew at once that trouble was in the offing. Strauss disagreed: he thought that the Nazis did not really mean what they said, that Zweig was an Austrian and therefore did not come under the ban, and that his own position was strong enough to force the issue. All the same, he wrote to Zweig on May 24, 1934: "I asked Dr. Goebbels directly whether there were any 'political accusations' against you, to which the Minister answered in the negative. So I do not think we will have any difficulties with *Morosus* [their original title for the opera], but I am glad you write that you 'do not allow yourself to be involved.' All attempts to soften the Aryan paragraph founder on the reply: 'Impossible! As long as such lying propaganda against Hitler is being spread abroad!' "

When Strauss was in Bayreuth, he informed Zweig—then working in London—"strictly confidentially" that Zweig was being spied upon, but that his exemplary behavior was judged "correct and politically unexceptional." What did neutral behavior have to do with the matter? Strauss was deluding himself and at the same time playing a game. Nor was he telling Zweig the whole truth. In Wahnfried, where Strauss was staying, Goebbels called on him to discuss the new opera. Strauss with a straight face told Goebbels that he had no wish to make difficulties either for Hitler or for his Propaganda Minister and that he was quite willing to withdraw the work. But, said he, in his opinion this would result in a horrible international scandal for the Reich. Goebbels answered evasively that though he could muzzle the press, he was not able to guarantee that somebody wasn't going to throw a stink bomb during the première. He then proposed that Strauss send the text to Hitler, and if Hitler found nothing objectionable, he would probably give his consent to the performance. Whether Hitler actually read that harmless little comedy we do not know. But he did give his consent, and announced that he would attend the première.

---

* The last line of *Jeremias:* "One cannot vanquish the invisible! One can kill men, but not the God who resides within them. One can subjugate a people, but never its spirit."

Later Strauss carefully noted all these details in a memorandum, which he locked in his safe. He wrote: "These are sad times when an artist of my rank has to ask a brat of a Minister for permission for what he may compose and perform. I belong to a nation of 'servants and waiters' and almost envy the racially persecuted Stefan Zweig, who now refuses definitely to work for me either openly or secretly. He wants no special favors from the Third Reich. I must confess I do not understand this Jewish solidarity and I regret that the artist in Zweig is unable to rise above political vagaries. . . ."*

The performance of *Die schweigsame Frau* was duly announced for June 24, 1935. What happened before the première is a well-authenticated incident told in full by Friedrich Schuch, the son of the conductor, who was then employed by the Dresden Opera House. Two days before the première, Strauss was sitting with him and two others in the Hotel Bellevue in Dresden, playing skat. Suddenly Strauss said, "I want to see the program." The intendant of the theater, Paul Adolph, was notified, and though he hesitated, he had no choice but to send over the proof sheet. Schuch hid it from Strauss as long as he dared but finally showed it. The name of Zweig had been eliminated from the the program, the text bearing the credit line: "Adapted from the English of Ben Jonson." Strauss looked at it, reddened deeply, and said, "You can do what you like, but I am leaving tomorrow morning. The performance will have to take place without me." Then he took the proof and wrote in the name of Zweig. The correct version of the program was restored, Strauss stayed, the première took place. But neither Hitler nor Goebbels was present. It was given out, and it might have been true, that a thunderstorm prevented the departure of their plane from Hamburg. Paul Adolph was soon dismissed from his post.

Strauss kept on beseeching Zweig to continue to work with him. If Zweig did not want to appear publicly in the matter, he, Strauss, would be willing to collaborate secretly and to lock the score away until times would return to normal. Not a single word to anybody would he let fall. What difference would it make? "In a few years, when our products will be ready, the world will probably look very different."†

---

* Memorandum of July 3, 1935.
† Letter to Zweig, August 24, 1934.

But Zweig persistently refused Strauss. He knew that these plans were not practical. He foresaw the harshening of the turmoil. He knew that these were times in which one had to "cancel the concept of security from our lives." He did not propose to appear in an equivocal light, much though he desired the continuation of their working together. He suggested other librettists. He brought forth ideas that he would willingly cede to other authors. (*Friedenstag* was one of these.) Strauss did not want other authors. "Don't recommend any other librettist to me. Nothing will come of it. It's a pity to waste the writing paper."* When conditions got worse, he suggested the childish expedient that they continue to correspond under assumed names: Zweig was to sign himself Henry Mor, he Robert Storch, the name he used in *Intermezzo.* As if anybody would have been fooled by that! In short: "I will not relinquish you because it so happens that we now have an anti-Semitic government."

With a blindness caused by his artistic egotism, Strauss refused to look the ugly facts in their ugly faces. He still thought he could "get away with it." Yet at the very time he was writing these letters, there appeared a book entitled *Fundamentals of the Development of National-Socialist Culture* by Dr. (practically all Nazi officials dealing with culture sported a Doctor title) Walter Stang. It propounded:

> We hold that a great difference exists between a Johann Strauss who aligned himself with a Jewish librettist, long ago at a time when National Socialism did not exist and one could hardly demand a perception of the importance of the racial question, and a composer who, working in the National Socialist State, refuses to sever his connection with Jewish poets of opera texts. We must regard the latter case as a disregard for the aims of the National-Socialist movement and we must act accordingly.

Incidentally, Dr. Stang goes on to praise a Dr. Siegfried Anheisser, who was "celebrated" as a pioneer of the "de-Judafication" of operetta librettos and of Mozart's librettos. Anheisser's new ver-

* Letter of May 24, 1935.

sions of the Mozart operas were "exemplary," the text "liberated from Jewish rant [*Floskeln*]."

How could Strauss stomach all this?

Finally, in answer to a renewed refusal by Zweig (in a letter now lost), Strauss lost his temper and replied: "Your letter of the 15th reduces me to despair! That Jewish stubbornness! It is enough to turn one into an anti-Semite! This pride of race, this feeling of solidarity—even I can sense its force! Do you think that any of my actions have ever been guided by the thought that I am a '*Germane*' (perhaps, *qui le sait*)? Do you believe that Mozart composed consciously in an 'Aryan' style? For me there are only two categories of human beings, those who have talent and those who have not. For me people exist only when they become the audience; whether that audience is made up of Chinese, Upper Bavarians, New Zealanders, or Berliners is all the same to me, as long as they pay the full price of a ticket." He then thanks him for the idea of *Capriccio*, refuses to work with Gregor, whom Zweig had suggested as his successor, urges him to continue to work, and tells him to let it be his concern as to how to keep the whole matter secret. He concludes: "Who ever told you that I am politically so active? Because I conducted a concert substituting for Bruno Walter? I did it for the orchestra, just as I substituted for that other 'non-Aryan' Toscanini: that I did for Bayreuth. All this has nothing to do with politics. How the gutter press interprets this is not my business. And you shouldn't worry about it either. That I mime the president of the Reichsmusikkammer? To do good and to prevent greater misfortunes. Yes, out of my consciousness of artistic duty! Under any government I would have accepted this troublesome honor, but neither Kaiser Wilhelm nor Herr Rathenau offered it to me. Be sensible then and forget Herr Moses and the other apostles for a few weeks and get to work on *your* two one-acters. . . ."*

This letter was mailed to Zweig in Zurich from Dresden. It never arrived. The Gestapo intercepted it, opened it, turned it over to the local police, who then forwarded a photocopy of it to Hitler with the following letter:

* Letter of June 17, 1935.

MEIN FÜHRER:

The enclosed photocopied letter of Herr Dr. Strauss to the Jew Stefan Zweig, which I bring to your kind attention, fell into the hands of the Geheime Staatspolizeiamt. In the matter of *Die schweigsame Frau,* I'd like to mention that the world première was given to a full house, including five hundred invited guests, that the second performance was so sparsely attended* that the intendant had to fill the house with free tickets, and that the third performance was canceled, allegedly because of the illness of the principal actress. Heil!

Your very devoted
MARTIN MUTSCHMANN†

Five days after this letter to Hitler, an official of the government appeared and demanded that Strauss resign as president of the Reichsmusikkammer in view of his "failing state of health." Strauss resigned at once.

Now obviously frightened, he wrote to Hitler:

MEIN FÜHRER:

The mail has just brought me the notification that my request to resign from the presidency of the Reichsmusikkammer has been granted. This request was initiated by Reichsminister Dr. Goebbels, who originally transmitted it to me through a special messenger. I hold my removal from the Reichsmusikkammer sufficiently noteworthy to feel obligated to recount to you, my Führer, in brief, the whole development of the affair.

The cause seems to be a private letter addressed by me to my last collaborator, Stefan Zweig, opened by the state police and handed over to the Propaganda Ministry. I willingly admit that without a precise explanation and taken out of context of a long artistic correspondence, without knowledge of its previous history nor of the mood in which the letter was penned, the contents of this letter could be easily misinterpreted and misunderstood. To understand my mood, it is first of all necessary to think oneself into my situation and to consider that I as a composer, like almost all my colleagues, suffer the continuous difficulty of not being able, in spite of frequent efforts, to find a German librettist of worth.

---

* A partial lie: the second performance was well attended, the opera having been favorably reviewed by the critics.

† Letter of July 1, 1935.

In the above-mentioned letter, there are three passages which have given offense. I have been given to understand that these were that I have little comprehension of anti-Semitism, as well as of the concept of a People's Community, and of the significance of my position as president of the Reichsmusikkammer. I was not given the opportunity for a direct and personal explanation of the sense, content, and meaning of this letter which, briefly put, was written in a moment of ill humor against Stefan Zweig and dashed off without further thought.

As a German composer, and in view of the sum total of my works, which speak for themselves, I do not think that I have to assert that this letter, in all its improvised sentences, does not represent my view of the world nor my true conviction.

Mein Führer! My whole life belongs to German music and to an indefatigable effort to elevate German culture. I have never been active politically nor even expressed myself in politics. Therefore I believe that I will find understanding from you, the great architect of German social life, particularly when, with deep emotion and with deep respect, I assure you that even after my dismissal as president of the Reichsmusikkammer I will devote the few years still granted to me only to the purest and most ideal goals.

Confident of your high sense of justice, I beg you, my Führer, most humbly to receive me for a personal discussion, to give me the opportunity to justify myself in person, as I take farewell of my activity in the Reichsmusikkammer.

I remain, most honored Herr Reichskanzler, with the expression of my high esteem,

Yours, forever devotedly,
RICHARD STRAUSS*

The letter represents the nadir of Strauss's morality. To it he received no answer. Further performances of *The Silent Woman* were forbidden.

Even as he was composing the plea to Hitler, three days before he sent it, he continued to write secretly his *apologia pro vita sua*. In a memorandum dated July 10, 1935, he told the story of the purloined letter. In a later memorandum, he wrote that he had been much misunderstood, that the foreign as well as the Viennese Jewish newspapers had derogated him in the eyes of decent people,

* Letter of July 13, 1935.

doing him more harm than the German government could ever make good. He had "always" been against the Streicher-Goebbels hunt of the Jews. He thought it a blot on German honor. He himself had received so much help, so much unselfish friendship, and so much intellectual stimulation from Jews that it would be a crime not to avow his gratitude. Indeed, his worst and most malicious enemies had been Aryans, and he named among others Perfall, Felix Mottl, Franz Schalk, and Weingartner.

Though he never again was entrusted with an official position (he was, however, the official composer and conductor of an Olympic Hymn for the opening of the Berlin Olympiad, as well as of the "Japanese Festival Music" already mentioned), though he was henceforth a man regarded with suspicion by the Nazis, he was too important a personality to be banished. Since his contemporary, Pfitzner, who was a convinced National Socialist, was virtually unknown abroad, his was the only name that stood for German music in the world. All the same, he was lucky not to end up in Dachau. For some unknown reason, the Gestapo sent a photostat of Strauss's incriminating letter to Stefan Zweig in London. Had he published it, the Nazis would have had to arrest Strauss.

As it was, it was desirable—for business reasons as well as others—to continue to let him be without interference. His operas continued to draw full houses, his tone poems continued as surefire successes. Hofmannsthal, to be sure, had been demoted from a "non-Aryan" classification to "Jew." But he was safely dead. So performances of Strauss's works continued unhampered, and the Grand Mogul of German music was able to conduct wherever and whenever he wanted.

He still wanted to very much. Even between the ages of seventy and eighty, he was active not only as a composer but as an executant musician as well. He suffered some disabilities of old age, now a touch of rheumatism, then a weakness of the respiratory tract, and an appendicitis operation, serious in a man of advanced age. But every time he rose from his sickbed to continue his work. When he was eighty, he recorded on tape almost all his orchestral works with the Vienna Philharmonic. The following year, in 1945, these tapes were destroyed by fire bombs.

As during the First World War, he showed apathy toward the

destruction of his country. As in his correspondence with Hofmannsthal, the war was hardly ever mentioned in his correspondence with Clemens Krauss. When he could not get enough meat, when travel was restricted, when Pauline didn't have enough soap to keep the house clean enough to suit her, when his chauffeur and gardener were requested for military duty, when communication with Krauss (with whom he worked on *Capriccio*) became difficult, then he complained. He called himself "a chronic querulant."

He had so little understanding of the seriousness of the situation during the war that he suggested to Krauss, after a poor performance of *Arabella* in Italy, that "all Italian intendants, conductors, singers and scenic designers" be transported by special train to Salzburg to witness Krauss's model performances of the work. (In 1942!)

A remarkable document exists, dated January 14, 1944, signed by Martin Bormann and distributed to the heads of the party associations (copy to Hitler, of course). It read:

> RE DR. RICHARD STRAUSS. *Confidential.*
>
> The composer Dr. Richard Strauss and his wife inhabit in Garmisch a villa with nineteen rooms. The property includes a lodge which contains, in addition to the porter's dwelling, two rooms with kitchen and bath.
>
> Dr. Richard Strauss has managed to sidestep all demands to give shelter to those who have been injured by bombs and to evacuees. When we pointed out to him that everyone must make sacrifices and that the soldier at the front is risking his life daily, he replied that that was none of his business: as far as he was concerned no soldier had to fight. He even refused peremptorily the politely voiced plea of the Kreisleiter to put two rooms of the lodge at the disposition of two engineers who were working for the armament industry. The whole matter is being actively discussed by the inhabitants of Garmisch and is being properly criticized.
>
> The Führer, to whom the case was submitted, has decided immediately to appropriate the entire lodge belonging to the property of Dr. Richard Strauss and billet there persons having suffered bomb damage and evacuees. In addition, the Führer directs that the leading personalities of the party, who have up to now had personal intercourse with Dr. Richard Strauss, are to cease having anything to do with him.

Perhaps the most remarkable part of this document is the fact that during a war that was already going badly Hitler paid attention to so trifling a matter and issued a directive.

Six months after the document was issued, Strauss became eighty years old. The Nazis were nervous about that. They speculated how far they were to go in paying him honor. They wished they could honor Pfitzner, who in the same year celebrated his seventy-fifth birthday. Unfortunately it was rumored that Hitler did not like Pfitzner, that he reminded him "in his whole behavior of a Talmudic rabbi." Dr. Schmidt-Römer (another Nazi *Kultur* custodian with a doctorate) believed that one day Pfitzner's personal characteristics would be forgotten, that the fact that he had a genius for making enemies would no longer be important, and that he would be counted "among the greatest personalities of our time."* In the meantime, what could they do? Strauss was famous.

Pfitzner's birthday remained almost unnoticed, while Strauss's was being celebrated, though mostly in Vienna. There he himself appeared on the podium, conducting *Till* and the *Domestica*, and Karl Böhm had prepared a special performance of *Ariadne* (an off-the-air recording of this performance was published by the Deutsche Gramophon Gesellschaft). Later in the same year (September 10), he celebrated his golden wedding anniversary. Shortly after that, all theaters in Germany and Austria were closed. The total war reached its final paroxysm.

At the beginning of 1945, the opera houses of Berlin, Dresden, and Vienna were destroyed. Then it was that Strauss mourned and wept. Then it was that the tragedy struck home to him. Then it was that he wrote to Willi Schuh, the critic in Zurich: "Perhaps sorrow and despair make us babble on too much. But the burning of the Munich Court Theater, where *Tristan* and *Die Meistersinger* received their first performances, where I first heard *Freischütz* 73 years ago, where my good father sat at the first horn desk for 49 years . . . it was the greatest catastrophe of my life; there is no possible consolation, and at my age no hope."† He even sketched out a composition, "Sorrow for Munich," which he left incomplete and themes of which he used later in the *Metamorphosen*.

* Minutes of a party meeting, November 1, 1943.
† Quoted in Ernst Krause, *Richard Strauss: Gestalt und Werk*.

But even then—and again, as during World War I—one looks in vain for any expressed sign of guilt, for any acknowledgment of responsibility, for any regret that though he might not have helped along Germany's shame, he had tolerated it. He wrote to his grandchild Christian:

> Your 12th birthday coincides with the grievous event of the almost complete destruction of the beautiful imperial city. 165 years ago people regarded the Lisbon earthquake as a turning point in history, ignoring the greater significance of the first performance of Gluck's *Iphigénie in Aulis,* which marked the conclusion of a process of musical development that had lasted for 3,000 years and called down from heaven the melody of Mozart, revealing the secrets of the human spirit to a greater extent than thinkers have been able to, over the course of thousands of years. . . . When you remember your last birthday you should always think with loathing of the barbarians whose dreadful deeds are reducing our lovely Germany to ruins and ashes. Perhaps you will understand what I am saying as little as your brother does. If you read these lines again in 30 years' time, think of your grandfather, who exerted himself for nearly 70 years on behalf of German culture and the honor and renown of his fatherland. . . .*

"Barbarians . . . dreadful deeds . . . lovely Germany." These are his phrases.

In short, Strauss's attitude to and relationship with National Socialism were as contradictory as Strauss's whole character. He swerved from pro to con; both the pro and the con were prompted by what he thought was better for him, not what was better for the world, for his country—or for music.

After the war, Strauss had to submit to an investigation of his Nazi status. He was classified as "Class I—principal guilty person," having held an official position under the Nazi government. Several witnesses came forward to exonerate him. One was C. B. Lievert, the art historian, who had been an inmate of Buchenwald but had after his pardon been a welcome guest in Strauss's home. Another was the Swiss Consul of Munich, who testified that no German had spoken more bitterly and contemptuously of Hitlerism than Strauss.

---

* Quoted in Krause, *op. cit.* The letter is owned by Franz Strauss.

Other foreign diplomats took his part. The Munich tribunal wisely decided not to be more papal than the Pope. Strauss was denazified.

It was easy to exonerate him. Was he not an artist and a great one? It was and is not so easy to excuse the man who, to protect his creative interest, could grovel and be callously devious.

Even before he obtained a bill of health, he was allowed to travel. He went to Baden, near Zurich (where he had been before), to take a cure. He was then slightly deaf, and as deaf men do, he spoke in a loud voice. In a restaurant he was overheard saying, "The Nazis were criminals—I have always known that. Imagine, they closed the theaters, and my operas could not be given." Such was the political *Weltanschauung* of Richard Strauss.

18

The Zweig and Gregor Operas

Stefan Zweig had two great interests in life: writing and collecting autographs. Zweig's collection of manuscripts was one of the best private ones in Europe until war and thievery scattered it. His treasures reflected his wide-roaming interest in the past, in the mind of man, in the "architects of the world," as he called them. He produced much biographical writing about diverse personalities, such as Mary Stuart, Mary Baker Eddy, Stendhal, Tolstoi, Dickens, Dostoevski, Fouchet, Magellan, and Marie Antoinette. He was fond of quoting Pope's "The proper study of mankind is man."

He was a lesser writer than Hofmannsthal, lacking the older poet's mystic vision. But in some ways he was a better storyteller: his short stories, such as "Amok," "Twenty-four Hours in the Life of a Woman," "The Invisible Collection," "Letter from an Unknown Woman," were gripping pieces and were read with avidity the world over. When the Nazis drove him away from his beloved Salzburg, he went first to London, then to the United States, and finally to Brazil. Nowhere could he feel at home. In 1942 he committed suicide, leaving a message for his friends that he hoped that they could manage to wait for better times; as for himself, he was too impatient to wait.

His adaptation of Ben Jonson's *Volpone* was a successful comedy. The Theater Guild played it in New York (with Dudley Digges and Alfred Lunt, 1928). He again turned to Jonson—a mind of the past he greatly admired—when he decided to adapt *Epicoene, or*

The Silent Woman for a libretto. He dumped sugar into a salty comedy. Jonson's play is a ribald satire of those young men-about-town who boast of having slept with women whom they have never known. Two of them, Sir Amorous La Foole and Sir Jack Daw, swear before a judge that they have enjoyed the favors of Epicoene, the wife of old Morose. She is then unmasked as a boy.

Nothing is left of this in the libretto: Morosus, having in his career as a ship's captain suffered an injury to his ear, bemoans the fact that he cannot escape from the noise that is everywhere, from carousing villagers, from church bells, from his chattering housekeeper; never can he find peace, never can he sleep soundly. Suddenly his long-lost nephew Henry appears with a newly acquired wife, Aminta. Morosus, the lonely old man, is overjoyed to see him, but his joy turns to fury when he learns that Aminta is a member of a theatrical troupe and Henry himself has joined the troupe. In order to get back into his uncle's good graces and, much more important, to assure himself of his uncle's inheritance, he and his friend the Barber concoct a plan: Aminta is to disguise herself and to play the role of a demure silent woman. She is to be recommended to Morosus as the ideal wife. The complications are the expected ones. No sooner has a fake marriage ceremony been performed than Aminta turns out to be a stormy, extravagant, chattering, impossible girl; and in the end Morosus is happy to get rid of her, welcome Henry back, and be left in peace.

The little play is as unoriginal as could be, but that, I think, was the purpose: to give Strauss a conventional text for which he could write old-fashioned music of the *Don Pasquale* or *The Barber of Seville* type. The characters are counterparts of the Pasquales and the Norenas and Ernestos. The only trouble was that Strauss could not write such music. He could not be a twentieth-century Donizetti or a Rossini in a stiff collar. The score of *Die schweigsame Frau* (The Silent Woman)—in spite of charming spots here and there—is as forced as the artificially naïve usually turns out to be. There is no simple laughter in it. A lot of boisterousness, much ingenuity, some fine lyricism—but laughter, no. It lacks the salient ingredient of Italian comic opera: sparkling melodies. There are melodies here, but they are tiny buds that never bloom. The composer knows too much. He quotes themes from early English music and anachronistic snatches from *Il Trovatore*. Even these do not sound in the theater and must be dug out of the score. *Die schweigsame Frau* is an anemic girl, debilitated by too many musicological capers. Yet there are delightful moments, such as Morosus' looking at Aminta before the marriage ceremony, the old man's heart being genuinely warmed by seeing this radiant young girl before him. At the close of the second act, Strauss writes a duet for the two young lovers—for which Morosus' falling asleep serves as a gentle pedal point—which is unashamedly sentimental. The end of the opera is masterful, as peace and contentment envelop Morosus and he tell us that music is beautiful, especially when it has stopped sounding, and a young wife is beautiful, especially when she marries someone else.

Yet—well, old Charles Burney, that knowledgeable commentator, said it in the eighteenth century: "The Italians are apt to be too negligent, and the Germans too elaborate; in so much, that music, if I may hazard the thought, seems play to the Italians, and work to the Germans." *The Silent Woman* seems work.

Nor is the libretto right. It is too verbose. It does not run on light feet. Zweig was not as expert a dramatist as he was a short story writer. Still, faulty though the libretto is, it seems vintage Hofmannsthal compared to the three texts that Strauss was to compose with the man whom he had at first brusquely refused and with whom he never came to a good understanding. This man, highly recommended by Zweig, was Joseph Gregor. He was a corpulent, good-natured bookworm, the curator of the Theater Library in Vienna* and a scholarly historian of the theater. With his rimless spectacles, his broad moon face, his pedantic manner, he looked exactly what he was, a professor: *Hofrat Professor Dr.* Joseph Gregor. His poetry is classroom poetry.

He stood even more in awe of Strauss than Zweig. Strauss treated him cavalierly. Demanding this and demanding that, he refused script after script with an old man's testiness, which often did not even make the pretense of being polite. "Stop playing the poet," he would say to him, "and get the action down on paper. Forget the elegant language and give me some characters." "Not literature—

* Is it mere coincidence that after Hofmannsthal's death Strauss chose Austrians as collaborators? Zweig, Gregor, and Clemens Krauss were all Austrians.

but theater!" "Your characters walk on stilts." "Don't poetize—just adapt." So it went on through three works, until in the final work Strauss dropped Gregor altogether and in midstream, without a by-your-leave.

The first of the three Gregor operas is a one-act hymnal piece based on an idea which Zweig had submitted. It was originally called "1648," deals with an episode of the Thirty Years' War, and was inspired by the Velasquez painting in the Prado, the *Surrender at Breda.* It was then retitled *Der Friedenstag* (Day of Peace). The Commander of a beleaguered town is instructed to hold the town under all difficulties, no matter how ferocious the enemy's attack. The populace is starving, the soldiers weary, the situation desperate. The Commander decides that rather than surrender he will blow up the entire bastion and kill himself and all those living within its walls. His wife, who represents the human and sunny element, contrasted with the war-induced bitterness of her husband, attempts to reason with him. A cannon shot is heard far away. All believe that the enemy is about to strike. Yet—no enemy appears. As they listen, they hear a distant bell, first one, then another, then still another, nearer and louder. An officer rushes in to report that the war is over, that the enemy approaches with the flag of peace. The Commander cannot believe this sudden turn of fortune, and at first refuses to welcome the enemy soldiers. Can they, whom he has hated for so long, be human beings exactly like himself? The two opposing leaders confront each other. The Commander struggles with himself. Then suddenly he throws away his sword and embraces the man who was his foe. A jubilant chorus ends the opera.

It is a hopeless piece of work. Its sentiments are elementary, its people representational shadows, the music uninspired, the central scene between husband and wife forced. The only exciting moment in the opera is the moment when the bells begin to peal—and that moment is more exciting dramatically than musically. Strauss's imagination could not be fructified by a subject that dealt with war and peace. The battlefield was not his terrain.

He tried again with what he called a "bucolic tragedy," *Daphne.* This was an an original idea by Gregor. The professor, as one might expect, gives the ancient legend a modern psychological twist.

Freud promenades in Arcady. Daphne becomes a creature who cannot respond to normal love. She feels herself at one with the purity of nature, the chaste beauty of tree and flower. She cannot give herself to her lover, a simple human shepherd. She is awakened by the kiss of the god, by the ray of the sun, only to turn away in fear and fright. Apollo kills the shepherd. Then he realizes his guilt. She, Daphne, shames the god. Daphne's purity is immortalized when she is released to Nature, when she is turned into the evergreen laurel tree. Apollo summarizes the theme:

Are we still the gods?
Or are we now obscured by the human heart?
Is our power extinguished by such purity?

Gregor's symbolism is squashy, his verses lumpish. Strauss's music throughout is lyrical and for the most part subdued. It is a refined distillation of very little. There lies but scant pleasure in this idyll played at dusk. The one passionate passage occurs in the duet of an Apollo and a Daphne who have been to a performance of *Tristan und Isolde.* Curiously enough, Strauss, who hated tenors, here composes main roles for two tenors, Apollo and the shepherd Leukippos. Still more curious, after we have sat through the whole opera, we are rewarded with a postlude that is well-nigh magical. When Daphne is transformed into a tree, only the orchestra describes that transformation. (At first Strauss had planned it differently. The idea of the final version came to him rather late in the day.)* A melody moves slowly in a still, serene air. It grows even as bark and leaves grow out of Daphne's body. It takes shape, it proliferates, in the orchestra. It sings with harps and strings until it is finally taken up by Daphne's voice in a wordless song. Then it fades away as the light dims and the curtain falls.

Die Liebe der Danae is several cuts above the other two operas. That is, musically; dramatically it is as inept. Whatever good music *Danae* does contain may forever be blotted out by the bad libretto. The story deals with the rivalry of Jupiter and King Midas for the

* It was actually Clemens Krauss who suggested that the original choral finale be given to the orchestra alone. Later Strauss set the text of the choral finale as a nine-part *a cappella* piece, "An den Baum Daphne."

love of a voluptuous girl who, at first at any rate, has one defect: she prefers gold to love. Midas has become the powerful, gold-encrusted king because Jupiter has made him so. He is part of Jupiter's scheme to win Danae, being originally nothing but a poor donkey driver. After several frustrations, Jupiter feels himself betrayed; as punishment, he reduces Midas to his former state. He puts the choice between himself and his rival up to Danae. Danae prefers, to no one's surprise, true happiness and simple, honest love to the embrace of a god.

The action takes place in a Greece in which the national dish seems to be *Schlagobers*. It is all quite ponderous, and one is never sure whether this Jupiter descended from Olympus or from Valhalla. The third act of the opera—musically the strongest and dramatically the weakest—is largely given over to a long scene between Danae and Jupiter, in which Jupiter renounces his love in favor of one who, to use Wotan's words, "is freer than I, the god."

The music is of uneven quality, sinking to an orchestral interlude that outglitters *Scheherazade* in describing the shower of gold of which Danae dreams. But at least two of the orchestral interludes are beautiful and the voice writing often rises to eloquence, chiefly because Strauss was able to compose sensuous and luscious music once more. Danae, outwardly cold, is an erotic creature.

It was supposed to be a "cheerful mythology," but the work is not really gay or joyous, and the comic supplementary figures, Mercury (playing Loge to Jupiter's Wotan), and four of Jupiter's former loves, such as Leda and Alcmene, add little to the festivities, being mostly mythological name-dropping.

Strauss stipulated that *Danae* was not to be produced until at least two years after the cessation of the war, which broke out while he was working on the opera. He called it "my posthumous work." In September, 1941, Clemens Krauss was appointed artistic head of the Salzburg Festival, and at once he asked Strauss to release *Danae* for Salzburg. Strauss promised the opera to Salzburg but still insisted on his former terms. However, as Strauss got to know Krauss better, and as the two collaborated on *Capriccio*, Krauss managed to obtain the composer's consent to a première at the 1944 Salzburg Festival, in honor of Strauss's eightieth birthday. The scores were printed in Leipzig by Johannes Örtel, the Aryan publisher who had succeeded Fürstner as Strauss's publisher. Fifteen hundred copies of the score were destroyed in an air raid on Leipzig. Nevertheless, it was decided to proceed with the production.

On July 20, 1944, an unsuccessful attempt was made by a group of generals to assassinate Hitler. In the preceding month the Allies had entered Rome and two days later had landed on the beaches of Normandy (June 6, 1944; Operation Overlord). Goebbels now decreed "total war" and the suspension of all theatrical festivals. Yet the Salzburg Festival was allowed to proceed, though in truncated form. Later it was decreed that the Festival was to be abandoned altogether, though *Danae* got to the stage of the final dress rehearsal (August 16, 1944). Strauss was present at the rehearsals. At one of them, according to an account written by Rudolf Hartmann, Strauss was visibly moved. He knew that the labor of the rehearsals was not to culminate in a performance. Toward the end of Act III Strauss rose from his seat and walked to the front, closely observing the Vienna Philharmonic Orchestra as well as the singers on the stage. Everybody on the stage and in the orchestra pit sensed the composer's emotion. Everybody—except perhaps a few diehards who still believed that Hitler was going to produce the "miracle weapon"—knew that the war was lost, the Reich doomed, the day of retribution near. There stood Germany's famed composer, his last work silenced by war's demands—who knew for how long? At the end of the rehearsal, Strauss raised his hands, and in a voice choked with tears he said to the orchestra, "Perhaps we shall see one another again in a better world."

A few days later, the final dress rehearsal was given before an audience of invited guests. Strauss took numerous curtain calls. Later he was discovered alone in one of the dressing rooms with a score of *Danae* in his hand. He lifted his eyes to heaven and whispered, "I shall be on my way soon and I hope that up there they will forgive me if I take this along." Knowing Strauss's antireligious feelings, one wonders if the composer of *Till Eulenspiegel* said this ironically.*

* The anecdote is taken from Franz Trenner (Ed.), *Richard Strauss: Dokumente seines Lebens und Schaffens.*

About a month after the dress rehearsal, Strauss wrote a long letter to Willi Schuh, which purports to be a factual and cool critique of his own opera. It is nothing of the kind, though the letter is fascinating just because it evidences a creator's lack of critical faculty. Strauss does point to what he felt were certain weaknesses in the opera, blaming some of them on the "dry text," and confessing that he always reacted strongly to "fortunate words." Yet he thinks that the third act "belongs among the best which I have written," and that a certain orchestral passage could be "placed on a high pedestal of honor in musical history."*

To round out the history of *Danae:* It was finally given in Salzburg in 1952, with Clemens Krauss conducting. The performance was broadcast. I have a tape of it; it is evident that neither the brilliant conducting of Krauss nor the beautiful playing of the Vienna Philharmonic nor the fine singing of Annelies Kupper as Danae nor the excellence of Paul Schöffler as Jupiter could make the work viable. Thomas Mann was present at the world première. He wrote to Emil Preetorius, who designed the costumes: "It is not a particularly fortunate work. . . . I doubt whether it will conquer the world. Gregor's poetry is bad; Hofmannsthal would have gazed at his nails [in listening to it]. The music has, of course, much that is beautiful and charming, yet an excess of percussion, pomp and emptiness. . . ."†

All the three Gregor operas, two of which are other-worldly, may represent a perhaps only subconscious effort on Strauss's part to flee into former times or into fable. Both *Daphne* and *Danae* seek a sunny mythical land. But his genius could no longer manage the "sea-change into something rich and strange."

Isolated in Garmisch, Strauss attempted to stop his ears against the ever-more-menacing noise that blared from a thousand loudspeakers. He tried to be deaf to the martial cacophony of daily history, with a cruel *sforzando* in every bar. Perhaps the enfeeblement that the music manifests, its turning away from people and characters—not one of the characters in the three operas is a delineated human being—is the result of a split between Strauss's imagination

* Letter of September 25, 1944.
† Erika Mann (Ed.), *Thomas Mann Briefe 1948-1955.*

and what was going on around him. While he was working on the *Friedenstag*, the Rhineland was being occupied and Italy ravaged Ethiopia. While he was working on *Daphne*, the Rome-Berlin Axis was drawn. When he began to work on *Danae*, the *Anschluss* of Austria was consummated. As he proceeded to compose, Germany invaded Czechoslovakia (March 15, 1939) and, being unopposed, stormed into Poland a few months later (September 1, 1939). Four days before Strauss completed Act I of *Danae*, England and France had declared war. Two weeks before Strauss finished *Danae* Paris had been taken, France had been vanquished (June 15, 1940). While all this happened, Strauss sat and neatly penned music of which the composer of *Ariadne* and *Salome** might well have been ashamed. "*Danae* was finished yesterday," he wrote to Krauss on June 29, 1940, "and I cannot bear to see an empty desk. (Perhaps that's senility.)" It was the same Strauss, but a different talent.

Once more, in fairness, I must mention dissenting judgments. Some critics believe that these three operas represent a fine and subtle old-age style of Strauss, that the public is wrong in rejecting them, and that one day they will be appreciated at their true worth. A fashion exists among certain "avant-garde" critics—at least among those who do not repudiate Strauss altogether—that Strauss's later operas are the very distillation of whatever is valuable in Strauss, that his musical thinking has been here cleared of his vulgar streak. One learns that *Friedenstag* is "Strauss's great and compelling diatribe against militarism, perhaps the finest of all his late operas" and that *Die Liebe der Danae* is "cheerful, mellow, unusually lyrical." One reads of the "self-involving humanity of the later operas." (These are British opinions.) One comes across the amazing statement that Strauss was, after 1910 (that is, after *Der Rosenkavalier*), "finally emerging as the composer he had been in flashes all along." (An American opinion.) *Friedenstag* is an opera "with a great future," and the time will come when *Danae* will become "one of the most successful operas of Richard Strauss." (A German opinion.) Willi Schuh, the Swiss authority on Strauss, speaks of "the beautiful, refined clarity in the style of *Daphne*. . . .

* Just before World War II began, *Salome* was performed in Paris for the *hundredth* time!

The realistic detail seems to be melted into the great flood of music that alternates between the lofty and the tender."* Well—Thomas Jefferson said, "Is uniformity of opinion desirable? No more than that of face and stature."

When Strauss finished *Danae,* he had just passed his seventy-sixth birthday. He was an old man:

> As I see him walking among the trees and past his little lakes, Strauss is an old man, yet extraordinarily tall. His thin topcoat sags in perpendicular lines to accommodate the hands he has thrust deep into his side pockets. His shoulders stoop together and he seems cadaverously, deceptively lean. The heavy head, square and shaggy as a mastiff's, comes as a surprise. It is in proportion to his height, yet not in proportion with his frame that has sunken and narrowed with the years. Dressed all in black, Strauss never fails to suggest a weird impression, as he moves slowly along, sauntering, slanting down the rows, like some giant bloom suddenly cut loose to become peripatetic and cruise about with its great head bowing on an inadequate stalk.†

Who, after listening to the Zweig and Gregor operas, would have thought that the old man still had a surprise up his sleeve? Who would have thought that he could get up in the middle of the night and, contrary to the gesture of the Marschallin, set the clock ticking anew?

---

* From the introduction to the DGG recording of *Daphne.*

† William Leon Smyser in *The New Book of Modern Composers,* edited by David Ewen.

19

Sunset

What cleared his gaze? What turned him again toward music in which brain and heart were co-equal? How did he manage, after spinning dry webs which crumble at a touch, to spin again the moist threads of romantic sounds? How did he regain lost eloquence?

Between the years when he reached seventy-six and his final work, composed at the age of eighty-four, he wrote one opera, two concertos, one orchestral piece, and four songs with orchestral accompaniment (to mention major efforts only). These are:

The opera *Capriccio*, finished August 3, 1941
The Second Horn Concerto, E-flat major, 1942
Metamorphosen, a study for 23 solo string instruments, 1945
Concerto for Oboe and Small Orchestra, 1946
The Four Last Songs, 1948

All are works of quality. They may not be "masterpieces," but they are deeply felt music. None is revolutionary, none breaks new ground. Rather, they are a recollection of times past, remembered in "a mild blue light." Artful though they are, the compositions are not pretentious. They do not raise the index finger to point at symbolic significance. They do not attempt to make a mythological mountain out of a tonal molehill. Though *Capriccio* has an intellectual thesis, its music is warmer and simpler than is the supposedly simple score of *The Silent Woman.*

No absolutely certain explanation can be given for the resurgence of Strauss's talent. It is probable that he reached the point when he, who had imbibed the wine of success for so many years, no longer cared for the ichor. He began to compose "for his own amusement"; he no longer wanted to compose "a practical opera" (or so he said). He may have considered the last works as a memorial; one he was not to hear. He ceased to ask himself, "Will it be successful?" He composed in a relaxed vein.

Retirement in Garmisch—forced or unforced—benefited him at the last. He no longer waved the baton or directed opera performances. Perhaps, too, interior change was at work: the sorrow and the suffering that swirled around him may finally have reached his soul. Almost alone, with travel become burdensome and then impossible, he looked into himself. He had long outlived most of his contemporaries, and though news from the outside did not easily penetrate a country ringed in by censorship, he probably knew that three men he had admired had died within three years: Stefan Zweig in 1942, Max Reinhardt in 1943, and Romain Rolland in 1944. Most of the men he had known were lying in their graves, or had gone far away from Hitler's Germany. He was old, often melancholy, sometimes cantankerous. He seemed like a monument, a monument to his former self. Yet, unlike a monument, he did not wish to keep silent. The creative vein still beat with an insistent pulse. He still wanted to, he still needed to, compose. He still had something to say.

He did have the good luck to meet a man who proved to be not only an intelligent collaborator but a stimulating friend. He, Clemens Krauss, spurred him on through the devotion and skill he expended on Strauss's music.

These explanations are to some extent conjectures. A mystery remains: the refreshment of a talent after years of sparse harvests.

Capriccio has a curious history, its libretto having been sired by several fathers, that is, Zweig, Gregor, Krauss, and Strauss himself.

After Zweig had completed work on *The Silent Woman* and was being importuned by Strauss for further ideas, he said that he had come across a libretto which a certain Abbé Giovanni Battista di Casti had produced for a little opera by Salieri entitled *Prima la musica e poi le parole* (First the Music, Then the Words). Salieri was a rival of Mozart's, and his opera included among its cast of characters a poet who was supposed to be a caricature of Mozart's librettist, Lorenzo da Ponte. The opera had been given in 1786 at a Carnival performance at Schönbrunn on a double bill, the other part consisting of Mozart's *Der Schauspieldirektor* (The Impresario). Both operas dealt with the trials and tribulations of producing an opera. Zweig felt that there was something in Casti's libretto that could be used. The suggestion evoked an immediate response from Strauss, for he had long been interested in the problem of the relative importance of words and music in opera. When Zweig knew that his collaboration with Strauss had to terminate, he passed the idea on to Gregor, and during a few days' stay in Switzerland the two men, Zweig and Gregor, worked out a plan for a scenario.

Gregor sent this scenario to Strauss, who recognized that it was largely Zweig's idea. It may have been this outline that prompted the strong letter Strauss wrote to Zweig, the letter that was intercepted by the Gestapo. At any rate, Strauss put the idea away. Not until 1939 did he reopen the question with Gregor. Then Gregor prepared an entirely new scenario and sent it to Strauss. Strauss responded negatively: it was "a disappointment," it contained "not a trace of what I envisaged." Yet he urged Gregor to keep at it, squeezing out of Gregor one sketch after another and himself making suggestions for plot details. Some time later, in 1939, Clemens Krauss entered the scene, criticized Gregor's latest scenario sarcastically, and advised changes. Strauss then asked Krauss if he would lend a hand. But he still continued to work with Gregor, suggesting such points as that the opera must end on a doubtful note, that the Count and the Countess should be twins, like words and music, that there should be a string quartet (eventually a sextet), and so on. On October 7, 1939, Strauss wrote Gregor a long letter in which he fixed the action very much as it eventually turned out to be. A few days later he discussed his plan with Krauss and the producer Rudolf Hartmann. As a result of this meeting, Krauss made a detailed sketch of his own and Strauss wrote the dialogue for the first scene. At this point, all three were working on the text, Gregor, Krauss, and Strauss, the composer thinking that he would extract the best material from the three versions. Eventually Strauss realized that Gregor was not equal to the task, and Krauss's collaboration, from being that of a prompter and critic, became that of an actual author. The final libretto, as near as one can tell, is about one-quarter Strauss and three-quarters Krauss. It is a wonder that this hybrid product is as good as it is.

The letters concerning the Krauss-Strauss collaboration have been published; they make lively reading. Krauss was an extraordinary man. As a conductor he had his limitations. He was flamboyant and not free of actorlike antics on the podium. With his long sideburns and his tall figure, he looked like "the artist"—as a middle-class female might picture an artist—until he became corpulent. As a personality he was demanding, cutting, even cruel. He was capable of embarrassing singers by conspicuously waving a white handkerchief to indicate that they were not following his beat properly. His chief interest lay in stage production, the appearance of every costume, the gesture of every chorister, the lighting of every scene. He was an accomplished stage director, and he trained his wife, the soprano Viorica Ursuleac, not only musically but in acting, so that she became one of Strauss's favorite interpreters. He had had extensive experience in the opera house, first as intendant in Frankfurt, then as the director of the Vienna Opera House (where he could satisfy the Viennese no better than Strauss had done); then in Berlin; and now (1937-44) as the general intendant of the Munich Opera. Because he conceived all music operatically, he conducted not only the Strauss operas but the tone poems superbly. The composer knew it.

Like Strauss, he was perfectly willing to serve Hitler. Unlike Strauss, he never had any trouble with the Nazis. He was quite happy to conform and snatch the best engagements in the Third Reich. His troubles began only after the war, when, much to Strauss's chagrin, he was for a time forbidden to appear publicly in Europe or the United States. Later he was reinstated, worked in Salzburg, recorded some of Strauss's tone poems and a complete *Salome.** He died in Mexico City in 1954.

---

* His recording of Johann Strauss's *Die Fledermaus* is still considered one of the milestones of the recording art.

It was this Caesar of the theater, a man of broad erudition and edgy character, to whom we owe *Capriccio,* at least partly. Without his counsel and collaboration the opera might never have been finished.

It is a very special opera. To enjoy it one must have an interest in the form of art it both represents and discusses. By and large, it is operatic shop talk, an intramural joke.

It plays in the house of Countess Madeleine in Paris. The period is eighteenth-century, at the time of Gluck. Two men are in love with the Countess: Olivier, a poet, and Flamand, a musician. One writes the words, the other the melody, of a sonnet that expresses this love. Supplementary characters adumbrate the action, among them La Roche, the impresario, who supposedly is modeled after Reinhardt; a famous actress, Clairon, with whom Madeleine's brother is in love; two comic Italian opera singers; a mysterious Prompter; and so on. Madeleine is the chief protagonist; she is the last of the charming and worldly female characters of whom Strauss was so fond. She cannot decide between the poet and the musician, as one cannot decide which comes first, words or music. The opera ends with the unresolved Madeleine looking at her image in the mirror—as many years before the Marschallin had looked in the mirror.

One must accept *Capriccio* for what Strauss meant it to be: he called it a "conversation piece." One either is interested in the conversation or one yawns over these eighteenth-century precious people sitting around, swapping epigrams over a question that is never answered. Accepting *Capriccio* for what it is, one perceives that the music is affectionate and tender, perhaps more admirable in manner than in matter, perhaps a bit abstract, yet all the same fine and mellifluous, with even here and there a touch of the old fervor. There are dull spots, such as the very long dissertation by the *Theaterdirektor* La Roche, who delivers a conceited lecture. What he has to say, when you come to examine it, is as self-evident as coming out against sin. His demand—

I want to people my stage with human beings!
With beings like us,
Who speak our language!

Their sufferings should stir us
*and their joys deeply move us!**

—had been too often ignored by Strauss himself.

The core of the opera lies in the sonnet which the poet Olivier writes and the musician Flamand sets to music and which the Countess repeats in her last monologue. (To me the music of the sonnet is better than the words, but I doubt whether that is intentional.)† The final scene—introduced by a moonlit orchestral intermezzo—is enchanting, an echo of a happier period of Strauss and of a happier period of the world.

Capriccio will never become a popular opera. How can two and a half hours of discussion be tolerated by a broad public? Yet there are those who love it, and with reason. The critic Winthrop Sargeant wrote recently: "I could with great pleasure simply listen to this score without paying any attention to the drama that accompanies it. Yet with the drama it becomes just that much more meaningful. . . ."‡

In the last years Strauss turned again to orchestral composing, though on a small scale. The Second Concerto for Horn (in E-flat Major) can be considered as a reminiscence of his father. It is a virtuoso piece for the horn, old-fashioned pretty music. Mendelssohn might almost have composed it.

More important is a study for 23 solo strings, the *Metamorphosen.* The work is in the form of a free fantasy and uses a theme from the slow movement of Beethoven's "Eroica" as well as an echo of Marke's monologue from *Tristan.* The mood is sad and elegiac throughout. Manuel Roland, the French composer and critic, biographer of Ravel and de Falla, wrote about the *Metamorphosen:*

> Perhaps Strauss lived for eighty-five years simply to create this glorious work. Perhaps his exaggerations, his excesses, his lack

* From a translation of the libretto by Walter Legge.

† The words are based on a sonnet of the French sixteenth-century poet Pierre Ronsard. The sonnet was found, at Krauss's instigation, by Hans Swarowsky, a young conductor who had been engaged by Krauss for Munich to supervise German adaptations of foreign operas. Swarowsky was an adept linguist and was one of Krauss's protégés, though at one moment he had been suspected of spying for the British. He seems to have been absolved from the suspicion.

‡ *The New Yorker,* April 2, 1966.

> of modesty, and his offenses against good taste have all been nothing but inevitable states on the road that has led to this old man's discovery of wisdom, and to the writing of this serene and nostalgic reverie.*

Such praise may be excessive. Still, this is touching music, springing from a sad heart.

He finished the composition on April 12, 1945. The day before, the Russians had entered Vienna and on the same day the British marched into Arnheim. Two days later, the Americans took Nuremberg and the great Russian offensive against Berlin began. Two weeks after that, Hitler was dead, a suicide in his bunker in Berlin. At the last he sputtered that the war had been "provoked exclusively by those international statesmen who either were of Jewish origin or worked for Jewish interests."† The Third Reich was over (April 30). The day before, the Americans had occupied Munich. War was at Strauss's doorstep, and though he was left more or less in peace, it is hardly likely that Pauline was successful in making the soldiers who called on him, partly just to gaze on the old celebrity, wipe their shoes on the doormat.‡

The following year, he wrote a little Concerto for the Oboe. It is evident that this is a plaything or, as Strauss dubbed it, a "wrist exercise." Its gaiety is somewhat wistful; the composer remembers *Till.*

The finest composition of his old age, indeed one of the finest compositions he produced, young or old, is the *Four Last Songs.* The song which in performance is usually sung last was composed first, in May, 1948. It is "Im Abendrot" (In the Glow of the Evening), set to a beautiful poem by Eichendorff, a song of such gentleness as to convey to us that the composer had made his peace with the world. Words and music fit together perfectly. When the larks take wing, one hears their flight through the flutes of the or-

---

* The World of Music Encyclopedia.

† Quoted by John Toland in *The Last 100 Days.*

‡ Among his American visitors were Irving Kolodin, the critic, and Joseph Kahn, the pianist. Strauss wanted to know "How are my friends in America?" and told them that by some chance he had heard during the war a shortwave rebroadcast of a Metropolitan Opera performance of *The Rosenkavalier.* Kahn sat down at the piano and played whatever music happened to spring to his mind. He played, among other things, Gershwin's "Summertime." Strauss said to Kahn, "That's very pretty; did you compose it?"

chestra, and when they reach the sky, a violin soars with them. The poem ends with the line "Can this perhaps be death?" and Strauss quotes pianissimo the Transfiguration motive. The other three songs were composed in September of the same year, to poems of Hermann Hesse. They are "Frühling" (Spring), "Beim Schlafengehen" (Going to Sleep), and "September." Neville Cardus, the English critic, considered the Four Songs "the most consciously and most beautifully delivered 'Abschied' in all music."* One marvels at the art with which Strauss, in "September," indicates the falling autumnal rain. One is deeply moved by the close of the song, when the poet speaks of eyes that have become weary.

The composer was never to hear these last songs. Their première was given some eight months after Strauss's death: Flagstad sang them, Furtwaengler conducted them, a London audience applauded them.

It remains only to finish the biographical details of a life the work of which was finished. Samuel Johnson detested biographies "that begin with a pedigree and end with a funeral," but the story of Strauss must be rounded off.

At the end of the war, it looked to Strauss, pinned down in Garmisch, as if he was never again going to be able to indulge his enthusiasm for travel, as if never again would he conduct, as if never again would he be able to contemplate the paintings he admired. A kindlier fate was in store for him, though the painting he perhaps loved most he never did see again.

Dresden, the town in which Strauss had seen his early triumphs, was destroyed. No other German city, not even Berlin, had been so thoroughly demolished. At least 100,000 people had been killed in a series of concentrated air attacks. The Opera House, the Castle, the Hofkirche, were burned-out ruins. So was the museum, the famous Zwinger. Its art treasures had been hidden away. But where? The Russian Marshal, Ivan S. Konev, had through some good detective work learned their probable whereabouts. Accordingly, in May, 1945, he drove east, crossing the Elbe River toward

* *Talking of Music.*

the Czech border. There, in an abandoned limestone quarry, a dank cavern amid pools of stagnant water, he unearthed the paintings, over seven hundred of them. Among these glorious treasures was Raphael's *Sistine Madonna.* This was the painting Strauss first saw when as a young boy he had been sent by his father away from home, and to which, all through his life, he made frequent pilgrimages. Now it was carted away by the Russians.

He himself longed to get away from the misery of Germany. His prestige was great enough for him to obtain unusual leniency. As I have mentioned, a few months after the end of the war, he applied for and received permission to travel to Switzerland for a cure. Pauline was ill, and the local commander, the American Major Hayl, permitted them to go. At the border it appeared that one of the necessary travel documents was missing. But the French authorities knew who this white-haired distinguished man was—he carried in his buttonhole the rosette of the Legion of Honor—and they allowed him to proceed. Strauss thanked them by offering the original manuscript of the *Alpensinfonie* to the National French Library. At the Swiss border, he and Pauline were required to undergo a disinfecting process; the humiliation was countermanded when he scattered autographs left and right.

Thus Strauss left Germany and spent three and a half years in various Swiss resorts, keeping in touch as best he could with all who could be useful to him. It was in the destroyed Dresden, in a hall that had escaped the burning, that the first postwar performance of one of his operas took place: *Ariadne,* on December 10, 1954. The following year Joseph Keilberth "rescued *Die schweigsame Frau* from the concentration camp"—as Strauss put it.

He sent chocolates and other edibles to his grandchildren in Garmisch, using much ingenuity to have the packages safely delivered by couriers. He asked Hugo Burghauser, formerly a member of the Vienna Philharmonic, who had for some time been a member of the Metropolitan Opera orchestra and who was now visiting Switzerland, for help in selling the scores of *Don Juan, Death and Transfiguration,* and *Till Eulenspiegel,* newly and carefully copied by himself. He said to Burghauser, "My son will soon become a millionaire through my operas, but now I am in urgent need of money." Burghauser was able to help sell these scores in the United States.

Then, unexpectedly, in 1947 he received an invitation from Thomas Beecham to come to London and to take part in a special Strauss festival. Beecham had obtained financial support from the BBC, and he had persuaded the Home Office to issue the necessary permit. The eighty-three-year-old Strauss immediately accepted, somewhat against the will of Pauline, who feared that the trip would be too much for him. What would he have to eat in an England that was virtually starving? Strauss said that he would eat oysters: "They are good for me and I like them."

On October 4, 1947, Richard Strauss undertook his first airplane trip. He traveled by himself, Pauline not being well enough to go. As soon as he stepped on the plane, ten years seemed to drop from his shoulders; he walked off the plane in London with a confident step. A number of acquaintances greeted him. Gerty Hofmannsthal was there, as well as Clemens Krauss, who was appearing at Covent Garden with the ensemble of the Vienna Opera. Maria Ceborati, who had sung Aminta in the fateful première of *The Silent Woman* in Dresden, was charged with the responsibility of taking care of Strauss. He stopped at the Savoy Hotel.

Thomas Beecham was the conductor of the first two concerts of the Royal Philharmonic at the Theatre Royal. On the program were three of the tone poems, *Macbeth, Don Quixote,* and *Ein Heldenleben;* excerpts from *Feuersnot* and *Ariadne auf Naxos; Le Bourgeois Gentilhomme* Suite; and a symphonic fantasy of *Die Frau ohne Schatten* music. Strauss attended all the rehearsals. When he entered the hall for the first concert, the whole audience stood up. He listened "with half-parted lips" to his music. *Time* magazine reported that "once, in his excitement after a brilliant violin solo, the old man interrupted the music of *Le Bourgeois Gentilhomme* Suite to clap. Conductor Beecham threw a silencing glance over his shoulder and Composer Strauss looked around apologetically. When the concert was over, the crowds stood applauding while Octogenarian Strauss climbed slowly down the stairs to the stage. He bowed and croaked '*Merci! Merci!*' "*

---

* *Time,* October 20, 1947.

Norman Del Mar recalls:

> During my own rehearsal of the *Frau ohne Schatten* Fantasia (Sir Thomas had generously assigned the work to me as part of my London début) he came up to the podium, glumly regarded the score for a few moments, muttered "All my own fault," and went away. Throughout the entire visit he was very terse and uncommunicative, and only twice do I remember him being roused to any liveliness. The first occasion was when the fireman at Drury Lane Theatre had inadvertently locked the communicating door between the house and stage, thus blocking Strauss's way when he wanted to come round to see Sir Thomas. I can still see him stamping and shouting about the "*Gottverdammte Tür.*" The second occasion was after the concert performance of *Elektra* which Sir Thomas gave in conjunction with the B.B.C. At the end the overjoyed Strauss came forward and embraced Beecham. This was an occasion I shall never forget. Nor shall I forget the embrace; I had not realized that Beecham was so small or that Strauss was so large.*

Other observers took a less grumpy view of him. Strauss was affable with the journalists, at ease with his companions, uncomplaining about the gushing social functions, patient at the honorary dinners. He carefully avoided the subject of Germany. He learned that his old acquaintance, George Bernard Shaw, now ninety-one years of age, was listening to the concerts over the radio. He had met Shaw years before on a holiday in Brioni. Shaw told Kessler that as long as the two of them were alone no one seemed to take notice of them. Then, when Gene Tunney, the boxer, joined them, they could not get away from the photographers.† In London Strauss spent most of his free time in the National Gallery, the Wallace Collection, and the Tate Gallery. Did he remember Reinhardt when he saw the Hogarth painting of *The Levee* once more?

The third concert Strauss conducted himself. It was given at the huge Albert Hall with the newly formed Philharmonia Orchestra. He conducted *Don Juan*, *Burleske*, and the *Sinfonia Domestica.* The fourth concert began with Adrian Boult conducting the "Jupiter" Symphony. Then it was Strauss's turn. Waiting in the Green

---

* *Richard Strauss: A Critical Commentary on His Life and Works*, Vol. I.

† Harry Graf Kessler, *Tagebücher*, entry of November 14, 1929.

Room, he got up a little stiffly, looked in the mirror, straightened his white tie, and said, "Well, the old war horse returns once again to the fray." He conducted *Till Eulenspiegel.* He could no longer hear the high tones of the orchestra; yet he conducted with utter assurance. It was not, however, the last time he held the baton.

In November of that year he began to suffer with a bladder ailment, and in December of the following year he was operated on. It was a severe operation; yet he, with his tremendous vitality, slowly recovered. He then returned from Switzerland to Garmisch. His eighty-fifth birthday (June 11, 1949) was the occasion for a round of honors: he became an honorary citizen of Bayreuth and of Garmisch, the same Garmisch where his grandchildren had been ostracized. He was awarded an honorary doctorate by the University of Munich. He was given a fine Tanagra figurine, and somebody had unearthed his school graduation diploma, which was now presented to him with heavy humor. To the festive speeches he replied with one of his own, but he got a little mixed up. To the Library of the Bavarian State he gave, as "counter-birthday gift," the manuscript of an unperformed little waltz entitled "Munich." In Munich, the evening before, he conducted at the dress rehearsal of a new staging of *Der Rosenkavalier* the finales of the second and third acts. Asked what birthday present he most wanted, he replied that he would like once again to see and hear *Le Bourgeois Gentilhomme.* It was performed for him at the Munich Gärtnerplatztheater on June 13. He then returned to his villa, to conduct a month later, for a radio performance, the little moonlight music from *Capriccio.* That was the last time he held the baton in his hand.

At the end of August his health worsened and he took to his bed. One of his last visitors was Rudolf Hartmann, with whom he discussed *Danae.* Strauss suddenly thought of *Siegfried,* and he sang and conducted an orchestral phrase. He began to weep and apologized for his weakness. When Hartmann was about to take his leave, Strauss said to him, "*Grüss mir die Welt*" (Greet the world for me). Then he asked, "Where is that from?" Neither Hartmann nor Strauss could remember at the moment. It is a quotation from *Tristan:* Isolde says it to Brangäne when she believes that she is about to quaff the potion of death. Those of us who are mystically inclined may find significance in the fact that the "world" was in his thought, and that the reminiscence that flashed through his mind was one of *Tristan.*

Strauss died on September 8, 1949, in the afternoon. When the world heard about it, many people were astonished. They thought he had died long ago. Was he not a "classic"? Pauline outlived him a scant eight months.

20

Summary View of Strauss as Musician and Man

Few would doubt that Strauss was an important composer. How important is he today? What part of his considerable output will remain alive? How golden is the coinage he minted?

It is the theme of this book that he appeared as a young composer and in middle age to be a greater genius than he eventually turned out to be.

His tone poems embrace a decade of youth (1888 to 1898, from twenty-four to thirty-four), the strong operas approximately another decade (1905 to 1915, from forty-one to fifty-one). Had one predicted his future after *Ariadne,* the prediction would have turned out to be erroneous, a promise unkept. Barring the tremulously luminous last works, the clouds hovered over him for over thirty years. It is the theme of this book that these clouds were caused by the German cultural weather, a worsening of the climate created by two wars and tyranny. One needs to be wary of connecting an artist's life with an artist's work. In his case, I believe, there was a connection; the world was too much with him. He began in a vigorously romantic world; he ended in an intellectually jejune and politically vicious world where the artist was supposed to behave himself and salute with a stiff right arm.

Decay, mental and moral, attacked him, as it attacked his people. Strauss's mind was not strong enough to wing above the times.

Even his early tone poems were tuned to the times, dealing with Nietzsche when Nietzschean philosophy—understood or misunderstood—was influential, dealing with The Hero when Wilhelm twirled his mustaches. Too often he exhaled the smog of German mysticism, a mysticism that is fatiguing at the least and crime-inciting at the worst.

To Strauss's detractors he is perhaps the George Moore of music, clever, a master craftsman, but a minor author, eventually to be forgotten.

I think he is much more than that.

At his best he dealt with the human heart in music that goes to the heart. He dealt youthfully with youth; these passages will remain green as the laurel tree. He gave daring expression to sexual attraction, his music being pervaded by hedonistic eroticism. He was bold. If this boldness eventually assumed classical respectability, as was inevitable, it still has the power to excite us. In at least three of the operas his theatrical sense vies with that of the best dramatists of the opera house. In *Elektra* he summoned a tragic power which, with all its nervousness, cleanses the bosom of perilous stuff. He could soar, as in the beginning of *Don Juan* or the Trio of *Der Rosenkavalier*. He could spin an ironic yarn or tell a joke gaily, as he did in *Till Eulenspiegel*. He created characters so explicit that they have become part of our standard literature, part of life. Life would be poorer without the Marschallin, Octavian, Zerbinetta, the Composer, or even mad bad Salome. This sanest of composers gave us "mad scenes" frightening and pitiful. The Klytemnestra scene is fraught with terror, and *Don Quixote* touches our sense of pity.

But it is his exuberant and adventurous romantic spirit that remains the part of him we like best. We seem to need it more than ever. That very quality, romantic warmth, indeed romantic passion, seems to be missing from modern music. Perhaps we cannot recapture it. If we cannot, too bad for music. Melody is an essential tool of romanticism. It must have tunes, not just ejaculations of sound. That Strauss was a melodist he proved early in *Don Juan* and proved again, after sixty years, in the *Four Last Songs*.

His songs are part of his romantic gift. The best of them continue the poignant tradition of the Lied, the tradition of Schubert, Schumann, and Brahms. He wrote a large number of songs and he was not very choosy in his texts. In addition to such famous and lovely songs as "Morgen" and "Traum durch die Dämmerung" and "Ständchen," he composed such fine though less famous songs as "Die Nacht," "Breit' über mein Haupt," "Du meines Herzens Krönelein," "Ach Lieb', nun muss ich scheiden," "Ich trage meine Minne," "Heimkehr," "Freundliche Vision"; such wistful songs as "Die Zeitlose" and "Wozu noch, Mädchen"; such overly operatic songs as "Wie sollten wir geheim sie halten," and such bad songs as "Ach, weh mir unglückhaftem Mann" and "Das Geheimnis."

What will last? My guess is *Don Juan, Till Eulenspiegel, Tod und Verklärung, Don Quixote, Salome, Elektra, Der Rosenkavalier, Ariadne auf Naxos,* many songs, including the four last ones, and for a special audience *Capriccio.* Enough to assure Strauss an important place in music's living repertoire.

For such music we are willing to accept the blots that spot even his best conceptions; a touch of vulgarity—indeed more than a touch—an occasional sugariness of melody and harmony, a tumult noisier than the thought warrants, and here and there polyphonic nodules, which his conservative father criticized in the early days. Strauss himself said that polyphony was Satan's gift to the Germans.

Though the enrichment he furnished the symphony orchestra—and no composer was a greater orchestrator than Strauss—became the common property of later composers, his style had remarkably little attraction for younger men. He did inspire the young Bartók to compose:

> From this stagnation I was aroused as by a flash of lightning, by the first Budapest performance of *Thus Spake Zarathustra.* . . . This work, received with shudders by musicians here, stimulated the greatest enthusiasm in me; at last I saw the way that lay before me. Straightway I threw myself into a study of Strauss's scores, and began again to compose. . . .*

But then Bartók took a different turn. So did Prokofiev, though it is clear that the Russian composer studied Strauss's scores. Schönberg and Berg abjured Strauss, and Stravinsky feels that all of

* Quoted in Halsey Stevens, *The Life and Music of Béla Bartók.*

Strauss's operas should be "condemned to purgatory." In *Themes and Episodes,* Robert Craft cites Igor Stravinsky's discomfiture at a performance of *Der Rosenkavalier* at the Staatsoper in Hamburg:

> The audience applauds I.S. as he takes his seat in the first row of the Staatsoper a moment before the lights dim for *Der Rosenkavalier.* He acknowledges this with a bow while whispering to me that "It is only because everybody is very happy to see me obliged to sit through four hours without syncopation." But he doesn't sit or, at any rate, doesn't sit still. "How long can this false counterpoint go on?" he says, and "How can anybody swallow all of that *Schlagsahne?* . . . Prurience is intolerable even in Mozart. The music has no highs or lows except too locally; it is too even, and Strauss always holds his breath too long . . . How well they go together, bad taste and vigor . . . It is an operetta—and as 'if Richard then Wagner,' so 'if Strauss then Johann.'" And the defamation keeps up after the performance: "Perhaps Strauss can charm and delight, but he cannot move. That may be because he had no commitment; he didn't give a damn . . . But I have a terrible thought. What if I am sentenced to Strauss in Purgatory?"

Such condemnations do not make Strauss any the less valid.

His gods were Wagner and Mozart—not such bad deities to worship. He understood Mozart profoundly. He said, "I wish I could compose as simply as Mozart." He knew he couldn't. His love embraced virtually all of Mozart's music, not only the operas. He particularly admired the piano concertos. Mozart brought him solace: Strauss went to Böhm one day while Pauline was lying ill with pneumonia. Tears were streaming down his face. Böhm took him to a concert in which some Mozart Serenades were performed. He lost himself completely in the music.

But it was Wagner who was the mentor from whom he could not escape entirely. Protest as he would that he had shaken off Bayreuth's shackles, he never did, not entirely. He idolized Wagner not merely as a composer but also as a theoretician and even as a philosopher. He said, "*Opera and Drama* is perhaps the most significant scientific book in world history." I have referred several times to his special relationship to *Tristan.* One can understand this affinity: in a sense *Tristan* is the most "modern" of Wagner's works. Its intensely articulated eroticism would touch the composer of *Don*

Juan; its preoccupation with death—which D'Annunzio had apostrophized—would touch the composer of *Death and Transfiguration.* Georg Solti remembers that after the war, in 1949, he traveled to Garmisch to discuss *Der Rosenkavalier* with the old Strauss. Strauss was not interested, but took down the score of *Tristan* from the shelf and said, "Let's talk about this."

Richard Strauss loved Johann Strauss. What musician does not? One is reminded of the charming incident when Brahms at a ball took the fan of a lady, wrote on it the opening bars of the "Blue Danube Waltz," and underneath, "Unfortunately not by Johannes Brahms." When Strauss was young, he sent Johann Strauss an admiring letter, and all through his career he was fond of conducting *Die Fledermaus, Perpetuum Mobile,* and the famous waltzes.

Of contemporary composers Strauss's judgment was as fallible as the judgments of creative people often are. (Didn't Tchaikovsky detest Brahms?) He liked Delius. He was astonished that "a British composer could write such agreeable music." He understood Debussy little, though he conducted *L'Après-midi d'un faune. Pelléas et Mélisande* was a closed book to him. So was Berg's *Wozzeck.* Nor did he understand Schönberg's revolutionary aims. All the same, and although he thought that Schönberg would be better off "shoveling snow," he cast his vote for Schönberg when he was asked which composer should receive a subsidy.

He respected his most famous contemporary, Gustav Mahler, and Mahler reciprocated this respect. We have seen that Mahler tried very hard to get *Salome* performed in Vienna, and Strauss conducted a number of performances of Mahler's symphonies, particularly the Fourth, which Strauss liked especially. Mahler and Strauss met frequently. Occasionally there reigned true cordiality between them; more often their attitudes were reserved, careful but distant, not without a trace of distrust. Their natures were antipodal. Mahler's gaze was forever raised to the sky; he was, as his wife once said of him in a moment of irritation, always telephoning to God, while Strauss had his eye fixed upon the world. Mahler's temperament, always idealistic and often naïve, swung from one extreme to the other, though his moments of depression were more frequent than his moments of joy. Strauss's even nature could not comprehend Mahler's dark-to-light oscillations.

Mahler thought Strauss cold and much too worldly. He felt in Strauss "a certain blasé quality." In a letter from Mahler to his wife, he tells of a visit he paid Strauss. Strauss was asleep, and Pauline took him into her boudoir ("very messy") and bored him to tears with local gossip, then explained that Strauss had had a strenuous rehearsal in Leipzig the day before and returned to Berlin in the afternoon to conduct *Götterdämmerung* in the evening, and she had promised not to disturb him. All of a sudden, however, she exclaimed, "Now we will have to wake up the sluggard!" and before Mahler could prevent it, she rushed into his room and yelled in her loudest voice, "Wake up! Gustav is here!" Strauss awakened with a start and smiled a long-suffering smile. Then the gossip began anew.*

On another occasion, Mahler wrote to Alma: "The atmosphere which one feels around Strauss is too dampening. I would rather eat the bread of the poor and walk in the light than be lost in the flatlands. . . . My time will come when his is ended." On the other hand, he reported to Alma that he had made a train journey with Strauss alone and they had conversed most amicably, "as in the old days." On still another occasion, Mahler took offense because Strauss did not come to one of his concerts, though he happened to be in the same city and Mahler had invited him. After the concert, Mahler found a little note of apology. "Probably Frau Pauline did not permit him to come" was Mahler's comment.†

One must be careful not to take all these remarks at their face value. Mahler, a sick man, was a moody reporter, and Alma was an unreliable retailer of anecdotes. Still, it is certain that Strauss and Mahler were two men out of tune with each other.

In 1911 Mahler returned from America a physically exhausted man; his final illness growing rapidly, he crawled back to the Vienna he had loved so much and which had treated him so shabbily, only to die there on May 18. Two days later, Strauss wrote to Hofmannsthal: "Mahler's death moved me deeply. Now he'll become a great man, even in Vienna."‡

---

* Letter written in January, 1907.

† The Mahler-Strauss relationship is more fully treated in Walter Thomas; *Richard Strauss und seine Zeitgenossen.*

‡ Letter of May 20, 1911.

He was out of sympathy with Stravinsky and did not appreciate the importance of *Le Sacre du Printemps*. And—as I mentioned—vice versa: Stravinsky loathes Strauss's music. In his autobiography Stravinsky claims that Strauss told him, "You make a mistake in beginning your piece *pianissimo;* the public will not listen. You should astonish them by a sudden crash at the very start. After that they will follow you and you can do whatever you like."* It is highly unlikely that the composer of *Till Eulenspiegel* or *Don Quixote* or *Ariadne,* all of which begin softly, should have told him any such thing.

"In my judgment, Richard Strauss was the most important conductor with whom I ever worked," said Sidney S. Bloch, who was a violinist at the Royal Opera in Berlin.† Not always did he conduct in an inspired vein. But when he did, a miracle of interpretation was likely to take place. No one could forget his conducting of *Tristan und Isolde.* In the Prelude he built the reiteration of the germinal motive to an almost unbearable tension. From beginning to end his interpretation of the work followed one sure dramatic design. Nor could anyone forget his conducting of *Così,* so much fun, fooling, and wit did he bring to it.

His behavior on the podium, after he had conquered the extravagances of youth, was dignity itself. He himself said that he conducted "with his necktie." A musician said he conducted with a toothpick. He did not have to change his shirt during intermission. He summoned the demons with a calm hand.

Strauss told Szell that a conductor must indicate the tempo beyond the shadow of a doubt with his first upbeat. He preferred fast tempos. Once he picked up the baton, and before giving the down beat he said to the orchestra, "Not fast enough." He disliked broadening of the tempo to render climaxes more impressive. He called that "amateurish."

In the main, he respected his public. He wrote in 1907: "One must not become confused by the fact that the same public which welcomes the superficially pleasant, the easily assimilated, and even

* Igor Stravinsky, *Autobiography.*

† Otto Zoff (Ed.), *Great Composers Through the Eyes of Their Contemporaries.*

the banal" can respond to the "artistically meaningful, the new, and even works which are in advance of their time. . . . Carl Maria von Weber once said of the public: 'Each one is an ass; together they are the voice of God.' "*

He was not a pedant when it came to his own works, which, by the way, he did not conduct by heart, having the score always in front of him. Erich Leinsdorf writes:

> I heard years ago a funny and authentic story about Strauss visiting a German opera group known as the Wanderbühne. They were preparing *Intermezzo* at the time, and the musical director of the group was very proud that the innumerable notes in their exact setting of German diction—at this Strauss was an unsurpassed master—had been rehearsed with the most precise, meticulous observation of every thirty-second and sixty-fourth, of every *piano, pianissimo,* of every accent and half accent. When he said to Strauss, who assisted at the rehearsal, "Master, every smallest note is being produced with the utmost exactness," Strauss, in one of his moods, said, "Tell me, my dear friend, why do you want it so exact?"†

In interpreting his operas, what he strove for again and again was the total impression. He was willing to transpose arias for a singer he valued and to adjust tempos to the capabilities of a singer, provided his or her interpretation as a whole pleased him. He was considerate of his artists. Lotte Lehmann speaks of the warmth and understanding that sometimes broke through his businesslike façade during rehearsals.

In the opera house, he insisted that the words be understood. He once—in 1925—wrote out "Ten Golden Rules" for a conductor. Rule Seven: "It is not sufficient that you hear every word of the singer. You know the text by heart. It is the public who must be able to follow effortlessly. If they do not understand the text, they will fall asleep."‡

In 1945, he sent to Karl Böhm what he called his "artistic testament." He suggested the need for two kinds of opera houses, one of

---

* Willi Schuh (Ed.), *Richard Strauss: Betrachtungen und Erinnerungen.*
† The *Atlantic,* August, 1965.
‡ Willi Schuh (Ed.), *op. cit.*

which he called the "Opera Museum," institutions equivalent to the Pinakothek or the Prado or the Louvre; and a smaller house, which he called the "Spieloper."*

His suggested repertoire for the Opera Museum of a German city was:

Gluck	*Orpheus, Alceste, Armide,* both *Iphigénies,* either in a new or in Wagner's version
Mozart	*Idomeneo* (in a version by Wallerstein and Strauss), *The Marriage of Figaro, Don Giovanni, Così fan tutte, Die Zauberflöte*
Beethoven	*Fidelio*
Weber	*Freischütz, Euryanthe, Oberon*
Berlioz	*Benvenuto Cellini, Les Troyens*
Bizet	*Carmen*
Verdi	*Aida, Simone Boccanegra, Falstaff*
R. Strauss	*Salome, Elektra, Der Rosenkavalier, Die Frau ohne Schatten, Friedenstag, Daphne, Die Ägyptische Helena, Die Liebe der Danae, Josephslegende*
R. Wagner	Everything from *Rienzi* (uncut) to *Götterdämmerung*

For the Spieloper, he proposed a larger repertoire:

Adam	*Le Postillon de Longjumeau*
D'Albert	*Tiefland, Die Abreise*
Auber	*La Muette de Portici, Fra Diavolo, Le Domino noir, Maurer und Schlosser* (I don't know which opera Strauss meant), *La Part du diable*
Bellini	*Norma, La Sonnambula*
Berlioz	*Beatrice and Benedict*
Leo Blech	*Das war ich, Versiegelt*
Boieldieu	*La Dame blanche, Jean de Paris*
Bizet	*Djamileh, The Pearl Fishers*
Chabrier	*Gwendoline, Le Roi l'a dit*†
Charpentier	*Louise*
Cherubini	*Les Deux journées*‡
Cimarosa	*The Secret Marriage*

* *Ibid.*

† Probably a mistake. Delibes wrote this; Chabrier wrote *Le Roi malgré lui.*

‡ Known in German as *Der Wasserträger.*

Cornelius	*Der Barbier von Bagdad, Der Cid*
Dittersdorf	*Doktor und Apotheker*
Donizetti	*Daughter of the Regiment, Don Pasquale, Elixir of Love, Lucia di Lammermoor*
Dvorak	*The Jacobin*
Flotow	*Alessandro Stradella*
Goldmark	*Die Königin von Saba*
Gounod	*Le Médecin malgré lui*
Humperdinck	*Hänsel und Gretel, Königskinder, Die Heirat wider Willen*
Kienzl	*Der Evangelimann*
Korngold	*Der Ring des Polykrates*
Kreutzer	*Das Nachtlager von Granada*
Leoncavallo	*I Pagliacci*
Lortzing	*Die beiden Schützen, Der Waffenschmied, Der Wildschütz, Zar und Zimmermann*
Marschner	*Hans Heiling, Der Holzdieb*
Mascagni	*Cavalleria rusticana*
Méhul	*Joseph*
Moussorgsky	*Boris Godunov*
Nicolai	*Die lustigen Weiber von Windsor*
Offenbach	*La Belle Hélène, Orphée aux enfers*
Pergolesi	*La serva padrona*
Pfitzner	*Palestrina*
Alexander Ritter	*Der faule Hans, Wem die Krone?*
Max Schillings	*Ingwelde, Der Pfeifertag*
Schubert	*Der häusliche Krieg*
Smetana	*The Bartered Bride, The Kiss, Two Widows, Dalibor*
Hans Sommer	*Loreley, Rübezahl*
Johann Strauss	*Fledermaus* (in the original!), *Zigeunerbaron*
Richard Strauss	*Guntram, Feuersnot, Ariadne, Intermezzo, Arabella, Die schweigsame Frau, Capriccio*
Tchaikovsky	*Pique Dame, Eugen Onegin*
Verdi	*Trovatore, Traviata, Rigoletto, Masked Ball* —in addition (a new thought!): since the early operas, which as complete works are for us today unbearable, such as *Macbeth, Luisa Miller, Sicilian Vespers,* contain isolated passages of genius, I recommend a sort of potpourri of scenes; for example, the Sleepwalking Scene of Lady Macbeth.

> These, with the ballet in costume and scenic representation, could be given on one historic Verdi evening.
>
> *Otello* I condemn altogether, as I do all opera texts which spoil the classical plays, as, for example, Gounod's *Faust*, Rossini's *Tell*, Verdi's *Don Carlos*. They do not belong on the German stage.*

These proposals are curious for both their inclusions and their omissions.That every single opera by himself is included we might have expected! He plumped, however, for second-rate operas fallen into disuse even in his time, such as Kreutzer's *The Bivouac of Granada*, a minor opera by Korngold, whom he detested, both operas by Alexander Ritter, and so on. Only two works by Bellini, only four by Donizetti, absolutely nothing by Rossini. And nothing whatever by the composer who in his day was and today is one of the pillars of operatic society: Puccini. If Strauss were alive today, he would have to accept the fact that Puccini is one of the most frequently performed composers on the German stage, *La Bohème* and *Tosca* far outranking any work by Wagner. Strauss's estimate of Verdi was erratic. He did include seven of Verdi's operas; yet he condemned *Otello*, misunderstanding Boïto's libretto completely, if indeed he read the libretto. He had no inkling of the greatness of that towering music drama. As to his suggestion that early Verdi operas be given as a "potpourri of scenes"—let us call it ingenuous, to be polite about it.

We have had occasion to observe his working habits. He was punctilious and fast. He told his publishers when each act of his major operas would be finished, and he kept to the due date almost to the day. He told Karl Böhm that one day he was reading the poem of "Traum durch die Dämmerung" and determined to set it to music. At this moment Pauline entered and told him that she wanted to go for a walk. He anwered that he was working. She said that he had exactly twenty minutes to complete whatever it was that he was doing. By the time she came to fetch him, he had finished the song.

---

* Strauss gives the titles of the operas mostly in German. I give them in the form in which they are more familiar to American readers.

Virtually up to the time he took to his deathbed, he could not leave off composing. After the *Four Last Songs* he still considered others, and in the final years he even toyed with still another operatic project, *Der Esels Schatten* (The Donkey's Shadow). He said that he could compose only in the summer. That was a self-delusion because he wanted to conduct in the winter. He could compose at any time.

As to Strauss the man—he can be summarized, if summary is needed, by a well-known Toscanini anecdote. When Strauss called on Toscanini in Toscanini's dressing room in Milan, Toscanini was getting ready to return home. He said to Strauss, "For Strauss the composer, I take my hat off. For Strauss the man, I put it on again."*

Toscanini was one of the early champions of Strauss's music. He wrote to Strauss—at the time that Strauss was finishing the score of *Salome*—that he had "long been imbued with admiration for his genius," that he would consider himself "the happiest man in the world" to make his personal acquaintance, that he ardently desired to conduct the Italian première of *Salome*, and that, even before seeing the score, he had managed to get hold of Oscar Wilde's original text in French, which he was studying. Toscanini thought the subject "a fine choice, beautiful and musical." † Strauss promised him the première, but changed his mind when Gatti-Casazza proposed what Strauss believed to be unsatisfactory conditions and when Turin offered Strauss 15,000 francs for the première with Strauss himself conducting, against Gatti's offer of 3,000 francs. Strauss explained all this to Toscanini on October 9, 1906, in a long letter. He regretted that Toscanini was "*fâché*" at him. (The early correspondence was written in French; it is difficult to say which of the two wrote worse French. Toscanini apologized for his bad French. Strauss answered that his own French was even more "barbaric.")

Fâché or not, Toscanini continued to play Strauss's music and Strauss continued to hold Toscanini in high regard. In 1928 Strauss

---

* Zweig, who admired both Strauss and Toscanini (he wrote an appreciative essay on Toscanini), denied that Toscanini was capable of forming such a judgment. Walter Toscanini confirmed that his father did say it.

† Letter of July 27, 1905, in the possession of Walter Toscanini.

sent Toscanini as a gift the first page of the *Salome* score, copied especially for him "as a small token of my veneration."

In judging Strauss as a man we must alternately take our hats off and put them on again. His contradictoriness is exemplified by his self-judgments, which ranged from the ridiculously modest to the arrogant. Self-deprecatingly he said, "My son will for a time piously play my compositions in four-hand arrangements from privately printed editions. Then even this will disappear and the world will go on its way."* He wrote to Clemens Krauss: "It is strange how much in need of revision one's own products seem after just a few years."† The year after, he wrote Krauss that "I have to admit to my horror that I will have to become ninety years old before I learn to write for the human voice and to orchestrate an opera properly."‡ When he was in New York for his second visit, he asked Stokowski to take him to the home of Lord Duveen. There he admired the works of art, particularly a Chinese screen, which he studied for a long time. Then he said, half to himself, "When I see such a work of art, I think I am only a rococo composer." Almost at the end of his life he summarized: "I know very well that my symphonic works do not touch the giant genius of Beethoven. I know exactly the distance (in greatness of conception, elemental melodic invention, and cultural wisdom) which separates my operas from the eternal works of Wagner. . . . Yet I claim an honorable place at the end of the rainbow." §

On the other hand, he wrote to Hofmannsthal: "I am really the only composer alive who has true humor, wit, and a talent for parody."|| Of *Ariadne* he wrote: "My score, considered as a score, is truly a masterpiece which nobody is going to surpass soon."¶

He was a salesman of his own wares. He promoted his own operas indefatigably. When in his opinion they were not given frequently enough, he fumed and spoke of "filthy intrigues" against

* Quoted by Ernst Krause, *Richard Strauss: Gestalt und Werk.*
† Letter of July 29, 1940.
‡ Letter of February 10, 1941.
§ Letter to Joseph Gregor, February 4, 1945.
|| Letter of June 5, 1916.
¶ Letter to Hofmannsthal, June 20, 1912.

himself. He carried on a long feud with the Munich Opera House. There were never frequent enough performances, and he was always speculating how the number could be stepped up. He once suggested to the singer Barbara Kemp that both *Salome* and *Elektra* should be given on the same evening, with herself playing both parts! In 1929 he wrote to Toscanini in America, recommending the pianist Paul Wittgenstein: Strauss had written two piano pieces for the left hand for Wittgenstein, the *Parergon to the Sinfonia Domestica* and the *Panatenäenzug.* Wittgenstein had played these works with "great success" and Strauss would be happy if they could be played "in America under your master baton."* The master baton never gave the down beat for these pieces.

"Originally destined for a musical career," wrote one spiteful critic, "Richard Strauss later took up a commercial career."

His avidity for money has been exaggerated. He did like money. (So did Voltaire, who even profited from a war.) What of it? Strauss earned a great deal of money from concertizing as well as from his performance fees. (His earnings have been estimated at $2,500,000, though some of his fortune was lost after both wars.) Only rarely did he "write for money." Instances of that are the additional music he composed for a *Rosenkavalier* film, and late in life, in 1945, a suite from the *Rosenkavalier* for the orchestra, both of these being potboilers cooked up for financial gains. He made copies of his scores to sell these manuscripts at high prices. Occasionally he composed for the sake of "diplomacy": a military march during World War I, a hymn or two for the Third Reich.

He was scrupulously honest in his dealings with librettists and publishers. He did not attempt to drive a hard bargain with his collaborators, even after Hofmannsthal. His interest in being adequately compensated was partly responsible for the organizational work he did, which was to benefit all German composers. At a lunch in Paris he tried to explain this plan to Debussy. (The lunch was given at the home of the music publisher Jacques Durand, who had promised himself that the meeting of the greatest composer of France and of Germany would prove a stimulating occasion. He

---

* Letter to Toscanini, September 29, 1929, in the possession of Walter Toscanini.

was disappointed.) Strauss spoke of nothing but financial matters, while Debussy, who did not understand a word of what Strauss was talking about, kept silent and pretended to be lost in his dreams.

Personally he was not particularly generous. When he entertained people he liked (or those he thought were important to his career) at his home, he was a gracious host, champagne flowing freely. When he went to a restaurant—he liked small restaurants where he would not be recognized—he scrutinized the bill carefully and sometimes left an insufficient tip. Barbara Tuchman, in her book *The Proud Tower,* in which she devotes an excellent chapter to Strauss,* tells the story that at the first Parisian performance of *Joseph* "the evening ended happily in a gala supper at Larue's given by the composer for his friends who had come from Germany, Austria and Italy for the première. After feasting on early strawberries and exquisite wines, each guest was presented by the waiter with his share of the bill." This, however, is not quite so shocking as Miss Tuchman thinks; in Germany and Austria it was often the custom to "invite" friends for a meal and have everybody pay his share.

On his concert tours, he was quite capable of camping in the house of friends, accepting their hospitality, knowing that their social standing could not fail to be enhanced by the presence of Richard Strauss. If he was in a good mood, he regaled everybody with stories and gossip of the opera house. If he was not, he would make a nest for himself of many pillows, stretch out on the couch, and go to sleep or pretend to. One hostess who invited him said, "Please come. It will be quite an informal evening—no fuss." To which he replied, "You may make a fuss when Richard Strauss comes."

More humor is to be found in the music than in the man. But he did have humor, jesting sometimes at his own expense. In a fulsome after-dinner speech Strauss was called the Buddha of music. He replied he was not quite sure who the Buddha was, but he knew very well that he was the Pest. Kaiser Wilhelm did not like *Falstaff.* There were no tunes in it. He said after a performance, "I hope, my dear Strauss, that when you are eighty you will compose a better opera than *Falstaff.*" Strauss replied, "Your Majesty, *so do I!*"

At an orchestral rehearsal of *Salome,* the oboist came to Strauss

* She portrays him as a representative of the period when "Neroism is in the air."

and declared that a certain passage might perhaps be playable on the piano but never on the oboe. Strauss looked at the score and said, "Don't worry. It's unplayable on the piano as well."

When in 1947, on his trip to England, a reporter asked him, "What are your future plans?" he answered, "I plan to die."

To the biographer's disappointment, his nature was not erotic. He was not highly sexed. He seems to have let it all out in the music. One is never quite sure when one makes so blanket a statement, yet it is fairly certain that he was not interested in flirtations or extramarital ventures.

We have observed that he had a deep feeling for the pictorial arts, a love for painting and an equal love for the monuments of Greek and Egyptian antiquity. However, in his own villa in Garmisch, he collected a hodgepodge of the good and the bad. He owned a Tintoretto of secondary quality, a good small El Greco, some beautiful South German wood carvings, some fine Gobelins; but with these he mixed ordinary bric-a-brac and such "objets d'art" as could have been prized by a German grocer—beer mugs and decorated coffee cups.

He was a prodigious reader, more international in his taste in literature than in music. Where did he get the time to read as much as he did? His reading was not confined to books or plays that somehow or other might furnish stuff for a libretto, but included the most diverse works of fiction and history. In 1944 he wrote to Ursuleac that he was tottering toward an "incurable old age and I am wasting my time reading Plutarch and Ranke, Shakespeare and Nestroy, and the least-read writings of Wagner."* In his last years, he systematically began to reread Goethe from beginning to end, including even Goethe's scientific writings. He read a great deal of the Russians—Tolstoi, Dostoevski, and Turgenev. In contemporary literature, he particularly admired Shaw.

That Shaw admired Strauss we have seen in connection with the *Elektra* controversy. After the London première of *Ariadne*, the editor of the *New Statesman*, Clifford Sharp, sent the galley of a review signed "X" (the review was written by G. C. Squire) to Shaw for his comments. Shaw replied in his best Shavian vein:

---

* Letter of October 29, 1944.

I have not heard *Ariadne* & can say nothing about it. But the passages I have underlined are silly impertinences. The writer is entitled to say that Strauss's music does not carry conviction of passion to him; but this "Strauss would like to believe" "he does not really believe" is simply bad manners. Strauss is a very great composer; and X is not his governess. It is this governess business that we must refuse to stand. I should tell the writer bluntly that we do not want a puppy to patronize Strauss and to undertake to explain him away, as we do not believe that Strauss got his European reputation for nothing.

Otherwise the article is all right; but it should be signed. The signature in no way commits the paper to the writer; and there should be a signature.

The writer should be perfectly free to declare to any extent that *Ariadne* or anything else has missed fire with him, or disappointed him, or bored him, or that he thinks Strauss an overrated humbug if he likes. But when, instead of telling us what he thinks & feels he proceeds to tell us what Strauss thinks & feels, he makes a fool of himself & of his editor.

G.B.S.*

(I owe the discovery of this letter, as well as that of the letter to Mapleson below, to Professor Dan H. Laurence, who is now engaged in the editing and publishing of all of Shaw's correspondence.)

Shaw continued to be one of Strauss's defenders. As a very old man, Shaw used to play *Ariadne* on the piano. Why did he never write a libretto for Strauss? The author of *Pygmalion* might have proved to be the ideal librettist. Shaw toyed with the idea. In 1907 the famous impresario Colonel Henry Mapleson proposed to Shaw that he write a libretto for Camille Saint-Saëns. Shaw declined:

My dear Colonel Mapleson,

Unfortunately I have a prior engagement with Richard Strauss, which is at present rather hung up by the fact that I want to write the music and he wants to write the libretto, and we both get along very slowly for want of practice.

I wonder whether Elgar would turn his hand to opera. I have always played a little with the idea of writing a libretto; but though I have had several offers, nothing has come of it. When one is past fifty, and is several years in arrear with one's own

* Letter to Clifford Sharp, May 31, 1913.

natural work, the chances of beginning a new job are rather slender.

Yours faithfully,
G. Bernard Shaw

(The letter was published in the *Pall Mall Gazette*, December 13, 1907.)

The composite picture, therefore, shows that Strauss was a man of high artistic intellect, broad knowledge, wide responsiveness to all the arts. His musical erudition occasionally led him into a coy playfulness that can be appealing only to a pedant. He was fond of quotations: he quotes *Rheingold* when Rhine salmon is served by the *Bourgeois Gentilhomme*, *Figaro* when the Singer speaks of strenuous rehearsals in *Intermezzo*.

Along with the qualities of his mind, there are the defects of character that we have noted, his opportunistic egotism, which transcended the self-preoccupation of many another composer, though Wagner could have given him cards and spades. When Vienna was being bombed, his anxious concern was for his manuscripts: he asked Gregor whether the original scores of *Der Rosenkavalier* and *Die Ägyptische Helena* were safely stowed away where the bombs could not touch them. Could Gregor see to it that his other manuscripts as well could be removed to a safe place? Gregor assured him that the scores were stored "in our very best storage rooms in company with Beethoven's and Mozart's."*

His was a closed personality, and there were few persons, very few, with whom he shared his inner joys and sorrows. In later years he felt that Hofmannsthal had been closer to him than anybody else. But this was not the truth; it was sentimental recollection. "My one and only Hofmannsthal," he called him then; and he wrote to Gregor: "This morning I dreamed that I was having breakfast in the house of a great lord who, however, was not present. Hofmannsthal entered and said to me, 'I have a one-act opera text for you: very tender—with nymphs!' "† We can imagine that Gregor was not overly flattered by this letter.

It is not difficult to theorize that his enormous success, achieved

* Letter of January 12, 1944.
† Letter of January 14, 1945.

early in life, could have aggravated the flaws of his character. I have mentioned that Romain Rolland modeled the figure of the composer Hassler on Strauss. There is a passage in *Jean-Christophe*—written before 1910—which describes Hassler after he has become famous. It is an apposite prediction, a look into the mirror of the future: "He accepted without examination every musical idea that came into his head, and he had a private conviction, however he might fall below his own level, he was still superior to all other musicians. And though that idea was only too true in the majority of cases, it did not follow that it was a very fit state of mind for the creation of great works."

He gave us much. He might have given us more.

He might have given us more, had not his judgments become warped by a degrading environment, had his character been immune to the dry rot that beset his country and his nation.

One can quote Shakespeare to any purpose. Enobarbus' comment on Antony may apply to Richard Strauss:

> *I see men's judgments are*
> *A parcel of their fortunes, and things outward*
> *Do draw the inward quality after them,*
> *To suffer all alike.*

BIBLIOGRAPHY OF PRINCIPAL SOURCES CONSULTED

Abell, Arthur M., *Talks with Great Composers*. New York, The Philosophical Library, 1955.

Aldrich, Richard, *Concert Life in New York 1902-23*. New York, G. P. Putnam's Sons, 1941.

Beecham, Sir Thomas, *A Mingled Chime: An Autobiography*. New York, G. P. Putnam's Sons, 1943.

Biancolli, Louis, and Peyser, Herbert F., *Masters of the Orchestra, from Bach to Prokofieff*. New York, G. P. Putnam's Sons, 1954.

Biancolli, Louis (Ed.), *The Opera Reader*. New York, McGraw-Hill Book Co., Inc., 1953.

Blaukopf, Kurt, *Great Conductors*. London, Arco Publications, Ltd., 1955.

Boehlich, Walter (Ed.), *Der Berliner Antisemitismusstreit*. Frankfurt, Insel Verlag, 1965.

Böhm, Karl, *Begegnung mit Richard Strauss*. Vienna, Doblinger, 1964.

Broch, Hermann, *Hofmannsthal und seine Zeit*. Munich, R. Piper and Co. Verlag, 1964.

Brockway, Wallace, and Weinstock, Herbert, *Men of Music: Their Lives, Times, and Achievements*. New York, Simon and Schuster, Inc., 1950.

———, *The World of Opera: The Story of Its Origins and the Lore of Its Performance*. New York, Pantheon Books, Inc., 1962.

Bülow, Hans Guido von, *Letters*, ed. Richard Du Moulin-Eckart. New York, Alfred A. Knopf, Inc., 1931.

———, and Strauss, Richard, *Correspondence*, ed. Willi Schuh and Franz Trenner. London, Boosey and Hawkes, Ltd., 1953.

Bülow, Marie von, *Hans von Bülows Leben/dargestellt in seinen Briefen*. Leipzig, Breitkopf and Härtel, 1921.

Bürgin, Hans, and Mayer, Hans-Otto (Eds.), *Thomas Mann—Eine Chronik seines Lebens*. Frankfurt, S. Fischer Verlag, 1965.

Busch, Fritz, *Aus dem Leben eines Musikers*. Zurich, Rascher Verlag, 1949.

Canaday, John, *Mainstreams of Modern Art*. New York, Holt, Rinehart & Winston, 1959.

Cardus, Neville, *Composers Eleven*. New York, George Braziller, Inc., 1959.

———, *Talking of Music*. London, William Collins Sons & Co., Ltd., 1957.

Cowles, Virginia, *The Kaiser*. New York, Harper & Row, 1963.

Delarue, Jacques, *The Gestapo: A History of Horror*. New York, William Morrow and Company, Inc., 1964.

Del Mar, Norman, *Richard Strauss: A Critical Commentary on His Life and Works*, Vol. I. London, Barrie & Rockliff, 1962.

Du Moulin-Eckart, Richard, *Hans von Bülow*. Munich, Rösl, 1921.

Engel, Eduard, *Geschichte der Deutschen Literatur*, 2 vols. Leipzig, G. Freytag, 1917.

Ewen, David (Ed.), *Composers of Today: A Comprehensive Biographical and Critical Guide to Modern Composers of all Nations*. New York, The H. W. Wilson Company, 1934.

———, *The New Book of Modern Composers*. New York, Alfred A. Knopf, Inc., 1961.

———, and Ewen, Frederic, *Musical Vienna*. New York, McGraw-Hill Book Co., Inc., 1939.

Farrar, Geraldine, *Such Sweet Compulsion* (autobiography). New York, Greystone Press, Inc., 1938.

Gal, Hans, *Johannes Brahms: His Work and Personality*. New York, Alfred A. Knopf, Inc., 1963.

Garden, Mary, and Biancolli, Louis, *Mary Garden's Story*. New York, Simon and Schuster, Inc., 1951.

Gatti-Casazza, Giulio, *Memories of the Opera*. New York, Charles Scribner's Sons, 1941.

Geiringer, Karl, *Brahms: His Life and Work*. New York, Oxford University Press, 1947.

Geissmar, Berta, *Two Worlds of Music*. New York, Creative Age Press, Inc., 1946.

Goléa, Antoine, *Richard Strauss*. Paris, Flammarion, 1965.

Götz, Klaus Kende, and Schuh, Willi (Eds.), *Richard Strauss: Clemens Krauss Briefwechsel*. Munich, C. H. Beck, 1963.

Gregor, Hans, *Die Welt Der Oper, Die Oper Der Welt*. Berlin, E. Bote and G. Bock, 1931.

Grout, Donald J., *A Short History of Opera*, 2 vols. New York, Columbia University Press, 1947.

Gutheil-Schoder, Marie, *Erlebtes und Erstrebtes*. Publisher unknown.

Haas, Willy, *Hugo von Hofmannsthal*. Berlin, Colloquium Verlag, 1964.

Hadamowsky, Franz, *Richard Strauss und Salzburg*. Salzburg, Residenz Verlag, 1964.

Hamburger, *see* Hofmannsthal.

Hamilton, Edith, *The Greek Way*. New York, W. W. Norton & Company, Inc., 1930.

Hederer, Edgar, *Hugo von Hofmannsthal*. Frankfurt, S. Fischer Verlag, 1960.

Hofmannsthal, Hugo von, *Ausgewählte Werke*, 2 vols. Frankfurt, S. Fischer Verlag, 1957.

———, *Carl J. Burkhardt Briefwechsel*. Frankfurt, S. Fischer Verlag, 1958.

———, *Selected Plays and Libretti*, ed. Michael Hamburger. New York, Bollingen Series, Pantheon Books, Inc., 1963.

Internazionale Mitteilungen, Richard Strauss Gesellschaft.

Kessler, Harry Graf, *Tagebücher 1918-1937*. Frankfurt, Insel-Verlag, 1961.

Kohn, Hans, *The Mind of Germany: The Education of a Nation*. New York, Charles Scribner's Sons, 1960.

Kolodin, Irving, *The Story of the Metropolitan Opera, 1883-1950*. New York, Alfred A. Knopf, Inc., 1953.

Korngold, Julius, *Deutsches Opernschaffen der Gegenwart*. Leipzig, Leonhardt-Verlag, 1921.

Kralik, Heinrich, *Richard Strauss—Weltbürger der Musik*. Vienna, Wollzeilen Verlag, 1963.

———, *The Vienna Opera*. Vienna, Verlag Brüder Rosenbaum, 1963.

Krause, Ernst, *Richard Strauss: Gestalt und Werk*. Leipzig, Breitkopf and Härtel, 1963.

Krehbiel, Henry Edward, *Chapters of Opera*. New York, Henry Holt, 1908.

Kusche, Ludwig, *Heimliche Aufforderung zu Richard Strauss*. Munich, Süddeutscher Verlag, 1959.

———, *Richard Strauss—Kultur-Karussell—1864 bis 1964*. Munich, Süddeutscher Verlag, 1964.

Lang, Paul Henry, *Music in Western Civilization*. New York, W. W. Norton & Company, Inc., 1941.

Lehmann, Lotte, *Five Operas and Richard Strauss*. New York, The Macmillan Company, 1964.

———, *Midway in My Song: Autobiography*. New York, The Bobbs-Merrill Company, Inc., 1938.

———, *My Many Lives*. New York, Boosey & Hawkes, Inc., 1948.

Lockspeiser, Edward, *Debussy: His Life and Mind*, 2 vols. New York, The Macmillan Company, 1965.

Mahler, Alma Maria, *Gustav Mahler: Memories and Letters*. New York, The Viking Press, Inc., 1946.

Mahler, Alma Maria (Ed.), *Gustav Mahler Briefe, 1879-1911*. Berlin, Zsolnay Verlag, 1925.

Mann, Erika (Ed.), *Thomas Mann Briefe 1889-1936*. Frankfurt, S. Fischer Verlag, 1961.

Mann, Golo, *Deutsche Geschichte 1919-45*. Frankfurt, Fischer Bücherei, 1961.

Mann, William, *Richard Strauss: A Critical Study of the Operas*. London, Cassell and Company, Ltd., 1964.

Marek, George R., *Opera As Theater*. New York, Harper & Row, Publishers, 1962.

Memorial de la Seconde Guerre Mondiale, 3 vols. Paris, Sélection du Reader's Digest, 1965.

Moore, Frank Ledlie (Ed.), *The Handbook of World Opera*. London, Arthur Barker, Ltd., 1962.

Natan, Alex, *Richard Strauss—Die Opern*. Basel, Basilius Presse, 1963.

Nettl, Paul, *The Book of Musical Documents*. New York, The Philosophical Library, Inc., 1948.

Newman, Ernest, *The Life of Richard Wagner*, 4 vols. New York, Alfred A. Knopf, Inc., 1933-46.

———, *More Essays from the World of Music*. New York, Coward-McCann, Inc., 1958.

———, *More Stories of Famous Operas*. New York, Alfred A. Knopf, Inc., 1943.

———, *Seventeen Famous Operas*. New York, Alfred A. Knopf, Inc., 1955.

———, *Testament of Music: Essays and Papers*. Ed. by Herbert Van Thal. New York, Alfred A. Knopf, Inc., 1963.

Nicoll, Allardyce, *World Drama: From Aeschylus to Anouilh*. London, George G. Harrap & Co., Ltd., 1949.

Niemann, Walter, *Brahms*. New York, Alfred A. Knopf, Inc., 1929.

Panofsky, Walter, *Richard Strauss: Partitur eines Lebens*. Munich, R. Piper and Co., 1965.

Pelzoldt, Richard, and Crass, Eduard, *Richard Strauss—Sein Leben in Bildern*. Leipzig, Veb Verlag, 1962.

Pfister, Kurt, *Richard Strauss: Weg—Gestalt—Denkmal*. Vienna, Bergland Verlag, 1949.

Pörnbacher, Karl, *Hofmannsthal-Strauss—Der Rosenkavalier*. Munich, R. Oldenbourg Verlag, 1964.

Priestley, J. B., *Literature and Western Man*. New York, Harper & Brothers, 1960.

Redlich, H. F., *Bruckner and Mahler*. London, J. M. Dent & Sons, Ltd., 1963.

Reinhardt, Max, *25 Jahre Deutsches Theater*. Munich, R. Piper and Co. Verlag, 1930.

Richard Strauss, catalogue of Centenary Exposition of the Austrian National Library. Vienna, 1964.

Richard Strauss und seine Zeit, catalogue of Centennial Exposition. Munich, Peter Winkler Verlag, 1964.

Rolland, Romain, *Correspondance; Fragments de Journal* (No. 3 in *Cahiers Romaín Rolland*). Paris, Albin Michel, 1951.

———, *Jean-Christophe*. New York, Henry Holt and Company, Inc., 1930.

Sayler, Oliver M. (Ed.), *Max Reinhardt and His Theatre*. New York, Brentano's, 1924.

Schonberg, Harold C., *The Great Pianists*. New York, Simon and Schuster, Inc., 1963.

Schrenk Walter, *Richard Strauss und die Neue Musik*. Berlin, Wegweiser Verlag, 1924.

Schuh, Willi, *Ein Paar Erinnerungen an Richard Strauss*. Zurich, Atlantis Verlag, 1964.

———, *Über Opern von Richard Strauss*. Zurich, Atlantis Verlag, 1947.

Schuh, Willi (Ed.), *Richard Strauss, Briefe an die Eltern 1882-1906*. Zurich, Atlantis Verlag, 1954.

———, *Richard Strauss: Betrachtungen und Erinnerungen*. Zurich, Atlantis Verlag, 1957.

———, *Richard Strauss Jahrbuch, 1954*. Bonn, Boosey and Hawkes, 1953.

———, *Richard Strauss—Stefan Zweig Briefwechsel*. Frankfurt, S. Fischer Verlag, 1957.

———, and Trenner, *see* Bülow.

Seaman, L. C. B., *From Vienna to Versailles*. New York, Harper & Row, Publishers, 1963.

Sedgwick, Henry Dwight, *Vienna: The Biography of a Bygone City*. New York, The Bobbs-Merrill Company, Inc., 1939.

Seltsam, William H., *Metropolitan Opera Annals—A Chronicle of Artists and Performances*. New York, The H. W. Wilson Company, 1947.

Shirer, William L., *The Rise and Fall of the Third Reich: A History of Nazi Germany*. New York, Simon and Schuster, Inc., 1960.

Slonimsky, Nicolas, *Lexicon of Musical Invective*. New York, Coleman-Ross Company, Inc., 1965.

Stefan, Paul, *Die Wiener Oper*. Vienna, Augartenverlag, 1932.

———, *Gustav Mahler*. Munich, R. Piper and Co. Verlag, 1912.

Steinitzer, Max, *Richard Strauss*. Berlin, Schuster and Loeffler, 1911.

———, *Richard Strauss in seiner Zeit*. Leipzig, Breitkopf and Härtel, 1914.

Sternfeld, Richard, *Hans von Bülow*. Leipzig, E. W. Fritsch, 1894.

Stevens, Halsey, *The Life and Music of Béla Bartók*. New York, Oxford University Press, 1953.

Strauss, Franz and Alice, and Schuh, Willi (Eds.), *Richard Strauss und Hugo von Hofmannsthal Briefwechsel*. Zurich, Atlantis Verlag, 1964.

Strauss, Richard, and Hofmannsthal, H. H. von, *A Working Friendship: Correspondence*. New York, Random House, Inc., 1961.

Stravinsky Igor, *Autobiography*. New York, Simon and Schuster, Inc., 1936.

———, and Robert Craft, *Themes and Episodes*. New York, Alfred A. Knopf, Inc., 1966.

Taubman, Howard, *The Maestro: The Life of Arturo Toscanini*. New York, Simon and Schuster, Inc., 1951.

Taylor, Deems, *Of Men and Music*. New York, Simon and Schuster, Inc., 1937.

Taylor, Edmond, *The Fall of the Dynasties: The Collapse of the Old Order 1905-1922*. New York, Doubleday & Company, Inc., 1963.

Tempo, Richard Strauss Centennial Number. London, Boosey and Hawkes Music Publishers, 1964.

Tenschert, Roland, *Richard Strauss und Wien*. Vienna, Verlag Brüder Hollinek, 1949.

———, *3 x 7 Variationen über das Thema Richard Strauss*. Vienna, Wilhelm Frick Verlag, 1944.

Tenschert, Roland (Ed.), *Richard Strauss und Joseph Gregor Briefwechsel*. Salzburg, Otto Müller Verlag, 1955.

Thomas, Walter, *Richard Strauss und Seine Zeitgenossen*. Munich, Langen-Müller Verlag, 1964.

Toland, John, *The Last 100 Days*. New York, Random House, Inc., 1966.

Tovey, Sir Donald Francis, *Essays in Musical Analysis*, 6 vols. New York, Oxford University Press, 1935-1939.

Trenner, Franz (Ed.), *Richard Strauss: Dokumente seines Lebens und Schaffens*. Munich, Verlag C. H. Beck, 1954.

Tuchman, Barbara W., *The Proud Tower: A Portrait of the World Before the War: 1890-1914*. New York, The Macmillan Company, 1966.

Van Thal, Herbert (Ed.), *Ernest Newman: Testament of Music*, essays and papers. New York, Alfred A. Knopf, Inc., 1963.

Vogt, Hannah, *The Burden of Guilt: A Short History of Germany 1914-45*. New York, Oxford University Press, 1964.

Wagner, Friedelind, and Cooper, Page, *Heritage of Fire: The Story of Richard Wagner's Granddaughter*. New York, Harper & Brothers, 1945.

Walter, Bruno, *Gustav Mahler*. New York, Alfred A. Knopf, Inc., 1958.
———, *Theme and Variations: An Autobiography*. New York, Alfred A. Knopf, Inc., 1946.
Weissmann, Adolf, *Die Musik in der Weltkrise*. Stuttgart, Deutsche Verlags-Anstalt, 1922.
Winwar, Frances, *Oscar Wilde and the Yellow Nineties*. New York, Harper & Brothers, 1940.
Wittkower, Rudolf and Margot, *Born Under Saturn*. New York, Random House, 1963.
World of Music Encyclopedia. New York, Abradale Press, Inc., 1963.
Wulf, Joseph, *Die Bildenden Künste im Dritten Reich, Musik im Dritten Reich, Literatur und Dichtung im Dritten Reich* (3 vols.). Gütersloh, Sigbert Mohn Verlag, 1963.
Zabel, Eugen, *Hans von Bülow—Gedenkblätter aus seinen letzten Lebensjahren*. Lucas Gräfe, 1894.
Zoff, Otto (Ed.), *Great Composers Through the Eyes of Their Contemporaries*. New York, E. P. Dutton & Co., Inc., 1951.
Zweig, Stefan, Biographical writings, plays and short stories.
———, *Die Welt von Gestern*. Berlin, G. B. Fischer, 1962.
———, *Romain Rolland: The Man and His Work*. New York, Thomas Seltzer, 1921.

Index

About the Author

George R. Marek, for many years Vice President and chief executive officer of the RCA Victor Record Division, is a native of Vienna. Most of his sources were, naturally, in German, and he visited and interviewed surviving members of the Strauss family as well as dozens of men and women who had worked with the composer. Mr. Marek's previous books have included *Puccini,* a biography; *Opera as Theater,* a critical study; *World Treasury of Grand Opera,* and others.